D0858797

Toward Assessing Business Ethics Education

A volume in
Ethics in Practice

Series Editors:
Robert A. Giacalone, *Temple University*
Carole L. Jurkiewicz, *Louisiana State University*

Ethics in Practice

Robert A. Giacalone and Carole L. Jurkiewicz, Series Editors

Positive Psychology in Business Ethics and Corporate Responsibility (2006)
edited by Robert A. Giacalone, Carole L. Jurkiewicz, and Craig Dunn

Human Resource Management Ethics (2006)
edited by John R. Deckop

Advancing Business Ethics Education (2008)
edited by Diane L. Swanson and Dann G. Fisher

Critical Theory Ethics for Business and Public Administration (2008)
edited by David M. Boje

Doing Well and Good: The Human Face of the New Capitalism (2009)
edited by Julian Friedland

Toward Assessing Business Ethics Education

edited by

Diane L. Swanson and Dann G. Fisher
Kansas State University

Information Age Publishing, Inc.
Charlotte, North Carolina • www.infoagepub.com

Library of Congress Cataloging-in-Publication Data

Toward assessing business ethics education / edited by Diane L. Swanson
    and Dann G. Fisher.
        p. cm. — (Ethics in practice)
    Includes bibliographical references.
ISBN 978-1-61735-162-4 (paperback) — ISBN 978-1-61735-163-1 (hardcover) —
ISBN 978-1-61735-164-8 (e-book)
    1. Business ethics. I. Swanson, Diane L. II. Fisher, Dann G.
    HF5387.T69 2010
    174'.40711--dc22

                                                        2010038051

Printed in the United States of America

Dedication

Diane L. Swanson dedicates this book to her parents, Harold A. Swanson and Betty Jo Swanson.

Dann G. Fisher dedicates this book to his parents, Larry Fisher and Judi Fisher.

We also dedicate this book to Dr. William C. Frederick, professor emeritus at the Katz Graduate School of Business at the University of Pittsburgh, in honor of his pivotal role in establishing and elevating business ethics research and education.

CONTENTS

FOREWORD

Robert A. Giacalone and Carole L. Jurkiewicz

The *Ethics in Practice* series is a forum for the exploration and discussion of organizational ethics issues that may otherwise be overlooked in the usual venues of academic journals and books. The focus of the series is interdisciplinary, which includes not only a focus on ethical issues in the public, private, and nonprofit sectors, but on the body of knowledge that can be found in nonorganizational disciplines as well. The series, therefore, seeks to help readers better understand organizational ethics from a variety of vantage points, including business, public and nonprofit administration, psychology, sociology, anthropology, criminology, and victimology. There is much these disciplines can learn from each other, with the common thread being organizational ethics.

As editors, our goal is to provide scholars, instructors, and professionals in ethics and social responsibility with a meaningful collection of books in key areas that will expand thinking on issues of research and pedagogy. We see the series as a consortium where new ideas can be surfaced and explored, future inquiry stimulated, and where old ideas can be seen through different lenses.

One of our early goals in the series was to focus on ethics education as a topic within the *Ethics in Practice* series. We were thrilled when Diane L. Swanson and Dann G. Fisher submitted *Advancing Business Ethics Educa-*

Toward Assessing Business Ethics Education
pp. ix–x
Copyright © 2011 by Information Age Publishing

tion for publication. We saw their volume as a leap forward in the dialogue on ethics education; an erudite contribution to a literature we see as critical not only to business ethics education, but to business education as a whole.

When *Advancing Business Ethics Education* went into press, we told Diane and Dann that if they wanted to do a second volume on ethics education, we would be thrilled to consider it for the *Ethics in Practice* series. The long, hard work on an edited or authored book often does not motivate the editors or authors to engage in a second volume, so we were pleasantly surprised when they came to us with another proposal for another book on ethics education.

Toward Assessing Business Ethics Education is the next, excellent volume focused on business ethics education. It is a comprehensive look at the delivery and assessment of business ethics education done by a group of authors who are among the most innovative, prolific, and distinguished in the area. We believe what these authors put forth will not only invigorate the dialogue on business ethics education, but will help lead to concrete new changes in business ethics education.

What we hope is that this book will help those who have remained on the sidelines of business ethics education to enter the dialogue. We hope that it will stir the positive imagination of educators and administrators to help encourage increased and better business ethics education. We hope that the authors' words stir the needed changes that will not only prevent future ethical infractions, but bolster business decisions that will make for a better world at large.

As always, we welcome your input and ideas surrounding organizational ethics education and welcome you to contact us with your suggestions and comments for future volumes.

CHAPTER 1

ASSESSING BUSINESS ETHICS EDUCATION

Starting the Conversation in Earnest

Diane L. Swanson and Dann G. Fisher

The conversation about business ethics is hardly new. After all, business ethics has a longstanding tradition as an academic field, as demonstrated by the accumulation of articles, books, textbooks, courses, seminars, journals, magazines, conference boards, careers, and associations that 6 decades of dedicated scholarship and practice have spawned, not to mention 2,000 years of ethics literature in Western culture alone. We cover these points in *Advancing Business Ethics Education,* our previous book with Information Age Publishing in the series *Ethics in Practice,* edited by Robert A. Giacalone and Carole L. Jurkiewicz. Although the conversation about business ethics is not new, a renewed concern about assessing business ethics education has captured the public's attention these past few years, fueled by recurring corporate scandals that have tarnished the reputation of business schools. But even this concern is not novel. One need only look back to independent reports issued in 1959 by the Ford Foundation and Carnegie Corporation to see scathing indictments of the medi-

Toward Assessing Business Ethics Education
pp. 1–12

1

ocrity of short-sighted, narrowly focused, and inward-looking business degree programs, sentiments that have been echoed by knowledgeable observers ever since (Frederick, 2006).

This introductory chapter is organized in four parts. First, we present a straightforward formula for sound business ethics education that can be used as a basis for assessment. Second, we discuss the resistance to this approach. Third, we outline the dangers of this resistance, including the risk of assessment errors. Finally, we point to the possibility of a renaissance in business ethics education. Along the way we introduce the subjects covered by our distinguished authors in the chapters that follow. But first we need to clarify that we take a broad approach to assessing business ethics education, similar to the view of Palomba and Banta (1999, p. 297) who define assessment as "the process of collecting, reviewing, and using information about academic programs in order to improve student learning and development."[1] Similarly, we deal not only with assessing ethics courses and classroom methods, but also curricular issues and attitudes towards ethics education that may ultimately impact ethics instruction and student learning and development.

Specifically, our aim in publishing this book is to advance the enterprise of assessing business ethics education in three ways. First, we provide a venue for scholars to share the innovative ways that they are assessing ethics coverage in courses and degree programs. Second, we offer an outlet for leaders in the field to identify what needs to be assessed and the means for doing so. Third, we hope that this book will serve not only as a guide to assessment, but also to expand and improve ethics coverage in business schools. Although one book alone cannot address all assessment issues, we hope that this one, replete with many authoritative voices, will help start the conversation in earnest.

BASING ASSESSMENT ON SOUND PEDAGOGY

In this section, we describe a three-part formula for sound business ethics education, followed by a discussion of resistance to this formula and the dangers posed by this resistance, including the risk of assessment errors.

Delivering Business Ethics Education Intact

As first set out by Swanson and Frederick (2005), the three-part formula for delivering business ethics education is quite straightforward, described below and also in chapter 16 by Swanson, Fisher, and Niehoff.[2]

1. A required foundational ethics course is necessary. (Often these courses are labeled "business and society," "corporate social responsibility," "social issues in management," and equivalent designations.)
2. Efforts to integrate ethics across the curriculum should be a goal.
3. Other initiatives, such as hosting guest speakers, offering service learning projects, and establishing endowed chairs in ethics, are highly desirable.

According to this formula, a required ethics course is a necessary foundation for solid business ethics education. According to Carroll and Buchholtz (chapter 15), one study found that students who took such a course said they learned the following, in order of importance:

1. Greater awareness of the ethical aspects of a business situation.
2. Ethical concepts that will help me analyze decisions.
3. Ethical principles that can help me make better decisions.
4. Ways to be a more ethical person.

These results substantiate our contention that a foundational ethics course should be required in the business curriculum. Truly, this approach should not be controversial. After all, what school would claim sound coverage of organizational behavior, strategy, operations management, accounting, marketing, finance, economics, and other traditional business areas if no freestanding coursework for these areas existed in the curriculum? Surprisingly, however, there is significant resistance to sound business ethics education, mostly from business schools and their accrediting agency.

The Resistance to Sound Business Ethics Education

Despite the longstanding history of business ethics scholarship and instruction, the conversation about assessing business ethics education that should have taken place by now has been sidetracked by curricular politics in business schools. This dynamic has been fueled by the decision of the accrediting agency, the Association to Advance Collegiate Schools of Business (AACSB). This agency in 2003, in the wake of Enron and other business scandals, rejected a modest proposal for mandating a standalone ethics course as a condition of graduation in favor of allowing the distribution of ethics across the curriculum (Willen, 2004).[3] We discuss the dangers of this distribution policy later. For now, it is important to note that the accrediting agency is one of the key groups resisting the formula for sound business ethics education.

William C. Frederick, one of the main founders of business ethics and corporate social responsibility research and education, describes the resistance to ethics education in business schools as mutually reinforcing, coming from both the accrediting agency and functionally trained faculty.

> In my view, there is a double layer of resistance to ethics in business schools. One, and the most important, is the general resistance among functional-field faculty that is found in most b-schools. Another is the officialdom of AACSB which represents the deanship component of b-schools, where the resistance is often more a matter of unconcern than outright philosophic opposition, given the deans' job of raising money, keeping alumni happy, and therefore keeping their own jobs. Over the years, AACSB has become so institutionalized and so inbred that it, in itself, has a vested interest in stabilizing the business schools and their curricula, in face of constantly changing business markets, new technologies, globalization, etc. Along the way, ethics instruction has become lost as a somewhat lesser matter than more immediate problems and issues of maintaining the institutional status quo, thereby justifying continuation of the AACSB's accrediting function (which is only another example of a failed self-regulatory system inasmuch as the member deans are the ones who do the accrediting). As faulty and misleading as they are, the various national ranking systems for business schools may give a truer assessment of any given business school's overall quality as does its accreditation by AACSB. But in both cases, ethics is given short shrift. (Personal correspondence, May 2, 2009)

The Dangers of Resisting Sound Business Ethics Education

There are at least four dangers of resisting sound business ethics education, discussed next as recreating the wheel, risking irrelevance, risking assessment errors, and diluting the power of summative and formative assessment.

Recreating the Wheel

First, the resistance to the requirement of an ethics course in the curriculum means that ethics champions are constantly called upon to recreate the wheel. That is, instead of being able to focus on advancing and assessing business ethics education, they are asked to defend the area itself, often to critics who seem unaware that courses dedicated to business ethics have existed in business schools for decades. Such diversionary queries include "Isn't business ethics an oxymoron?", as if that question was not put to rest long ago by textbooks, journals, conferences, coursework, and associations dedicated to the subject. Perhaps some of the ignorance is due to the attrition of standalone ethics courses in many business schools that resulted from the accrediting agency's shift to flexible mission-driven standards in the 1990s (see Swanson, 2004). Prior to that, AACSB's accreditation standards clearly pointed to the requirement of a freestanding ethics course, often labeled "business and society" and equivalent nomenclatures (Windsor, 2002). The many business schools that cut these courses to make room for others are now in poor positions to advance knowledgeable discussions about ethics education. Hence, these discussions tend to reflect uninformed viewpoints that waste energy recreating the wheel. Ethics education is not advanced and sound assessment languishes.

Perhaps the most diversionary question of all is "Can ethics be taught and learned?" This interminable question puts ethics on the defensive by expecting a demonstration of changed behavior when no other business courses face such onerous burden of proof. For instance, there is no call for verification that courses in economics, finance, accounting, strategy, and marketing ensure that students make accurate predictions of economic trends, good investments, reliable audits, sound strategic decisions, and successful sales, respectively. That is because, as Petrick notes in chapter 18, education is but one link in a complex chain of inputs that can influence behavior over time. The responsibility of business schools is to ensure that subjects deemed important are delivered as strong links in this chain, not as bits of incoherent information scattered across the curriculum.

Risking Irrelevance

Besides the wasted time and energy spent recreating the wheel, the second danger of resisting sound ethics instruction is that business education will fail to keep pace with the needs of its students. As McGaw at the Aspen Institute reports in chapter 5, graduating MBA students now place greater emphasis than before on a company's responsibility to create value for local communities. Coursework that deals with this issue should be required in the curriculum, just as finance courses that emphasize shareholder value are. Otherwise, business schools ignore important student and societal interests.

Another way business schools risk irrelevance is by failing to keep pace with ethics delivered in continuing education programs. This is already the case, since the majority of states in the United States now require an ethics course as a condition for certified public accountant relicensing (Fisher, Swanson, & Schmidt, 2007), whereas only one third of accredited business schools offer an ethics course, and presumably fewer require one (Willen, 2004). This gap between continuing education and business schools did not always exist. Collins and Wartick (1995) found that the number of ethics courses grew greatly from 1973 to 1986 with more than half of the business schools polled requiring an undergraduate and graduate ethics course by the mid-1980s. Presently, however, it appears that business schools are letting continuing education take the lead, which is like putting the cart before the horse. Students in continuing education programs will be expected to build upon ethics material they never saw whole cloth in their degree programs, despite their reported interest in the subject (see chapter 5 by McGaw).

Corporate recruiters have told college placement officials that they want not only functional expertise, but also breadth in general management and behavioral skills (Rynes, Trank, Lawson, & Ilies, 2003). Moreover, business students repeatedly confirm that they expect to encounter values conflicts in their professional lives, as reported by McGaw in chapter 5. Therefore, as Stewart and Freeman discuss in chapter 4, business ethics education should encourage students to clarify their own values, figure out where they stand on a variety of potential challenges, and determine what type of future leaders they will aspire to become. These endeavors are particularly important in light of the most recent Aspen Institute finding that educational experience does impact the attitudes of MBA students about the responsibilities of companies (see chapter 5 by McGaw).

Failing to ensure that students get solid road maps for ethical reasoning breaks faith with their needs as well as the needs of business school constituents. It also breaks faith with the university's core mission to expose students to useful knowledge and ideals, as Swanson, Fisher, and Niehoff discuss in chapter 16. To risk such irrelevance is to fuel the crisis of legitimacy for business schools (Vidaver-Cohen, 2008).

Risking assessment errors

The third danger of resisting ethics education is that of inadequate assessment, which goes directly to the theme of this book. The distribution policy endorsed by the accrediting agency assumes that ethics topics will be handled sufficiently across the curriculum, absent a required course. Typically, this practice will not add up to any particular standard (see Swanson, 2004; Swanson & Frederick, 2005). Instead, superficial, uninformed coverage can be judged equivalent to a standalone course delivered by knowledgeable faculty. Moreover, when ethics topics are scattered across the curriculum, assessing learning outcomes becomes difficult. Two assessment errors will be unavoidable at most schools.

1. Ethics coverage will be assessed as being sufficient when it is woefully inadequate or even missing in action.

2. Ethics content can be distorted, diluted, or trivialized but still pass inspection (Swanson & Frederick, 2005).

To complicate matters, most schools lacking in standalone ethics coursework will not have trained ethicists on hand to advise other faculty on how to distribute ethics across the curriculum. This almost ensures that ethics coverage will be garbled, incoherent, or otherwise meaningless. Again, the formula for sound ethics education is to deliver ethics cohesively in a standalone course while encouraging the distribution of topics across the curriculum, particularly in courses taught by receptive faculty. This latter point is very important. As Frederick noted earlier, faculty members in functional areas tend to resist ethics. To rely on these resistors is tacitly part of AACSB's distribution policy which, among other things, renders it fatally flawed.

Diluting the Power of Summative and Formative Assessment

By unlinking assessment from a standalone ethics course, the accrediting agency has discouraged the use of summative and formative assessment to improve instruction and student learning. As outlined by the Aspen Institute Education and Society Program (AIESP), summative assessment is generally done infrequently, such as at the end of the semester or school year, in order to evaluate students' performance against some defined set of content standards (Perie, Marion, Gong, & Wurtzel, 2007). Typically this is done as a basis for assigning a grade. Although teachers may use the data as feedback that informs future instruction, summative feedback occurs too far down the learning channel to make a difference in the present learning process. Formative assessment, on the other hand, is carried out throughout a semester to aid learning by providing students with more immediate feedback on their work (Ames, 1992; Angelo & Cross, 1993) and instructors with timely information that can be use to determine the next steps in the learning process.

In addition to summative and formative assessment, the Aspen Institute Education and Society Program also recognizes interim assessment, usually consisting of items that can be aggregated and reported at a broader level than the classroom. Often labeled "benchmark assessments," these instruments and the data they generate are typically controlled by administrators for centralized uses (e.g., prediction and diagnosis) and, in many cases, are purchased from commercial outlets. Some business schools may rely on assessing ethics in this way, even though there is no research base to support the claim that interim assessment improves student learning (Perie et al., 2007). Nevertheless, generating some type of centralized report is encouraged by AACSB. After all, the agency includes "ethical understanding and reasoning abilities" in its

Assurance of Learning Standards while calling for a "well documented, systematic processes to develop, monitor, evaluate, and revise the substance and delivery of the curricula of degree programs and to assess the impact of the curricula on learning" (AACSB International, 2010, p. 72). Yet because the agency does not require a specific ethics course in the curriculum, business schools are left to their own devices to assess ethics education, especially since AACSB does not (to our knowledge) provide a benchmark (interim) assessment instrument. As a result, schools may attempt to produce a centralized report, which may consist of simply adding up the ethics topics listed on various course syllabi as proof of meeting the learning standard. The two assessment errors, identified earlier, are all but assured by this approach. It doesn't take much imagination to envision an interim assessment process that is motivated not by evaluative or predictive purposes, but rather by a need to check a box in order to pacify accrediting bodies. It would be more straightforward to require a standalone ethics course that could easily provide for formative and summative assessment rather than relying on a centralized report designed to prove ethics coverage when, unlike formative and summative assessment, such reports are not known to improve instruction and student learning.

Our view is that the accrediting agency has backed itself into a corner by (1) insisting on an ethics learning standard, (2) not insisting on a standalone ethics course that leverages formative and summative assessment, while (3) not providing schools with a valid instrument for benchmarking learning outcomes absent such a course. It adds up to a mixed message, at best. It will now be up to university administrators, faculty, students, alumni, and other business school constituents to insist on a clearer signal. The potential for a renaissance in delivering and assessing business ethics education is at stake.

THE POTENTIAL FOR A RENNAISSANCE IN DELIVERING AND ASSESSING BUSINESS ETHICS EDUCATION

The authors featured in this book represent a considerable sum of experience, expertise, and vision. Their voices in union represent innovative and forward looking views on what business schools need to do to bring about a renaissance in ethics education. One of the broadest statements about this potential is the Principles of Responsible Management Education, described by Waddock, Rasche, Werhane, and Unruh (chapter 2). Because these principles call for graduates to be equipped with broad social skills, they challenge business schools to reflect on the purpose and role of business in society as a starting point for preparing students for their careers. This impetus for reflection is consistent with Buchholz's assertion (chapter 3) that what must be assessed is business education itself, prompted by a rethinking of what a business school is all about. Specifically, he queries: What are business schools trying to accomplish and what kind of values are being imparted to students in these schools? Similarly, Stewart and Freeman (chapter 4) call on business schools to ask: What is the fundamental view of business ethics at the institution? What is being assessed and what is the purpose of the assessment? In answering these questions, business schools would do well to keep in mind the findings of the Aspen Institute, reported by McGaw (chapter 5), which portend that business schools may not be doing enough to nurture and sustain students' self-reported aspirations to contribute to society. Collins (chapter 14) demonstrates how business professors can respond to these aspirations by teaching an interdisciplinary ethics course designed to deliver and assess service-learning team projects as an active learning experience.

Addressing what it takes for business schools to transform themselves into socially responsible institutions, Martell and Castiñeira (chapter 6) propose a process by which they can incorporate the Principles of Responsible Management Education as an organizing component while striving for inclusion in the Aspen Institute's Beyond Grey Pinstripe alternative ranking of ethics and social issue coverage. These authors also detail the criteria for this alternative ranking (chapter 7) and report on those schools that have obtained it. This kind of assessment is important, as a renaissance in ethics education will undoubtedly be fueled by examples of schools that go beyond insufficient accrediting standards for ethics education. As schools look to these standard bearers, they should consider business ethics education at Duquesne University. In chapter 10, Weber describes how Duquesne's two schools of business have implemented the three pronged approach of requiring foundational ethics courses, infusing ethics across the degree programs, and offering extracurricular ethics projects. Furthermore, he details a longitudinal assessment of this approach in both schools. Other examples of potential role models for ethics education can be found in the survey of ethics coverage in top U.S. business schools by Litzky and MacLean (chapter 8). This report, along with the finding of growth in corporate social responsibility education in Europe by Orlitzky and Moon (chapter 9), suggests that business schools that do not keep pace with the vanguard may eventually be viewed as outdated by comparison.

Babson College is clearly among the vanguard in business ethics education. This college went through the daunting, time-consuming process of mobilizing faculty and administrators to integrate ethics throughout the curriculum and design an assessment process that fit. As described by Mandel and Chase (chapter 11), this infusion method does not default merely to counting ethics topics on various syllabi, an approach we have criticized as a superficial shortcut for meeting AACSB's weak accreditation standards. Instead, Babson College changed its curriculum so that ethics is truly integrated throughout. We applaud this accomplishment, with the caveat that the majority of business schools are not likely to revamp their curricula so profoundly. For the majority of business schools, the alternative is to require a standalone ethics course that capitalizes on the power of formative and summative assessment that improves instruction and learning. Ultimately, this tried-and-true method of delivering foundational knowledge could lead to the fuller integration of ethics across the curriculum, similar to what Babson College has accomplished admirably by redesigning its curriculum. As a reality check on what such redesign involves, Niehoff (chapter 12) gives an administrative accounting of what it takes to mobilize faculty to formulate student learning objectives and develop applicable rubrics for assessing them. His experience corroborates our view that most business schools will need to approach implementation and assessment changes incrementally. The three part formula for ethics education (discussed above and also in chapter 16) allows for such flexibility.

In other words, the first step for most schools that strive to deliver sound ethics education is to require a standalone course as proof that ethics knowledge is being assessed in the curriculum. The next step is to identify measurable learning objectives for the course that can be used for class-based assessment. Payne (chapter 13) weighs in on what is involved in planning, personalizing, and reporting on this level of assessment.

Specific learning objectives for a standalone ethics course are provided by Carroll and Buchholtz (chapter 15), along with the results of a survey of student learning in sampled classes. Swanson, Fisher, and Niehoff (chapter 16) also identify specific learning objectives for a standalone ethics course and provide the results of a pilot study designed to assess them. Given the goal of integrating ethics across the curriculum, it is also important to define ethics learning objectives for functional areas within business, which Kidwell, Fisher, Braun, and Swanson do for accounting in chapter 17.

Finally, we believe that an emphasis on professionalism will necessarily be part of a renaissance in business ethics education. Speaking to this imperative, Buchholz (chapter 3) discusses what professional standards would mean for assessing business ethics education. As if to reply, Waddock, Rasche, Werhane, and Unruh (chapter 2) describe how The Thunderbird School of Global Management has institutionalized a Professional Oath of Honor that parallels the inclusion of Principles of Responsible Management in its curriculum. Closely related to the call for professional standards is the need for business schools to attend to the moral competencies and character development of its students. Along these lines, Petrick (chapter 18) demonstrates improved moral competencies in students, based on his 5-year study at a Midwestern public university designed to assess the effectiveness of applying a model of change to business ethics teaching. In keeping with this accent on student moral development, Wright (chapter 19) defines character, discusses the importance of assessing it in business education, and proposes using the classroom to encourage positive character development. Stuebs (chapter 20) details how to use the technique of journaling to this end, specifically to advance students' moral motivation and moral character through reflection and assessment.

It can be seen that the views of the thought leaders featured in this book synergistically point to a potential renaissance in delivering and assessing business ethics education.

NOTES

1. Although we take a broad approach to assessment, others draw distinctions between measurement (gathering and quantifying data), assessment (analyzing and interpreting data), and evaluation (judging assessment efforts) (see Palomba & Banta, 1999, p. 297). Readers will find all these dimensions addressed in the chapters that follow.
2. The material discussed in this section is on a continuum with previous research by Swanson and Frederick (2003); Swanson (2004); Swanson and Frederick (2005); Fisher, et al. (2007); and Swanson and Fisher (2008).
3. We invited AACSB officials to present their recommendations for assessing business ethics education based on the agency's claim that distributing ethics across the curriculum is sufficient coverage, absent a standalone course. Our offer was declined.

REFERENCES

Association to Advance Collegiate Schools of Business (AACSB) International. (2010). *Eligibility procedures and accreditation standards for business accreditation.* Retrieved from http://www.aacsb.edu/accreditation/AAACSB-STANDARDS-2010.pdf.

Ames, C. (1992). Classrooms: Goals, structures, and student motivation. *Journal of Educational Psychology, 84,* 261-271.

Angelo, T. A., & Cross, K. P. (1993). *Classroom assessment techniques: A handbook for college teachers* (2nd ed.). San Francisco, CA: Jossey-Bass.

Collins, D., & Wartick, S. L. (1995). Business and society/business ethics courses: Twenty years at the crossroads. *Business and Society, 34,* 51-89.

Fisher, D. G., Swanson, D. L., & Schmidt, J. J. (2007). Accounting education lags CPE requirements: Implications for the profession and a call to action. *Accounting Education, 16*, 345-363.

Frederick, W. C. (2006). *Corporation, be good! The story of corporate social responsibility.* Indianapolis, IN: Dog Ear.

Palomba, C. A., & Banta, T. W. (1999). *Assessment essentials: Planning, implementing, and improving assessment in higher education.* San Francisco, CA: Jossey-Bass.

Perie, M., Marion, S., Gong, B., & Wurtzel, J. (2007). *The role of interim assessments in a comprehensive assessment system: A policy brief.* New York, NY: Aspen Institute.

Rynes, S. L., Trank, C. Q., Lawson, A. M., & Ilies, R. (2003). Behavioral coursework in business education: Growing evidence of a legitimacy crisis. *Academy of Management Learning & Education, 2*, 269-283.

Swanson, D. L. (2004). The buck stops here: Why universities must reclaim business ethics education. In D. Reed & R. Wellen (Eds.), Special issue on universities and corporate responsibility. *Journal of Academic Ethics, 2*, 43-61.

Swanson, D. L., & Frederick, W. C. (2003). Campaign AACSB: Are business schools complicit in corporate corruption? *Journal of Individual Employment Rights, 10*, 151-165.

Swanson, D. L., & Frederick, W. C. (2005). Denial and leadership in business ethics education. In O. C. Ferrell & R. A. Peterson (Eds.), *Business ethics: The new challenge for business schools and corporate leaders* (pp. 222-240). Armonk, NY: M.E. Sharpe.

Swanson, D. L., & Fisher, D. G. (Eds.). (2008). Business ethics education: If we don't know where we are going, any road will take us there. In *Advancing business ethics education* (pp. 1-23). Charlotte, NC: Information Age.

Vidaver-Cohen, D. (2008). Architectures of excellence: Building business school reputation by meeting the ethics challenge. In D. L. Swanson & D. G. Fisher (Eds.), *Advancing business ethics education* (pp. 67-84). Charlotte, NC: Information Age.

Willen, L. (2004, March 8). *Kellogg denies guilt as B-schools evade alumni lapses.* Retrieved from http://www.cba.ksu.edu/archives/41/kellogg.pdf

Windsor, D. (2002, October 8). *An open letter on business school responsibility.* Retrieved from http://info.cba.ksu.edu/swanson/Call/Call.pdf

CHAPTER 2

THE PRINCIPLES FOR RESPONSIBLE MANAGEMENT EDUCATION

Implications for Implementation and Assessment

**Sandra Waddock, Andreas Rasche,
Patricia H. Werhane, and Gregory Unruh**

INTRODUCTION

In July 2007, a new set of Principles for Responsible Management Education (PRME, pronounced "prime") were launched at the United Nations Global Compact Leaders Summit in Geneva, Switzerland. The PRME were developed by an international task force consisting of 60 deans, university presidents, and official representatives of leading business schools in collaboration with the United Nations Global Compact (UNGC), the Association to Advance Collegiate Schools of Business (AACSB), the Aspen Institute's Business and Society Program, the European Foundation for Management Development (EFMD), the Globally Responsible

Toward Assessing Business Ethics Education
pp. 13–28
Copyright © 2011 by Information Age Publishing
All rights of reproduction in any form reserved.

Table 2.1.   Glossary of Terms

- AACSB: Association to Advance Collegiate Schools of Business
- EABIS: European Academy of Business in Society
- EFMD: European Foundation for Management Development
- GMAC: Graduate Management Admission Council
- GRLI: Globally Responsible Leadership Initiative
- MNCs: Multinational corporations
- NGOs: Nongovernment organizations
- PRME: Principles for Responsible Management Education
- SA 8000: Social Accountability 8000
- SIOP: Sharing information in progress
- UNGC: United Nations Global Compact
- WBCSD: World Business Council for Sustainable Development

Leadership Initiative (GRLI), and NetImpact, a student organization with more than 13,000 members, all of which remain partners. In addition, the Graduate Management Admission Council (GMAC) and the European Academy of Business in Society (EABIS)[1] are part of the steering committee that guides PRME. (See Table 2.1 for a list of relevant terms and acronyms.) Only 3 years later (as of August 2010), 323 business schools or management education programs from around the world had already signed on to the principles.

PRME represent a set of voluntary standards to which management schools and programs agree to adhere in the interest of developing future leaders with the necessary insights, skills, and competencies to deal with the issues that businesses and other institutions are facing in the twenty-first century. The six principles focus on the (1) purpose of creating sustainable value and an inclusive, sustainable global economy, (2) values of responsibility, as illustrated by initiatives like the UN Global Compact's 10 principles around human rights, labor rights, ecological sustainability, and anticorruption, (3) method of creating pedagogies and education approaches that develop effective and responsible leaders, (4) research that advances understanding about the impacts of companies in creating sustainable social, environmental, and economic value, (5) partnership that fosters interactions between managers and academics to explore challenges in meeting environmental and social responsibilities, and (6) dialogue that facilitates debate among representatives of the multiple sectors that constitute society around key social and sustainability issues (see Table 2.2. and www.unprme.org for the complete principles).

Like the UNGC, which focuses on principles for responsible business, the PRME are aspirational in their intent. Inspired by the UNGC principles, PRME seek to develop "a new generation of leaders capable of man-

Table 2.2.   The Principles for Responsible Management Education

As institutions of higher learning involved in the education of current and future managers we are voluntarily committed to engaging in a continuous process of improvement of the following Principles, reporting on progress to all our stakeholders and exchanging effective practices with other academic institutions:

- **Principle 1. Purpose:** We will develop the capabilities of students to be future generators of sustainable value for business and society at large and to work for an inclusive and sustainable global economy.

- **Principle 2. Values:** We will incorporate into our academic activities and curricula the values of global social responsibility as portrayed in international initiatives such as the United Nations Global Compact.

- **Principle 3. Method:** We will create educational frameworks, materials, processes and environments that enable effective learning experiences for responsible leadership.

- **Principle 4. Research:** We will engage in conceptual and empirical research that advances our understanding about the role, dynamics, and impact of corporations in the creation of sustainable social, environmental and economic value.

- **Principle 5. Partnership:** We will interact with managers of business corporations to extend our knowledge of their challenges in meeting social and environmental responsibilities and to explore jointly effective approaches to meeting these challenges.

- **Principle 6. Dialogue:** We will facilitate and support dialog and debate among educators, business, government, consumers, media, civil society organizations and other interested groups and stakeholders on critical issues related to global social responsibility and sustainability.

We understand that our own organizational practices should serve as example of the values and attitudes we convey to our students.

aging the complex challenges faced by business and society in the 21st century" (www.unprme.org). The UNGC asks companies to support global consensus documents about how the planet is to be governed in recognition of the increasingly important role that companies play in global governance. The PRME grew in part because business leaders, having accepted the challenge of the UNGC, looked to business schools—and asked the question: What are you doing to help future business leaders understand what they really need to know in the future?

In light of the economic meltdown that began in 2008 with the subprime mortgage crisis and collapse of financial institutions that had a casino mentality, we believe that the PRME are more important than ever as markers for business schools. The PRME emphasize continual improvement, transparency (including annual sharing of information on progress of implementation), curriculum change to incorporate more materials emphasized by PRME, and encouragement of research on PRME-related issues. The PRME have been endorsed by two leading management education proponents. The board of the accrediting body AACSB International unanimously endorsed the PRME in September 2007 as a complement to and continuous improvement framework for management education, and has committed to promoting the PRME among its member institutions. Similarly, EFMD formally endorsed PRME at its September 2007 meeting.

Fundamentally, PRME are designed to "inspire and champion responsible management education" (PRME, 2008, p. 2), much as the UNGC Principles hope to inspire responsible management practices. They serve as a framework for continuous—and voluntary—improvement in global citizenship education and research, but are not (yet) part of any accreditation process. The premise behind PRME is that management education is a powerful force for change in the world, since management in practice frequently commands more resources and employs more people than governments of smaller nations. Never has this force for change been needed more than in the face of the serious ethical lapses and system failures that triggered the collapse of investment banking, shaking the foundations of the financial services industry and posing global ramifications for all industries. Significantly, the global scientific consensus on climate change that has emerged also highlights the need for future leaders with a far broader understanding of system dynamics in terms of ethics, responsibility, and accountability than was needed in the past. The PRME's founders hope that adopters will share best practices and that adoption will provide recognition and potential reputational benefits. There is growing recognition of the important roles that businesses can and should play in fostering not just economic value, but also ecological sustainability, social justice, and peace in a troubled world. Yet there are questions about whether current approaches to management education can fully meet the emerging needs of businesses—or, for that matter, of the world itself.

The PRME are designed to help educate future managers and leaders who can quite explicitly link social and ecological considerations directly to business matters to foster a more cohesive and inclusive global economy, and who can combine profitability with social justice and sustainability. An underlying assumption is that management education actually does work to effect change in understanding, attitudes, and practice among learners. If that is true, then what management students need to learn to meet the needs of the future has to be broadened considerably beyond what is offered today in most management education programs.

Thus, behind PRME is an understanding that management education programs need to take leadership roles today to educate future leaders to be capable of coping with the kinds of social, ecological, and governance issues that their organizations will increasingly face in this troubled and resource-constrained world. The key, of course, is implementation of the principles in management programs. Yet many questions remain about how to best implement them, which we will address later.

Behind the PRME lies a sense that the world is changing rapidly. New demands face business leaders to deal with the planet itself more sustainably, to deal with the numerous societies their organizations operate in more equitably and with greater cultural understanding, and to be more open, transparent, and responsible with respect to their stakeholders. As the recent credit crisis has shown, questions abound about whether current management education, with its strongly functional, problem-solving orientation, develops future leaders with the requisite skills to meet these new demands. The PRME fundamentally ask management schools to ensure that graduates are equipped with the globally oriented, broad thinking, societally and ecologically based skills needed to cope with these demands.

About a year after the PRME were launched, the authors of this chapter organized an All-Academy Professional Development Workshop at the annual Academy of Management meeting in Anaheim, California. The initial aim of the meeting was to identify and share the questions that emerged in the early phases of adopting and beginning to implement the PRME, as well as those answers concerning PRME implementation already formulated. Early adopters were invited to discuss their experiences and best practices and share these with others who had just adopted or were considering adopting PRME, with the aim of facilitating shared experiences and best practices regarding responsible management education. In addition, jointly developing innovative solutions to implementing PRME were discussed.

What follows is a synthesis of some of the issues raised with respect to implementation at that meeting along with our understanding of how the PRME addresses those issues. We have organized these issues into four major areas of concern: (1) reasons for signing on to PRME, (2) particularly important questions about PRME and its current status, (3) reflections about critical issues within the implementation process, including an example of how one school, the Thunderbird Global School of Management, has handled these issues, and (4) a reflection on how PRME can influence assessment issues with regard to responsible management education.

WHY SIGN THE PRINCIPLES FOR RESPONSIBLE MANAGEMENT EDUCATION?

There are numerous rationales that can be offered for becoming a PRME signatory. One of these rationales is student- or applicant-demand for a more globalized curriculum or for corporate responsibility initiatives within management programs. A recent survey of over 2,000 MBAs by NetImpact concludes that more than 75% of all students want to learn more about topics such as corporate social responsibility and environmental sustainability. Another rationale is the potential to brand a program, or at least enhance a program's brand, by leading with the PRME's values. The well-known Beyond Grey Pinstripes ranking of the Aspen Institute demonstrates that schools can compete with regard to their inclusion of social, environmental, and governance issues in their curricula. We think that PRME adopters can benefit from potential positive reputational effects which, however, should be judged carefully because there is also the risk of negative public exposure if a business school decides to sign up without doing much to implement the six principles. We will address the issue of signatory risk more in the sections that follow.

Further, because companies need leaders and managers equipped with an understanding of the complexity and constraints of the environment they are facing, employers are beginning to demand more attention to these issues in management curricula. For example, the World Business Council for Sustainable Development (2009) argues that:

> Tomorrow's leaders will need new skills and competencies to cope with increasing social and environmental challenges across a changing landscape. A sustainability perspective will be critical to managing relationships, creating change, and planning for the future.

In a similar vein, the GRLI notes that the leadership challenge of the future contains four key challenges: (1) being able to act in a global context, (2) broadening corporate purpose to reflect accountability to societies everywhere, (3) putting ethics at the heart of management practice and thinking, and (4) transforming "business education to give corporate global responsibility the centrality it deserves" (Globally Responsible Leadership Initiative, 2005, p. 2). The PRME fit neatly into these and related agendas.

Most importantly, signing on to the PRME allows institutions to set the issue of responsible management education on the agenda of the business school and thus gather support among top-level decision makers (e.g., deans). Building on this, schools can use the six principles to start a discussion about how to change the status quo with regard to responsible management education and/or develop courses and programs from scratch. Last but not least, the PRME provide a platform for exchanging ideas and learning among institutions that integrate social and environmental issues into research and teaching. PRME participants can profit from a strong global network of committed schools that are willing to jointly look for innovate solutions to better prepare students for tomorrow's markets.

UNANSWERED QUESTIONS ABOUT THE
PRINCIPLES FOR RESPONSIBLE MANAGEMENT EDUCATION

Among the obvious questions about the PRME are the ones about purpose. Is the goal simply to create dialogue, ultimately to change business school education, to create some sort of brand that could be a model for other business schools, or help with student placement in the global economy? Of course, at some level, all of these could be answered positively, but our understanding of the PRME is that, like the UNGC, the ultimate goals involve dialogue, learning, and change of management education so that graduates—future leaders and managers—have the skills needed to understand the truly complex world they will face. Thus, we want to explicitly point out that the PRME do not aim to be a compliance measurement system. The six principles are deliberately designed in a rather broad way so that adopting institutions have the necessary free space to come up with contextualized solutions that fit their respective context (e.g., with regard to existing national regulations and/or administrative structures). One risk, of course, is that signing is simply what is called "bluewashing" in the case of United Nations initiatives (i.e., wrapping one's organization in the blue UN flag without really changing much internally, with the result that signing is rhetoric without reality). Naturally, the PRME organizers hope that there will be substance and some degree of curriculum, research, and organizational change resulting from signing the PRME.

Because the PRME represent a new initiative, numerous issues can be raised, particularly with respect to implementation. For example, is there some sort of paradox associated with implementing the PRME simultaneously with the need to maintain academic freedom? Although we do not believe that the PRME, which are derived in part from the globally agreed principles of the UNGC (all of which come from international treaties signed by the countries of the world), limit academic freedom in any way, perhaps they do suggest more of a societally rather than solely economically based orientation toward management education. In the PRME there is an acceptance of the need for both sustainability and social equity in a globalized world that is consistent with progressive thought on such issues. It is notable in this context that the PRME were constructed by a task force drawn from all parts of the planet so as to avoid potential problems of bias toward any one part of the world's thinking on these issues.

For us, as for many others, the key question however is the one of implementation: How do adopters actually bring the six principles to life? What reforms with regard to existing curricula and programs are necessary? How do we ensure that courses on responsible management education are not static but constantly improving? These questions have content (What do we teach within responsible management education?), process (How do we teach responsible management?), and context (What is the business school and general economic context shaping responsible management education?) dimensions, all of which are heavily interrelated. We will reflect on implementation and assessment issues in the next section.

IMPLEMENTATION AND ASSESSMENT ISSUES

Approaching Implementation

Signing on to the PRME is relatively easy to do, with the major requirement being a letter from the dean or other authority in the management school indicating a desire to participate. The other conditions of being signatories are to (1) begin the process of implementing the principles in the institution's operations, research, and curriculum, (2) communicate annually to the PRME office on progress, and (3) publicly advocate PRME values. Reports are relatively simple, because the initiative is not meant to be bureaucratic, and, as with the UNGC, there are no enforceable sanctions that the PRME office has (with the exception of possible de-listing, as has happened with UNGC signatories that failed to submit communication on progress reports).

To deal with issues of implementation and communication of learning among signatories, the PRME office launched a Global Forum for Responsible Management Education in December 2008. This forum, similar to UNGC learning forums, brought signatories (and potential signatories) together to discuss their learning with respect to implementing the PRME in their institutions, issues associated with PRME, and related matters. PRME is a small initiative, housed within the UNGC office, which itself is a relatively small operation by United Nations standards.

Strategies for Implementation

There is, of course, some risk in being an early signatory. Taking the lead in saying that a business school will teach and act responsibly creates a degree of visibility that demands consistency between rhetoric and action, but the reality is that no institution is perfect. Companies that have set themselves up as leaders in corporate responsibility face much the same type of risk, but have moved ahead because of the potential for reputational advantage and differentiation that such leadership provides. Business schools are likely to follow much the same strategy.

In the process, political savvy is necessary, since approaching issues of curriculum redesign and inclusion of new materials in courses already overloaded with content can be tricky. Questions of whether business in society content should be delivered in a stand-alone course or integrated into all other courses have perennially been asked about related topics like ethics—with the answer typically given that it is not an either/or situation. Both are needed. For business and society content to be considered sufficiently it needs to be delivered in graded modules or courses. At the same time, the very nature of globalization, ethics, and business in society content and what Joseph Stiglitz has called its "discontents" means that the best approach is also to incorporate such issues in functional and integrative courses, where students can see these issues in context.

In many respects the PRME present an alternative perspective to the traditional neoclassical economics model, suggesting that businesses do have responsibilities to the societies and natural environment in which they reside that go significantly beyond economic values. Because these issues can be controversial, it is likely that processes of dialogue, combined with the commitment of the dean, will be necessary parts of the implementation process in some schools.

Schools that have adopted the PRME can approach implementation strategically in a number of different ways. The top-down way is for the dean to sign the PRME and then announce the signing to the faculty, with the expectation that changes will then occur. Sometimes this approach is taken because the dean recognizes, as companies have done with respect to the UNGC, that there is already significant alignment between the management school's existing values and those articulated in the PRME. Hence, signing the PRME is very consistent with what is already being done. Another path followed by Thunderbird, one of the early signatories, is to move quickly to incorporate the PRME into operations and curriculum while generating dialogue among the faculty, department chair, and others in the governance structure to ensure buy-in in a more bottoms-up approach. The example of how the Thunderbird Global School of Management has handled the implementation process is given at the end of this chapter. Another possible bottoms-up approach is for schools to respond to employer demands for inclusion of PRME-related content in programs. In this vein, students are another source of strategic pressure for implementation, since many of them join management programs with such interests already in mind, while others seek job opportunities where they can put those interests to work. To create demand on the student side, it is important for management schools and programs to enlist companies known as responsible to recruit on campuses, as well as to include non-governmental organizations with similar leanings.

As a further strategic consideration, we recommend auditing and publicizing related work already being done by faculty that represents "low hanging fruit" on which the local case for PRME can be established, as well as finding local champions to guide the implementation process. Another possibility is to create discipline-focused modules that can be embedded in the different disciplines, and then reward faculty for creating and teaching those modules. Additionally, certifications might be offered to doctoral students who have mastered related subject areas, including business ethics, corporate responsibility, and business in society issues related to PRME. Other possibilities for changing curriculum content might be to incorporate mandatory (or elective) courses in sustainability, business responsibility, business ethics, business in society, or courses with similar foci. Experientially based courses and extracurricular experiences that incorporate PRME related values and principles are other potentially excellent sources of new material for curricula.

At a broader level of strategy, there is a political task to be done to ensure that major associations adopt the PRME principles for their constituencies and work with them to ensure that either accreditation processes or membership requirements take note of the school's or program's stance toward the PRME. As noted above, most of the major business education institutions are already part of the steering committee for the PRME; however, more academically oriented organizations have yet to become fully aware of the PRME, including various divisions of the Academy of Management (especially the Social Issues in Management Division), the Society for Business Ethics, the International Society for Business in Society, the International Society for Business, Economics, and Ethics, and similar professional associations.

Assessment Dimensions and Issues

With regard to assessment issues, there are two major dimensions where the PRME can make a difference. First, the PRME can help to hold all faculty members (i.e. traditional ethics-focused faculty members, but also, and most importantly, faculty members who do not have a traditional ethics focus) accountable for student learning on issues related to sustainability, ethics, responsibility, accountability, and governance. We believe that the PRME can support this process of establishing accountability by encouraging participating faculty members to translate the six principles into specific learning objectives for students. These objectives can then be used as a starting point for more precise assessments. For instance, Principle 2 (regarding values) in Table 2.2 asks institutions of higher learning to incorporate and communicate universal values (e.g., as promoted by the Global Compact) into teaching. A resulting learning objective which can guide assessment is that students establish familiarity with the content and nature of universal agreements, such as the Universal Declaration of Human Rights. Ensuring that students become familiar with important declarations and treaties, which have formed the normative basis of compliance based standards like SA 8000 as well as principle-based initiatives like the UNGC, can guide teaching (and also research; see Principle 4). Then, given this familiarity, students can be given a case study and tested as to whether or how Principle 2 can be implemented in a specific situation relevant to the course and its application.

As another example, Principle 5 (regarding partnerships) can be translated into a more process-oriented learning objective geared to incorporating the views of key stakeholders in classroom discussions. According to Principle 6, this translates into a dialogue with institutional partners as well as other stakeholders, such as NGOs and unions. Guided by this learning objective, field visits, practitioner presentations, and moderated discussions with external stakeholders can act as important stimuli to facilitate students' interests and allow for a more practice-based discussion in the classroom. The bottom line is that the PRME can act as an important starting point for formulating learning objectives which, in turn, can influence pedagogy and, ultimately, an assessment of it.

Sharing information on progress (SIOP) is an important element of implementing and assessing the progress of the PRME as it provides annual evidence of continuous improvement. Instead of being an additional burden, reporting is supposed to be seen as an opportunity to share information, foster mutual learning, and provide information on how well initiatives are being implemented. The overall purpose of SIOP is to share experiences, provide information to the market, and create a sense of community. To achieve maximum transparency (also for students), SIOP can be delivered in any language; it may but does not have to be English. As of this writing, a PRME discussion group is developing a web-based template which is supposed to be used by signatories. The template focuses on the following aspects of an organization's PRME efforts: (1) key initiatives, (2) key challenges, and (3) objectives for the coming year.

The second dimension of the relation between assessment issues and the PRME is, from our perspective, the installation of effective and efficient feedback mechanisms to advance the experience that students have while attending courses. We believe that the above-mentioned mandatory SIOP, which is required from all PRME signatories, allows (and to a certain extent forces) adopting schools to permanently reflect on their practices. The required annual reporting, thus, should be seen less as an extra burden, but as an opportunity to constantly review and improve a school's performance with regard to responsible management education.

Once there is a common reporting framework, which would make the different reports more comparable, the PRME can be used to gather feedback internally. It can also be used to benchmark one's own practices against other schools in the same region. We believe that the mandatory SIOP can help to foster assessment in the sense that responsible management education is kept on the agenda of top-level decision makers within schools.

CONCLUDING REFLECTIONS ON RESPONSIBLE MANAGEMENT EDUCATION

At one level, the PRME offer an unusual opportunity for business schools: a chance to reflect seriously on the purpose and role of businesses in society—and of business schools and management programs for preparing leaders for the future they actually face. In light of the numerous challenges facing humanity—the financial meltdown, climate change, pandemics, a growing gap between rich and poor, and increased local violence to name only a few issues—the PRME present an opportunity for business schools to think seriously about the nature of the leaders they are developing and what their perspective on making change in the world is. Business as usual has become business unusual in this time of multiple crises. A critical question in this regard is: What do you want your school to look like in this new century of globalization? This question can help future managers anticipate the need to deal with various complex global issues, which is only fitting, given the dominance of business as an institution in the world.

The key issue is that the PRME will be what each school and its faculty want them to be. If we take this initiative seriously, we can start a dialogue within and among business schools and also with other important parties such as accreditation agencies, student organizations, and NGOs. The six principles themselves need to be filled with context specific meaning in each institution; they need to be brought to life by serious reflections among students, faculty, alumni, and other stakeholders. Just as the 10 principles of the UNGC need reflection and commitment to make something out of them, the PRME by themselves are only as good and useful as we make them by reflection and action in each of our institutions. It is our responsibility to accept the challenges posed by these principles. For, how can we research and teach about responsibility without accepting responsibility for education ourselves? This, dear reader, is a question that *you* have to answer.

APPENDIX

Case Example: Thunderbird's Approach to Principles for Responsible Management Education

Although different universities obviously require implementation approaches specific to their situations, the experience of one institution, Thunderbird School of Global Management (Glendale, AZ), which is comprehensive, may be instructive for other institutions. Hence some details are provided here. Thunderbird, which by its nature is a globally oriented institution, began its implementation process with a recognition of the setting in which business today exists, including the current state of global governance.

As background, the seeds of the current international governance system of nation states emerged in the seventeenth century with the Treaty of Westphalia and, for about 300 years, nation states have been the bedrock of the international system of law. In the twentieth century, however, emerging problems such as HIV/AIDS, climate change, and other transborder environmental and social issues have revealed the limitations of the nation state and its boundaries. While the decisions made in the United States, and in the future by emerging nations like China and Brazil, will have important implications for the long-term viability of humanity, there are in addition a variety of actors other than national governments that are increasingly influential in global governance. These include multinational businesses and nongovernmental organizations like Transparency International, Greenpeace, and Oxfam, not to mention terrorist organizations, all of which can influence the course of global political evolution.

Of all these nonstate actors, it is arguably MNCs that have the greatest influence in global governance, since these corporations are among the biggest institutions in the world, with greater privileges and liberties in many cases to operate globally than most nation states. With their global sourcing networks and marketing practices, it is sometimes difficult to determine whether MNCs have any national allegiance that would root them. Because of these factors, MNCs play an important structural role in the global economy, making them more powerful in some ways than many nations, who despite this reality, are loathe to cede any preeminence in global governance.

The UNGC, on which the PRME are partially based, represents an interesting new development for the United Nations. Prior attempts to develop codes for companies mostly failed because they were prescriptive and MNCs perceived that the UN was dictating behavior to executives. The UNGC, on the other hand, is derived directly from existing international law, and instead asks MNCs to sign onto the same rules and norms that nation states accept—that is, to principles endorsed by humanity about how the planet is to be governed. The UNGC also explicitly recognizes the important role corporations play in solving some—although certainly not all—of the challenges facing the planet. In fact, many of humanity's most pressing global concerns cannot be adequately addressed without the participation of global business.

Business leaders have responded to the UN's invitation for corporations to become constructive participants in enacting the elements found in international law by signing on to the UNGC in large numbers. However, it has been the experience at many UNGC network meetings where business leaders and business school educators meet that there has been a disconnect between what corporations are committing to in the UNGC and how business schools are training young managers. Quite literally in these meetings, business leaders have looked at business educators and asked the following questions:

We've committed ourselves to fulfilling these principles, but what are you doing to help ensure that we can meet our commitments? Future managers and leaders need a solid understanding of the global problems addressed in the Compact's principles, like those related to human rights and the environment. So, what are you, the business schools, doing to ensure that the people we will be hiring know what they need to know?

Thunderbird felt compelled early on to respond to these calls from UNGC signatories and, therefore, became part of the process of both developing and ultimately implementing the PRME. In contrast to the benign dictator approach to signing the PRME, whereby a senior university official unilaterally commits the school to the PRME, Thunderbird began a broad consultative process that included students, faculty, administrators, and alumni. The process revolved around internal dialogue that asked: How would we approach management education if we consider management to be a true and honorable profession, like medicine or law?

The question forced Thunderbird to recognize that as a professional endeavor, management education has two important aspects. The first is the knowledge and skills practitioners need to perform the profession's responsibilities, something business schools are very adept at imparting to their graduates. But professionals also understand that misuse of those same skills can cause harm to society. A doctor's skills can be used to cure or kill, for instance. In recognition of this, the profession of medicine has a Hippocratic Oath which enjoins its practitioners to do no harm in the pursuit of their professional duties. Management has no equivalent code, yet the consequences of managerial decisions are often more far-reaching than a single doctor's, amplified by the power of corporations to leverage capital, labor, and other resources globally. This reality led Thunderbird to develop its own Professional Oath of Honor in 2006, drafted by the student-led Thunderbird Honor Council after this body was challenged by the school's President Angel Cabrera in 2005 to establish an oath that could guide students through their business careers (see the Thunderbird Professional Oath of Honor below). The oath recognizes that professions exist to serve more than simply the practitioners and that while maximizing shareholder wealth is an important goal for management, the oath recognizes that managerial professionals need to also be guided by a super-ordinate goal. For Thunderbird this higher goal has been framed as creating sustainable prosperity worldwide or prosperity that can be shared intragenerationally and intergenerationally.

Thunderbird Professional Oath of Honor

As a Thunderbird and a global citizen, I promise:
I will strive to act with honesty and integrity,
I will respect the rights and dignity of all people,
I will strive to create sustainable prosperity worldwide,
I will oppose all forms of corruption and exploitation, and
I will take responsibility for my actions.
As I hold true to these principles, it is my hope that I may enjoy an honorable reputation and peace of conscience.
This pledge I make freely and upon my honor.

The process of having the code broadly adopted by the larger Thunderbird community involved debate among students and alumni, and then with the faculty. Student leaders from the Honor Council met individually with each faculty member (there are only about 50 in the school), getting their feedback and input and then using it to refine the oath. The refined proposal was then presented for debate in the faculty senate, which ultimately voted unanimously to approve the document, thanks largely to the inclusive deliberative process that preceded the vote. From there, the oath went to the president's office, from which it was presented to the school's board of trustees. Following presentations by students, faculty, and administrators, the board unanimously adopted the oath as an institutional pillar of the school.

Within this process, it was important to allow concerns to be voiced and incorporated as changes into the document. As a result, when the PRME were brought to the various university constituencies, the approval process was much easier, because the passage of the oath had already paved the way. The harder work, of course, is making changes to the curriculum to live up to the principles. Part of the challenge is making space in an already crowded curriculum and addressing the concern that class time for PRME coverage will be allotted at the expense of the functional areas. But the PRME proved to be a credible lever because they provide a platform for the type of metrics that the accrediting body, AACSB, is now seeking. The process has effectively institutionalized PRME content in the curriculum by the inclusion of global citizenship as one of Thunderbird's core learning outcomes, which is assessed and reported on internally and externally on both an individual course and overall program basis. In addition, Thunderbird incorporates the oath and the PRME into marketing materials so that candidate students are pre-advised about the expectations of the Thunderbird community. In fact, one of the application essays requires students to read and reflect on the principles. Once students are accepted into the program, they encounter the Oath and principles throughout their degree programs, starting in student orientations and continuing in the core module in the curriculum and in a range of electives. Finally, at the end of their degree studies, students are invited to formally sign the oath and principles upon graduation, leaving them with a distinct impression about the professional nature of their roles as future managers.

NOTES

1. The European Academy of Business in Society (EABIS) is now simply The Academey of Business in Society although still recognized as EABIS.

REFERENCES

Globally Responsible Leadership Initiative. (2005). *Globally responsible leadership: A call for engagement.* Brussels, Belgium: EFMD (The International Network for Excellence in Management Education).

Principles for Responsible Management Education. (2009). Retrieved from http://www.unprme.org

Principles for Responsible Management Education. (2008). *A global initiative, a global agenda: The principles for responsible management education.* New York, NY: United Nations Global Compact Office.

World Business Council for Sustainable Development. (2009). *Future leaders team.* Retrieved from http://www.wbcsd.org/web/flt/fltbrochure.pdf

CHAPTER 3

ASSESSING BUSINESS EDUCATION IN RELATION TO AN ETHIC OF SERVICE

Rogene A. Buchholz

INTRODUCTION

Assessing business ethics education is at best a difficult undertaking. Some years ago in speaking to a Rotary Club meeting about the efforts that were being undertaken to incorporate ethics into business school education, I was asked the question as to whether all this activity that I mentioned was really doing any good. This was a question I could not answer directly and could only reiterate that surely all this activity had to be having some impact. Thus I could only point to input measures as a way of assessing business ethics education. And this was before Enron and the other scandals that took place at the beginning of the century. If I had been asked that question after these scandals, I would have had a better answer.

So how does one assess business ethics education? Determining whether there is a required course on ethics in the curriculum doesn't seem to be enough, as this course might not have any impact whatsoever on student's ethical sensibilities. Nor would assessing whether ethical

Toward Assessing Business Ethics Education
pp. 29–47
Copyright © 2011 by Information Age Publishing

issues are integrated into existing functional courses. Giving some kind of ethics exam at the end of the program would seem to be a superficial way of determining whether ethical courses have had a positive impact. Outcome assessments of this kind are always problematical, which is why the Association for the Advancement of Collegiate Schools of Business gave up on outcome assessments of business school education in general some years ago.

Assessment of any kind must be done in light of the goals and objectives that are hoped to be attained by some kind of activity. For those who teach business ethics these goals and objectives are most likely something like increasing the ethical sensibilities of business school students, making students aware of the ethical dimension of management decision making, giving students some kind of a theoretical framework that is useful in analyzing ethical issues, imparting whatever skills are relevant to making ethical decisions, and similar objectives. These are important objectives for those who teach business ethics, but are they important objectives for the business school curriculum as a whole? Or are ethical concerns merely peripheral matters that only get attention when corruption becomes front page news or the system fails to function effectively?

In response to the financial crisis of 2008-2009, there was renewed criticism of business schools, particularly given the fact that the top schools routinely sent more than 40% of their graduates into the financial industry (Holland, 2009). Some of the critics focused on the scientific orientation, claiming that business schools had become too scientific and detached for real-world concerns. Others said that students in these schools were taught to oversimplify management problems and come up with hasty solutions to more complicated problems that should have taken more time and thought. Still others contended that students received a limited and distorted view of their role in society and that they graduated with a focus on maximizing shareholder value with only a limited understanding of the social and ethical factors that are essential to business leadership.[1]

Answering these criticisms involves a reexamination of the purpose of schools of business and management in modern society. Some authors have suggested that business schools have become nothing more than highly sophisticated trade schools to prepare students for careers in organizations whose sole purpose is to create wealth for themselves as agents and for shareholders as principals (Khurana, 2007). It is believed that one of the primary purposes of gaining a business school education is to develop a social network that can give access to a job in one of the top companies in the country, if not the world. The MBA program is seen to be more like an exclusive fraternity or country club that gives students an advantage in the labor market.

> If academic credentialing and providing a social network are now the primary functions of business schools, then the role of the institution is that of a gatekeeper rather than a transmitter of knowledge and values ... a student invests in higher education simply to purchase a signal that is received by prospective employers as an indication of the likelihood that he or she is committed to a business career and will perform productively. (Khurana, 2007, pp. 352, 348)

It seems that students see the MBA degree as opening up opportunities to climb the corporate ladder that is not available to nondegree people. They do not have to start in the mail room or on the factory floor but can start on the middle rungs of the ladder, so to speak.

> The business schools' most important purpose is to serve the corporate labor market by screening, disciplining, training, and mentally conditioning its graduates so they may be minimally ready for life within the corporate system. Never mind that most of the knowledge acquired by MBA students is irrelevant to the actual conditions and challenges to be encountered in the workplace, as countless critics have demonstrated. Getting in the corporate door is what it's all about. (Frederick, 2006, p. 248)

Others (Etzioni, 2002; Mitroff, 2004; Swanson & Frederick, 2003) have criticized the MBA program as being an enculturation process where students learn to accept the basic values found in corporate culture and become committed to the goals and practices that are needed to achieve marketplace success. An Aspen Institute study (Frederick, 2006) found that students entering an MBA program who may have initially believed that customer needs and product quality were top priorities of the company changed their top priority to shareholder value by the time of graduation.

The perception is that the corporate system is currently geared toward making a profit and maximizing shareholder wealth. Nothing else really matters including corporate social responsibility, ethics, ecology, or any other subject not directly related to the central objective of meeting the financial goals of the organization. Once in the corporation one has to play the game to get ahead, and the game consists of meeting financial goals, not being socially or environmentally responsible or making a contribution to society. As Khurana (2007) states: "Notions of sustained effort to build companies that create useful products and services, provide employment, and contribute to their communities are less and less a part of the aspirations American business school students" (p. 380).

What these comments suggest is that assessing business ethics education is too narrow a focus. What must be assessed is business education in general, and this involves a rethinking of what a business school is all about and what goals and objectives are important to its faculty and administration. What are business schools, as a whole, trying to accomplish and what kind of values are being imparted to students in these schools? Are business schools merely sophisticated vocational schools that are teaching students how to maximize shareholder wealth by making as much profit as possible? And if so, what are they doing as part of a university setting dedicated to a search for knowledge?

THE NEED TO PROFESSIONALIZE MANAGEMENT

One of the most important questions related to this issue is whether or not management can be considered a profession akin to law or medicine or even education itself. If it is a profession rather than a vocation, then it has ample justification for being in a university setting along with the more traditional professions. This question also has implications for assessment of business school education, as it would entail some way of determining whether or not business schools are truly imparting the values and attitudes that go with being a profession rather than just imparting the knowledge that is useful to running a business organization in a profitable manner. This is a whole different way of thinking about management and its responsibilities to society and how one would determine whether or not professional goals and objectives are being attained.

This question of whether management is a profession has been discussed many times over the years, but one of the most insightful articles of recent origin was written by Warren Bennis and James O'Toole (2005), two management professors at the University of Southern California. In this article they analyze the reasons for the alleged failure of business schools to adequately prepare their graduates for the world of business. In the beginning of the article they enumerate recent criticisms of MBA programs that include failing to impart useful skills, failing to prepare leaders, failing to instill norms of ethical behavior, and even failing to lead graduates to corporate jobs. These criticisms came from many different groups including students, employers, the media, and deans of some of the country's most prestigious business schools. Attempts to address these problems resulted in many efforts to revise the curriculum to be more relevant to the business world, but Bennis and O'Toole believe that the curriculum is the effect, and not the cause, of what ails the modern business school.

The actual cause of today's crisis in management education, they believe, can be traced to a dramatic shift in the culture of business schools that has taken place over the past several decades as many leading business schools have come to measure their success solely by the rigor of their scientific research rather than in terms of the competence of their graduates or how well faculties understand important drivers of business performance. This scientific model, they argue, is predicated on the faulty assumption that business is an academic discipline like chemistry or geology, when in fact it is a profession akin to medicine and the law. Business schools should be professional schools, and this distinction between a profession and an academic discipline is crucial and no curricular reforms will work, in their opinion, until the scientific model is replaced by a model that is more appropriate to the special requirements of a profession.

The rest of their article discusses how business schools came to embrace the scientific model of physicists and economists rather than the professional model of doctors and lawyers. The problem is not that business schools have embraced scientific rigor, but rather that they have forsaken other forms of knowledge that are relevant to business organizations. To regain relevance, according to Bennis and O'Toole, business schools must realize that business management is not a scientific discipline, but a profession, and they must deal with the things a professional education requires. There must be a balance between rigor and relevance.

Citing Rakesh Khurana, an associate professor at the Harvard Business School, Bennis and O'Toole point out that the professions have at least four key elements: (1) an accepted body of knowledge, (2) a system for certifying that individuals have mastered that body of knowledge before they are allowed to practice, (3) a commitment to the public good, and (4) an enforceable code of ethics. Professions are oriented toward practice and focused on client needs, and above all integrate knowledge and practice. While not proposing making management a gated profession requiring credentialing and licensing, they do believe these elements of a profession are critical to business school education.

The most important element in the above list for purposes of this chapter and perhaps for a profession in general is commitment to the public good. What does this mean in a business context and what implications does this criterion have for management education? Is it possible for business management to be committed to the public good or is this something that is more akin to the traditional professions that have an obligation to focus on their clients' needs? What is expected of management in our society in the kind of economic system in which business functions? What does it mean for business management to be a profession in the context of a free enterprise or capitalistic system?

According to Albert William Levi (1964) writing in an article entitled "Ethical Confusion and the Business Community," the aim of a profession is the performance of a service and the true professional keeps his or her eye on the activity. Commitment and responsibility are thus a mark of the professions. The aim of business, on the other hand, is profit and the true businessperson keeps his or her eye on the reward. This is a logical distinction according to Levi, and calls attention to the diametrically opposed point of view between a business and a profession as ordinarily understood. The major problem with a professional model for business is the conflict between the professional demand for service and the exclusively business demand for profits.

This distinction is largely a matter of emphasis, according to Levi. For instance, if a doctor thinks more of his fee than of the patient, then he can be deemed a businessperson, even if he spent 6 years in the best medical school in the country. Likewise, if the owner of a bakery takes pride in her bread and is less interested in the volume of her yearly profit than in the quality and reputation of her merchandise, then she is a professional, even if she never graduated from college. Levi recognizes that this distinction may sound utopian to many people and squares badly with the practice of many fee hungry doctors and lawyers. But this does not impair the logic of the position, and only indicates the deterioration of standards which results when business mentality at its worst corrupts the traditional professions.

For business to become a profession, then, it must embody methods whereby emphasis upon the activity, commitment, and responsibility become the common property of members of the business community. But this change of emphasis in business goes against the grain of the mentality of Western civilization and requires a psychological reorientation of that mentality in terms of a rethinking of the purpose of business and society itself. As Levi (1964, p. 27) states, "the ethical behavior of any segment within society is generally not without roots in the more general aspiration of that society as a whole." And our society is infused with a philosophy of individualism and rights that forms the basis for our understanding of modern capitalism. It is this philosophy that must be broadened to include community and responsibility in order for management to be considered a profession.[2]

THE PROFESSIONALIZATION PROJECT

The emergence of management as an identifiable function within the corporation was congruent with the rise of the modern corporation. These enterprises grew in size and complexity by combining the various stages of production within a single industrial establishment. The integration and synchronization of these stages allowed output to be controlled and managed in a manner that was not possible in an economy composed of many smaller enterprises. Thus the economy changed after the Civil War from one composed mostly of small organizations in competition with each other to one dominated by the large corporations we see in today's economy that operate in a different competitive environment.

The management of this kind of organization involves a great many administrative tasks, such as directing the labor force, organizing the production process, defining procedures to get the work done, and numerous other tasks of this nature. The performance of these tasks fell to an emerging function within the corporation called "management" that was not identified as either labor or capital, but over time came to control the modern corporation. These managers had a great deal of discretion regarding the use of corporate resources and were not subject to the discipline of the market in the same way as smaller enterprises. This led Alfred Chandler (1977), a former professor at the Harvard Business School, to argue that the visible hand of management had replaced the invisible hand of the market. Managers were making administrative decisions about the employment of resources that would have been made by the market in a more competitive environment composed of smaller, less integrated enterprises.

Managerial capitalism thus involved the emergence of a managerial class that did not derive its legitimacy from the ownership of stock, but rather from its ability to administer and coordinate the tasks that needed to be done in large and complex organizations. It took over the authority from the entrepreneurs who may have started the business and from the owners of the corporation who had certain property rights. Managers controlled the corporation, called the shots, and their authority within the corporation was unquestioned. Their legitimacy, however, was always in question, and the argument that they derived their authority from stockholders through the board of directors was largely fictional. They came to control the board of directors, and until recent times, shareholders were largely shut out of the governance process. But by what right did they take over control of the corporation?

> One must also concede that both the Founding Fathers and Adam Smith would have been perplexed by the kind of capitalism we have.... They could not have interpreted the domination of economic activity by large corporate bureaucracies as representing, in any sense, the working of a "system of natural liberty." The large, publicly owned corporation of today which strives for immortality, which is committed to no line of business but rather seeks the best return on investment, which is governed by an anonymous oligarchy, would have troubled them, just as it troubles and puzzles us. And they would have asked themselves the same questions we have been asking ourselves for almost a century now: Who "owns" this new leviathan? Who gov-

erns it, and by what right, and according to what principles? (Kristol, 1978, pp. 4-5)

This legitimacy question continued to haunt managers as they needed to find some basis for the authority they exercised over the use of corporate resources. One of the ways this was attempted, according to Rakesh Khurana (2007), an associate professor of organizational behavior at the Harvard Business School who published an extremely interesting history of business schools in the United States, was the establishment of business schools within the American university. The primary purpose of these schools at their inception, according to Khurana, "was to legitimate and institutionalize the new occupation of management" (Khurana, 2007, p. 6). The achievement of this purpose was attempted by presenting management as an emerging profession like the traditional professions of medicine and law and thus dedicated to serve the broader interests of society rather than the more narrowly defined interests of either capital or labor.

This professionalization project as a decades-long goal for business schools began to be abandoned after the end of World War II. This trend was accelerated with the publication of the Gordon and Howell (1959) and Pierson (1959) reports, funded by the Ford Foundation and Carnegie Foundation, respectively, both of which were extremely critical of business school education as being too vocationally oriented and, consequently, lacking in academic respectability. These reports argued that management had become more of a science with the development of decision making tools during the war years. Subsequently, these two foundations provided generous funding to promote reforms of teaching and research along these lines.

These efforts, based on the notion of a science-based professionalism, contained an inherent contradiction that eventually led to the demise of the professionalization project. For if management is truly a science that can be reduced to a set of fundamental scientific principles, what need is there for management to be viewed as any kind of a profession with broader responsibilities to society? What finally led to the demise of the professionalization project for good was the emergence of what Khurana (2007, p. 368) calls "investor capitalism" as a replacement for managerialism. Managers were seen as standing in the way of the efficient operation of competitive markets and were accused of mismanaging corporate assets. Takeovers were justified on this basis and to ward off hostile takeovers managers had to improve the performance of their companies by divesting themselves of unrelated businesses, cutting out layers of middle management, outsourcing noncore functions, downsizing, and other measures to improve the economic situation of their firms. Loyalty to workers, products, communities and the like went out the door, as the only thing that mattered was the creation of shareholder value.

According to Khurana, the rise of agency theory supported this change to investor capitalism and ended any concern about the professionalization of management. Agency theory holds that managers serve as merely agents of shareholders and are bound to manage corporate assets in their interests. Managers are seen as nothing more than hired hands with no permanent responsibilities to any collective interests of society. Agency theory is clearly based on individualism and does not incorporate any notion of a collective responsibility, but instead views managers as distinct individuals dissociated from one another who have no responsibilities to any collective entity, including the organization itself. The organization is viewed simply as a nexus of contracts among individuals with no sense of community. Such a view is opposed to any notion of professionalization.

> the promise that business schools would socialize managers into a culture of professionalism—thereby legitimating managerial authority in the face of competing claims to corporate control from the socially disruptive forces of capital and labor ... gave rise to the university business school in the first place. The autonomy and authority of professional managers would be rooted not only in expert knowledge but in their obligation not to represent the interests of either owners or workers—much less of themselves—but to see that the corporation contributed to the general welfare. Agency theorists, however, dismiss any such framing of managerial work as tender-hearted do-gooding. Agency theory also excludes from consideration any notion of collective identity—a fundamental attribute of professions in any sociological framing of the phenomenon—let alone collective responsibility. On the contrary, it frames managerial agents as distinct and dissociated from one another, defining an organization as simply a nexus of contracts among individual agents. (Khurana, 2007, pp. 324-325)

Khurana goes on to say that managers were thus cut loose from any moorings to the organizations they led and to the communities in which these organizations were embedded. In the final analysis, they were ironically cut loose from shareholders who were unable to prevent these managers from taking a greater and greater share of corporate wealth to enrich themselves, regardless of their performance, at the expense of shareholders and employees. It also opened the door to a series of corporate scandals involving misstatement of earnings, backdated stock options, and a host of other malpractices in a number of companies, all of which undermined public trust in the integrity and fairness of the capitalistic system.

Managers have become loose individuals in that they do not feel constrained by constructive social values, such as fairness and equity, while having no allegiance to anyone else but themselves. When relationships are anchored only in such utilitarian self-interest, they can play fast and loose with other individuals in relationships that involve trust and responsibility. To counter these trends, Khurana advocates reviving the notion of professionalism for management, as professions are a vital part of the economic and social order. When they are compromised or corrupted, society is harmed. But any new professionalization project must be rooted in community rather than individualism, for professions derive their basic structure and logic from communities, according to Khurana. What should also be pointed out is that a community-based professionalism would involve a sense of responsibility on the part of managers to something other than themselves.

TOWARD REVIVING A PROFESSIONAL MODEL FOR MANAGEMENT

What would a professional model for management based on community and responsibility rather than individualism and rights look like? The problem with a professional model for business, as was stated by Levi (1964), is the inherent conflict between inclusively society-regarding responsibilities of the professional on the one hand and the exclusively business-centered demand for profits on the other. The true professional is committed to serve his or her client, and although profits are necessary for lawyers and doctors to continue to serve their clients, profits are not supposed to be the overriding objective for them, as they are for business. In contrast, the businessperson keeps his or her eye on the reward and overriding objective of making a profit which, in theory, increases the economic wealth of nations. The exact nature of the goods and services produced and provided are secondary to this objective. Levi thinks this way of thinking is largely a matter of emphasis. That is, it is a kind of mentality that pervades the business community while not necessarily a function of capitalism itself.

Levi did not seem too optimistic that a change in this mentality would ever take place, as it would go against the way Western civilization thinks of business activity. It would require a rethinking of the purpose of business and society, as well as the nature of the self. In other words, the current mentality is pervasive. As stated before, Levi thinks that the ethical behavior of any segment within society is generally not without roots in the more general aspiration of that society as a whole. This is one of the most important insights that he provides and must be kept in mind as the discussion about business as a profession proceeds. The notion that wealth is primarily if not exclusively economic in nature is widely shared in Western industrialized societies. The creation and acquisition of material wealth are what these societies are all about and money is what an acquisitive society values above everything else.

Business managers are, of course, a part of this money oriented society and, therefore, it is not surprising that they should seek profits as the overriding goal of their organization. Money is the measure of their success and that of the organization. Profits are taken to be an indicator of how well the company has contributed to the well-being of society, even if those profits come at the expense of people's health and the environment. If a company is profitable, then it is generally taken that the organization has performed a useful role in society and is given society's blessing to continue in existence because it is believed to have served the public good in some sense. But profits in-and-of themselves are not the problem, it is the profit motive that Levi is concerned about.

To be a professional in the true sense of the word, managers must put profits in a broader context and recognize that their major objective is to serve the clients of the organization. These include the people who consume the organization's products, work for the organization, invest in it, and depend on it for various things in the community. To be a true professional, managers must change their focus to one of putting service to these clients foremost in their decisions. If they do this and produce products that truly enhance people's lives, provide good jobs for their employees with adequate wages, and exhibit a concern for environmental impacts, then profits are bound to follow in a society that keeps money in its proper perspective.

One of the first and most important tasks in construing business as a profession is to place the corporation in the context of society. This involves a decentering of the corporation; a recognition that the corporation is not the center of the universe around which society revolves, but that the corporation is but one element, albeit an important one, of the total social context in which humans work out a meaningful and fulfilling existence for themselves (Frederick, 2006; Giacalone & Thompson, 2006). Business exists to serve society and enhance the well-being of the members of that society; the society does not exist to serve business and its interests. This involves a change of worldview on the part of business people who tend to think of the organization as being at the core of the universe.

The elements that go toward the making of this corporate-centric worldview are consistent with each other and have long informed our understanding of capitalism and the role of the corporation in society. An emphasis on individualism and rights is consistent with the notion that the use of private property to increase material wealth is the most important undertaking in society, and that society must see to it that the organization, which is the primary generator of this wealth, namely the corporation, is given priority in this concern. In the process, the economy is artificially separated from the rest of society, with production and consumption, which keep the economy going, seen as ends in themselves needing no further moral justification.

This idea that society and all its elements exist to serve corporate interests has to change in order for business to be seen as a profession. Managers of business organizations have to broaden their perspective to think of society in their decisions and how the corporation can enhance the well-being of society's members in ways that involve more considerations than just the creation of economic wealth. After all, economic wealth is something of an illusion or fiction in that it merely reflects the value society places on economic entities. Business, as a social enterprise, must serve a wider spectrum of values and interests than just economic ones, and this broader perspective must be considered when managers formulate business policies and practices.

It is important for managers to think in terms of an array of clients and attempt to determine these clients' interests and the impacts that the actions of the corporation has on their existence. The traditional view of business would hold that the stockholder is the major client, that managers are agents of the owners, and therefore managers have a primary responsibility to earn the highest rate of return that can be earned on the owner's investment in the business. But a case also can be made that the major client is the consumer, since business exists to produce goods and services to satisfy consumer demand. From this viewpoint, the focus should be on producing goods and services that make the lives of consumers better and more satisfying. One could also make a case for employees being the major client, as they spend the better part of their waking hours working for the company. The corollary is that the enhancement of employees' experience could well be the focus of corporate activity.

It seems then that business has multiple clients, but this is actually no different from the traditional professions. Private hospitals have stockholders to satisfy; lawyers have staff to keep happy as do large doctors' offices with many nurses and clerical personnel. Every decision will probably affect all of these clients to some degree, but most decisions will most likely affect one of more clients to a greater degree than the others. Thus, a stakeholder model would seem to be an appropriate way to approach the client question. Yet if stakeholders are viewed through an individualistic, corporate-centric lens, then they will not be seen as integral to the functioning of the organization. To overcome this individualistic view, the corporation must instead be seen as a community within a community with multiple responsibilities that enrich the total community experience.

Management must then be concerned with (a) producing goods and services that are going to better the lives of consumers and provide them with enriching experiences, (b) providing employees with meaningful experiences and the opportunities to grow and develop as human beings during the time they spend working for the corporation, and (c) providing stockholders with an ample return on their investment. It is not a matter of balancing these various interests against each other, but rather giving all of them attention at the same time. They are all part of the same community nexus and tied together in a quest for a better life with more enriching experiences. And it is not only the human community that is of concern, but also the natural world that must be taken into consideration in corporate decisions. This is what an ethic of service is all about.

ASSESSING PROFESSIONALIZATION IN BUSINESS SCHOOLS

What would it take for the professionalization project to be revived in business schools? Currently the business school curriculum reflects the traditional philosophy of individualism and rights in its courses, and the stated or unstated purpose of most courses is still to emphasize the maximization of shareholder wealth despite many years of teaching and research on social responsibility, ethics, and stakeholder management. There has been no significant change in the economic, social, and moral philosophy that informs the courses that are taught in the traditional business school. Even business ethics, to the extent that it is based on the "good ethics is good business" idea, reflects this traditional philosophy.

If management is no longer considered to be a profession, and managers are nothing more than hired hands, then in what sense can business schools be considered professional schools on the same level as schools of law and medicine? In what sense can business schools be aligned with the mission of the university as a whole? The place to begin an appropriate alignment would seem to be in the business schools themselves where business school students are trained and acculturated. Change has to start somewhere, it will not happen by magic, and the educational process is one place where students can be encouraged to think differently about their lives and future occupation and adopt the values that may lead to a more fulfilling and enriching life for themselves and society. Reviving the notion of management as a profession that makes managers the primary link between the narrow concerns of business and the broader concerns of society is seen to be essential for business schools to gain respectability within the university and regain a sense of mission and purpose that goes beyond that of a trade school (Khurana, 2007).

> If university business schools...are to continue to play any role in the educa-
> tion of managers that could not be filled equally well by corporate training
> programs or for-profit, purely vocational business schools, they belong in
> the forefront of the discussions now taking place among informed and
> thoughtful citizens all around the globe about the shape that capitalism
> should take in the twenty-first century. (Khurana, 2007, p. 366)

To effect this change and regain a sense of professionalism, business
schools must change their worldview. According to Giacalone and
Thompson

> We teach students to perpetuate business' importance and its centrality in
> society, to do so by increasing wealth, and to assume that by advancing orga-
> nizational interests, they advance their own and society's overall best inter-
> ests. (Giacalone & Thompson, 2006, p. 267)

Again, the corporation must be decentered and placed in the context of
society at large. Business exists to serve society and not the other way
around. This entails the adoption of a different philosophy of business
based on community and responsibility that would be reflected in the
courses that are taught in the business school curriculum.

What would have to change to reflect this philosophy is not so much a
matter of content but rather a matter of emphasis.[3] The rationale or
objective of courses would have to be restated and taught with a different
focus. An ethic of service would have to permeate the entire curriculum.
For example, marketing courses would have to focus on how products
could be sold in such a way as to maximize consumer satisfaction and take
into account the interest of consumers in bettering their lives rather than
an exclusive focus on how the consumer can be persuaded to purchase the
company's products so that a profit can be made for the company. Advertising would have to focus on providing the consumer with the information they need to make an informed decision that will work to make their
lives better rather than trying to manipulate the consumer to buy things
they may not want or need in order to better the company.

Likewise strategy courses would have to focus on how the company can
do better things to enhance the entire society rather than focus on how to
beat the competition and attain a greater market share. Finance courses
would focus on using financial resources efficiently and effectively to better society rather than on the maximization of shareholder wealth. Organizational behavior courses would have to be concerned with providing
experiences in the workplace that enhance workers' lives rather than on
how to make them more productive. And accounting courses would have
to broaden their perspective to focus on accounting for the use of society's
resources as a whole and not just for narrow financial gain, as well as

develop means for reporting on the use of human and physical resources in a meaningful and accurate manner that could be audited in the way financial information is audited.[4]

Other courses that are not now a part of most business schools could be added, such as a course in science and technology that gives business students a better understanding of how science works and the importance of technological concerns in decision making. An important course would be one that deals with ecology and environmental concerns so that students could gain an understanding of the ways in which nature is connected with human well-being and how corporate activities affect the environment. Although liberal arts courses are important to broaden a student's perspective, these kinds of courses would show the relevance of science and technology and the environment to business concerns. While ethics should be a part of every course where appropriate, a separate course that focuses on conflicts of interest, fraud and deception, and other strictly ethical issues is a necessity.[5]

An additional course to be added, if it is not already in the curriculum, is a leadership course that should come in the final semester. This course should focus on the qualities of leadership and stress how leadership is different from just managing a corporate organization. It should look at how leaders in business, politics, and other areas have used their power to effect change in the organization and society. The most important project in this course should be a required paper that would make students articulate their philosophy of management. Every student in an MBA program graduates with some kind of philosophical understanding of management, but in most cases it is unarticulated. This project could serve as kind of a capstone to the entire MBA experience and would give students the opportunity to reflect on their business education and set down on paper what it all means. This could be the most important project in the entire curriculum.

Such a curriculum would most likely have little appeal to students who are currently in or to faculty currently teaching in an MBA program who see maximization of shareholder wealth as the overriding objective of business organizations and the pursuit of profits as the major responsibility of managers. But over time such a curriculum could appeal to a plurality of students who have an interest in serving society and devoting their lives to something more than just making profits for the organization in which they spend the majority of their lives. A curriculum designed around an ethics of service should have an appeal to more socially minded students who want to do something more fulfilling for themselves and who recognize that their well-being is tied up with the well-being of society as a whole.

So what does all this mean for assessment of business ethics education? It must be emphasized again that the focus on business ethics education is too narrow and does not get at what is most important. Ethics is not separated from everything else; it is not a functional area that can be assessed on its own terms. The implication of this chapter is that the assessment of business education in general must focus on the ability of business schools to produce true professional managers who see their primary responsibilities as enhancing the quality of life for multiple constituencies, not just shareholders. This entails a responsibility to enhance the multiple environmental conditions in which these clients live; their social, political, cultural, and natural environments. Assessment of business school education must focus on how well such an ethic of service has been acculturated in its students.

Such assessment could consist of some kind of exams or tests given to students in their last semester to assess what kind of attitudes they will carry with them into the corporate world. Such exams are subject, of course, to a socialization bias in that students' answers to the questions may reflect what they think the faculty wants to hear. Even so, if students are required to write a paper reflecting on their own philosophy of management, as suggested above, then this could provide an indication of what kinds of values students take away from the program. A complementary, overriding perspective on assessment would be a focus on mission-driven standards, which is similar to the approach the accrediting agency, the Association to Advance Collegiate Schools of Business, uses in its accreditation process. In this case, the process would be focused on ensuring that schools have a stated mission that elevates professionalism and the coursework to match.

CONCLUSION

The change to an ethic of service in business school education could not be more important. We are at one of those times in our nation's history when change seems to be inevitable. The financial and economic crisis brought about by defaulting on sub-prime loans has resulted in an unprecedented involvement of government in bailing out financial institutions and taking an ownership interest in private companies. Unregulated capitalism is being questioned and the current administration will undoubtedly press for additional regulations on the financial industry in particular and the economy in general. The era of free market capitalism seems to be over and something else is emerging that contrasts with the era of bashing government and praising the free market that has gone on for several decades. The question is whether the emerging view is in the best interest of the society as a whole.

Many will oppose a new regulatory effort, but something needs to be done to prevent more upheavals in the future. The question is whether an ethic of service—and the changes in thinking about capitalism it involves —represents a viable alternative to increased government involvement or whether it is hopelessly utopian. The answer to this question has important implications for the future of our society. Business schools can take the lead on this issue by changing the focus of their efforts and developing corresponding assessment tools.

NOTES

1. In response to this last criticism, there has been some effort to professionalize management to make it more like law and medicine with the development of a code of conduct, a certification examination, and continuing education. The Dean of Thunderbird's School of Global Management, Angel Cabrera, has been working with the United Nations Global Compact, which promotes standards for world-wide business practices, and has led a task force to develop a set of Principles for Responsible Management Education that are said to follow a similar philosophy. Thus far about 200 business schools worldwide, including Thunderbird, have adopted them, although there is considerable skepticism that these principles will have a major impact on business school education (Holland, 2009).

2. Efforts to broaden the responsibilities of business that contained some notion of community, such as social responsibility and stakeholder theory, have floundered on the shoals of this philosophy. While there was a broadening of responsibilities through the public policy process, which supposedly reflects community interests, this effort ran up against the limitations of a rights-based approach. Likewise, ethical approaches have been limited in affecting corporate behavior because of their individualistic emphasis. Changing this focus on individualism and rights entails a new theoretical framework for capitalism based on a philosophy of community and responsibility. This framework, which is beyond the scope of this chapter, leads to a different way of interpreting and understanding the capitalistic system and the function of management. Ultimately, it points to a reorientation of our thinking about capitalistic economic activity (Buchholz, 2009).

3. The content of courses in the curriculum of business schools could still be science-based, depending on the nature of the course itself. Bennis and O'Toole (2005), while critical of the scientific orientation of business schools as a whole, do not advocate throwing the baby out with the bath water. Science would still be important in providing a rigorous analysis of business problems. But the scientific base would have to be placed in the context of business as a profession and broadened to include other aspects

of human and organizational behavior. Agency theory and a strictly economic view of the firm overlooks such organizational phenomena as power, coercion, exploitation, discrimination, conflict and related issues while relieving managers of any meaningful responsibilities to other members of the organization and to society as a whole. But people are not just contracting agents. They relate to coworkers in the organization and to society in a variety of ways and have a nexus of responsibilities for which the disciplines of sociology, political science, and psychology are just as important as economics and agency theory in understanding how people behave in organizations and the behavior of organizations in society.

4. It is interesting to note that the current accounting curriculum in schools of business and management is geared toward helping accounting students meet CPA requirements so that they can become a certified public accountant and attain the professional status that goes with this certification. Thus these students have some exposure to professionalism that other students in the business school do not have. Moreover, they must engage in continuing education to maintain this certification, including some exposure to the American Institute of Certified Public Accountants code of ethics. Yet, ironically, accounting research is dominated by the agency model which prevents a full measure of professionalism from being imparted to these students (Fisher, Swanson, & Schmidt, 2007).

5. A campaign was mounted in 2002 that took aim at the Association for the Advancement of Collegiate Schools of Business which is the international accrediting agency for business schools. This campaign, which sought to upgrade and strengthen ethics accreditation standards, charged that the AACSB's weak ethics standards unwillingly contributed to corporate crime and corruption by failing to mandate a required ethics course as a condition of accreditation (Swanson, 2004; Swanson & Frederick, 2001-2002; Swanson & Fisher, 2008).

REFERENCES

Bennis, G. W., & O'Toole, J. (2005). How business schools lost their way. *Harvard Business Review, 83*, 96-104.

Buchholz, R. A. (2009). *Rethinking capitalism: Community and responsibility in business.* New York, NY: Routledge.

Chandler, A. (1977). *The visible hand: The managerial revolution in American business.* Cambridge, MA: Belknap Press.

Etzioni, A. (2002, August 4). When it comes to ethics, B-schools get an F. *The Washington Post*, p. B4.

Fisher, D. G., Swanson, D. L., & Schmidt, J. (2007). Accounting education lags CPE requirements: Implications for the profession and a call to action. *Accounting Education: An International Journal, 16*, 345-363.

Frederick, W. C. (2006). *Corporation be good!* Indianapolis, IN: Dog Ear.

Giacalone, R. A., & Thompson, K. R. (2006). Business ethics and social responsibility education: Shifting the worldview. *Learning and Education, 5*, 266-277.

Gordon, R., & Howell J. (1959). *Higher education for business*. New York, NY: Columbia University Press.

Holland, K. (2009, March 15). Is it time to retrain B-Schools? *New York Times*, pp. BU 1-2.

Khurana, R. (2007). *From higher aims to hired hands: The social transformation of American business schools and the unfulfilled promise of management as a profession*. Princeton, NJ: Princeton University Press.

Kristol, I. (1978). *Two cheers for capitalism*. New York, NY: Basic Books.

Levi, A. W. (1964). Ethical confusion and the business community. In J. W. Towle (Ed.), *Ethics and standards in American business* (pp. 20-29). Boston, MA: Houghton Mifflin.

Mitroff, I. (2004, June). An open letter to the deans and faculties of American business schools: A call for action. *Academy of Management Newsletter*, 7-8.

Pierson, F. C. et al. (1959). *The education of American businessmen*. New York, NY: McGraw-Hill.

Swanson, D. L. (2004). The buck stops here: Why universities must reclaim business ethics education. *Journal of Academic Ethics*, *2*, 43-61.

Swanson, D. L., & Fisher, D.G. (2008). Business ethics education: If we don't know where we're going, any road will take us there. In D. L. Swanson & D. G. Fisher (Eds.), *Advancing business ethics education* (pp. 1-23). Charlotte, NC: Information Age.

Swanson, D. L., & Frederick, W. C. (2001-2002). Campaign AACSB: Are business schools complicit in corporate corruption? *Journal of Individual and Employment Rights*, *10*, 151-165.

Swanson, D. L., & Frederick, W. C. (2003, Spring). Are business schools partners in corporate crime? *The Journal of Corporate Citizenship*, *9*, 24-27.

CHAPTER 4

ASSESSING BUSINESS ETHICS EDUCATION

Assessment *From Where* and *For What*?

Lisa A. Stewart and R. Edward Freeman

Now more than ever—in the midst of a worldwide economic crisis and with the public's trust in business at an historic low—the spotlight is focused on the responsibility of MBA programs to equip students with core business ethics knowledge and the courage to be leaders in building and maintaining ethical cultures at their companies even when this may go against the grain. A recent *New York Times* article, "Is it time to retrain B-Schools?" (Holland, 2009) explored questions of the responsibility of business schools in relation to their graduates' future endeavors. We believe that before releasing newly minted MBA students into the business world, business educators must take responsibility for equipping these new business leaders with necessary tools to navigate an increasingly complex business environment.

That said, business ethics programs are not magical and cannot take unethical students and miraculously transform them into ethical leaders in 2 years. What business ethics programs reasonably can be expected to

Toward Assessing Business Ethics Education
pp. 49–56

accomplish, however, is helping MBA students gain a better understanding of how business and ethics are connected and how both need to be applied in the real world of complex and often no-right-answer types of situations. Business ethics programs can and should be expected to encourage students to clarify their own values, to figure out where they stand on a variety of potential challenges, and to determine what type of future leader they will aspire to become. Business ethics programs, among other things, can be expected to provide students with opportunities where they can develop skills that will help them to push back against a future manager who may request them, as new junior associates, to perform an unethical act.

It is equally reasonable to expect that business schools assess these types of learning goals and objectives to determine if—at some meaningful level—the business ethics programs are successful in teaching students these concepts and skills and in changing student attitudes on these dimensions. Assessments can also be expected to explore how existing teaching methods can be improved to strengthen the program's effectiveness.

In a widely accepted definition, assessment is described as "the systematic collection, review, and use of information about educational programs undertaken for the purpose of improving student learning and development" (Palomba & Banta, 1999). We believe that the real starting point for any useful assessment process should be in determining the answers to two more basic and fundamental questions:

1. Assessment from where: What is the fundamental view of business ethics at the institution?
2. Assessment for what: What is being assessed and what is the purpose of the assessment?

Once these two questions have been substantially addressed, then it is possible to move forward to the subsequent steps of developing program goals, objectives, and meaningful assessment tools and processes to directly measure the effectiveness of the program. Just as the assessment for an MBA program is based on the overall business program, in our view, so too the assessment of business ethics education must consider the program in its entirety when embarking on the assessment process.

A program's assessment must start at a place of common understanding of the foundational purpose. This core understanding can help to ensure alignment around the program goals, to develop measurements that ensure student progress on the program's learning objectives, and to meet the Association to Advance Collegiate Schools of Business (AACSB) standards of accreditation.

For it to be most effective, a discussion of a business ethics program's fundamental purpose must be a sustained community-wide process, one that engages students, faculty, staff and the school's business and other organizational partners over time. Our aim is not to provide specific guidance on how to proceed with developing the specific tools for completing the assessment. AACSB's website Assessment Resource Center (Association to Advance Collegiate Schools of Business, 2009) offers thorough and in-depth information on assessment, along with numerous examples of leading practices in this area from a variety of educational institutions. Information on the creation of measurement tools based on specific program goals and objectives, including the how to and what to assess, is readily available.

The challenges we raise are for institutions to remain ever mindful of both the overall purpose of business education—to prepare ethical business leaders, along with the goal of assessment—to improve student learning. To best reach these ends, it is necessary for the entire academic community to engage in business ethics conversations on an ongoing basis, continuing to challenge each other to grow and to look for positive change.

ASSESSMENT FROM WHERE: WHAT IS THE FUNDAMENTAL VIEW OF BUSINESS ETHICS AT THE INSTITUTION?

Business ethics can be viewed as a way to understand the value creation process in a manner that explores the connection between business and ethics. For instance, one view of business ethics is that it creates value for stakeholders. In the process of performing its "regular" business, a firm: (a) provides good jobs; (b) treats customers, employees, and suppliers fairly; (c) creates wealth; and (d) offers valuable goods and services to the community. Business ethics is at the core of good business strategy and decision making, and business is fundamentally all about value creation.

Simply put, we believe business ethics conversations should be the norm for all business conversations, not just when there is a special guest speaker at the end of a course or for a one-day highlighted content area. Students should learn in business school that the default mode for business decision making includes ethical dimensions, whether they happen to be sitting in a finance course or in an ethics course. For example, when assessing the valuation model for building a factory in an offshore location, a manager might be able to predict the financial merits through a spreadsheet model. Yet, clearly that is only part of a good business decision in this case. A spreadsheet will not be able to predict how the community will react to having the factory there, the commitment and engagement of the workforce, or what the reaction from any number of the firm's other stakeholders might be. Ethical leaders would consider various dimensions of a business decision. Such ethical business leaders are what the world is now demanding from business educators.

The assessment process itself can make a useful contribution to developing an ethical business mindset by leading conversations about the role of business ethics within the educational institution. Assessment from where: what is the fundamental approach to teaching business ethics within the institution? When coming from a place where business ethics is an inextricable part of business strategy and decision making, an assessment is far more likely to be helpful in identifying new and innovative ways to teach business ethics.

If an institution mostly views ethics as an add-on and the assessment is done in part to legitimize the role of teaching business ethics within the organization, then it is a fundamentally different exercise. This is simply another version of the question, does ethics pay? And this is the wrong question to ask. The assessment process, based on this underlying perspective, is frankly far less valuable and less likely to yield positive and useful results.

It is critical to determine what the term "business ethics" means at your institution before developing any of the particular assessment goals and objectives. What is the place of business ethics within the overall MBA program? What other aspects of business does it relate to and encompass, and how is it incorporated into the overall educational experience? Is business ethics viewed as a core and fundamental discipline within business?

Do faculty, administrators, and students routinely incorporate ethical perspectives into course discussions and business decision making? Do business ethics conversations also happen in the hallways and in all of the functional classes, such as accounting, marketing, and finance? Is there a required ethics course placed early in the curriculum, in addition to elective courses and ethical concepts integrated across the curriculum into different subject areas? Is research supported across disciplines that include ethical dimensions? Alternatively, do most faculty, students, and administrators at your institution think of business ethics as something that is fundamentally separate from the core and "hard" disciplines of business or as more of an add-on subject or elective? Do students need to put on their "ethics hat" for specific discussions that involve ethical dimensions, or are these conversations happening so frequently and seamlessly as to be ordinary?

ASSESSMENT FOR WHAT: WHAT IS BEING ASSESSED AND WHAT IS THE PURPOSE OF THE ASSESSMENT?

Program assessments must look deeply into the full business ethics program to attempt finding ways to measure real value creation. The entire program of business ethics education, not just a specific course, should be included in the assessment process. Business ethics education can happen in a business ethics class, but it also can happen across the curriculum in other core courses and within the broader academic and surrounding community. All of these components must be incorporated into the assessment process to get a more accurate measure of the program's effectiveness.

Once again, the assessment process itself can serve a useful purpose here. The occasion of the assessment can drive a process by which the institution can have the necessary meaningful conversations that will clarify the program and the myriad ways that business ethics education is—or can be—most effectively conveyed to students. It is critical to engage key members of the entire institutional community in the conversation about a business ethics program's ongoing development and assessment process. Once the program becomes more clearly defined, assessment goals and objectives should be developed to capture and measure progress in student learning from the overall teaching of business ethics.

Assessment—viewed as an ongoing, long-term process—can help to guide and shape the direction of a program over time. One purpose of the assessment is to measure a program's effectiveness at a specific point in time—how well are we doing with teaching business ethics where we are today? Another perhaps more important purpose in assessment should be to strive toward improvements over time—where are we today against where we would like to be 5 or 10 years from now? The overarching goal of the assessment process should be to continually move the entire ethics program toward its longer-term goals and objectives, targeting both short-term and long-term program improvements.

Starting with a set of aspirational principles—such as the overarching institutional Principles for Responsible Management Education developed by the United Nations Global Compact (United Nations Global Compact, 2007) or the specifically focused business ethics program framework (given below) presented in *Shaping Tomorrow's Business Leaders: Principles and Practices for a Model Business Ethics Program* (Business Roundtable Institute for Corporate Ethics, 2007)—can help to target future growth and improvement areas for a business ethics program. The assessment process will be most useful when it aims to seek new ideas, find novel ways to improve current practice, and identify innovative opportunities to create value. As a business ethics program continually strives for improvement and cohesion, the following set of principles may be useful for providing solid benchmarks for leading practices in this area, and for helping to stay on course toward progress over time.

Principles of a Model Business Ethics Program: Course, Curriculum, and Community[1]

Course

An ethics course should be:

1. Grounded in the leading thinking and practice about ethics and moral philosophy from academia, business, and other organizations;
2. Connected deeply to all other disciplines of business, including management, leadership, strategy, finance, business law and organizational behavior, based on a belief that business ethics is inherently interdisciplinary;
3. Required as a foundational course placed early in the curriculum, taught by ethics-trained faculty or a multidiscipline faculty team including ethics-trained faculty;
4. Designed to promote highly engaged student participation through a variety of teaching tools and techniques such as small class size, outside speakers, experiential components, and case studies; and
5. Aimed at preparing students for understanding their roles as ethical leaders, managers, and followers.

Curriculum

As an integral part of the curriculum:

1. Ethics should be a core and fundamental business discipline;
2. Ethics content should be integrated into all other business disciplines, and other business content should be integrated into the ethics discipline;
3. Ethics content should be equally weighted and valued with other disciplines through early semester introduction, required graded content, the offering of ethics electives, and other methods that that demonstrate that ethics is an integral part of the curriculum.

Community

The entire academic community (students, faculty, administration, and business partners) should:

1. Demonstrate commitment to ethical practices;
2. Support ethics program through an active research process that produces leading-edge field research, practice aids, published works, and teaching materials; and
3. Collaborate on issues such as recruiting, role models, and relevant research.

Current State of Assessment for Business Ethics Education

The current state of assessment likely falls somewhere between the far ends of this continuum --from an ongoing, long-term process on the one end to taking an inventory or a snapshot of superficial information on the other—as do the attitudes toward business ethics programs themselves. Assessment in the ideal situation could be an extraordinarily useful process. It could point to areas for improvement and be a useful tool to guide important conversations. We should, however, continue to remain constructively skeptical of the process and always ask the questions: assessment from where? and assessment for what? The reality is likely to fall somewhere between these extremes: either viewing ethics as a core and fundamental discipline of business or as simply an add-on tagged onto the business curriculum. Additionally, we should always target our assessment toward our program aspirations and keep student learning in the forefront of our efforts.

NOTE

1. The principles of the model business ethics program in terms of course, curriculum, and community were establishing by the Business Roundtable Institute for Corporate Ethics (2007).

REFERENCES

Association to Advance Collegiate Schools of Business. (2009). *Assessment Resource Center.* Retrieved rom http://www.aacsb.edu/resource_centers/assessment/default.asp

Business Roundtable Institute for Corporate Ethics. (2007). *Shaping tomorrow's business leaders: Principles and practices for a model business ethics program.* Retrieved from http://www.corporate-ethics.org/pdf/mbep.pdf and http://www.corporate-ethics.org/Ethics_curriculum_report_principles.htm

Holland, K. (2009, March 15). Is it time to retrain B-Schools? *New York Times.* Retrieved from http://www.nytimes.com/2009/03/15/business/15school.html

Palomba, C. A. & Banta, T. W. (1999). *Assessment essentials: Planning, implementing, and improving assessment in higher education.* San Francisco, CA: Jossey-Bass.

United Nations Global Compact. (2007). *The principles for responsible management education.* Retrieved from http://www.unprme.org/index.php

CHAPTER 5

ASSESSING MBA ATTITUDES ABOUT BUSINESS AND SOCIETY

Implications for Business Education

Nancy McGaw

THE MISSION OF THE ASPEN INSTITUTE'S BUSINESS AND SOCIETY PROGRAM

The Aspen Institute's Business and Society Program (Aspen BSP) opened its doors in January 1998. Since then, understanding the role of management education in preparing the next generation of leaders to tackle the social and environmental challenges faced by business has been at the heart of our mission to catalyze fresh thinking, teaching, and research at the intersection of business needs and social concerns.

Business schools then, as now, were producing well over 100,000 MBA graduates each year in the United States, accounting for roughly one out of every four master's degrees granted annually. Competition among the schools was intense. Issues of business magazines with the latest rankings

Toward Assessing Business Ethics Education
pp. 57–71
Copyright © 2011 by Information Age Publishing
All rights of reproduction in any form reserved.

of business schools were flying off the shelves as students around the world tried to figure out how they could best turn their expensive graduate education into earnings. In 1998, these business school rankings tended to give most weight to two factors: GMAT scores of accepted students and salaries of graduates. These metrics were easy to plug into formulas for success, but they told us nothing about how well the schools were preparing students to be financial, social, and environmental stewards. Nor did they tell us how business school education influenced students' thinking about how business should operate within society.

At Aspen BSP, we set out to discover new metrics. In 1999, working with the World Resources Institute, we introduced a biennial survey and ranking of MBA programs called *Beyond Grey Pinstripes*.[1] Using self-reported data from schools, we began to assess the extent to which these programs were integrating ethical, social, and environmental content into their teaching and research. In 1999, we also began a series of student attitudinal surveys designed to learn how students view the role of business in society.

Since that time, we have found much to celebrate in many schools— some at the top of the mainstream business rankings and some that are less well known. Extensive content from business schools around the world can be viewed at our Center for Business Education website, www.AspenCBE.org. However, despite the important innovations and commitments at many business schools to prepare students to make decisions in the best interests of all stakeholders of the firm, we have also found that students in most MBA programs are still taught that shareholders come first. Moreover, the dominant model in management education continues to be one that favors "rules-plus-analytics" rather than "principles-plus-implementation" (Gentile, 2008, p. 91).

> The rules-plus-analytics model teaches that the rules governing corporate behavior ... are simply constraints to be overcome; the analytic tools represent ways to work within or around any rules in your own way, for the sake of winning the most immediate competitive game. This model emphasizes impersonal aggressiveness, in which managers walk as close to the legal and ethical line as possible—even crossing over it when they expect they won't get caught. It encourages students to interpret Adam Smith's 'invisible hand' theory ... to mean that in any given situation they do not have to consider the wider implications of their choices because the market will. (Gentile, 2008, p. 91)

The mindset rewarded by this model promotes short-term thinking and disregard for the impact these choices have on communities and the environment—and often on employees as well. According to Gentile, a principles-plus-implementation model takes a different approach:

A principles-plus-implementation model of management education, by contrast, starts with the fundamental questions of why a business exists and how it builds and deploys wealth. It teaches the reasons for the rules ... and offers the challenge and the opportunity to practice decision making in the service of the goals that the rules were designed to achieve. (Gentile, 2008, p. 91)

It is the latter approach that is required if business schools are to prepare students to tackle the critical goals management must strive to achieve if they are to run successful businesses ready for the future. These goals are outlined in Hamel's article, "Moon Shots for Management" (Hamel, 2009). Serving a higher purpose is first among the management goals listed, and Hamel explicitly notes the need for management practices to be linked to goals that are noble and have social significance. Focusing on shareholder primacy as the dominant endgame or relying on a rules-plus-analytics model will certainly cause managers to fall short.

To ensure that the next generation of leaders is ready for these challenges, Aspen BSP continues to call for a new rigor in management education which also elevates the importance of preparing students to think in terms of a larger purpose for business—beyond the concept of *homus economicus*. This new approach explicitly values morals and ethical reasoning and is built on holistic, systems-based analysis that incorporates the measurement of externalities (Samuelson, 2006). Is this new rigor taking hold in business schools? Our *Beyond Grey Pinstripes* data collected over the past decade document that change is happening but that huge challenges remain, as many thoughtful critics have asserted (see, for example, Bennis, 2005; Ghoshal, 2005). Our research on the attitudes of MBA students, the focus of the analysis presented in this chapter, offers a further perspective on whether business schools are meeting their full potential for preparing graduates to have the will and skill to be financial, social, and environmental stewards in the businesses where they work.

SURVEYING MBA STUDENT ATTITUDES TOWARD BUSINESS IN SOCIETY

To complement the data we receive from the business schools, we have also sought to understand how MBA students view the role of business in society and how their attitudes toward the roles and responsibilities of the company are shaped by the MBA experience. This research began in 1999 when we initiated an attitudinal survey at thirteen leading graduate business schools.

For our first study, published in 2001, we surveyed students at the beginning of their MBA programs (fall, 1999), after 1 year (spring, 2000), and toward the end of the second year (spring, 2001). A second study, published in 2003, surveyed first and second year students in the fall of 2002 to see how their attitudes had changed following the collapse of Enron, the demise of a generation of dot.com companies, the attack on the World Trade Center in New York, and a sharp economic decline. Five years later, in 2007, we conducted a further study of MBA students, which was published in the spring 2008 (see Aspen Institute, 2001, 2003, 2008).[2] Then, in the fall of 2008, we collaborated with Net Impact to conduct another student attitudinal survey that was published in March, 2009.

In the sections that follow, we present selected findings from all of these surveys and pose some questions for business school students, faculty, and administrators suggested by this research.

Primary Responsibilities of Companies

A headline from our first student attitudinal research report in 2001 was that as students continued through their MBA studies, they appeared to shift from a customer mode to a business manager mode. When asked to identify the top three "primary responsibilities of the company," incoming students in 1999 chose "satisfying customer needs" more than any other option. However, students midway through their MBA program, surveyed in 2000, and students about to graduate, surveyed in 2001, chose "maximizing value for shareholders" more than other options, although satisfying customers remained their second most favorite choice.

Recent surveys suggest that students are taking a more nuanced view. In the fall of 2007, as in previous surveys, we asked students to choose the top three "primary responsibilities" of a company from a list of 10 options. Maximizing value for shareholders continues to be the top choice among students. However, its dominance has decreased, as 64% of students in 2007 selected that option as one of their three choices, down from 71% in 2002 and 75% in 2001. These responses suggest that today's MBA students, in general, are looking at companies with a much broader view of their role and the stakeholders they serve.

When we look at the responses of students at different stages in their MBA program, it appears that their educational experience does have some impact on their attitudes about the responsibilities of companies. The data indicate that both second-year students and those graduating soon are more likely to chose "maximize value for shareholders" and "satisfy customer needs" as primary responsibilities of a company than are first-year students. However, graduating students also place greater

Table 5.1.   Primary Responsibilities of Companies

What do you believe are the primary responsibilities of a company? Please choose a maximum of three alternatives.

	All Students	Just Started	Halfway Through	Will Graduate Soon
Comply with all laws and regulations	34%	34%	36%	30%
Create value for the local community in which it operates	**33%**	**34%**	**31%**	**40%**
Enhance environmental conditions	6%	7%	4%	11%
Ensure confidentiality in the use and transfer of information	3%	3%	3%	1%
Invest in the growth and well-being of employees	45%	47%	42%	43%
Maximize value for shareholders	**64%**	**60%**	**69%**	**66%**
Offer equal opportunity employment	4%	5%	4%	1%
Other	2%	2%	2%	1%
Produce useful and high-quality goods/services	48%	53%	43%	40%
Satisfy customer needs	**51%**	**47%**	**58%**	**54%**

Source: Aspen Institute survey conducted in fall, 2007.

emphasis on the company's responsibility to "create value for the local community in which it operates" in that 33% of all students—and 40% of graduating students—selected this option as one of the top three responsibilities. This is a marked change from earlier surveys. In 2001 and again in 2002, only 25% of all respondents selected this responsibility as one of their three choices. These data suggest that students arrive in MBA programs more inclined to accept creating value for communities as a central corporate responsibility than they did in earlier years—and that their MBA experience further reinforces this idea.

Defining Well-Run Companies

Our survey also asks MBA students to evaluate various factors that could be used to define a "well-run" company and judge each factor as to

Table 5.2.   Defining a Well-Run Company

In your definition of a well-run company, how important are the following? Please indicate whether it is "very important," somewhat important," or "not important at all." (Only "very important" responses shown below.)

	Just Started	Halfway Through	Will Graduate Soon
Adheres to a strong mission	**51%**	**49%**	**42%**
Adheres to progressive environmental policies	**44%**	**42%**	**46%**
Attracts and retains exceptional people	**90%**	**92%**	**90%**
Creates products or services that benefit society	49%	44%	47%
Has efficient and flexible operations	**77%**	**75%**	**72%**
Invests in employee training and professional development	69%	71%	64%
Is a stable employer	**43%**	**38%**	**30%**
Offers high financial return to shareholders	47%	49%	46%
Operates according to its values and a strong code of ethics	**79%**	**77%**	**71%**
Produces high-quality products and services	79%	77%	78%
Provides competitive compensation	57%	55%	48%
Provides excellent customer service	**82%**	**82%**	**84%**

Source: Aspen Institute survey conducted in fall, 2007.

whether it is "very important," "somewhat important," or "not important at all." When we compare data collected in 2007 from students starting their MBAs against graduating students, we find that students' responses remain relatively consistent in many areas. Management education seems to have little impact on the priority they assign to most factors. Their beliefs in the importance of environmental policies, employee management ("attracts and retains exceptional people"), efficient operations, and customer service hold fairly constant. Although aggregate percentages decline, it is reassuring to see that over 70% of students at every stage in their MBA program judge ethics to be very important. However, there are two notable changes. First, 51% of students just starting their MBA program say adhering to a strong mission is very important. The percentage drops to 42% amongst students who are graduating soon. The second change pertains to the importance students place on whether or not a company is a stable employer. Along these lines, 43% of students starting MBA programs say this factor is very important. Only 38% of second-year students and 30% of students graduating soon agree.

The Role of Business in Society

Further insights about students' attitude toward the role of business in society were gathered from the Net Impact/Aspen BSP survey conducted in November, 2008 in the midst of severe economic turmoil (Net Impact, 2009). In that survey we asked students to indicate whether they agree or disagree with several statements regarding the role that business plays in society. Responses to the first statement, "I believe that most corporations are currently working toward the betterment of society," indicate a rather surprising degree of skepticism. Only 31% agreed with that statement. Remarkably, 44% disagreed. And one fourth (25%) of all respondents said they were neutral or had no opinion. A whopping 88% of students agreed with the second statement that "The for-profit sector should play a role in addressing social and environmental issues," suggesting that students believe corporations can do a better job of serving society. Students also overwhelmingly affirmed their belief that "Corporate social responsibility makes good sense because it leads to financial profits," since 77% of respondents agreed with that statement.

Do business schools have any impact on what students think about these three questions? Evidently not. There is no statistical difference between the responses of those students who are just starting their MBA degree programs compared to those who report that they will graduate soon.

Questions for Business Schools

Students' responses to questions that reveal their attitudes about companies prompt us to ask a number of questions of business school faculty and administrators. We wonder, for example, whether faculty and administrators share a consensus view about how they hope their MBA graduates will define the primary responsibilities of companies. Similarly, we wonder if they have a common expectation that their students will gain a particular perspective during their MBA experience about what characteristics best define a well-run company.

Over the years, through our *Beyond Grey Pinstripes* surveys, we have accumulated evidence that participating schools are placing greater emphasis on teaching about sound environmental practices in business.

So it was somewhat puzzling to see that this MBA coursework had little influence on the percentages of students who place high importance on progressive environmental policies. Do schools expect that the coverage of corporate environmental practices and policies now included in MBA curricula will prompt students to link environmental policies with management excellence? If so, they may want to survey their own students to make sure they are connecting the dots.

Finally, should business schools attempt to counter the somewhat discouraging view that students hold about whether or not corporations actually work toward the betterment of society? Does it matter if nearly 70% of students do not respond affirmatively to this perspective, even though they agree overwhelmingly that the for-profit sector should address social and environmental issues?

UNDERSTANDING HOW MBA STUDENTS VIEW VALUE CONFLICTS

An important goal for educating the next generation of business leaders is to help them learn to make decisions in the face of incomplete data and significant complexity. Many of the decisions these leaders will be called on to make will involve value judgments. Our research indicates that the MBA track record in giving students the confidence to manage these judgments, and the ability to know when value conflicts may occur, is mixed.

Student Responses

One thing is clear. Students repeatedly confirm that they expect to encounter values conflicts in their professional lives. When asked to respond to the statement "I anticipate that my own values will sometimes conflict with what I am asked to do in business," 29% of respondents to the 2007 survey strongly agreed, while 54% somewhat agreed. In the survey conducted by Net Impact/Aspen Institute in the fall of 2008, students provided further confirmation in that 34% strongly agreed and 47% somewhat agreed with that statement.

In an effort to identify where students see the potential for values conflicts, the 2007 survey included a question that asked respondents to rate the likelihood of values conflicts arising in various business activities. Somewhat surprisingly, less than a quarter of students thought values conflicts were very likely in some of the business activities that have been exposed by the current economic crisis to be problematic from a values point of view: awarding stock options, financial reporting, and raising or

Table 5.3.   Likelihood of Values Conflict

Assume you are engaged in each of the following business activities/practices. How likely do you think it is that values conflicts would arise? Please indicate whether it is "very likely," "somewhat likely," or "not likely at all" that values conflicts would arise. (Only "very likely" responses shown below.)

	All Students	Just Started	Halfway Through	Will Graduate Soon
Awarding stock options	**17%**	**17%**	**17%**	**12%**
Conducting performance reviews	21%	22%	21%	14%
Downsizing	56%	58%	55%	41%
Financial reporting	**22%**	**24%**	**21%**	**13%**
Interacting with government officials	24%	26%	23%	20%
Investing in less-developed countries	50%	52%	50%	39%
Managing personnel in manufacturing facilities/plants	19%	19%	19%	19%
Natural resource exploration	41%	42%	40%	38%
Negotiating with suppliers or customers	18%	19%	17%	16%
Outsourcing production operations	38%	38%	39%	39%
Raising or borrowing capital	**12%**	**13%**	**11%**	**12%**
Setting executive compensation levels	29%	30%	27%	27%

Source: Aspen Institute survey conducted in fall, 2007.

borrowing capital. In fact, the percentage of students who said values conflicts are "not likely at all" in these areas were 30%, 28% and 37%, respectively.

Table 5.3 illustrates the correlation of "very likely" responses with the time spent in MBA programs. The data indicate that students' perspectives regarding situational values conflicts are not greatly affected by what they learn in business schools.

Since these responses raise more questions than they answer, we invite further speculation and, ultimately, more research along the following lines. Does the failure to recognize situational value conflicts as "very likely" on the part of the majority of respondents reflect a lack of imagination on their part? Do the faculty who teach courses on the best management practices in these activity areas systematically explore the values judgments that may be required? Do faculty then identify approaches for tackling them? If so, the survey results may reflect that students simply feel confident as they move toward graduation that values conflicts in the workplace won't be very likely because they already have the tools to manage them.

Even so, the responses to the question of value conflict seem curious when we look at other survey responses. For example, 44% of respondents "strongly agree" and 49% "somewhat agree" that "managers place too much emphasis on short-term performance measures when making business decisions." To the statement "Most companies accurately report their earnings and profits," just 12% said they "strongly agree" although another 53% say they "somewhat agree". Given these results, we have the following questions: Doesn't student ambivalence regarding these statements suggest that values—and inevitably values conflicts—play a huge role in management decision making? How confident are students that their MBA programs are preparing them to manage values conflicts in general?

The good news is that survey responses in 2007 reflected more confidence than those from the 2002 survey, the last time we broached the values issue. Specifically, in 2007, 43% of all students said their business school is doing "a lot" to prepare them to manage value conflicts. This percentage compares very favorably with the 2002 data in which only 23% of students gave that response. The worrying news is that the students' confidence appears to decline as they progress through their MBA programs. In 2007, 48% of the students who were just stating their MBA programs said their school is doing "a lot." This percentage falls to 37% for those halfway through and to 28% for those students graduating soon.

Questions for Business Schools

It is unwise to read too much into responses to surveys that students are completing online and perhaps quickly in the middle of the night when taking a break from studying. However, we are nevertheless inclined to ask if students' responses to these questions about values conflicts reflect a real unease on their part about their preparedness to wrestle with the complex, competing stakeholder demands they will face in the world of work. We ask the following questions as well. Is it the responsibility of business schools to make sure that their students have a chance to practice responding to these conflicts in a safe educational environment that permits "do overs"?[3] Does the dominant rules-plus-analytics approach in business schools give students a sense that they can use the decision-making frameworks they have learned to get to the "right" answers without having to accommodate value ambiguity? Or, worse yet, are students' survey responses confirmation of Ghoshal's proposition that "by propagating ideologically inspired amoral theories, business schools have actively freed their students from any sense of moral responsibility?" (Ghoshal, 2005, p. 76).

Many faculty and administrators would surely argue against that suggestion. But to support their opposition, it would be useful for business schools to explore systematically what opportunities they offer their MBA students to practice values-based decision making and whether or not ample opportunities are provided to do so within the context of the core disciplines. The data from students at various stages of the MBA program seem to suggest that values and ethics may be featured more during orientation to the program than they are in the core and elective courses that follow. Faculty and administrators should step back and ask exactly where in the MBA programs their students are acquiring the skills they need to manage values conflicts as they move into the workforce.

MAKING CAREER CHOICES

MBA students are a career-oriented lot. So it is interesting to get a better understanding of what drives their employment choices, especially whether they are taking social and environmental practices of employers into consideration and how and/or whether their MBA experience influences their thinking about these practices.

A Shift in MBA Student Attitudes

Over time we have seen a shift in MBA student attitudes about which factors will be most important in their job selection. In 2002, we asked second-year students to select three factors among 15 options. "Challenging and diverse job responsibilities" was the option selected most often by 63% of students. "Work/life balance" was next at 53%. "Potential to make a contribution to society" was well down the list.

In surveys conducted in 2007 and 2008, we condensed the number of options to 10 but continued to give students three choices. Challenging and diverse job responsibilities remained the top factor, with compensation and work/life balance in second and third slots respectively. The fourth most popular choice among MBAs, however, had become "potential to make a difference to society." In 2008, one out of three students (32%) selected that factor as one of the top three considerations, compared to 26% in 2007 and just 15% in 2002.

Table 5.4.   Job Selection Factors

What factors will be most important in your job selection? Please choose a maximum of three alternatives.

	All students 2008 Survey*	All Students 2007 Survey**	Just Started 2007 Survey	Halfway Through 2007 Survey	Will Graduate Soon 2007 Survey
Challenging and diverse job responsibilities	51%	64%	65%	63%	54%
Colleagues whom I respect	26%	24%	22%	27%	22%
Compensation	49%	48%	47%	49%	50%
High ethical standards	19%	13%	13%	14%	14%
Job security	19%	4%	4%	3%	3%
Opportunities for rapid advancement	22%	22%	22%	22%	20%
Opportunities for training and development	26%	24%	21%	26%	30%
Opportunities to travel/work internationally	20%	18%	19%	17%	18%
Other	3%	3%	2%	4%	1%
Potential to make a contribution to society	32%	26%	28%	23%	25%
Work/life balance	56%	45%	45%	44%	46%

Sources: *Net Impact/Aspen BSP survey conducted in November 2008. **Aspen Institute survey conducted in fall, 2007.

Perhaps we are seeing a millennial generation effect here, but it is one that business schools would do well to watch closely. Our data from 2007 suggest that business schools may not be doing enough to nurture and sustain students' aspirations to contribute to society, especially among male MBAs. Data from 2007 show that as men go through the MBA experience their interest in the "potential to make a contribution to society" option declines. Specifically, 25% of men starting their MBA programs selected this option, but this dropped to 19% for those halfway through their programs and to 16% of those soon to graduate. Compare these data to those of women MBAs. For those starting their programs, 34% select this option, for those halfway through, 29%, and finally for those graduating soon, 39%.

A similar response was given to a question asking students to anticipate the relative importance that various factors would have to them 1 year after receiving their MBAs. For men, "having a positive impact on society" declines in importance as they approach graduation.

In focus groups conducted after the survey, many students—men and women—said that as they got closer to selecting a job, they struggled with the following tradeoff. They want to make money, pay off student loans, and work for prestigious firms. However, they also felt that making these choices was inconsistent with a higher purpose. They were inclined to believe that in order to make a contribution to society, they would need to select a job, for example, in environmental consulting or, perhaps, with a nonprofit organization. It appears that neither firms nor business schools are helping them see how all of these objectives could converge.

Questions for Business Schools

Much has been said over the last decade about the importance of integrating ethical, social, and environmental issues into the core and elective curricular offerings at business schools. Less has been said about integrating content about how to align best practices in every discipline, including accounting, marketing, and information technology, with personal aspirations for making a difference.

How often, for example, in a rigorous finance course that teaches students to be financial engineers are students asked to assess how to balance financial innovation with long-term community impacts? Moreover, courses in taxation are designed to help students master complex tax codes. Getting an "A" in the course means they know the rules. However, it does not assure that they have had opportunities to reflect on the professional decisions they may be called on to make that could have implications far beyond their institution's financial bottom line. How do schools of business help students who place a premium on being able to have a positive impact on society in their work realize that opportunities for the greatest impact may lie in what seem to be unlikely places? Should business schools even address this issue? In this vein, imagine how history might have been changed if derivatives specialists over the last 5 years raised their voices to suggest that booking more risk at the margin was not a pathway to greater profitability but rather a straw that might break the camel's back.

CONCLUSION

The economic crisis that took hold in countries around the world in mid-2008 has prompted renewed calls for fundamental reform in business schools. Business school graduates were pervasively present in the institutions that played some role in creating the environment that led to the economic crisis that exists at the time of this writing. As one way to hold business practitioners to greater account for their actions, many experts are urging that we take steps to make business a profession more akin to law and medicine (e.g., Khurana & Nohria, 2008). (See also the chapter by Buchholz in this book.) Khurana suggests that to rebuild trust in business, "business leaders must embrace a way of looking at their role that goes beyond their narrow responsibility to shareholders to include a civic and personal commitment to their duty as institutional custodians" (Khurana & Nohria, 2008, p. 70).

The professionalizing of business would have enormous, long-term and perhaps beneficial implications for management education. Whether or not broad consensus on this point is reached, business schools can take immediate steps to prepare graduates to act more in line with the kinds of standards typically associated with the professions. Our student attitudinal research suggests a number of areas where business schools could influence students to think along these lines. It may be useful for business schools to survey their own students when they enter their degree programs and then do so again when these students graduate and become alumni. The point would be to collect data on whether or not student perceptions of business stewardship evolve. Stakeholders of the schools—students, faculty, administrators, and alumni—may also find it useful to engage in open dialogue asking: Do we want to offer a holistic and integrated view of the different activities that make a company great? What does this stance look like in practice? This kind of conversation can go a long way toward helping schools recognize how to build on their unique strengths. It can also produce a collective vision for developing the kinds of graduates they most want to represent them.

NOTES

1. In 1998, The World Resources Institute (WRI) created *Grey Pinstripes with Green Ties*, a report that examined the inclusion of environmental management topics in 37 MBA programs. In 1999, WRI partnered with the Aspen Institute's Business and Society Program (Aspen BSP) to balance the report by examining MBA programs for the teaching of social impact management. This led to the creation of *Beyond Grey Pinstripes*. In 2007, Aspen BSP took over management of the survey and the ranking of MBA programs which is produced every 2 years.
2. A total of 1,943 students responded to the 2007 survey. Fifty-five percent said they were just starting their MBA; 37% reported they were "half way through" and 8% said they "will graduate soon."

3. One example of how schools can offer students this opportunity is the *Giving Voice to Values* curriculum, available online at www.GivingVoiceToValues.org. This curriculum was developed by Dr. Mary Gentile and launched by the Aspen Institute Business & Society Program and Yale School of Management with ongoing support from Babson College. Drawing on both the actual experience of business practitioners as well as cutting-edge social science and management research, this curriculum helps students identify the many ways that individuals can and do voice their values in the workplace. It also provides them the opportunity to script and practice this voice in front of their peers.

REFERENCES

The Aspen Institute. (2001). *Where will they lead? 2001 MBA attitudes about business & society.* New York, NY: Author.

The Aspen Institute. (2003). *Where will they lead? 2003MBA attitudes about business & society.* New York, NY: Author.

The Aspen Institute. (2008). *Where will they lead? 2008 MBA attitudes about business & society.* New York, NY: Author.

Bennis, W., & O'Toole, J. (2005, May). How business schools lost their way. *Harvard Business Review, 83*(5), 96-104.

Gentile, M. (2008, Summer). The 21st-century MBA. *strategy+business, 51*, 88-99.

Ghoshal, S. (2005). Bad management theories are destroying good management practices. *Academy of Management Learning & Education, 4*(1), 75-91.

Hamel, G. (2009). Moon shots for management. *Harvard Business Review, 87*(2), 91-98.

Khurana, R., & Nohria, N. (2008, October). It's time to make management a true profession. *Harvard Business Review, 86*(10), 70-77.

Net Impact (in partnership with the Aspen Institute). (2009, March). *New leaders, new perspectives: A survey of MBA student opinions on the relationship between business and social/environmental issues.* Available at www.NetImpact.org

Samuelson, J. (2006). The new rigor: Beyond the right answer. *Academy of Management Learning & Education, 5*(3), 356-365.

CHAPTER 6

ASSESSING A VIRTUOUS CIRCLE FOR SOCIALLY RESPONSIBLE BUSINESS SCHOOLS

Janette Martell and Ángel Castiñeira

INTRODUCTION

You see things; and you say, "Why?"
But I dream things that never were; and I say, "Why not?"

—George Bernard Shaw, *"Back to Methuselah"* (1921, part 1, act 1)

The infamous lack of personal and business values that induced the recent financial market chaos and the global economic crisis has strengthened the need for immediate and decisive changes in business education. Consequently, global initiatives for business education with the capabilities of the Principles for Responsible Management Education (PRME) have become essential, as well as the adoption of more congruent standards by the leading accreditation bodies: the Association to Advance Col-

Toward Assessing Business Ethics Education
pp. 73–99

legiate Schools of Business (AACSB), the Association of MBAs (AMBA), and the European Quality Improvement System (EQUIS). Such specifically revised standards, along with an extension of the Beyond Grey Pinstripes (BGP) survey, sponsored by The Aspen Institute (2009), to include new criteria for the evaluation of social responsibility at the organizational level, can impel business schools to become socially responsible institutions.

In response to this concern we are proposing the model of a virtuous circle for the development of socially responsible business schools, with the participation and roles that PRME, AACSB, AMBA, EQUIS, and BGP would play concurrently in a process of transformation toward socially responsible business education. Since PRME may be a coalescing factor in the virtuous circle, we additionally examine the response and commitment this initiative has had from the business schools accredited by AACSB, AMBA, and EQUIS as well as the ones ranked in the BGP 2009-2010 Global 100.

Related to the transformation of academic institutions, François Vallaeys (2008) defines university social responsibility as follows:

> It is a policy of continuous improvement of the university towards the effective fulfillment of its social mission through four processes: ethical and environmental management of the institution, training of responsible and socially committed citizens, production and dissemination of socially relevant knowledge, and social participation in the promotion of a more human and sustainable development. (p. 209)

Responsible business education implies much more than the transmission of knowledge; it means working with people in terms of their behavior, mindfulness, motivations, emotions, and values (Losada, 2009). Referencing John Elkington's book *Cannibals with Forks: The Triple Bottom Line of 20th Century Business*, Lozano (2009a) states:

> The current crisis also causes business schools to question whether their function is simply to teach people to eat with a fork, and to question whether their job is only to improve the instruments that are used, the capacities and skills that are acquired, the technologies that are applied, and the concepts that are learnt. It is obvious that instruments, capacities, skills, technologies, and concepts are fundamental, and the more developed and refined they are the better. However, mixed in with these elements there is also an ideological and evaluative debate which asks them, and will ask them in an increasingly frequent manner what enterprise model and, above all, which successful business model do they transmit in all of their messages and activities, both educational and non-educational. (p. 1)

Lozano's words strengthen our argument for the need to transform business schools thoroughly into becoming socially responsible institutions. Transformation means to shift the educational *weltanschauung* (Payne, 2000, cited in Giacalone & Thompson, 2006, p. 266) and train persons with a transcendent education (see Giacalone, 2004). Our proposal refers to a comprehensive transformation, as suggested by Vallaeys (2008), making substantial changes in business schools' management, education, research, and extension (social participation). Transformation involves the introduction of new types of behavior which inevitably lead to cultural change. Vidaver-Cohen (2008, p. 68) considers it to be "like building a culture of ethics and professional responsibility within the business school," and it means integrating social responsibility into the strategy and competitiveness model (Lozano, 2009b, p. 1). Transformation also requires a new definition of the mission, vision and values of the schools and universities, along with the creation of a strategic plan that will ensure the alignment of objectives towards a common purpose: to offer responsible business education. In the transformation process the conviction and commitment of presidents, deans, and faculty are certainly essential, and also essential that their actions and rhetoric become impregnated with a purposeful meaning of social responsibility.

Barely 9 days after being sworn in as President of the United States of America, Barack Obama stated: "We must have the courage and commitment to change.... Year after year, decade after decade, we've chosen delay over decisive action" (Hechtkopf, 2009). His words underscore the reality at academic institutions. For the past 50 years urgent calls to action have been made to academic institutions to deliver responsible business education: a half century of discussion and concern among stakeholders who, in different forms of expression and levels of intensity, have called for ethics, social responsibility, and sustainability in business education (Martell, 2008). For this reason we must have the courage and commitment to implement a process of change, with the aim of transforming business schools to ensure a socially responsible education.

We propose the following reflection: What kind of additional or greater crises, distressing events, and billionaire rescues will society and corporations have to endure in the future, in order for business leaders, business schools, and accreditation bodies to finally accept their ethical responsibilities and undertake decisive actions for a responsible business education, and strive for the inculcation of ethical convictions in students through the transformation of business schools into socially responsible institutions?

THE VIRTUOUS CIRCLE MODEL AND ITS INSTITUTIONAL FACTORS

We propose a model that can generate a virtuous circle for the transformation of business schools. By "virtuous circle" we mean a set of self-reinforcing, interconnected relationships among different entities which produces a beneficial effect beyond the ability of any single one of the entities acting independently. The synergic coordination of PRME, AACSB, AMBA, EQUIS, and BGP is suggested through the implementation of common objectives, congruent standards and criteria. Figure 6.1 represents our model of the virtuous circle.

We suggest that the component institutions of our proposed virtuous circle coordinate and share common objectives for

- Achieving the renovation of AACSB, AMBA, and EQUIS's accreditation standards to evaluate ethics, social responsibility, and sus-

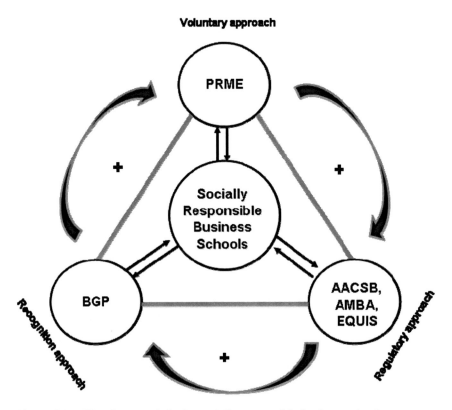

Figure 6.1.   The virtuous circle for socially responsible business schools.

tainability as basic requirements in business schools' essential processes: management, education, research, and extension (social participation).

- Attaining BGP's inclusion of the fundamental aspects of socially responsible business schools into its ranking methodology.
- Motivating business schools to adhere to PRME by adopting and implementing its principles.
- Developing a collective synergy to promote a planned process for transforming business schools into socially responsible institutions.
- Facilitating the submission of a single comprehensive annual report from each of the PRME signatories, including accredited and ranked schools, on their transformation progress, in order to fulfill transparency and accountability requirements.
- Achieving an equitable balance between voluntary, regulatory, and ranking-recognition approaches.

We will now examine each of the five institutional components of the proposed virtuous circle—PRME, AACSB, AMBA, EQUIS, and BGP—as the key factors in the transformation process.

Principles for Responsible Management Education (PRME)

We have faith in PRME and in its enormous potential for becoming the coalescing factor of business schools around the world, to join together in a common purpose for transforming themselves into socially responsible institutions, capable of instilling in their students a high standard of business ethics and a conviction in terms of social responsibility and sustainability.

PRME was conceived in October 2006, in Cleveland, Ohio by the Academy of Management, the UN Global Compact Office (UNGC), and the Case Weatherhead School of Management. The principles were drafted thereafter by six coconvening institutions: AACSB International, Aspen Institute Business and Society Program (BSP), European Foundation for Management Development (EFMD), Globally Responsible Leadership Initiative (GRLI), and Net Impact, together with the United Nations Global Compact (UNGC). The significant collaboration of an international taskforce of almost 60 deans, university presidents, and official representatives of leading academic institutions from 29 countries, contributed successfully to the creation of the initiative. It is currently led by a steering committee made up of the six original coconveners, three of whom are institutional components of our proposed model; the fourth component of our virtuous circle is AMBA, which adhered to PRME on June 30, 2009. The six PRME principles are transcribed in the Appendix.

The mission of PRME, presented at the United Nations in 2007, is to inspire and champion responsible business education, research, and thought leadership globally. PRME signatories commit themselves voluntarily to developing the capabilities of students to be future generators of sustainable value for business and society; to incorporating values of global social responsibility in their curricula; and to aligning their missions, strategies, and core competencies with United Nations' values regarding human rights, labor, environment, and anticorruption, as embodied in the principles. Signatories also commit themselves to reporting annually to stakeholders on the progress they have attained, and to exchanging effective practices with other academic institutions (see www.unprme.org). It is evident that signing on to PRME implies a responsibility (Martell & Castiñeira, 2009).

One of the most significant merits of PRME is that it is a global initiative. As United Nations Secretary-General Ban Ki-moon (2008, p. 4) stated: "PRME has the capacity to take the case for universal values into classrooms on every continent" (www.unprme.org). Basing itself on the Global Compact experience, PRME offers platforms to discuss issues related to the development and implementation of social responsibility, and it may induce learning processes through interaction and cooperation (Runhaar & Lafferty, 2009). It fosters the creation of local and worldwide networks to develop new practices, such as disseminating information through web pages, newsletters, scientific papers, and best practice studies, as well as bringing them together for meetings, conferences, and seminars (Cetindamar & Husoy, 2007), and it encourages the implementation of more transparent social responsibility systems and responsible accountability. We believe that PRME's greatest asset may be its catalytic impact on academic institutions by promoting, as Kell (2005, p. 70) declares, "a new era of cooperation [with the academic community], thus constituting a platform for the need of dialogue, learning, and action."

However, we find that PRME lacks an important element that refers to guidance on how to implement the six principles, and we are concerned that the implementation process has been left too open and discretional for academic institutions. This laxness may generate the pursuit of diverse isolated actions and ineffective activities without first reflecting on, and sharing the meaning of, fundamental aspects. Some examples: What does it mean to be a socially responsible business school? What is our purpose? What are our day-to-day values for faculty, students, and staff members? How should we live a culture of social responsibility? What type of professionals and persons do we intend to form? What do we expect from our alumni after they graduate? What practices must we implement for the socially responsible management of our school?

When these reflections begin to be defined and fathomed, we may say that the transformation process has started, and then we may be able to attain the PRME principles effectively within a purposeful process of change.

We recently attended an academic conference in the United Kingdom where in a session focused on PRME a concern was expressed about the apparent emptiness of the six principles. It was said they left their materialization practically open to the interpretation of their readers, thus giving rise to two possibilities. First, they may lead to the desired transformation if they are clearly interpreted with a definition of objectives, strategies, goals, action plans, and performance indicators for each principle. The second possibility, however, if the principles are not clearly interpreted, is that they may only produce actions with a rhetorical label of social responsibility but no consequence of substantial change, turning out to be window dressing.

We further believe that the absence of guidelines might curb the participation of academic institutions who may conclude that they are not prepared to commit themselves to the principles. However, we infer the possibility of positive amendments in the future from PRME's announcement on December 3, 2009, by which the steering committee has changed the introduction to the foundational document "in order to dispel misunderstandings by potential signatories." It will henceforth read:

> As institutions of higher education involved in the development of current and future managers, we declare our willingness to progress in the implementation, within our institution, of the following Principles starting with those that are more relevant to our capacities and mission. We will report on progress to all our stakeholders and exchange effective practices related to these principles with other academic institutions. (PRME communication, 2009)

It is opportune to mention, however, that GRLI has developed a Community of Responsible Action (CoRA) around PRME with five important categories whose objective is to stimulate an ongoing discussion about the many different ways that academic institutions can create a stronger focus on responsible management education in different contexts around the world (see Aspling & Thiesgaard, 2009). These categories are:

- Getting started with PRME;
- Implementing PRME in management education;

- Implementing PRME in management research;
- Developing partnerships with business organizations; and
- Creating a broad-based dialogue about PRME.

Finally, we believe that along with the social and environmental responsibilities, which are fundamental concepts expressed in the principles, the precept of business ethics education should be recurrently stated in a precise and emphatic manner in order not to take such an essential component for granted.

Leading Accreditation Bodies

Julio Urgel (2007, p. 77), director of the Quality Services Department at the European Foundation for Management Development (EFMD), notes that the value added by accreditation systems stems from three main interrelated areas: assessment of the quality of the school based on several criteria, enhanced brand recognition from being granted a distinctive accreditation label, and contribution to the actual improvement of the school. Other factors that underpin the importance of accreditation are the increasingly competitive global market for the most promising business students, and an ever-increasing number of business programs that deliver management education (Trapnell, 2007, p. 67). Accreditation is of strategic importance inasmuch as accreditation processes help business schools gain clarity about the markets they serve and the services they offer (Zammuto, 2008, p. 256).

According to John J. Fernandes (2008), president and chief executive Officer, AACSB International, his research staff has estimated a total of 11,767 business schools in over 200 countries, although no one knows the exact number of schools offering higher education degrees in business. AACSB and EQUIS accredit only about 5% of them, which means that 95% of the world's business schools are operating without recognized quality assurance and continuous improvement. We do emphasize, however, that the minute 5% encompasses most of the leading and prestigious business schools in the world that are accredited by AACSB and/or EQUIS, a fact which, we believe, underlines the significance of accreditation.

We have included a third accreditor in our proposed virtuous circle, AMBA, because along with AACSB and EQUIS, they constitute the three major management education accreditation bodies well known internationally as the Triple Crown accreditation for outstanding research, education, and career-building qualities.

AACSB International

AACSB is the world's oldest and largest accrediting organization for undergraduate, master, and doctoral degree programs in business; their accreditation represents the highest standard of achievement for business schools worldwide. Founded in 1916 by a consortium of 16 business schools including Columbia University, Dartmouth College, Harvard University, New York University, Northwestern University, Ohio State University, Tulane University, University of California at Berkeley, University of Chicago, University of Illinois, University of Nebraska, University of Pennsylvania, University of Pittsburgh, University of Texas, University of Wisconsin-Madison, and Yale University (www.aacsb.edu), AACSB celebrates its 94th anniversary in 2010.

Analyzing AACSB's eligibility procedures and accreditation standards for business accreditation, which were revised on July 1, 2009, we find two criteria that contribute to the virtuous circle's objectives: "The mission driven philosophy, by which the viewpoint of the school's stakeholders is required for the definition and review of its mission statement" (AACSB, 2009, p. 16), and the stipulation that "the institution must establish expectations for ethical behavior by administrators, faculty, and students, which is paramount to the delivery of business education" (p. 13). However, among the AACSB's standards that are fundamental for a socially responsible education we have unfortunately identified the following, related to core learning goals and course-embedded measurement, that barely contribute to our objectives:

- The general knowledge and skills goals, while not management specific, relate to knowledge and abilities graduates will carry with them into their careers. Such learning areas as communications abilities, problem-solving abilities, and ethical reasoning skills ... are the types of general knowledge and abilities that schools might define as part of the core learning goals. (p. 62)
- A school with learning goals that require students to integrate knowledge across business functional areas, or to incorporate ethical considerations into decision making, may embed the measurement of accomplishment on those goals into a capstone business-strategy course. (p. 66)

The above standards unfortunately leave their application entirely to the discretion of the school by employing words such as "might define" or "may embed." Various authors have qualified these and other requirements set by AACSB as vague (Etzioni, 2002), and flexible (Casile & Davis-Blake, 2002; Navarro, 2008; Swanson & Frederick, 2003; Vidaver-

Cohen, 2008; Windsor, 2002), which are not therefore impelling the transformation of business schools into socially responsible institutions.

AACSB standards repeatedly refer to recommendations and examples of ethics issues to be included as components in courses, learning goals, demonstrations of achievement, and curricula management, but in none of the topics are those issues mentioned as specific subjects or requirements for assessment purposes, remaining at the level of recommendations, and leaving to the schools' discretion their incorporation as core or embedded courses. The standards refer to every aspect of business education in detail, but they omit ethics and social responsibility as basic requirements in business education which is regrettable for students' formation and the protection of society, and certainly, for the materialization of our proposed virtuous circle. Furthermore, the many paragraphs devoted in the Standards to the analysis, definition, and requirements of the mission statement do not include the concepts of ethics or social responsibility at all, even though they are fundamental to the schools' strategic management. We earnestly wish that AACSB will include the requirement for these concepts in future revisions of their standards, thus contributing with their prestige and influence to the successful transformation of business schools and the materialization of the virtuous circle.

The vision of AACSB board chair 2008-2009, Richard Cosier, significantly expresses one of the most frequently called for changes in the accrediting body's standards. Cosier (2008) states that:

> It is more vital than ever that AACSB and its members incorporate ethics and integrity into business school curricula. It is equally important to emphasize to our new AACSB members, regardless of geographic location, that our students, faculty, and administrators be held to the highest standards of ethical conduct.... We must ensure that our high standards of management education are upheld, without exception. (p. 56)

Transferring Cosier's vision to AACSB's accreditation standards would ensure that business schools generate substantial changes in their organizational culture.

Through its history, performance, and influence, AACSB has been acknowledged as the institutional actor most capable of influencing business schools (Evans, Treviño & Weaver, 2006, p. 288). The participation of AACSB in the virtuous circle model would therefore be absolutely indispensable and determinant for its synergic success. However, AACSB would have to believe in the transcendence of transforming business schools into socially responsible institutions through the decisive influence of its accreditation standards.

AMBA

AMBA was organized in 1967 as a global accreditation institution for masters of business administration (MBA), masters in business and management (MBM) programs, and doctorates in business administration (DBA). In 2009, according to its webpage, its vision was updated in order to be recognized internationally as the authoritative voice in postgraduate management education. It is the only worldwide professional membership organization for MBA students and graduates; and it provides support and services to prospective and current students and graduates, as well as business schools and MBA employers, in a network of 9,000 members in 88 countries (see www.mbaworld.com).

We were very pleased to learn that on July 30, 2009, AMBA officially declared its participation in, and support for PRME which, according to the PRME Secretariat, adds a new powerful partner in terms of global outreach and international inclusiveness (www.unprme.org).

In its MBA accreditation criteria, dated August 2007, AMBA requires all programs to ensure that candidates acquire a firm understanding of the major areas of knowledge that support general management, such as ethical, social, economic, and technological change issues, as well as globalization and sustainability, including the impact of environmental forces on organizations (p. 4). This accrediting institution specifically requests the inclusion of ethics, social, environmental and sustainability issues in its standards, at the institutional strategy level and across the curricula, and therefore contributes effectively to the objectives set out in our proposed model. Its contribution to the virtuous circle would be significantly valuable because of the importance it attributes to social responsibility, and the number of business schools that it accredits in 72 countries.

EQUIS

EQUIS has gained prestige and recognition worldwide since it was founded in 1997 by a mandate of EFMD members, with the support of top business schools in Europe: Bocconi, HEC Paris, Helsinki School of Economics, IESE, IMD, INSEAD, Instituto de Empresa, London Business School, and Rotterdam School of Management (see www.efmd.org). EQUIS is EFMD's international system of quality assessment, improvement, and accreditation of higher education institutions in management and business administration. At the time of its creation there were no international accreditation systems established in the field of management (Urgel, 2007, p. 73) and therefore, the need became evident to develop an accreditation system targeted at those business schools around the world that were trying to make an impact beyond their domestic frontiers. Miles, Hazeldine and Munilla (2004, p. 29) suggest that as a strategic response to EQUIS and other emerging accreditation bodies, and because of a more global, diverse, and technology-driven environment, AACSB revised its accreditation standards and transformed its reaffirmation framework. It is possible that EQUIS' international scope stimulated AACSB's international expansion.

In 2005, EFMD launched the Globally Responsible Leadership Initiative (GRLI), with support from the UNGC, to promote understanding of globally responsible leadership and develop its practice. Anders Aspling, EFMD board member and chair of the initiative (2005, p. 1), explains that their aim is to establish the norms and expectations of business behavior for the twenty-first century and ensure that the emerging generations of business leaders live by them. He stresses the need to overhaul business education worldwide to provide a foundation of global responsibility in every area of learning. GRLI's specific action targets include making global responsibility a foundational requirement within the accreditation systems for business schools, and piloting new best practice approaches to learning within leading business schools and companies so that business leaders not only know what is expected of them, but also practice it.

Since both EQUIS and GRLI stem from EFMD, their principles strengthen EQUIS' accreditation standards which in their latest revision, in January 2009, evaluate an institution's compliance with the following criteria:

- The school's clear understanding of its core values and the inclusion of an explicit commitment to ethical and socially responsible behavior in the management profession, as well as the broad acceptance of those values and the adherence to them across the school (EQUIS, 2009, p. 11).
- The process by which the mission, vision, values, and strategic objectives are converted into strategic and operational plans (p. 11).
- The extent to which programs integrate the main challenges in business and society, such as global responsibility and sustainable development (p. 21).
- The means by which issues relating to business ethics and corporate social responsibility are integrated into personal development, giving special importance to the processes by which the school helps students to develop both personally and professionally, along with the key personal skills that the school aims to develop in individuals (p. 29).

We believe that EQUIS is reaching a position of leadership in the accreditation requirements related to fostering socially responsible business schools, and we therefore hope they will generate influence and example to be followed by AACSB and AMBA in the near future. Jointly, with a common conviction, the three accreditation bodies will ideally turn the proposed virtuous circle into a successful reality.

Beyond Grey Pinstripes (BGP) Project

In a different chapter of this book we describe the BGP project and its contribution to the assessment of socially responsible business education. The integration of BGP, as the fifth component of our virtuous circle, creates a perfect balance among voluntary (PRME), regulatory (AACSB, AMBA, EQUIS), and ranking-recognition (BGP) approaches to the integration of social responsibility in business schools.

Presently, BGP focuses exclusively on coursework and faculty research (see www.beyondgreypinstripes.org). However, the issue of business school responsibility cannot be limited to asking what curriculum is offered. Social responsibility certainly includes curriculum but does not end there. Socially responsible business education must transmit a culture of responsibility as an essential part of the identity of the business school itself; therefore, the fundamental question is not about the curriculum but about the business school's identity/raison d'être (Losada, Martell, & Lozano, in press).

Being ranked in BGP is certainly a matter of pride for the selected business schools, but we deem that distinction should also entail the responsibility of living up to the values for which those schools are ranked. We believe that BGP and PRME share common ideals in challenging business schools to form ethical and socially responsible business leaders for the twenty-first century. As a result, it is intensely hoped that all the business schools that are ranked in the BGP Global 100 will adhere to PRME and be distinguished, additionally, as leading promoters of change.

In our proposed virtuous circle we have stressed the necessary contributions of PRME, AACSB, AMBA, EQUIS, and BGP to promote the transformation process leading to socially responsible business schools. We believe that PRME can be the coalescing factor in the virtuous circle, provided that AACSB, AMBA, EQUIS, and BGP act jointly with a common conviction, establishing requirements in their respective standards and criteria to ensure that academic institutions transform their essential processes to become socially responsible.

ASSESSMENT OF PRME'S DEVELOPMENT
AND ITS INFLUENCE ON THE VIRTUOUS CIRCLE

The transcendence of PRME as a global initiative with the mission to inspire and champion responsible management education, and its potential catalytic effect, merits a detailed analysis of its evolution with regard to the response from the business schools accredited by AACSB, AMBA and EQUIS, as well as by the schools ranked in the BGP 2009-2010 Global 100. This assessment allows us to ascertain the level of commitment of business schools in regards to their transformation into socially responsible institutions. Considering the pivotal position that we have attributed to PRME in the virtuous circle, it is pertinent to mention that this initiative is currently led by a Steering Committee of eight internationally prestigious members, three of whom are proposed components of our virtuous circle.

We have examined the evolution of the total number of PRME signatories, starting from the launch of the initiative in July 2007, in order to assess their potential level of commitment to drive forward their transformation process, and their contribution to the realization of the virtuous circle. The academic institutions' decisive and committed participation in PRME will support the success of the synergic coordination of the virtuous circle components.

Development of PRME Signatories

In his speech at PRME's First Global Forum, on December 4, 2008, Manuel Escudero, head of academic initiatives and executive director of the Research Center for the Global Compact, stated that the goals that had been set on September 8, 2007 at the first meeting of the PRME Steering Committee, to recruit 150 academic participants, had been successfully reached. In January 13, 2010, PRME counts a total of 280 signatories of whom 72% are business schools and 19% are universities. Figure 6.2 shows the development of PRME signatories.

The voluntary endorsement of PRME by 280 academic institutions in two and a half years attests to the significant concern for ethics and social responsibility, and suggests the potential of PRME. We nonetheless consider that the initiative deserves a greater recruitment dynamism and support, and feel that the number of signatories should have reached a higher level by the date mentioned above. However, it is appropriate to indicate that applications from some institutions were rejected because their nature did not fulfill PRME's basic screening criteria; that is, to be recognized publicly and to be degree-granting institutions. On the other hand, applications were accepted from several supporting organizations that can contribute a new outreach capacity to the Steering Committee's efforts.

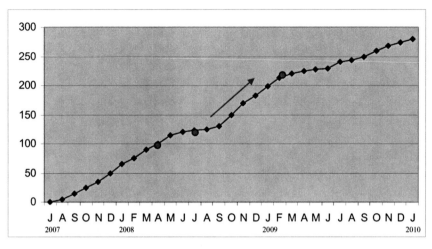

Figure 6.2.   Development of PRME signatories. January 13, 2010.

Surprisingly, many prestigious business schools have not signed up, and even the First Global Forum was not as well attended as PRME merited. The representative of the U.S. region, Carolyn Woo, dean of Mendoza College of Business, expressed disappointment at seeing only 27 deans of U.S. schools in attendance, noting that of the top 20 business schools, only one dean was present at the forum (2008, p. 2).

We analyzed the 280 signatories up to January 13, 2010 (www .unprme.org/participants/index.php); Figure 6.3 shows their distribution in 61 countries on that date.

As the map shows, PRME has signatories in 61 nations of which eight concentrate almost 60% of all signatory institutions: United States 73, United Kingdom 25, France 16, Spain 13, Germany 13, Canada 10, China 8, and India 7.

Our findings regarding the commitment of accredited and ranked business schools to PRME reveal an important growth potential in relation to other components of the virtuous circle:

- AACSB has granted accreditations to 570 schools in business programs as of September 2009, according to its website (www.aacsb.edu/accreditation/accreditedmembers.asp). Only 87 of those schools (15%) have signed on to PRME while 483 (85%) have not, as yet. Of the 280 signatories counted on January 13, 2010, 87 schools (32%) were accredited by AACSB. It is important to note that only two of the 16 prestigious universities that founded AACSB

Figure 6.3.   PRME signatory institutions in the world (January 13, 2010).

in 1916 (Ohio State University and University of Pittsburgh) have signed on to PRME.

- By December 2009, AMBA had accredited a total of 161 business schools. We found that of these, 47 (29%) had signed, while 114 (71%) had not. Of all 280 PRME signatories, 17% are schools accredited by AMBA.

- According to EFMD's website, by November 2009, 122 business schools had been awarded accreditations by this institution (www .efmd.org/index.php/accreditation-/equis/accredited-schools).   Of those schools, 48 (39%) are PRME signatories and 74 (61%) are not, while 17% of all 280 signatories hold EQUIS' accreditations.

- Our analysis of the BGP 2009-2010 Global 100 ranking indicates that 48 of the ranked business schools have signed on to PRME, while 52 have not. Only 18% of PRME signatories are BGP ranked.

Figure 6.4 illustrates the degree of adhesion and commitment to PRME from accredited and ranked schools.

Notwithstanding the low commitment levels of schools accredited by AACSB, AMBA and EQUIS, or the ranked schools in the BGP Global 100, this should not be seen as a bad sign for PRME's future. Instead, it should be regarded as the outset of the most promising initiative ever conceived for the integration of social responsibility in academic institutions, and as a great opportunity for them, as Lozano asserts, "to define and declare the values they defend" (2009a, p. 1).

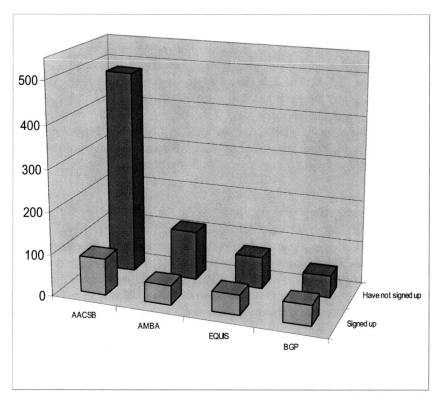

Figure 6.4.   Accredited and ranked business schools that have and have not signed PRME (January 13, 2010).

It is important to acknowledge the continuous efforts of the co-convening organizations that have been using their communication channels to advocate PRME, including a joint campaign where AACSB, EABIS, EFMD, GRLI, Net Impact and UNGC presented PRME to their respective constituents (Escudero, 2008), and it is worthy of mention that the BGP 2009-2010 survey included a pertinent question that probably prompted several schools to adopt the initiative thereafter: "Has your business school signed up for PRME?"

The international taskforce that drafted PRME was made up of almost 60 deans, university presidents, and official delegates representing 51 leading academic institutions and two nonacademic institutions from 29 countries (http://www.unprme.org/resources-docs/PRME.pdf). We would have expected to find all 51 academic institutions of the taskforce to be PRME signatories. However, this was not the case: only 32 of them, 63%

of the total, committed themselves to this initiative whereas 19 academic institutions, 37% of the taskforce members, did not.

The country with the highest number of members in the taskforce is the United States, with 12 academic institutions of which only five (42%) signed on to PRME. The fact that a high number of taskforce members from the United States have not committed themselves to upholding PRME is a cause for concern, and it is surprising to find that business schools of considerable significance, such as Columbia, Harvard, Haas, MIT, Stephen M. Ross, Wharton, and Yale who were members of the Taskforce have not upheld an initiative of such significance.

Reasons for Opting Out of PRME

Our research was expanded in order to understand the reasons why 37% of the taskforce members had not adopted the initiative, and we personally contacted several of them who voluntarily and candidly shared their opinions with us. The reasons were of various kinds, from basic and simple, to others more elaborate; some not too supportive, but many others very favorable.

Several direct comments merit mention, but we shall maintain the identity of the respondents in confidence:

- We have not signed up for two reasons, none of which reflects negatively on PRME. First, I had some other policies to accomplish, namely getting ethics required in the MBA program. That has taken me over a year, and I plan now to introduce the dean to PRME after the New Year. The second reason, and probably why not everyone has signed up, is the onerous task of reporting every year. There are so many things to report about that this just seems like overkill. However, there are probably ways around that and I am working on that (personal communication, December 15, 2008).
- The universities I have worked at, in [name of country withheld], tend to react very slowly to initiatives of this nature, but I believe that in the long term they will adhere to PRME. One reason that now prevents universities in my country from signing up is probably the socially responsible support to labor rights that the UN Global Compact strongly upholds. The universities I refer to strongly depend on the corporate sector which is reluctant to support unions in their companies. It is hoped that our corporations will change their position on this issue, and thereafter, universities

will have less reticence to adhere to the initiative (personal communication, December 15, 2008).

- My assistance in the formulation of the principles was given in my individual capacity and not as a formal assignment from [name withheld] business school or its dean (personal communication, December 15, 2008).

- I stepped down as dean a year and a half ago. I'm copying my successor, who may not know what PRME is (personal communication, December 16, 2008).

- The PRME has the potential to influence the development of management education. It has highlighted the importance and urgency of the need for, in your own words, a "common purpose of forming ethical and socially responsible persons." There will be many ways of going about that but the PRME recognizes the importance of education in the formative years of a management professional's education. The PRME encourages learning institutions to commit to that process. I don't think you have overvalued the PRME initiative. It is, however, important that PRME be evaluated in substance. We should not be overly concerned with bean-counting the number of signatories. Many signatories of the UN Global Compact are not necessarily model companies. The main thing is that business schools are increasingly mindful of the type of graduates they produce. The KPIs (key performance indicators) for the UNGC office vis-à-vis the PRME are different from the KPIs of the universities. Nevertheless, the PRME is a catalyst in the common purpose you talked about (personal communication, December 17, 2008).

- PRME represents a useful initiative in enriching and broadening the purpose of management education. It reinforces the larger shift in management practice toward adding social value generation to the traditional business role of economic value generation. Any international initiative to set forth and then have adopted universal principles faces a multitude of challenges that you are undoubtedly aware of, and in the process of discovering in your research. Whether or not an individual institution adopts the principles is not necessarily an indicator of the degree of agreement with or support for them. Every business school has its particular organizational culture, policies, and politics that might impede adoption on process rather than substantive grounds. In fact, it might be valuable to ascertain to what extent organizations adopting or not adopting actually differ in their practices relative to the principles. There may even be some non-adopters that are more congruent with the principles or even exceed them than adopters (personal communication, December 19, 2008).

- Even though I was interested in adhering to PRME in my capacity as dean, with the desire to implement positive changes, I encountered resistance from officials in my university involved in issues of social responsibility, who objected my recommendation alleging that the network of (name withheld) universities, to which we belong, was considering other alternatives (personal communication, December 20, 2008).

- Although (name withheld) university has not signed up to the PRME, it does not mean that we do not subscribe to the principles and values of the PRME. At the heart of every undergraduate degree program is the university core curriculum. The core curriculum includes analytical skills and creative thinking, leadership and team building, ethics and social responsibility, business, government and society, and technology and world change. The courses underline the importance of these subjects as part of the overall education in [name withheld] University. In addition, students have to complete 60 hours of community service as part of their degree program. In short, business ethics and social responsibility are integral part of the core courses in the curriculum. The amount of faculty resources devoted to the teaching of the courses is a representation of the university's commitment to a holistic education. At (name withheld) university, ethics and social responsibility are managed and taught by faculty from the school of law. At the MBA level, all students have to take an exam in the course of managing ethical dilemmas and corporate governance. I suppose the way forward is for the school of law to work with the other five schools, especially the school of business, to achieve buy-in for the PRME. As the law school's remit is not management education, there are internal channels to navigate to have (name withheld) university sign on to the PRME. Nevertheless, we are doing as much as many of the PRME signatories in promoting and sensitizing students on the importance of ethical and responsible conduct in the business realm (personal communication, January 2, 2009).

- I recall that I helped (name withheld) draft and edit some text for the development of these principles. I was involved in the Global Compact at the beginning but I did not think that it was doing anything; rather, it simply put on a series of big show conferences where very little substance/change was taking place. As a result, I stopped attending and have focused my work on the research and meetings I have been organizing/doing around the (name withheld) project (personal communication, January 8, 2009).

Regional Initiatives Beyond PRME

The foregoing comments we received regarding other alternatives to PRME, such as the network of universities engaged in a project of their own, led us to research other developing initiatives for socially responsible universities:

- A network of 14 Chilean universities launched in 2001 a socially responsible university project named Universidad Construye País [Universities Build a Country], to expand the concept and practice of social responsibility through jointly coordinated actions across the entire Chilean university system.
- The Iberoamerican Network of Universities for Corporate Social Responsibility (REDUNIRSE) was launched in 2006. It constitutes an area for exchange between Iberoamerican universities which, with the support of institutions promoting social responsibility such as the Agencia Española de Cooperación Internacional (Spanish Agency for International Cooperation) (AECI) and the United Nations Development Program (UNDP), aims to link up the different social actors involved in social responsibility. The objective is to promote social capital in Iberoamerica and help create a socially responsible community, promote ethical human development, spread information, and raise awareness about social responsibility, as well as encouraging training, research and extension (social participation) in this area.
- The Association of Universities Entrusted to the Society of Jesus in Latin America (AUSJAL), created in 2007, has brought together 31 universities located in 15 Latin American countries; its main objective is to create the first university network in Latin America with an identity, shared leadership and common strategy, in order to carry out educational and social reform in that region.

The projects mentioned above are worthy of enthusiastic praise for their initiatives and efforts to create socially responsible universities. There are other laudable projects in action, but they all are either regional or belong to one university or to a network of several universities. On the one hand, PRME is an initiative which does not exclude other constructive projects but is, by its origin, nature and principles, a project that can unite schools towards common ideals and purposes. Isolated efforts disperse and weaken overall objectives. Contrariwise, PRME fosters the creation of local and worldwide networks to develop a new era of cooperation within the academic community and the constitution of a shared platform for dialogue, learning and action. Additionally, the exceptional support and formal recognition that the United Nations has granted to the PRME initiative deserves endorsement—with conviction and commitment—from business schools (PRME News, 2009).

We know that taking the decision to implement changes in academic institutions has never been easy (see Cohen, 2003); planned change, affecting the entire system is unusual (Burke, 2008, p. 1) and takes much longer than expected. However, current challenges are demanding immediate and decisive action and, paraphrasing President Barack Obama's words, "We [that is, the business schools] must have the courage and commitment to change."

A suitable recommendation for all academic institutions that have not yet adhered to the commitment of implementing PRME is Judith Samuelson's statement, made in 2003, which is quite pertinent to our proposal:

> Build on your school's strengths, whether that means key faculty, or research, or an innovative approach to curriculum, or close ties to the community, or global reach, or something else. You don't have to start with a full-blown program, you can start where the energy and ability already exists and build from there. (Gentile & Samuelson, 2005, p. 504)

Taking the first step is the fundamental action: Signing on to PRME and becoming committed to implementing the principles for a process of change towards the transformation of business schools into socially responsible institutions.

CONCLUDING REMARKS

Greed and lack of values contributed to the recent financial chaos and the global economic crisis, which revealed a lack of ethics for the business executives involved. Many of them, skillful business practitioners, graduated from prestigious business schools with the goal of attaining prominent positions in the corporate world. However, they did not seem to be equipped with the ethical compass that such positions require. We call for business schools to fill this void and encourage their students, society's future managers, to attend to ethics in their decision making. We believe that such effort to deliver socially responsible business education and inculcate a conviction for ethical professionalism in students can have positive repercussions for society.

In short, we advocate that business schools integrate social responsibility into their curricula as an essential philosophy. We realize that this process is a complex one, and attempting it in an individual, isolated manner is difficult. Hence, it is timely that PRME was created over two and a half years ago as a global initiative with the capability of joining business schools together in a common purpose through a set of principles and common ideals that emphasize the fundamental normative connections between business, the environment, and society.

To further this initiative, we have proposed a virtuous circle, integrated by PRME as the central component in conjunction with three accreditation institutions, AACSB, EQUIS and AMBA, and the BGP ranking project as the fifth component. These prestigious institutions, as founders and supporters of PRME, conscious of their responsibility and influence, are in positions to synergistically encourage all the business schools that they accredit or rank to sign up to PRME and engage thereafter in a process of change aimed at delivering socially responsible education.

ACKNOWLEDGMENTS

The authors gratefully acknowledge helpful comments from William C. Frederick and Manuel Valles on an earlier draft of this chapter.

APPENDIX

Principles for Responsible Management Education (PRME)

- Purpose: We will develop the capabilities of students to be future generators of sustainable value for business and society at large and to work for an inclusive and sustainable global economy.
- Values: We will incorporate into our academic activities and curricula the values of global social responsibility as portrayed in international initiatives such as the United Nations Global Compact.
- Method: We will create educational frameworks, materials, processes and environments that enable effective learning experiences for responsible leadership.
- Research: We will engage in conceptual and empirical research that advances our understanding of the role, dynamics and impact of corporations in the creation of sustainable social, environmental and economic value.
- Partnership: We will interact with managers of business corporations to extend our knowledge of their challenges in meeting social

and environmental responsibilities and to explore jointly effective approaches to meeting these challenges.

• Dialogue: We will facilitate and support dialogue and debate among educators, business, government, consumers, media, civil society organizations and other interested groups and stakeholders on critical issues related to global social responsibility and sustainability (Source: PRME A Global Initiative—A Global Agenda, UNGC, http://www.unprme.org).

Glossary

• AACSB: Association to Advance Collegiate Schools of Business
• AECI: Spanish Agency for International Cooperation
• AMBA: Association of MBAs
• AUSJAL: Association of Universities Entrusted to the Society of Jesus in Latin America
• BGP: Beyond Grey Pinstripes
• BSP: Business and Society Program
• DBA: Doctorates in Business Administration
• EABIS: European Academy of Business in Society
• EFMD: European Foundation for Management Development
• EQUIS: European Quality Improvement System
• GMAC: Graduate Management Admission Council
• GRLI: Globally Responsible Leadership Initiative
• KPI: Key performance indicators
• MBA: Masters of Business Administration
• MBM: Masters in Business and Management
• PRME: Principles for Responsible Management Education
• REDUNIRSE Ibero-American Network of Universities for Corporate Social Responsibility
• UNDP: United Nations Development Program
• UNESCO: United Nations Educational, Scientific and Cultural Organization
• UNGC: United Nations Global Compact

REFERENCES

Aspen Institute Center for Business Education. (2009). *Beyond Grey Pinstripes 2009-2010 Global 100 ranking*. Retrieved from http://www.beyondgreypinstripes.org/pdf/2009-2010BGP_Brochure.pdf

Aspling, A. (2005, October 18). *Globally responsible leadership initiative launched.* Retrieved from http://www.unglobalcompact.org/newsandevents/news_archives/2005_10_18.html

Aspling, A., & Thiesgaard, P. J. (2009, Summer). Providing guidance for the enactment of the UN Global Compact PRME. *GRLI Magazine*, 15-16. Retrieved from http://www.grli.org/images/stories/newletter/aspling_thiesgaard.pdf

Association of MBAs. (2007). *MBA accreditation criteria. August 2007.* Retrieved from http://www.mbaworld.com/MBAWorld/jsp/images/accreditation/pdf/MBA_criteria_0807.pdf

Association of MBAs. (2009). *Accredited academic institutions.* Retrieved from http://www.mbaworld.com/index.php?option=com_content&view=article&id=474&Itemid=132

Association to Advance Collegiate Schools of Business. (2009). *Eligibility procedures and accreditation standards for business accreditation* (Revised July 1, 2009). Retrieved from http://www.aacsb.edu/accreditation/standards.asp

Burke, W. (2008). *Organization change: Theory and practice* (2nd ed.). Thousand Oaks, CA: Sage Publications.

Casile, M., & Davis-Blake, A. (2002). When accreditation standards change: Factors affecting differential responsiveness of public and private organizations. *Academy of Management Journal, 45*(1), 180-195.

Cetindamar, D., & Husoy, K. (2007). Corporate social responsibility practices and environmentally responsible behavior: The case of the United Nations Global Compact. *Journal of Business Ethics, 76*, 163-176.

Cohen, A. (2003). Transformational change at Babson College: Notes from the firing line. *Academy of Management Learning & Education, 2*(2), 154-180.

Cosier, R. (2008, September/October). Ethical objectives. *BizEd Magazine for Business Education.* Retrieved from http://www.aacsb.edu/publications/Archives/sepoct08/52-57%20Ethical%20Objectives.pdf

Escudero, M. (2008). *Report on 2008 activities and 2009 strategy and goals.* Retrieved from http://www.unprme.org/resources-and-reporting/index.php

Etzioni, A. (2002, August 4). When it comes to ethics, B-schools get an F. *The Washington Post*, p. B4. Retrieved from http://amitaietzioni.org/documents/B399.pdf

European Quality Improvement System. (2009). *Standards and criteria.* Retrieved from http://www.efmd.org/images/stories/efmd/EQUIS/equis_standards_and_criteria_jan09.pdf

Evans, J. M., Treviño, L. K., & Weaver, G. R. (2006). Who's in the ethics driver's seat? Factors influencing ethics in the MBA curriculum. *Academy of Management Learning & Education, 5*(3), 278-293.

Fernandes, J. (2008, October). *eNEWSLINE, 7*(10). Retrieved from http://www.aacsb.edu/Publications/ENewsline/archive_print/vol7-issue10.pdf

Gentile, M. C., & Samuelson, J. F. (2005). Keynote address to the AACSB International Deans Conference, February 10, 2003: The state of affairs for management education and social responsibility. *Academy of Management Learning & Education, 4*, 496-505.

Giacalone, R. A. (2004). A transcendent business education for the 21st century. *Academy of Management Learning & Education, 3*(4), 415-420.

Giacalone, R. A., & Thompson, K. R. (2006). Business ethics and social responsibility education: Shifting the worldview. *Academy of Management Learning & Education, 5*(3), 266-277.

Hechtkopf, K. (2009, January 26). Obama calls for new energy policy. *CBS News.* Retrieved from http://www.cbsnews.com/blogs/2009/01/26/politics/politicalhotsheet/entry4753446.shtml

Kell, G. (2005). The Global Compact selected experiences and reflections. *Journal of Business Ethics, 59,* 69-79.

Ki-moon, B. (2008). *PRME a global initiative—A global agenda.* Retrieved from http://www.unprme.org/resourcedocs/PRMEBrochureFINALlowres.pdf

Losada, C. (2009, April 23). La (de)formación directiva [The (de)formation directive]. *Expansión.* Retrieved from http://www.expansion.com/2009/04/23/opinion/1240482458.html

Losada, C., Martell, J., & Lozano, J. (in press). Responsible business education: Not a question of curriculum but a raison d'être for business schools. ESADE Working Paper.

Lozano, J. M. (2009a, January 8). Y si habláramos de las escuelas de negocios. *NetworkedBlogs.* Retrieved from http://www.josepmlozano.cat/Bloc0/PersonaEmpresaySociedad/tabid/218/EntryID/770/language/es-ES/Default.aspx

Lozano, J. M. (2009b, January 27). La RSE en el gobierno corporativo. *NetworkedBlogs.* Retrieved from http://www.josepmlozano.cat/Bloc0/PersonaEmpresaySociedad/tabid/218/EntryID/786/language/es-ES/Default.aspx

Martell, J. (2008). Socially responsible business schools: Collective stakeholder voices demand urgent actions. *Journal of the World Universities Forum, 1*(6), 115-126.

Martell, J., & Castiñeira, A. (2009, April). *Who's who in PRME: The rhetoric of involvement vs. the reality of commitment.* Paper presented at the 13th European Business Ethics Network UK Conference, Bristol, UK.

Miles, M., Hazeldine, M., & Munilla, L. (2004, September/October). The 2003 AACSB accreditation standards and implications for business faculty: A short note. *Journal of Education for Business, 80*(1), 29-34.

Navarro, P. (2008). The MBA core curricula of top-ranked U.S. business schools: A study in failure? *Academy of Management Learning & Education, 7*(1), 108-123.

Payne, S. L. (2000). Challenges for research ethics and moral knowledge construction in the applied social sciences. *Journal of Business Ethics, 26*(4), 307-318.

Principles for Responsible Management Education Communication (2009, December 3). *Important change in PRME foundational document.* Retrieved from http://www.unprme.org/resource-docs/December 2009.pdf

Principles for Responsible Management Education (PRME) News (2009, December 8). *PRME receives official support from the United Nations General Assembly.* Retrieved from http://www.unprme.org/news/index.php?newsid=120

Runhaar, H., & Lafferty, H. (2009). Governing corporate social responsibility: An assessment of the contribution of the UN Global Compact to CSR strategies in the telecommunications industry. *Journal of Business Ethics, 84,* 479-495.

Swanson, D. L., & Frederick, W. C. (2003). Campaign AACSB: Are business schools complicit in corporate corruption? *Journal of Individual Employment Rights, 10*(2), 1-28.

Trapnell, J. (2007). AACSB international accreditation: The value proposition and a look to the future. *Journal of Management Development, 26*(1), 67-72.

Urgel, J. (2007). EQUIS accreditation: value and benefits for international business schools. *Journal of Management Development, 26*(1), 73-83.

Vallaeys, F. (2008, September). Responsabilidad social universitaria: Una nueva filosofía de gestión ética e inteligente para las universidades. Instituto Internacional de UNESCO para la Educación Superior en América Latina y el Caribe (IESALC) [University social responsibility: A new philosophy of ethical and intelligent management for universities]. *Revista Educación Superior y Sociedad: Nueva Época, 13*(2), 191-219.

Vidaver-Cohen, D. (2008). Architectures of excellence. Building business school reputation by meeting the ethics challenge. In D. L. Swanson & D. G. Fisher (Eds.), *Advancing business ethics education* (pp. 67-84). Charlotte, NC: Information Age.

Windsor, D. (2002). *An open letter on business school responsibility, to AACSB Blue Ribbon Committee on accreditation quality and Milton Blood, director of AACSB accreditation services.* Retrieved from http://info.cba.ksu.edu/swanson/Call/Call.pdf

Woo, C. (2008, December 5). *Global Forum concluding session: Address to Secretary General Mr. Ban Ki-moon.* Retrieved from http://www.unprme.org/resources-and-reporting/index.php

Zammuto, R. (2008). Accreditation and the globalization of business. *Academy of Management Learning & Education, 7*(2), 256-268.

CHAPTER 7

ASSESSING WHAT IT TAKES TO EARN A BEYOND GREY PINSTRIPES RANKING

Janette Martell and Ángel Castiñeira

INTRODUCTION

If the next generation of business leaders is to excel at managing enterprises of greater competitiveness, then they will need the knowledge and skills to tackle not only the financial but also the ethical, social, and sustainability challenges faced by today's corporations. The scope and reach of business education demand that business schools understand the significance of these concepts and how to introduce them to students. The Beyond Grey Pinstripes[1] survey and alternative ranking seeks to identify the business schools that have taken the greatest strides to prepare their students to manage the complex social, environmental, and ethical issues they will face in their business careers as entrepreneurs and innovators. The aim is for future business leaders to be conscious of the social impacts of their decisions and keep ethical principles "at the center of their thoughts, words and deeds" (Globally Responsible Leadership Initiative, 2004, p. 2).

Toward Assessing Business Ethics Education
pp. 101–131

Ever since *Business Week* introduced its ranking of full-time MBA programs in 1988, there has been an explosion of other rankings from business publications around the world. MBA rankings of business schools, published yearly by prestigious periodicals, have become of utmost importance to universities, MBA candidates, corporations, and recruiters (Peters, 2007; Policano, 2007). Although these rankings do not necessarily capture the complexity of business education, most business schools view their position in these rankings as synonymous with quality and achievement. In this way, the rankings may encourage schools to strive to excel in the merits for which they are ranked.

The diverse rankings are compiled on many different bases: graduates' salaries, recruiters' perceptions, faculty research, students' satisfaction, opportunity cost, return on investment, and the potential to network, among others. Our interest in assessing the Beyond Grey Pinstripes (BGP) survey and ranking is because it focuses solely on the curricula and research content of ethics, social responsibility, and sustainability. No other ranking survey considers these areas as priorities. The distinction associated with being ranked in the BGP Global 100 is indeed a matter of pride for the selected business schools and contributes to efforts to improve MBA education around the world. It may also be a factor in attracting prospective students, since rankings are viewed as an important criterion for choosing a business school.

We are ever mindful of those presidents, deans, and faculty members who have the conviction and earnest desire to influence a new generation of responsible business leaders. Those who have a particular interest in the BGP survey will find this chapter to be an assessment of it from the standpoint of methodology, requirements, and qualities.

HELPING LEADERS REFLECT AND ACT ON IDEAS AND VALUES

Sixty years ago, Chicago businessman and philanthropist Walter Paepcke created in Aspen, Colorado "a place where the human spirit can flourish" (Aspen Institute, 2009, p. 3). Known today as The Aspen Institute, this organization has provided a platform for leaders from around the globe in many disciplines to discuss contemporary issues. The vision and reach of the Aspen Institute extend today far beyond its original roots, but in all of its work since inception, it has remained committed to the power of thoughtful dialogue about enduring human values. The many events, seminars, programs, networks, and leadership initiatives that the Institute delivers around the world have attracted statesmen, Nobel laureates, businesspersons, intellectuals, scientists, scholars, technology pioneers, and other leaders. All these participants seek to resolve dilemmas, advance policy solutions, examine the social and moral values underlying human problems, and strengthen their capacity for self-knowledge and mutual understanding (p. 3).

The Aspen Institute's mission is to foster values-based leadership and provide a neutral and balanced venue for discussing and acting on critical social issues (www.aspeninstitute.org). The institute enacts this mission in four ways.

- Seminars are aimed at helping leaders reflect on what makes a good society. Among them, the Aspen Seminar (formerly the Executive Seminar) challenges leaders in every field to think more critically and deeply about leadership. The Socrates Society is another program that has provided a forum for emerging leaders.
- Young-leader fellowships around the globe bring together a select group of proven leaders for an intense multiyear program.
- Policy programs serve as nonpartisan forums for analysis, consensus building, and problem-solving on a wide variety of issues, among which the Business and Society Program creates opportunities for executives and educators to explore new routes to business sustainability and values-based leadership.
- Public conferences and events provide a common forum for people to share ideas about the values that help create a good society.

THE ASPEN BUSINESS AND SOCIETY PROGRAM

Given its premise "change the way you educate people and you can change the world" (Aspen Institute, 2009, p. 29), the Aspen Business and Society Program (BSP)[2] creates opportunities for executives and educators to explore new routes to business sustainability and values-based leadership through dialogue, research, and curriculum development. For this program, the goal is to develop leaders for a sustainable global society. Judith Samuelson is the executive director of the Aspen BSP (www.aspeninstitute.org/policy-work/business-society).

Center for Business Education

As part of the Aspen BSP program, the Center for Business Education (CBE) works with business schools to serve as a source for innovative curricula. It equips students, the future business leaders, with a new management paradigm: the vision and knowledge to integrate corporate profitability and social value with the goal of radically reorienting the MBA degree to embrace the principles of corporate citizenship and sustainability. The CBE, under the directorship of Rich Leimsider, offers a range of programs, resources and initiatives in three areas.

- Business and faculty networks that cultivate new curriculum and emerging research agendas.
- Academic resources aimed at introducing new ideas about social and environmental issues in the classroom.
- Awards programs that recognize exceptional teaching, research, and thought leadership in MBA programs (www.aspencbe.org).

In the past 9 years, the CBE has surveyed MBA students three times about their attitudes toward the relationship between business and society. The results have revealed that MBA programs definitely influence the way students think about the role of business and its relationship to society, once they become managers and leaders.

A unique program of the CBE is Beyond Grey Pinstripes (BGP), a survey and ranking of business schools that integrate social and environmental stewardship into curricula and research. Our purpose is to assess the merits and objectives of the BGP survey, its contribution to socially responsible education and, mainly, what it takes to earn recognition in the survey's Global 100 ranking. We will deliver this material in four parts. First, we give a detailed description of the BGP survey and ranking methodology. Second, we offer recommendations for fulfilling BGP ranking requirements. Third, we analyze the 2009-2010 ranking and the programs that earned six top business schools their positions. Finally, we reflect on BGP methodology.

BEYOND GREY PINSTRIPES

Overview

In 1998, the World Resources Institute (WRI) created Grey Pinstripes with Green Ties, a report that examined the inclusion of environmental management topics in 37 MBA programs. In 1999, WRI partnered with the Aspen Institute Business and Society Program (BSP) to balance the WRI report by examining MBA programs for the teaching of social impact management.[3] This led to the creation of Beyond Grey Pinstripes (BGP), a survey and consequent ranking of business schools that spotlight innovative full-time MBA programs that encourage the integration of social and environmental stewardship into curricula and research. The ranked schools are thus distinguished for preparing students for the reality of tomorrow's markets and for equipping them with the social, environmental, and economic perspectives required for business success in a competitive and fast-changing world. In 2007, the Aspen BSP took over the management of the survey and the business school ranking.

MBA rankings are a controversial topic in business education. Although they are typically popular among schools, alumni, corporations, recruiters, and prospective students, they can also contribute to a myopic view of what makes a business school "the best." Additionally, the rankings "may sometimes be based on unsound research and can lead to a misallocation of student interest and alumni funding, and faculty and administrator attention" (Aspen Institute Center for Business Education, 2009, p. 1).

The primary difference between the BGP Global 100 and other business school rankings is one of perspective. It is the only survey and ranking to focus directly on courses and research at each school with the aim of ensuring that MBA programs are preparing future business leaders to identify the opportunities, and mitigate the costs, of business' relationship with society and the environment. BGP's specific goals are as follows.

- To promote and celebrate innovation in business education.
- To inform prospective students about environmental and social impact management programs.
- To raise the bar by challenging business schools to incorporate social and environmental impact management topics into their curricula.
- To inform corporate recruiters of business schools that provide training in social and environmental skills as part of business decision making.
- To disseminate best programs in teaching, research, and extracurricular activities.
- To facilitate conversations about social issues among students, faculty, administrators, and business leaders.

BGP casts a broad net in an effort to promote and support schools and faculty. Prospective students, current students, alumni, faculty, administrators, corporate recruiters, business executives, and the media can use the information and ideas available via Aspen's website to highlight the goal of integrating social and environmental issues into business practice.

The survey and Global 100 ranking provides several unique benefits to business schools and their stakeholders.

- It allows public recognition of the faculty, departments, and schools that are doing excellent work in the ranked areas.
- It signifies a matter of pride for those schools recognized for fulfilling the social mission of educating society's future leaders in responsible management practices.
- It can augment the public relations and marketing efforts of ranked schools.
- It provides a detailed map of what is currently taught, so that schools can be benchmarked and best programs from around the world identified.
- It provides information for benchmarking schools in terms of extracurricular activities related to the social and environmental impacts of business.
- It can be used to inform alumni about how their schools rank on social and environmental issue coverage.

The BGP survey and ranking is conducted and published every 2 years, after 18 months of rigorous research on how well MBA programs incorporate social, environmental, and ethical issues into their curricula. What follows is a summary of BGP's research methodology (see also www.beyondgreypinstripes.org).

Research Methodology

Outreach

Working with the Association to Advance Collegiate Schools of Business (AACSB), the European Foundation for Management Development (EFMD) and other international MBA accrediting bodies, the BGP team assembles a roster of approximately 600 accredited full-time MBA programs throughout the world to whom initial invitations are sent to participate in the survey. All schools in the United States must have AACSB accreditation. To be ranked by BGP, schools that meet a certain set of qualifying criteria can opt into the process and submit data, and those that subsequently become eligible can access the online survey site, generally starting in October and ending in mid-December. Aspen CBE staff members offer participating schools two online tutorials at the beginning of the survey period and continue support services throughout the data collection period. Survey questions are refined every 2 years, with the last update occurring in 2008, in consultation with an advisory group of 30 business school faculty members. This last survey incorporated ethical components not previously included.

The survey, which is managed by the Aspen CBE, tracks only information about accredited full-time, in-person MBA programs. In some cases, information is accepted from part-time programs that have a significant full-time enrollment, but only numbers associated with full-time students are included in the survey. Articles written by professors who are not teaching at the MBA level may not be included; however, articles written by researchers working in centers housed in the business school may be included. The 2009-2010 Global 100 ranking was determined by the scores obtained from data submitted by 149 business schools in 24 countries, of which 63% are located in the United States. The remaining 37% were from 23 other countries. Most of the final report is available on the BGP website.

Data Collection/Survey

The survey data are collected in three broad categories, as explained below.

- *MBA Coursework.* This category focuses on core and elective courses that include social, environmental, or ethical topics for which Aspen uses the umbrella term "social impact management." The survey asks schools for data from the two academic years preceding the survey, including the department, instructor, number of MBA students enrolled in each course, credit hours for each course, and total school enrollment. Schools must indicate the percentage of pertinent content in each course, although such information is not validated. Submissions of course descriptions, supporting syllabi, or a uniform resource locator (URL) link are required, with syllabi preferred.

- *Faculty Research.* Schools are asked to submit a spreadsheet containing all scholarly articles written by faculty members that address social, environmental, or ethical topics in any peer-reviewed business journal during the previous two calendar years, as well as journal details.

- *Institutional Support.* Schools are asked to report exemplary noncurricular activities and programs that specifically address social and environmental impact management. Information is requested about external speakers, internships and consulting programs, student clubs, career development services, university institutes and centers, joint degrees, specializations, and other such activities.

The data on institutional support are not used for ranking calculations. The same applies to the 500-word narrative from each school on how it prepares students for environmental and social stewardship. This information is published on the Aspen CBE and BGP websites, which get one million visits each year. It is also published in the CBE Closer Look series of white papers for faculty. Notably, the school's profile and pertinent information are featured in the Aspen guidebook, *The Sustainable MBA: The 2010-2011 Guide to Socially Responsible MBA Programs.*

Data Cleaning

Attempts are made to clean all data for obvious errors. If necessary, Aspen CBE contacts schools for corrections and clarification. Except for obvious errors, CBE does not attempt to assess the validity of self-reported data. However, the transparency and accuracy of data reporting are supported in the following ways.

1. An online signature is required from the reporter, pledging honesty and accuracy.
2. All reported data are made publicly available so that peer schools, students, and alumni can review them.

Data Not Evaluated

Although extracurricular activities can make a difference in a student's experience, data on these activities are not considered in the ranking. Again, in an effort to make comparisons consistent, the BGP methodology focuses exclusively on coursework and research. Information on extracurricular activities of all participating schools is available on the Aspen CBE website. Student opinions regarding their education are also not used in ranking calculations.

Scoring/Ranking Calculations

The Aspen ranking focuses on the following four areas of scoring and ranking calculations.

1. Availability of relevant courses;
2. Student exposure;
3. Relevant courses on for-profit impact; and
4. Faculty research.

The ranking is tabulated directly from the self-reported survey data, and researchers at Aspen evaluate the responses using a rigorous evaluation protocol. Some survey metrics are calculated directly from the data reported, while others require a subjective review.

Availability of Relevant Courses counts the number of courses offered with ethical, social, and/or environmental content. An evaluative question is asked: How much opportunity do students have to take courses with this content?

Student Exposure measures teaching hours and student enrollment in these courses. The evaluative question is: To what extent are students actually exposed to such content? The formula for each course is: [(percent of course time dedicated to such issues) × (course credits/total degree credits) × (course enrollment / total school enrollment)]. This formula adjusts for the size of the student body, length of courses, enrollments in courses, and whether the courses are required or elective.

Relevant Courses on For-Profit Impact is a simple count of the number of courses that specifically address the intersection of social and environmental issues with mainstream, for-profit business. The evaluative question is: Do any of the courses being taught on campus explicitly discuss how business can be an engine for improving social and environmental conditions? This metric measures an MBA program's possible impact on business's role in society, which is the central focus of Aspen CBE.

Faculty Research counts the number of scholarly publications by faculty in peer-reviewed journals containing some degree of ethical, social, or environmental material. The evaluative question is: To what extent do professors on campus explore these issues in their own research? The CBE Research Fellows, whose characteristics and responsibilities are explained below, review all articles and abstracts using criteria similar to that applied to relevant coursework.

Final Computation

The various raw score metrics are then adjusted by using a statistical smoothing process called square-root standard deviation about the mean, which produces numerical values that represent how well a school has done relative to the other schools in the survey. Each of the above-mentioned values, or z scores, are weighted at 25% and then summed to arrive at an overall point total. The final ranking is an ordinal list of the Global 100 schools by total points received.

For subjective reviews, Aspen CBE uses a team of 12 PhD and PhD candidates as research fellows selected in a competitive process from leading institutions around the world. Research fellows are trained carefully on the survey protocol, and in any review by them scoring is done blindly— without school or faculty names associated with data—and in pairs to obtain inter-rater reliability, consistency, and minimize possible biases.

In mid-February 2009, CBE announced the 2009 class of research fellows who reviewed the coursework and research for scoring calculations of the 2009-2010 Global 100 ranking. They came from Alberta, Darden, ESADE, Fuqua, Interpolitecnica, McGill, New York, North Carolina, Schulich, Washington State, Wharton, and Zurich business schools.

RECOMMENDATIONS FOR FULFILLING BGP REQUIREMENTS

The following suggestions are directed to the presidents, deans, faculty, students, and administrative members of business schools who are committed to a process of transforming their schools into socially responsible institutions.[4] That is, we are addressing those members of academic communities who strive to inculcate social responsibility into every aspect of their schools.

The process described in Figure 7.1 suggests four avenues of analysis that schools should undertake in order to implement actions that lead to successful BGP ranking.

1. The first box in Figure 7.1 indicates that schools striving for BGP recognition should review the most recent Global 100 information in the areas of coursework, faculty research, and extracurricular activities. This information can be useful in striving to meet benchmark standards in these areas.

2. The second box in Figure 7.1 shows that analyzing the projects and initiatives of key international organizations can also inform implementation. These organizations include AACSB, Aspen Institute, European Academy of Business in Society (EABIS), EFMD, Globally Responsible Leadership Initiative (GRLI), Principles for Responsible Management Education (PRME), and United Nations Global Compact (UNGC).

3. The third box in Figure 7.1 illustrates that schools need to analyze their own coursework, research output, and extracurricular activities, especially in light of the information gleaned from the above two steps. Such analysis should entail a deep look into the business school's culture and the commitment to ethics and environmental responsibility on the part of faculty, students, administrators, and alumni. These constituents will need to be involved in the process of change and be committed to it. The internal diagnosis should also include an evaluation of systems and procedures with the goal of ensuring that they can provide the necessary support to comply

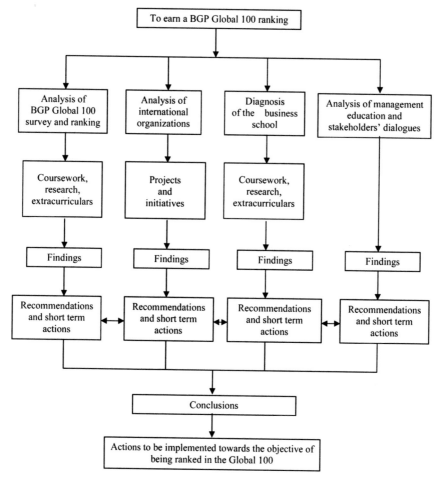

Figure 7.1.   Process of analysis for the implementation of actions.

with the mission of training socially responsible business leaders in line with the school's vision, mission, values, and strategies.

4. The fourth box in Figure 7.1 indicates that schools need to engage continuously in open-ended dialogue with internal and external stakeholders about what constitutes socially responsible management education in light of emerging social trends and challenges.

It is necessary to bear in mind that the fundamental areas for the BGP ranking are ethics, social responsibility, and environmental sustainability. Therefore the following aims are indispensable.

- To have these concepts fully integrated in the curricula in a transversal manner.
- To achieve an enrollment of the highest possible number of students in elective courses with a high content of these concepts.
- To encourage faculty to consistently publish peer-reviewed journal articles in these areas.

Additional Resource Analysis

Related to the second step given above, the following resources can be useful in achieving the desired benchmark.

- Case studies related to ethics, social responsibility, and sustainability can be obtained from CasePlace.org (Aspen CBE), EABIS, and the European Case Clearing House (ECCH).
- Ideas for the integration of new courses can be found at Giving Voices to Values (www.aspencbe.org) and Peace Through Commerce Program (www.aacsb.edu/resource_centers/peace/default.asp).
- For program transformation and redesign, it would be beneficial to refer to the experiences of other institutions that have radically redesigned their MBA programs. These include HEC Paris, Stanford Graduate School of Business, Yale School of Management, the College of Business at Washington State University, and the Daniels College of Business at the University of Denver.
- Detailed examples of courses, extracurriculars, and university centers can be found at beyondgreypinstripes.org, the world largest MBA database.

Suggestions for Implementation Actions

Figure 7.1 shows that the analysis undertaken by business schools should culminate in implementation actions. An important aspect of implementation is to communicate to faculty and staff the decision to participate in the BGP survey, the benefits that the institution will derive, and the objectives and goals of the ranking project. The participation and engagement of these internal constituents will be necessary for a successful outcome. Administrators should keep in mind that successful change involves generating trust, forging new organizational capabilities, gaining emotional commitments, and fostering motivation through inspiration (Wheatley, 2003). In short, leadership matters. We suggest that a task force that includes faculty, administrators, and students use the steps indicated in Figure 7.1 to identify short term actions for enhancing coursework, research, and extracurriculars. Subsequently, this task force should pull together all findings and recommendations to formulate an action plan for pursuing BGP ranking. Since leadership is important to a successful outcome, the dean should attend all informative meetings and take part in the decision processes.

ANALYSIS OF THE 2009-2010 GLOBAL 100

The 2009-2010 Global 100 ranking is composed of business schools from 17 different countries. Sixty-eight schools are located in the United States; seven are in Canada, six in the United Kingdom, three in Spain, three in France, and two in Australia. The remaining 11 schools are in 11 different countries.

Table 7.1 shows the 100 ranked schools, the countries in which they are located, the rankings reports published in 2009, 2007, 2005, 2003, and 2001, and the bodies that accredited these schools in 2009.

The Global 100 incorporates the scores obtained by the schools in each of four areas in accordance with established calculations (www.beyondgreypinstripes.org/rankings/index.cfm). Listed below are the schools that obtained first, second, and third position in each of the categories in the 2009-2010 edition.

1. Availability of Relevant Courses: 1st York, 2nd Stanford, 3rd Yale.
2. Student Exposure: 1st IE Business School, 2nd Simmons, 3rd RSM Erasmus.
3. Relevant Courses on For-Profit Impact: 1st Michigan, 2nd Stanford, 2nd U. of North Carolina.
4. Faculty Research: 1st York, 2nd Michigan, 3rd Notre Dame.

York University (Schulich) was ranked number one in the most recent Global 100, displacing Stanford's primacy in the past two editions. The only business school that has been steadily ranked among the world's top three in each ranking period is York University. Otherwise, the top rankings change constantly from year to year with only 12 schools indicated in the past five editions. Of those schools, nine are in the United States, one in Canada, one in Finland, and one in Mexico.

The five consecutive evaluations of the Global 100 reveal the first-place business schools in five Top 10 categories:

Table 7.1. BGP 2009-2010 Global 100 Business Schools

	Business School	Location	Aspen's Evaluation of MBA Programs					Accreditations 2009 ✓ Accredited ✗ Not accredited		
			2009(5)	2007(4)	2005(3)	2003(2)	2001(1)	AACSB	AMBA	EFMD
1	York (Schulich)	Canada	1	3	3	Distinction	Distinction	✗	✗	✗
2	U. of Michigan (Ross)	USA	2	2	7	Distinction	Distinction	✓	✗	✗
3	Yale School of Management	USA	3	9	21	Distinction	Distinction	✓	✗	✗
4	Stanford Graduate School of Business	USA	4	1	1	Distinction	Distinction	✓	✗	✗
5	Notre Dame (Mendoza)	USA	5	5	5	Distinction	-	✓	✗	✗
6	UC Berkeley (Haas)	USA	6	4	11	Distinction	Distinction	✓	✓	✗
7	RSM Erasmus	Netherlands	7	15	16	Distinction	-	✓	✓	✓
8	NYU (Stern)	USA	8	11	-	-	-	✓	✗	✗
9	IE Business School	Spain	9	10	-	-	-	✓	✓	✓
10	Columbia Business School	USA	10	6	13	Distinction	-	✓	✗	✗
11	U. of Virginia (Darden)	USA	11	24	13	Distinction	-	✓	✗	✗
12	Cornell (Johnson)	USA	12	7	9	Distinction	-	✓	✗	✗
13	George Washington School of Business	USA	13	13	6	Distinction	Distinction	✓	✗	✗
14	U. of North Carolina (Kenan-Flagler)	USA	14	12	8	Distinction	Distinction	✓	✗	✗
15	Simmons School of Management	USA	15	32	-	-	-	✓	✗	✗
16	Duke (Fuqua)	USA	16	26	-	-	-	✓	✗	✗
17	Wisconsin School of Business (Madison)	USA	17	33	28	-	-	✓	✗	✗
18	Duquesne (Donahue)	USA	18	8	-	-	-	✓	✗	✗
19	U. of New Mexico (Anderson)	USA	19	18	18	Distinction	Distinction	✓	✗	✗
20	U. of Denver (Daniels)	USA	20	47	-	-	-	✓	✗	✗
21	U. of San Diego SOB Administration	USA	21	36	-	-	-	✓	✗	✗
22	Loyola U. Chicago Graduate SOB	USA	22	62	-	-	-	✓	✗	✗
23	Nottingham U. Business School	UK	23	28	12	-	-	✗	✓	✗

	Business School	Location	Aspen's Evaluation of MBA Programs					Accreditations 2009 ✓ Accredited ✗ Not accredited		
			2009(5)	2007(4)	2005(3)	2003(2)	2001(1)	AACSB	AMBA	EFMD
24	Ohio State (Fisher)	USA	24	-	-	-	-	✓	✗	✗
25	Portland State U. SOB Administration	USA	25	22	20	-	-	✓	✗	✗
26	Babson (Olin)	USA	26	31	-	-	-	✓	✗	✓
27	Griffith Business School	Australia	27	-	-	-	-	✓	✗	✗
28	INSEAD	France	28	43	24	Distinction	-	✓	✓	✓
29	San Francisco State U. College of Business	USA	29	37	-	-	-	✓	✓	✗
30	UC Davis Graduate School of Management	USA	30	29	-	-	-	✓	✗	✗
31	McGill (Desautels)	Canada	31	45	22	Distinction	-	✗	✗	✗
32	ESADE Business School	Spain	32	14	2	Distinction	-	✓	✓	✓
33	Case Western Reserve (Weatherhead)	USA	33	57	23	Distinction	Distinction	✓	✗	✗
34	Concordia (John Molson)	Canada	34	59	-	-	-	✓	✗	✗
35	Georgetown (McDonough)	USA	35	73	30	-	-	✓	✗	✗
36	U. South Florida St. Petesburg COB	USA	36	34	-	-	-	✓	✗	✗
37	U. of Colorado at Boulder (Leeds)	USA	37	20	17	Distinction	-	✓	✗	✗
38	Monterey Institute of Int. Studies	USA	38	40	-	-	-	✓	✗	✗
39	U. of Stellenbosch Business School	South Africa	39	70	-	-	-	✗	✗	✓
40	U. of Oregon (Lundquist)	USA	40	-	-	-	-	✓	✗	✗
41	U. of Navarra (IESE)	Spain	41	66	27	Distinction	-	✗	✓	✓
42	U. of South Carolina (Moore)	USA	42	51	-	-	-	✓	✗	✗
43	Wake Forest (Babcock)	USA	43	30	10	Distinction	Distinction	✓	✗	✗
44	Dartmouth (Tuck)	USA	44	25	24	Distinction	-	✓	✗	✗
45	Brandeis (Heller)	USA	45	19	-	-	-	✓	✗	✗
46	HEC Genève	Switzerland	46	61	-	-	-	✗	✓	✗
47	Willamette (Atkinson)	USA	47	58	-	-	-	✓	✗	✗
48	U. of Jyväskylä SOB and Economics	Finland	48	35	26	Distinction	Distinction	✗	✗	✗

	Business School	Location	Aspen's Evaluation of MBA Programs					Accreditations 2009 ✓ Accredited ✗ Not accredited		
			2009(5)	2007(4)	2005(3)	2003(2)	2001(1)	AACSB	AMBA	EFMD
49	U. of British Columbia (Sauder)	Canada	49	23	-	-	-	✓	✗	✓
50	Carnegie Mellon (Tepper)	USA	50	27	-	-	-	✓	✗	✗
51	U. of Calgary (Haskayne)	Canada	51	16	25	Distinction	-	✓	✗	✗
52	Boston University - School of Management	USA	52	54	-	Distinction	-	✓	✗	✗
53	U. of Western Ontario (Ivey)	Canada	53	21	14	-	-	✗	✗	✓
54	Northwestern (Kellogg)	USA	54	-	-	Distinction	-	✓	✗	✗
55	Villanova U. School of Business	USA	55	-	-	-	-	✓	✗	✗
56	Wright State (Raj Soin)	USA	56	-	-	-	-	✓	✗	✗
57	Arizona State (W.P. Carey)	USA	57	-	-	-	-	✓	✗	✗
58	Michigan Tech. SOB and Economics	USA	58	94	-	-	-	✓	✗	✗
59	Thunderbird School of Global Management	USA	59	44	-	-	-	✓	✗	✓
60	IESA	Venezuela	60	75	-	-	-	✓	✓	✓
61	U. of Southern California (Marshall)	USA	61	-	-	-	-	✓	✗	✗
62	Pepperdine (Graziadio)	USA	62	50	-	-	-	✓	✗	✗
63	Copenhagen Business School	Denmark	63	41	-	-	-	✗	✓	✓
64	UT Dallas School of Management	USA	64	-	-	-	-	✓	✗	✗
65	CUNY, Baruch College (Zicklin)	USA	65	82	-	-	-	✓	✗	✗
66	U. of Colorado at Denver Business School	USA	66	-	-	-	-	✓	✗	✓
67	Bentley (McCallum)	USA	67	55	-	-	-	✓	✗	✗
68	Lamar University College of Business	USA	68	85	-	-	-	✓	✗	✗
69	U. of Vermont SOB Administration	USA	69	78	-	-	-	✓	✗	✗
70	Vlerick Leuven Gent Management School	Belgium	70	-	-	-	-	✓	✓	✓
71	University of Glasgow Business School	UK	71	-	-	-	-	✓	✓	✗
72	Western Washington U. CBE	USA	72	87	-	-	-	✓	✗	✗

	Business School	Location	Aspen's Evaluation of MBA Programs					Accreditations 2009 ✓ Accredited ✗ Not accredited		
			2009(5)	2007(4)	2005(3)	2003(2)	2001(1)	AACSB	AMBA	EFMD
73	Boston College (Carroll)	USA	73	46	15	Distinction	-	✓	✗	✗
74	Vanderbilt (Owen)	USA	74	49	-	Distinction	Distinction	✓	✗	✗
75	U. Mass Boston College of Management	USA	75	-	-	-	-	✓	✗	✗
76	Saint Joseph's University (Haub)	USA	76	-	-	-	-	✓	✗	✗
77	Kansas State U. COB Administration	USA	77	-	-	-	-	✓	✗	✗
78	University of South Australia IGSB	Australia	78	-	-	-	-	✗	✗	✓
79	HEC Paris	France	79	64	-	-	-	✓	✓	✓
80	Dalhousie SBA	Canada	80	39	-	-	-	✓	✗	✗
81	Cranfield School of Management	UK	81	56	-	-	-	✓	✓	✓
82	Massachusetts Institute of Tech. (Sloan)	USA	82	71	-	-	-	✓	✗	✗
83	U. of Bath School of Management	UK	83	60	-	-	-	✗	✓	✓
84	EGADE Tecnológico de Monterrey	Mexico	84	17	4	Distinction	Distinction	✓	✓	✓
85	Georgia State University (Robinson)	USA	85	-	-	-	-	✓	✗	✗
86	Tulane (Freeman)	USA	86	74	-	-	-	✓	✗	✗
87	Oregon State U. College of Business	USA	87	89	-	-	-	✓	✗	✗
88	Ashridge Business School	UK	88	84	-	-	-	✓	✓	✓
89	Claremont Graduate U. (Drucker)	USA	89	-	-	-	-	✓	✗	✗
90	Washington State U. College of Business	USA	90	76	-	-	-	✓	✗	✗
91	U. of Arkansas (Walton)	USA	91	-	-	-	-	✓	✗	✗
92	IEDC (Bled)	Slovenia	92	-	-	-	-	✗	✓	✗
93	U. of Maryland (Smith)	USA	93	-	-	-	-	✓	✗	✗
94	Illinois Institute of Technology (Stuart)	USA	94	48	-	Distinction	Distinction	✓	✗	✗
95	London Business School	UK	95	-	-	-	-	✓	✓	✓
96	Audencia Nantes School of Management	France	96	90	-	-	-	✓	✓	✓

	Business School	Location	Aspen's Evaluation of MBA Programs					Accreditations 2009 ✓ Accredited ✗ Not accredited		
			2009(5)	2007(4)	2005(3)	2003(2)	2001(1)	AACSB	AMBA	EFMD
97	Asian Institute of Management	Philippines	97	42	19	Distinction	-	✓	✗	✗
98	Baylor University (Hankamer)	USA	98	-	-	-	-	✓	✗	✗
99	North Carolina State U. (Jenkins)	USA	99	68	-	-	-	✓	✗	✗
100	aSSIST	South Korea	100	-	-	-	-	✗	✗	✗

Notes:

1 **The Aspen and World Resource Institute 2001 Leading MBA Programs Report** was the first attempt, preceding BGP, to survey how environmental and social issues intersect and merge with one another and with traditional management concepts in the business curriculum. The report spotlighted 21 business schools and faculty at the forefront of incorporating social and environmental stewardship issues into the fabric of their MBA programs.

2 **The Aspen and World Resource Institute 2003 Leading MBA Programs Report** was the second attempt, preceding BGP, that emphasized the importance of preparing students for a more comprehensive approach to social and environmental stewardship. The report compared 36 business schools on the basis of their accomplishments across both domains, rather than excellence in one or the other.

3 **The Aspen and World Resource Institute 2005 Ranking of MBA Programs.** The first biennial ranking of the Top 30 business schools, preceding the BGP Global 100, spotlighted innovative full-time MBA programs and faculty that lead the way in integrating issues of social and environmental stewardship into business school curricula and research.

4 **Beyond Grey Pinstripes 2007-2008 - The Global 100,** Aspen's first research survey and alternative ranking of business schools, spotlights innovative full-time MBA programs leading the way in curricular integration of issues concerning social and environmental stewardship.

5 **Aspen's Global 100 - Beyond Grey Pinstripes 2009-2010.** The most recent biennial survey and alternative ranking of business schools. Its mission is to spotlight innovative full-time MBA programs that are integrating issues of social and environmental stewardship into curricula and research.

- United States Schools: 1st place, University of Michigan (Ross).
- International Schools: 1st place, York University (Schulich).
- Coursework (Availability of Relevant Courses, Student Exposure, Relevant Courses on For-Profit Impact): 1st place, Yale School of Management.
- Faculty Research: 1st place, York University (Schulich).
- Small Schools: 1st place, Simmons School of Management.

Analysis of Accreditations

Considering the importance for business schools to be accredited, not only to be eligible to participate in the BGP survey, but also fundamentally because accreditation promotes reputational quality in education, we analyzed the bodies that accredited the schools ranked in the 2009-2010 Global 100.

- All U.S.-based schools (68) are accredited by AACSB, fulfilling the eligibility requirement.
- The Global 100 indicates that 12 schools have the designation of Triple Crown, meaning that they are accredited by AACSB, the Association of MBAs (AMBA), and EFMD. According to Table 7.1, the criteria for obtaining all three accreditations are recognition for outstanding research, education and career-building qualities. The Triple Crown schools are Ashridge, UK; Audencia Nantes, France; Cranfield, UK; EGADE Tec de Monterrey, Mexico; ESADE, Spain; HEC Paris, France; IESA, Venezuela; INSEAD, France; IE Business School, Spain; London Business School, UK; RSM Erasmus, Netherlands; and Vlerick Leuven Gent, Belgium.
- The Global 100 includes 87 schools accredited by AACSB, 20 by AMBA, and 21 by EFMD.
- Besides the 12 schools accredited by all three bodies, another school is accredited by both AACSB and AMBA, three schools are accredited by AACSB and EFMD, and four by both AMBA and EFMD.
- Seventy-one schools are accredited exclusively by AACSB, three by only AMBA, and two by only EFMD.
- It is notable that four ranked schools do not have their MBA programs accredited by AACSB, AMBA or EFMD. These are Schulich, Canada; McGill, Canada; Jyväskylä, Finland; and aSSIST, South

Korea. Of these schools, only Schulich offers a reason on its webpage, as follows.

> In Canada, education is the responsibility of the provinces, not of the federal government. All degree programs in business or management must meet the quality-control criteria of their respective provincial governments. There is no separate accreditation body for university degree programs in business or most other disciplines. Universities in the province of Ontario offer one third of all Canadian MBA programs and enroll one half of the country's MBA students. Before a new program is established in Ontario, it must be approved by a special council, the Ontario Council for Graduate Studies (OCGS). Then, to ensure that quality is maintained, the program must be reassessed every seven years by the OCGS. In 1998, the Schulich School of Business graduate degree programs: Master of Business Administration (MBA), Master of Public Administration (MPA), International Master of Business Administration (IMBA), and Joint and Dual Programs, were reappraised by the OCGS. Each was awarded the Council's highest level of quality (www.schulich.yorku.ca).

An Analysis of Six Top Ranked Business Schools

We selected six top business schools from the ranking and four areas of the Global 100 in order to identify the most relevant programs. Table 7.2 provides general information about those schools. Readers may benchmark additional criteria from other select schools, according to disciplines.

Table 7.3 lists the scores obtained by the six selected schools in the disciplines which fulfill BGP's requirements. These schools are scored for ranking in three coursework categories: relevant courses, student exposure, and relevant courses on for-profit impact. The faculty research scores, which represent the number of published articles from each school, are included in the table.

Our analysis of coursework with social, ethical, and environmental coverage suggests that the most popular vehicle for this coverage is not Corporate Social Responsibility or Business Ethics courses. Instead, the following courses were indicated, listed in order of the highest to lowest frequency of coverage.

1.   Finance
2.   Management

Table 7.2. General Information About the Selected Top Schools (February 20, 2010)

Global 100 Rank	Business School	Location	Full-Time MBA Enrollment	Core and Elective Courses(*)	Relevant Courses Rank	Student Exposure Rank	For-Profit Impact Rank	Faculty Research Rank	Leading Rank	Website
1	York (Schulich)	Canada	412	162	1	40	10	1	Relevant Courses and Faculty Research	www.schulich.yorku.ca/
2	U. of Michigan (Ross)	USA	843	80	8	23	1	2	For-Profit Impact	www.bus.umich.edu
3	Yale School of Management	USA	382	110	3	4	4	16	Coursework	www.mba.yale.edu
4	Stanford Graduate SOB	USA	740	121	2	14	2	18	-	www.gsb.stanford.edu
5	Notre Dame (Mendoza)	USA	313	96	4	5	14	3	-	www.nd.edu/~cba/
9	IE Business School	Spain	500	73	9	1	14	59	Student Exposure	www.ie.edu

Note: *Courses with social, environmental, or ethical content.

Table 7.3. Coursework by Discipline and Faculty Research With a Content of Business in Society (February 20, 2010)

Disciplines	Coursework and Faculty Research, BGP 2009-2010					
	York (Schulich)	Michigan (Ross)	Yale School of Management	Stanford Graduate School of Business	Notre Dame (Mendoza)	IE Business School
Accounting	15	6	8	8	5	5
Business and Government	4	0	3	7	0	1
Business Law	10	5	2	1	3	6
CSR/Business Ethics	6	1	5	2	17	2
Economics	7	7	9	7	2	5
Entrepreneurship	4	8	4	2	4	7
Environmental Management	3	0	10	6	3	0
Finance	23	4	14	14	14	6
Human Resource Management	0	0	1	1	1	6
Inf. Technology and Systems	4	3	0	0	4	2
International Management	14	1	4	3	8	0
Management	16	16	11	5	12	6
Marketing	16	3	11	7	11	10
Organizational Behavior	13	0	6	22	1	1
Production and Operations Mgmt	3	4	4	19	2	6
Public and Non-Profit Management	14	2	6	3	4	0
Quantitative Methods	3	0	1	0	1	0
Strategy	7	20	11	14	4	10
Total Coursework	162	80	110	121	96	73
Total Faculty Research	52	38	16	15	34	10

3. Strategy
4. Marketing

Relevant programs and outstanding qualities of the six selected schools were identified on their webpages, in addition to the information about them on the BGP webpage. Our review of this self-reported information substantiates that the ranking of schools in the Global 100 is determined by the provision of courses and faculty research with ethics, social, and environmental content. The following paragraphs summarize the public profiles of the six select schools.

- *The Schulich School of Business at York University* (Toronto, Ontario, Canada) has been an early pioneer of integrating social impact management and environmental management into core course and across the curriculum. Schulich provides students with the opportunity to select a significant number of courses from the more than 100 business ethics and business and sustainability electives it offers in 18 cutting-edge specializations. In addition to courses, the school has a number of in-house research institutes and centers, including Transparency International Canada, Inc., a business corruption watchdog organization; the York Centre for Applied Sustainability; and the Centre for Practical Ethics. The Erivan K. Haub Program in Business and Sustainability at Schulich is at the cutting edge of current best practices in executive education.

- *The Stephen M. Ross School of Business at the University of Michigan* (Ann Arbor, MI) features social and environmental responsibility as a cornerstone of broad-based management education. Its MBA program prepares students to address fundamental issues of social responsibility and environmentally sustainable business whether they work in the public, private, or nonprofit sector. The schools' commitment to responsible business is woven organically into the core curriculum. All students are required to complete a course dedicated to ethics and governance, as well as a course on the world economy that addresses the civic and cultural landscape of global business. Many electives focus on environmental and social responsibility, including corporate environmental strategy, finance for sustainable enterprise, sustainable manufacturing, and systems thinking for sustainable enterprise. Ross is also a leader in addressing the relationships between development and poverty alleviation.

The Frederick and Barbara Erb Institute offers a dual degree: an MBA from Ross and a Master of Science (MS) from the School of Natural Resources & Environment (SNRE), which focuses on Global Sustainable Enterprise. The Nonprofit and Public Management Center, a partnership with the schools of Public Policy and Social Work, is dedicated to providing expertise for public, private, and nonprofit management. The Ross School also shares many resources with the William Davidson Institute, which has a mission to improve social welfare and facilitate economic transition in developing countries.

- *The Yale School of Management* (New Haven, CT) has a mission to educate leaders for business and society. For more than 30 years this program has been known for its commitment to social and environmental issues and ethical leadership. These areas are included in the majority of courses in the integrated MBA curriculum, developed in 2006, as part of an effort to move away from the typical "siloed" teaching approach. As part of this effort, the Case Research Department produced the first web-based, multimedia case study, opening up pedagogical opportunities consistent with the new integrated curriculum. The Center for Business and the Environment joins the strengths of two world-renowned institutions, the Yale School of Management and the Yale School of Forestry and Environmental Studies, two schools that have been at the forefront of addressing the business environment for more than a quarter of a century. Yale has also partnered with The Aspen Institute to develop Giving Voice to Values, an innovative curriculum for developing the skills, knowledge, and commitment required to implement values-based leadership.

- *The Stanford Graduate School of Business* (Stanford, CA) has a new curriculum that is hailed as representing a revolutionary change in management education. Introduced in 2007, four key elements characterize this educational model: a customized program, a more engaging intellectual experience, a more global curriculum, and expanded leadership and communication development. At Stanford, issues and cases related to corporate responsibility and social impacts are integrated throughout the required curriculum as well as in electives. One of the hallmarks of this curriculum is a course in critical analytical thinking for all first-year students. The School of Business also continues to develop courses that recognize the role of public policy and management knowledge for nonprofit and for-profit organizations. The Center for Social Innovation provides critical support to sustain research, course development, and executive education in these areas. The Leadership in Focus Video Case

Series at the Center for Leadership Development and Research houses a collection of 170 cases used at 427 colleges in 41 countries, and is now available for corporate training.

- **The Mendoza College of Business at Notre Dame University** (Notre Dame, IN) has long served as an advocate for the United Nations Global Compact (UNGC). A sustained emphasis on corporate social responsibility and business ethics in teaching and research lead to support for the Principles for Responsible Management Education (PRME) among students, faculty, and administrators. A new MBA curriculum, launched in 2005, focuses on problem-solving opportunities related to ethics, organizational effectiveness, and the greater good. All 14 required courses and 93 electives integrate social, ethical, or environmental issues in their coverage of topics. Two new courses, issues in sustainability and ethics in investing, are dedicated to examining the importance of ethical, social, and governance (ESG) investment criteria. Through these courses, Mendoza seeks to sensitize its students to the ethical dimensions of professional responsibilities, domestically and globally. The Mendoza Institute for Ethical Business Worldwide assists the academic community by providing business ethics material in Accountancy, Finance, Management, and Marketing.

- **The IE Business School** (Madrid, Spain), one of the 12 schools with the distinctive Triple Crown accreditation, covers social and environmental issues in more than 60 core and elective graduate courses. In the area of entrepreneurship, IE offers a social entrepreneurship track to promote the creation of social companies. All MBA students are required to prepare a business plan that includes an analysis of the social and environmental impact of their project. IE's initiatives include a chair in ethics funded by the IE Business School Alumni Association, The Corporate Governance Centre, and The Eco-Intelligent Management Centre. The PwC & IE Center for Corporate Responsibility is a joint initiative of IE and Pricewaterhouse-Coopers focused on disseminating material that advances responsible governance, environmental sustainability, and diversity.

REFLECTIONS ON BEYOND GREY PINSTRIPES METHODOLOGY

Our aim in this section is to reflect briefly on the BGP survey and ranking methodology in terms of several criteria.

Eligibility

The following eligibility criteria were extracted from the Aspen website, specifically the methodology and frequently asked questions sections. We also used questionnaire material that Aspen provided prior to survey applications.

1. Eligible schools must confer MBA degrees.
2. Only accredited MBA programs are eligible.
3. Only in-person MBA programs are eligible.
4. The MBA program must have full-time enrollment.
5. United States-based schools must have AACSB accreditation in order to participate.

We suggest specifying this qualifying criteria in the CBE *Our Closer Look at Business Education* series (Aspen CBE, 2009), with exact reference to the accreditation agencies. Sometimes AACSB or EFMD are noted but, at other times, AACSB is simply implied. To further complicate matters, unnamed international accrediting associations or programs are also implied. Finally, a prestigious accreditor, AMBA, is not mentioned at all; yet, 20 schools were accredited by this body in 2009.

Accreditation

In analyzing the Global 100, we found that four non-U.S. schools were ranked without fulfilling the eligibility requirement of accreditation: two in Canada, one in Finland, and one in South Korea. This data is surprising, considering that out of the 32 non-U.S.-based ranked schools, 28 do fulfill the requirement. Furthermore, the arguments that Canadian business schools are subject to accreditation by their provincial governments, or that there is no separate accreditation body for degree programs in business, should not exempt the two mentioned schools from being accredited by AACSB or EFMD (or AMBA, if accepted) because there are five other ranked Canadian schools accredited by these bodies. It is also worth mentioning that, although AMBA is not explicitly accepted as an accreditor, three schools in the Global 100 are exclusively accredited by this body in the United Kingdom, Switzerland, and Slovenia (as shown in Table 7.1).

Data Transparency, Accuracy, and Feedback

We believe that certain reporting practices may undermine the fairness of the ranking process. Notably, the data submitted for coursework would be more accurate and reliable if syllabi and course URLs were required, thus eliminating the option for course descriptions. The latter may inaccurately inflate course content and encourage other schools to follow suit. We make the same observation for the self-reported course content percentage, which may lead to an imprecise calculation of student exposure to social, ethical, and environmental coverage. Self-evaluations of for-profit impact courses, based on unrestricted descriptions, may also be inaccurate. Finally, we suggest that the Aspen Institute provide all participating schools with postsurvey feedback so that the schools can identify areas for improvement.

Faculty Research

In the most recent ranking, published research in any peer-reviewed business journal was allowed. Yet for the previous survey, only 80 leading academic journals were acceptable. This expanded range of journals allows schools to include a larger number of articles, which may dilute the legitimate recognition of publications that contribute more directly to advancing ethics, social, and environmental issues in research. At the same time, non-peer-reviewed works are not allowed, even though some have attained a reputation for quality, the most notable being *Harvard Business Review* (which relies an editorial review process). This state of affairs has prompted Adler and Harzing (2009, p. 75) to ask: "Why only journal articles?" A more encompassing diversity of publications, including books and book chapters, would certainly be worthy of consideration in scoring.

Principles for Responsible Management Education (PRME)

We believe that BGP and Principles for Responsible Management Education (PRME) represent common ideals that challenge business schools to advance ethical and socially responsible business leadership. The 2009-2010 survey poses a question regarding PRME: "Has your business school signed the PRME?" However, no data regarding this question is provided in the post survey period. We recommend that all the business schools ranked in the Global 100 sign up to PRME and, by committing to its principles, be distinguished as leading promoters of socially responsible education.

CONCLUDING REMARKS

The Beyond Grey Pinstripes ranking is uniquely significant because it encourages business schools to deliver high quality education in ethics, social responsibility, and environmental stewardship. And it recognizes those that do so. The process we have suggested for becoming ranked requires that schools follow a number of steps, including an objective benchmarking of their courses, research, and extracurriculars. This process, led by committed faculty and administrators, should ideally result in a school's transformation into a socially responsible educational enterprise. In this way, being ranked in the Global 100 is not only a matter of pride for selected schools, but also an incentive to strive continuously for excellence in the targeted areas.

NOTES

1. The texts in this chapter that pertain to the Aspen Institute, Aspen Business and Society Program, Aspen Center for Business Education, Beyond Grey Pinstripes survey and ranking methodology, as well as all information related to these subjects, were extracted from the Aspen Institute's webpage. The texts were transcribed, condensed, and paraphrased while the highest possible degree of exactness was observed. Any error or omission in the information is involuntary and the absolute responsibility of the authors. A list of the consulted websites is included in the Appendix.

2. Instead of business *and* society, we favor the expression business *in* society. Instead of business intersecting with society, we believe that business is a full member of society and exists to create value for it.

3. Social impact management focuses on the complex interdependencies between business needs and wider societal concerns. If these interdependencies are not understood well and managed intelligently, neither business nor the society in which it operates can thrive (Gentile, 2002).

4. How can business schools be responsible? Through reflective processes of management, teaching, research, and social participation that can guide business schools to respond thoughtfully to social contingencies. In this way, business school responsibility is not an extracurricular activity; it is part and parcel of the university's essence, ethos, and way of being (see http://web.guni2005.upc.es/news/detail.php?chlang=en&id=1135).

ACKNOWLEDGMENTS

The authors gratefully acknowledge helpful comments from William C. Frederick on an earlier draft of this chapter. We also thank Diane L. Swanson and Dann G. Fisher for their review of the chapter and Xènia Guardia and Manuel Valles for their generosity in sharing valuable material for our research.

APPENDIX

AACSB Accredited Members	www.aacsb.edu/accreditation/AccreditedMembers.asp
AMBA Accredited Academic Institutions	www.mbaworld.com/index.php?option=com_content&view=article&id=474&Itemid=132
Aspen Institute	www.aspeninstitute.org/about
Beyond Grey Pinstripes	www.beyondgreypinstripes.org/index.cfm
Business and Society Program	www.aspeninstitute.org/policy-work/business-society
CasePlace.org	www.aspencbe.org/teaching/caseplace.html
Center for Business Education	www.aspencbe.org/
Closer Look Series	www.aspencbe.org/about/library.html#closerlooks
Coursework Search	www.beyondgreypinstripes.org/search/search_coursework.cfm
EABIS Case Studies	www.eabis.org/index.php?id=119
EQUIS Accredited Schools	www.efmd.org/index.php/accreditation-/equis/accredited-schools
European Case Clearing House	www.ecch.com/about/Cases.cfm
Extracurricular Activities Search	www.beyondgreypinstripes.org/search/search_ activities.cfm
Giving Voice to Values	www.aspencbe.org/teaching/gvv/index.html
Guide to Socially Responsible MBA Programs	www.aspencbe.org/teaching/MBA_Guide.html
Peace Through Commerce	www.aacsb.edu/resource_centers/peace/about.asp
Research Search	www.beyondgreypinstripes.org/search/search_faculty.cfm
Students Attitudes Survey	www.aspencbe.org/teaching/Student_Attitudes.html
The Global 100	www.beyondgreypinstripes.org/rankings/index.cfm
Top Ten Lists	www.beyondgreypinstripes.org/rankings/topten.cfm

Glossary

- AACSB: Association to Advance Collegiate Schools of Business
- AMBA: Association of MBAs
- BGP: Beyond Grey Pinstripes
- BSP: Business and Society Program
- CBE: Center for Business Education
- CSR: Corporate Social Responsibility
- EABIS: European Academy of Business in Society
- ECCH: European Case Clearing House
- EFMD: European Foundation for Management Development
- EQUIS: European Quality Improvement System
- ESG: Ethical, Social, and Governance
- FAQs: Frequently Asked Questions
- GRLI: Globally Responsible Leadership Initiative
- IMBA: International Master of Business Administration
- MBA: Master of Business Administration
- MPA: Master of Public Administration
- MS: Master of Science
- OCGS: Ontario Council for Graduate Studies
- PRME: Principles for Responsible Management Education
- PwC: PricewaterhouseCoopers
- SNRE: School of Natural Resources & Environment
- UNGC: United Nations Global Compact
- URL: Uniform Resource Locator
- WRI: World Resources Institute

REFERENCES

Adler, N. J., & Harzing, A. (2009). When knowledge wins: Transcending the sense and nonsense of academic rankings. *Academy of Management Learning & Education, 8*(1), 72-95.

Aspen Institute. (2009). *The Aspen Institute celebrating 60 years: 2009 overview and 2008 annual report.* Retrieved from www.aspeninstitute.org/sites/default/files/content/docs/about/2008-annual-report.pdf

Aspen Institute Center for Business Education, Closer look report (2009, November). A closer look at business education series: Beyond Grey Pinstripes. Retrieved from www.aspencbe.org/documents/BeyondGreyPinstripes CloserLook.pdf

Gentile, M. C. (2002, Fall). *Social impact management: A definition.* Retrieved from http://www.aspeninstitute.org/policy-work/business-society/publications-speeches/publications-archives/social-impact-management-de

Globally Responsible Leadership Initiative. (2004). *Globally responsible leadership: A call for engagement.* Retrieved from http://www.efmd.org/attachments/tmpl _3_art_060614xvqa_att_060614trmw.pdf

Peters, K. (2007). Business school rankings: Content and context. *Journal of Management Development, 26*(1), 49-53.

Policano, A. (2007). The rankings game: And the winner is…. *Journal of Management Development, 26*(1), 43-48.

Wheatley, M. J. (2003). Change: The capacity of life. *Business leadership: A Jossey-Bass reader* (pp. 496-517). San Francisco, CA: John Wiley & Sons.

CHAPTER 8

ASSESSING BUSINESS ETHICS COVERAGE AT TOP U.S. BUSINESS SCHOOLS

Barrie E. Litzky and Tammy L. MacLean

INTRODUCTION

The rash of corporate scandals over the past decade has sparked intense debate among business school faculty and administrators about whether their curricula ameliorates or abets the bad behavior of business school graduates (Etzioni, 2002; Jacobs, 2009; "Top Business," 2002). Outside of scholarly circles, corporate and government institutions are weighing in on the discussion of whether or not more emphasis should be placed upon business ethics in business school curricula. Although there seems to be little disagreement that business schools need to elevate the role of ethics in their curricula, the question of just how to do this has ignited vigorous debate in academe (Swanson, 2004). The road maps of this discussion is the question of whether or not universities should require students to take a standalone, foundational business ethics course. Although most parties appear to agree that ethics should be integrated throughout business school curricula by embedding ethics-related material throughout all relevant courses, the discourse has crystallized into a debate over

Toward Assessing Business Ethics Education
pp. 133–142
Copyright © 2011 by Information Age Publishing
All rights of reproduction in any form reserved.

whether or not stand-alone ethics courses are also necessary components of effective business ethics education.

The argument has polarized into two opposing points of view. One position argues that business ethics is best taught by infusion, or by integrating business ethics into the core courses of the curriculum such as marketing, strategy, accounting, and other functional subject areas. The other position asserts that infusion is necessary but insufficient, and argues that to effectively teach business ethics, a foundational stand-alone required ethics course is necessary for students to develop a common language and common understanding of the fundamentals of business ethics before they will be able to effectively apply these concepts in the functional courses.

At present, MBA programs in the United States deliver ethics education both through infusion and through foundation courses. In this chapter we highlight the types and numbers of ethics courses offered at the top U.S. business schools at three points in time over the last decade. We note which university courses infuse ethics into their subject matter and which are foundation courses. We gathered data on the top MBA programs recognized by *Business Week* and the *Wall Street Journal* in 2002, and *Business Week* in 2004 and 2008. We chose these schools based upon the assumption that the top schools act as benchmarks and role models for other institutions in terms of many issues, including business ethics education. In our analysis, business ethics courses were defined as those courses addressing right and wrong or normative actions taken by corporations or their employees, including courses that inclusively address normative areas as they relate to business law (e.g., Sarbanes-Oxley), public policy (e.g., Securities and Exchange Commission guidelines), organizational ethics (e.g., corporate governance) and corporate social responsibility (e.g., obligations to community and stakeholders) (Swanson & Frederick, 2003). In contrast, other courses that are more narrowly content specific, such as business law and corporate governance, are not stand-alone ethics courses per se, but can easily be used as vehicles for the infusion of ethics topics across the curriculum.

DATA COLLECTION

Data were collected at three points in time from university websites which listed curriculum requirements and electives along with course descriptions.[1] We categorized universities according to whether or not they offered a required or elective stand-alone ethics course and whether or not they offered any required or elective courses that explicitly infused ethics in course descriptions and syllabi (if available).

Stand-alone courses—sometimes referred to as survey, core, foundation, or threshold courses—offer a foundation in business ethics by providing a broad overview of the normative relationships between business, government, and society. Course titles include, but are not limited to: business and public policy, business ethics, ethical issues in the biotech industry, ethics, ethics and global business, ethics and responsibility, making ethical decisions, managerial ethics, social and ethical responsibility of business, socially responsible business practices, strategic corporate citizenship, and the moral leader.

Infused courses are those that are used as vehicles for embedding ethics across the curriculum. They can be context specific, as in business law, corporate governance, finance law, managers and the legal environment, social enterprise, social and nonprofit marketing, and sustainability. Infused courses may also specify in the course description that they address relevant ethical issues as related to the course topic, including but not limited to: social entrepreneurship, strategy in the business environment, strategic issues in philanthropy, and transnational business and human rights.

FINDINGS

Time 1

In 2002, data were collected as talking points for a symposium, part of a larger research effort that explored the level of integration of business ethics into the MBA curriculum at top U.S. business schools (MacLean & Litzky, 2003).[2] The universities included were from a combined list of the top 13 U.S. business schools ranked by both *Business Week* and the *Wall Street Journal* ("2002 b-school," 2003; "Top Business," 2002). Findings are presented in Table 8.1.

As shown in Table 8.1, in 2002, three of the top 13 U.S. business schools (23%) had a stand-alone requirement in business ethics. Four out of 13 (31%) had an integrated business ethics requirement. Two of 13 (15%) had both one stand-alone and one integrated requirement. One school, University of Michigan, required students to take one business ethics or one business law course. In essence this allowed the student to choose either a stand-alone or an integrated elective. Twelve of the top 13 (92%) business schools offered at least one stand-alone course as an elective.

Time 2

Data were collected during the summer of 2004 from the top 50 U.S. business programs ranked by *Business Week* ("2004 b-school," 2006). We

Table 8.1.   Ethics Coverage at 13 Top U.S. Business Schools in 2002

University	Stand-Alone Courses Offered		Infused Courses Offered	
	Required	Elective	Required	Elective
Carnegie Mellon		1	1	
Columbia		1		7
Dartmouth		1		1
Duke		1		4
Harvard	1			8
MIT		1	1	4
Northwestern		2	1	4
Stanford	1		1	6
University of Chicago		1		9
University of Michigan[a]		1		16
University of Texas, Austin		3		6
Wharton	1	1	1	
Yale		1	1	24

Note: This list is presented in alphabetical order. The 13 schools represent a combination of the top 10 ranked by both *Business Week* and the *Wall Street Journal*.
[a]Requires students to take one business ethics or one business law course.

placed follow-up phone calls to the universities in an effort to validate the accuracy of the website information. Data were missing from Boston University and University of Georgia; therefore, we report our findings out of a sample of 48, rather than 50, universities. The findings are presented in Table 8.2.

In 2004, 35 of the top 48 (73%) U.S. business schools did not require a stand-alone ethics course. Specifically, only 13 of the top 48 (27%) schools required one stand-alone ethics course, eight of those were listed in the top 30 (27%), and the other five categorized as second-tier universities. At least one infused course was required by 27 of the top 48 (56%) schools, with six of those 48 (12%) requiring two infused courses in the curriculum. Of the schools requiring at least one infused course, 14 ranked in the top 30 (47%). Four of the top 30 (13%), along with four second-tier schools, required at least one stand-alone and one infused course as part of the curriculum. Sixteen of the top 48 (33%) schools had neither a stand-alone nor infused ethics requirement; 12 of those universities ranked in the top 30 (40%). In terms of electives, 32 of the top 48 (66%) offered at least one stand-alone elective and 46 out of 48 (96%) offered at

Table 8.2. Ethics Coverage at 50 top U.S. Business Schools in 2004

	University	Stand-Alone Courses Offered		Infused Courses Offered	
		Required	Elective	Required	Elective
1	Northwestern		2	1	5
2	University of Chicago		1		9
3	University of Pennsylvania	1	1	1	
4	Stanford	1	2	1	6
5	Harvard	1	2		8
6	Michigan		1		16
7	Cornell		1		6
8	Columbia		1		7
9	MIT		1	1	4
10	Dartmouth		1		1
11	Duke		1		4
12	Virginia		3		3
13	NYU			1	3
14	UCLA				4
15	Carnegie Mellon		1	1	
16	UNC	1			4
17	UC Berkeley	1	1		5
18	Indiana		1	1	3
19	Texas-Austin		3		6
20	Emory		1	1	3
21	Purdue		1	1	3
22	Yale		1	1	24
23	Washington		2	1	3
24	Notre Dame	1	3		6
25	Georgetown	1		1	1
26	Babson			2	2
27	University of Southern California				4
28	Maryland			2	5
29	Rochester				1
30	Vanderbilt		1		6
2nd tier	Arizona State			1	1
2nd tier	Boston College[a]			2	4
2nd tier	Boston University[b]				
2nd tier	Brigham Young	1	1	1	1
2nd tier	UC Irvine		2		5
2nd tier	Case Western Reserve[a]		1	2	5
2nd tier	Georgia[c]				
2nd tier	Georgia Tech[a]		1		6
2nd tier	Illinois at Urbana-Champaign		1	2	1
2nd tier	Iowa			1	1
2nd tier	Michigan State	1		1	1
2nd tier	Minnesota	1			4

(Table continues on next page)

Table 8.2.   (Continued)

	University	Stand-Alone Courses Offered		Infused Courses Offered	
		Required	Elective	Required	Elective
2nd tier	Ohio State		2	1	1
2nd tier	Penn State[a]		2		5
2nd tier	Rice[a]	1		1	2
2nd tier	Southern Methodist				4
2nd tier	Thunderbird		1	1	2
2nd tier	Wake Forest[a]	1		1	3
2nd tier	University of Washington	1	1	2	2
2nd tier	Wisconsin[a]		1	1	3

Note: Business Week denotes the top 30 universities by numerical rank and groups the next 20 into a second-tier category.
[a]Not listed in 2008.
[b]Data missing in 2004, listed in 2008.
[c]Data missing in 2004, not listed in 2008.

least one infused elective, with most universities offering multiple infused electives.

Time 3

The data collection process for the universities listed as the top business schools in 2008 took place over the fall 2008 and spring 2009 time period ("2008 business," 2008). In 2008, *Business Week* categorized 15 rather than 20 schools as second tier. We therefore gathered data from 45 schools in total. The findings are presented in Table 8.3.

In 2008, 27 of the 45 (60%) top business schools required a stand-alone ethics course. Within the top 30 universities, 17 (57%) required as least one stand-alone and four (13%) required two stand-alone ethics courses. Four of the 15 (27%) schools categorized as second tier required two stand-alone ethics courses as well. Within the top 45 programs, 12 (27%) required an infused course, with seven (15%) schools requiring at least one stand-alone and one infused course. There were 13 out of 45 (29%) schools with neither a stand-alone nor an infused ethics requirement; 10 of those ranked in the top 30 (33%). Almost half (22) of the top 45 schools (48%) offered at least one stand-alone ethics elective, and 28 of the 45 (62%) offered at least one infused elective, with many universities offering multiple stand-alone and infusion elective choices.

Table 8.3.   Ethics Coverage at 45 Top U. S. Business Schools in 2008

	University	Stand-Alone Courses Offered			Infused Courses Offered		
		Required	Required in 2004	Elective	Required	Required in 2004	Elective
1	Chicago		No	1		No	2
2	Harvard	1	Yes	2	1	No	8
3	Northwestern[a]		No	3	1	Yes	8
4	University of Pennsylvania	1	Yes	2	1	Yes	4
5	Michigan		No	2		No	1
6	Stanford	1	Yes		1	Yes	
7	Columbia	1	No			No	1
8	Duke[b]	1	No	1		No	3
9	MIT		No			Yes	9
10	UC-Berkeley	1	Yes	5		No	
11	Cornell		No	3	1	No	
12	Dartmouth		No	2		No	3
13	NYU	1	No			Yes	5
14	UCLA		No			No	1
15	Indiana		No	1	1	Yes	
16	Virginia	1	No	2		No	3
17	North Carolina	1	Yes			No	1
18	Southern Methodist		No	1		No	
19	Carnegie Mellon	2	No			Yes	
20	Notre Dame	2	Yes	3		No	
21	Texas-Austin		No	2		No	1
22	Brigham Young	1	Yes			Yes	2
23	Emory		No	1		Yes	1
24	Yale	1	No		1	Yes	7
25	University of Southern California		No			No	
26	Maryland	2	No			Yes	
27	University of Washington	1	Yes			Yes	2
28	Washington University		No	3		Yes	1
29	Georgia Tech	1	No		1	No	
30	Vanderbilt	2	No			No	5
2nd tier	Arizona State	1					
2nd tier	Babson	1					
2nd tier	Boston University	1					5
2nd tier	Connecticut[c]	2					

(Table continues on next page)

Table 8.3.   Ethics Coverage at 45 Top U. S. Business Schools in 2008

		Stand-Alone Courses Offered			Infused Courses Offered		
	University	Required	Required in 2004	Elective	Required	Required in 2004	Elective
2nd tier	George Washington[c]	2			1		
2nd tier	Georgetown	2					2
2nd tier	Illinois-Urbana Champaign			2	1		1
2nd Tier	Iowa						
2nd tier	Michigan State	1					
2nd tier	Minnesota[d]	2		1			2
2nd tier	Ohio State			2			
2nd tier	Purdue[e]	1		1			1
2nd tier	Rochester						2
2nd tier	Thunderbird			1	1		1
2nd tier	UC-Irvine	1		3	1		2

Note: *Business Week* denotes the top 30 universities by numerical rank and groups the next 15 into a second tier category.
[a]Required infused course is a pre-term, half credit course.
[b]Three-week seminar format.
[c]Not listed in 2004.
[d]One of the two required stand-alone courses delivered as a 2-week international immersion.
Required stand-alone delivered each Friday during year one for zero credit hours.

SUMMARY OF FINDINGS

In the 4 years between 2004 and 2008 there appears to have been a solid shift in the offerings of ethics courses within the top MBA programs we sampled. In 2004, 40% of the top 30 business schools had no ethics requirement, whereas in 2008 that percentage dropped to 30%. The percentage of the top 30 business schools that required at least one stand-alone ethics course rose from 27% in 2004 to 57% in 2008. During the same period the percentage of schools in the top 30 requiring at least one infused ethics course dropped from 47% in 2004 to 27% in 2008, possibly suggesting that schools were responding to the business environment by focusing more attention on ethics vis-à-vis required stand-alone courses.

STUDY LIMITATIONS

The means of data collection may limit our findings in a number of ways: First, it is unlikely that the degree to which ethics is embedded into various courses can be assessed solely through course descriptions. Second, our categorization scheme counts the number of required and elective courses. However, a count of electives, for example, does not detect a difference between schools that offer one elective versus schools that offer 12 to 15. Furthermore, many of the websites indicated that only a partial list of electives was provided. Third, a variety of schools offer courses which cover nonprofit businesses. These mission-based businesses by their very nature could fall into our definition of infused business ethics courses, although we did not include them in this research. Finally, there may be a better way to categorize courses that are not stand alone. For example, the infused category includes courses which cover a variety of topics because this category encompasses both context specific and integrated courses.

Despite these limitations, it is our hope that this study will contribute to efforts to assess and strengthen ethics education in business schools.

NOTES

1. In most instances we only included courses with descriptions unless the course title was extremely specific (e.g., business ethics, business law, corporate governance, etc.).
2. This audit of business ethics education is affiliated with the Business Ethics Education Initiative at Kansas State University (http://www.cba.k-state.edu/index.asp?NID=332).

REFERENCES

2002 b-school rankings and profiles. (2003). *Business Week.* Retrieved from http://www.businessweek.com/bschools/02/full_time_rank.htm

2004 b-school profiles and rankings. (2006). *Business Week.* Retrieved from http://www.businessweek.com/bschools/04/

2008 business school rankings and profiles. (2008). *Business Week.* Retrieved from http://www.businessweek.com/bschools/rankings/index.html

Etzioni, A. (2002, August 4). When it comes to ethics, b-schools get an F. *The Washington Post.* Retrieved from http://www.washingtonpost.com/ac2/wp-dyn/A38323-2002Aug2

Jacobs, M. (2009). How business schools have failed business. *Wall Street Journal.* Retrieved from http://online.wsj.com/article/SB124052874488350333.html

MacLean, T., & Litzky, B. E. (2003, June). *Task force on integrating ethics and business in society in the U.S. management curriculum. The business in society curriculum in Europe and the United States: A comparative analysis and conversation.* Presented at the The International Association for Business and Society 14th annual conference, Rotterdam, The Netherlands.

Swanson, D. L. (2004). The buck stops here: Why universities must reclaim business ethics education. *The Journal of Academic Ethics, 2*(1), 1-19.

CHAPTER 9

ASSESSING CORPORATE SOCIAL RESPONSIBILITY EDUCATION IN EUROPE

Trends and Comparisons

Marc Orlitzky and Jeremy Moon

There is growing evidence of European translations of corporate social responsibility (CSR) from its American roots. This chapter presents and discusses findings from the Second European Survey of CSR Education in 2007. It finds overall growth in CSR education in European business schools by several measures (including enrollments, modules, and programs) since the First European Survey of CSR Education in 2003. It provides insights into different drivers of European CSR education, particularly the importance of individual faculty and school-level CSR research capacity. Although there has been a growth in the importance of university leadership and student demand as key success factors, faculty interest and dedicated teaching and research centers are regarded as the most critical success factors overall. Our evidence also points to a maturation of CSR as an academic field within European business schools, both in terms of in-house teaching capacity, the consolidation of CSR research, and the integration of CSR issues into other business school courses. Comparisons are made with findings from a similar

Toward Assessing Business Ethics Education
pp. 143–175

study of leading business schools, a worldwide cohort of business schools, and business schools within different national business systems.

INTRODUCTION

Corporate social responsibility (CSR) might reasonably be described as a managerial and academic creation of the United States of America. However, its recent growth in Europe, both as a management and an academic concept, has also been noted, albeit with some distinctive features, such as an emphasis on the greater role of governments and business associations (Aaronson & Reeves, 2002; European Commission, 2001, 2002, 2006; Habisch, Jonker, Wegner, & Schmidpeter, 2005; Matten & Moon, 2008). Given that one of the recurring questions in the debate about CSR is "how to do it?" ("Corporate Social," 2008, p. 12), we need to understand the status, drivers, key success factors and barriers, teaching techniques, and research focus of CSR in European management education.

This chapter is based on the Second European Survey of CSR Education.[1] In this chapter, CSR education refers to both teaching and research about the responsibilities of business in society (see also Russell, 2007). Our objective is to understand the current state and nature of CSR education in Europe by identifying developments since the first survey (Matten & Moon, 2004) and examining teaching techniques and research topics in Europe. This introduction continues by contextualizing the issue of CSR education.

Our contribution is timely in that there is an increased interest in CSR education from a number of quarters. For example, an increasing number of business students participate in extracurricular organizations such as Net Impact, which claims a membership of over 10,000 MBAs, graduate students, and professionals across six continents. In addition, for several years the Aspen Institute has been highlighting best practices in CSR education, recognizing faculty pioneers, and formally rating or providing a ranking of business schools. This biennial report describes various efforts by business schools to address corporate responsibility and sustainability topics in their research and teaching.

Despite the Aspen Institute's index of the best schools and its forum to share ideas about teaching innovations regarding CSR topics, little systematic empirical evidence has been collected to date about the extent to which social and environmental responsibility topics have become integral to management education. For instance, Mahoney's (1990) comparison of teaching practices in the United States, United Kingdom, and continental Europe showed that there were significant differences in the maturity of business ethics disciplines, financial support, and typical disciplinary foci. Mahoney argued, among other things, that ethics teaching in continental Europe tended to be more oriented toward a critical analysis of entire economic systems than the more corporate or individualist focus of ethics teaching in the United Kingdom and United States (see also Enderle, 1996; Nash, 1994). Similarly, Preuss (1999) identified a relatively high degree of theory development of business ethics at the macro level of analysis in Germanic countries. In addition, contributors to Zsolnai's (1998) book suggested a diversity of conceptualizations of business ethics in eight European countries (Czech Republic, Denmark, France, Hungary, Netherlands, Spain, Sweden, Switzerland), although it is unclear to what extent the researchers' observations reflected systematic differences between countries or idiosyncratic differences of the contributing authors' home institutions (Spence, 2000).

In their analysis of the First European Survey of CSR Education, Matten and Moon (2004) found a remarkable interest in topics related to business in society and corporate responsibility (including sustainability).[2] Approximately two thirds of respondents offered CSR courses in one of their programs (e.g., undergraduate/ diploma, masters, MBA, or executive), albeit taught with highly diverse approaches. We will further describe this study when we compare it to our findings.

A more recent study focused on the MBA programs of the top 50 business schools ranked by the *Financial Times* (Jones Christensen, Peirce, Hartman, Hoffman, & Carrier, 2007). In a survey of the deans and directors of these premier business schools, the researchers found that 84% of the responding schools exposed students to ethics, CSR, or sustainability topics in at least one mandatory course in their MBA programs. In addition, a relatively large proportion (66%) of their respondents reported having established a research/teaching center or institute in one of the three topics. Over half the respondents (55%) indicated that their schools integrated ethics, CSR, and sustainability offerings in some way in their MBA programs. Also, the inclusion of sustainability topics in MBA programs appears to be a growing trend. Several schools relied on experiential learning and immersion techniques to teach ethics-, CSR-, or sustainability-related course content. The various descriptions showed that teaching innovations, such as those described in Muijen (2004) and Moratis, Hoff, and Reul (2006) have been implemented in an increasing number of business schools. Finally, in the top ten schools, student interest in these topics in their extracurricular activities (e.g., Net Impact) was especially strong.

The present study builds on these previous research efforts in the following ways. First, it focuses on European trends and changes in CSR education by comparing the present findings to those of Matten and Moon (2004). Second, it examines differences in levels of commitment to

CSR education between different European regions. Third, it is broader than Jones Christensen et al.'s (2007) study because it analyzes a wider range of CSR education initiatives at the undergraduate, masters (particularly the masters of arts and masters of science), and generic and tailored executive levels, as well as CSR research in business schools. Fourth, in line with our comparative focus, we describe the program-specific levels of CSR, teaching foci and methods, as well as other features that might reflect or facilitate CSR mainstreaming, which we define as the full integration of CSR education in the curricula.

Hence, this chapter presents more detailed and broader analyses than several previous studies of CSR education in Europe and around the world. It consists of the following sections: (1) sample characteristics in the Second European Survey; (2) trends in European CSR education; (3) key success factors and barriers to CSR education; (4) CSR teaching techniques; (5) CSR research in Europe; (6) a discussion of findings (study limitations and suggestions for future research); and (7) concluding remarks. First we describe the sample on which our analysis and conclusions are based.

SAMPLE CHARACTERISTICS OF THE SECOND SURVEY

In our second survey of CSR education at European universities, conducted in 2007, we received responses from 77 organizations out of 384, for a response rate of 20.1%. Thus, our sample size was larger than those used by Jones Christensen et al. (2007) and Cornelius, Wallace, and Tassabehji (2007). For instance, our sample included members of the European Association for Business in Society (EABiS) as well as nonmembers who were on the mailing list of EABiS. As is typical in survey research, not all respondents answered all questions, which explains the variability in question-specific sample sizes shown in our tables. Our definition of Europe followed the description on the official web site of the European Union (http://europa.eu), which includes EU members, European nonmember countries, and EU candidate countries. The one exception is that we excluded Turkey because we consider it to be part of the Middle East for cultural and political reasons. Table 9.1 shows the geographic spread of respondents.

Although the response rate was higher than many social science surveys and comparable to that of the first survey (Matten & Moon, 2004), our sample may not be representative of all European business schools in general, but instead may be more representative of those regarding themselves as CSR best practice schools, as suggested by two main indicators. First, there was a 17% overlap between the respondents in this sample and the Aspen Institute's Beyond Grey Pinstripes (BGP) top 100 rankings of

**Table 9.1.   Number and Proportion of
European Survey Respondents by Geographic Region**

Region	Frequency	Percent
Nordic countries (Denmark, Sweden)	2	2.6
British Isles (UK and Ireland)	18	23.4
France	14	18.2
Benelux	6	7.8
Central Europe (Austria, Bosnia-Hercegovina, Germany, Hungary, Poland, Slovakia, Slovenia, Switzerland)	16	20.8
Southern Europe (Greece, Italy, Portugal, Spain)	16	20.8
Russia and Ukraine	5	6.4
Total	77	100.0

outstanding MBA programs in terms of CSR education in 2007. Second, the vast majority of survey respondents (77.6%) were also members of associations, networks, and partnerships (e.g., EABIS, European Foundation for Management Development, or the European Business Ethics Network) which are committed to the mainstreaming of CSR. The combination of these factors leads to our conclusion that ours is a sample of CSR champions in one way or another.[3] Our focus on the behavior of best practice schools may therefore yield insights into broader future patterns and trends because lower tier schools may emulate higher tier schools and, consequently, offer more proactive ethics and/or CSR courses in the future (see also Cornelius et al., 2007).

The sample was later expanded to allow for some broader international comparisons, which will be discussed in later sections. After European replies were compiled, an online survey was developed to survey institutions of higher education worldwide. This second research phase resulted in 54 more responses from non-European countries. Twenty-two of these non-European responses were from North America (United States and Canada).

TRENDS IN EUROPEAN CORPORATE
SOCIAL RESPONSIBILITY EDUCATION

This section describes trends in European CSR education since the 2003 study.[4] It does so by first considering changes and trends in the levels of CSR educational provisions and, second, by reviewing the drivers of CSR education, CSR teaching tools, and CSR research. As mentioned before, the objective of this chapter is to track changes and trends rather than test hypotheses. Pursuing this descriptive objective, we seek to advance knowledge and understanding by inductive rather than deductive means (see Hambrick, 2007; Locke, 2007).

In our description of trends, we largely avoid reliance on statistical significance testing, which has been described as "the most bone-headedly misguided procedure ever institutionalized in the rote training of science students" (Rozeboom, 1997, p. 335) because it leads to numerous misinterpretations and false conclusions (Cohen, 1990, 1994; Hunter, 1997; Schmidt, 1992). For example, whenever a statistical test comes out nonsignificant, there is a temptation to conclude that this indicates no change. However, such a conclusion would be false. As methods expert Frank Schmidt forcefully argued:

> The third false belief [about statistical significance testing] is the most devastating of all to the research enterprise. This is the belief that if a difference or relation is not statistically significant, then it is zero, or at least so small that it can safely be considered to be zero. This is the belief that if the null hypothesis is not rejected, then it is to be accepted. This is the belief that a major benefit from significance tests is that they tell us whether a difference or effect is real or "probably just occurred by chance." Oakes (1986) has shown empirically that the operational decision rule used by researchers is indeed "if it is not significant, it is zero." Researchers must be disabused of the false belief that if a finding is not significant, it is zero (Schmidt, 1996, p. 126)

So, when in our present study we find a difference of, let's say, 8% compared to the 2004 results, the best estimate of this change is 8%, not 0%, even if a significance test indicates a lack of statistical significance (see Armstrong, 2007; Cohen, 1994; Harlow, Mulaik, & Steiger, 1997; Kline, 2004; Schmidt, 1992; Schmidt & Hunter, 2002). In contrast, many researchers and readers falsely equate nonsignificant change/difference to no change/difference whenever such significance tests are used and reported (Oakes, 1986; Schmidt, 1996). For this reason, we decided to report effect sizes (such as percentage changes), which is consistent with the advice from the methods literature (e.g., Cohen, 1994; Harlow et al., 1997; Kline, 2004). At the same time, we refrain from the ritual of statistical significance testing whenever possible because statistical significance tests control for errors that, strictly speaking, cannot, or are at least unlikely to, occur (Type I errors) (Cohen, 1990, p. 1308; Cohen, 1994, p. 1000; Tukey, 1991) and ignore such issues as statistical power (i.e., Type II error, which is the error of falsely concluding that there is no difference when there really is one) (Cohen, 1988, 1992). With small sample sizes,

Type II error rates often are prohibitively high, and statistical significance tests only exacerbate the problem (Schmidt, 1996; Sedlmeier & Gigerenzer, 1989).

Level of CSR Education in European Institutions: Changes and Trends

According to our data, the amount of teaching devoted to CSR topics generally increased in European business schools and universities since 2003, but the change was uneven across programs. The changes described with reference to Table 9.2 are based on a comparison with the findings reported previously by Matten and Moon (2004).

First, Table 9.2 suggests that the proportion of schools offering optional CSR modules increased at all levels and was most pronounced in masters programs,[5] where it increased from 35% to 66%. In other programs, the trend was similar, though not as pronounced. For examples, the following increases were observed in other programs: 51% to 73% in undergraduate/diploma programs, 32% to 59% in the full-time MBA programs, 32% to 36% in the part-time MBA programs, and 17% to 27% in Executive education. Also, we found that optional CSR modules are much more likely to be featured in full-time MBA than part-time MBA programs. This might be because many business schools market their full-time MBA program as their flagship program and are therefore likely to adjust this course content more quickly in response to industry trends and student demand.

Furthermore, average enrollments in optional CSR courses have only grown in masters and undergraduate programs (statistically significant increase at $p < .05$). They have slightly dropped in MBA programs (from 45 to 32 in full-time programs). Interestingly, as shown in Table 9.2, European business schools now enroll a disproportionately larger number of students in tailored executive education than in generic, or open, Executive education courses. This suggests that most business organizations probably consider CSR to be firm-specific activities that require customized attention in business schools while requiring large cohorts of managerial employees to attend tailor-made courses. If more than a quarter of European business schools offered tailored short courses in CSR, enrollments would, most likely, be less concentrated (i.e., decrease) among those executive education vanguard schools.

Table 9.2 also indicates that changes in the proportion of European schools with dedicated CSR programs were uneven across program types. Consistent with trends described by Balch (2007), dedicated CSR program offerings at the masters level, usually master of arts (MA) and mas-

Table 9.2. CSR Modules and CSR Programs in European Business Schools Proportions and Enrollment Figures

	Undergrad (Bachelor, etc.)		MA/MSc[a]		MBA (Full Time)		MBA (Part Time)		Executive		Tailored Executive	
	2003	2007	2003	2007	2003	2007	2003	2007	2003	2007	2003	2007
Proportion of schools with optional CSR modules	51%	73%[+]	35%	66%[+]	32%	59%[+]	32%	36%[ns]	17%	27%[ns]	17%	27%[ns]
Average enrollments	45	180[+]	34	132[+]	45	32[ns]	NA	35	87	3-	NA	713
Proportion of schools with dedicated CSR programs	9%	14%[ns]	11%	31%[+]	12%	7%[ns]	12%	12%[ns]	13%	11%[ns]	13%	3%[ns]
Average enrollments	240	256[ns]	200	74[ns]	74	30[ns]	NA	105	87	2-	NA	250
Proportion of schools with majors or "tracks" in CSR	NA	20%	NA	28%	NA	17%	NA	12%	NA	47%	NA	39%
Average enrollments	NA	53	NA	34	NA	1	NA	2	NA	3	NA	61
Proportion of schools with compulsory CSR classes or modules	NA	68%	NA	63%	NA	62%	NA	56%	NA	44%	NA	41%
Average enrollments	NA	264	NA	172	NA	191	NA	76	NA	3	NA	97

Note. [a] MA = Master of arts, MSc = Master of science degree (see also endnote 5). N ranged from 49 to 61 in 2007, and was 166 in 2003. An alpha level of .05 was used for all statistical tests. + = statistically significant increase since 2003; - = statistically significant decrease since 2003; ns = statistically nonsignificant change. Based on z values ($z = \dfrac{\hat{\pi}_1 - \hat{\pi}_2}{\sqrt{\hat{\pi}(1-\hat{\pi})\left(\dfrac{1}{n_1} + \dfrac{1}{n_2}\right)}}$, where $\hat{\pi} = \dfrac{x_1 + x_2}{n_1 + n_2}$). For the enrollment figures, t tests were used. Where no super-scripts appear, incomplete information prevented calculations regarding statistical significance.

ter of science (MSc), nearly tripled since 2003, from 11% to 31%. However, dedicated CSR MBA programs dropped from 12% of full-time MBA programs to 7% (and remained constant at 12% for part-time programs, as shown in Table 9.2). Similarly, there was a slight decline for dedicated CSR programs in executive programs. Among undergraduate programs, there was an increase from 9% to 14% in dedicated programs. Average enrollments dropped in executive and masters dedicated CSR programs (but only the decrease in executive enrollments was statistically significant at an alpha level of .05). The decrease in masters enrollments (from 200 to 74, which is a statistically nonsignificant decrease) suggests that the recruitment pool of motivated and talented master of arts and master of science students, who most likely are research oriented, may be limited. Therefore, if no new research talent can be tapped by these new CSR programs, average student numbers will likely drop when a larger proportion of universities start offering dedicated masters CSR programs. Average undergraduate and full time MBA enrollments in dedicated CSR programs were fairly stable in the last four years. Interestingly, average enrollments seem to have been over three times higher in part-time MBA programs (105 students) relative to full-time MBA programs (30 students).

We cannot present any trends for majors, tracks, and mandatory courses in CSR because Matten and Moon (2004) did not include proportions for these two categories. In 2007, more schools offered majors in CSR at the undergraduate and masters level (20% and 28%, respectively) than in the MBA program (17% in full time MBA, 12% in part time MBA), although none of these differences were statistically significant. CSR majors or tracks are most popular in executive programs (47% and 39%), despite quite lower enrollments. In contrast, average enrollments in the CSR major were highest in undergraduate (53) and masters programs (34).

Interestingly, the proportion of European schools requiring CSR coursework was lower than the figure presented by Jones Christensen et al. (2007), who reported mandatory ethics, CSR, or sustainability coursework at 84.1% of the *Financial Times* top 50 (or, more precisely, of their 44 respondents). In our study, however, fewer than 70% of all schools required CSR coursework in their programs. Given the compulsory nature of these courses, enrollments were naturally quite high.

Table 9.3 presents European respondents' views on trends in CSR teaching, courses, and activities since 2003. On average, they indicated an increase of over 75% in CSR education programs. The data pertaining to holistic, self-reported perceptions of changes in CSR education showed a bimodal distribution, with 29.1% of respondents reporting a doubling in CSR coursework and an equal proportion of respondents reporting an

Table 9.3.   Increase in Number of European CSR Teaching, Courses, and Activities since 2003 (Self-Reports)

Description of Increase	Percentage in Europe	N
More than 300%	14.5	8
More than 200%	5.5	3
More than 100% (i.e., doubled)	29.1	16
More than 75%	3.6	2
More than 50%	5.5	3
More than 25%	29.1	16
No change	12.7	7
Decrease since 2003	0	0

Notes: Mean change since 2003: > 75% (4.1)[a]; Median change: > 75% (4.0)[a]; Mode: >25%. [a]Scale ranging from 1 (more than 300%) to 8 (decrease since 2003). Total N = 55 because of missing responses.

increase of over 25%. Thus, compared to the overall average of dedicated CSR programs and optional CSR courses (an average increase of 56% relative to the results reported by Matten and Moon in 2004), the increase in CSR courses seems to have been overestimated by at least 19 percentage points, or 34%, when respondents were asked directly about their perceptions of changes in CSR education. This highlights the importance of conducting follow-up replication studies (like this one) to track changes instead of relying on respondents' retrospective accounts of perceived changes (see also Golden, 1992, 1997).

CSR Education in Four European Regions: British Isles, France/Benelux, Central Europe, and Southern Europe

Previous research (e.g., Enderle, 1997; Habisch et al., 2005; Mahoney, 1990; Matten & Moon, 2008; Vogel, 1993; Zsolnai, 1998) suggests that different countries within Europe institutionalize business-and-society relations and patterns differently. The National Business Systems (Whitley, 1997) and Varieties of Capitalism (Hall & Soskice, 2001) literature, for example, would lead us to expect more explicit corporate responsibilities toward society in more market-based countries in which business has greater discretion with respect to its social commitments (as in the United Kingdom, for instance). Conversely, this literature would lead us to expect more implicit corporate responsibilities in countries where the social obligations of business are more embedded in wider institutional forms, be these state-led (as in, France) or the product of neocorporatism (as in Germany) (see Matten & Moon, 2008).

To examine the influences of these cross-cultural institutional forces, we investigated whether these differences might also be manifest in differential emphases on dedicated CSR by business schools and, consequently, examined responding educational institutions' commitment to CSR by European region. Toward this end, we developed two aggregate survey measures for commitment to CSR coursework offered across all six program levels (from undergraduate programs to tailored Executive programs) in terms of commitment to (a) dedicated CSR programs and (b) optional CSR modules. This focus on dedicated and optional CSR coursework is consistent with a previous study of business school web sites (Cornelius et al., 2007). According to our measures, CSR commitment could range from a minimum of 0 (no dedicated degree/optional CSR course at any program level) to a maximum score of 6 (dedicated degrees/optional CSR courses at all six program levels). Internal consistency (calculated using the Kuder-Richardson Formula 20, which is the equivalent of Cronbach's alpha for nondichotomous items) of this commitment variable was .77.

Figures 9.1a and 9.1b show mean plots for the two CSR commitment variables. Although the mean plots might, at first glance, suggest differences between the four European regions, the associated statistical tests indicate that these regions are remarkably homogeneous with respect to their commitment to CSR. For both commitment variables, the ANOVA F-statistics (.749 and .387, respectively) and the Welch and Brown-Forsythe statistics (associated with the robust tests of equality of means) are all nonsignificant. This means that, at least with respect to the commitment variables, differences between the different European regions should not be overemphasized. In other words, the average levels of commitment to CSR education can be assumed to be fairly similar (i.e., similarly low) in the British Isles, France/Benelux, Central Europe, and Southern Europe. Still, consistent with our expectations, schools in the British Isles exhibited the greatest commitment to CSR education, an observation that may reflect the wider view that CSR in the United Kingdom is relatively advanced (Aaronson & Reeves, 2002; Vogel, 2005).

Drivers of CSR Education in Europe

As in 2003, respondents were asked what they considered the main drivers of CSR teaching in business schools to be, though in the second survey they were specifically asked about drivers of (a) introduction and development and (b) successful mainstreaming of CSR education (i.e., its full and effective integration in the business school curriculum). Tables 4 and 5 show that individual faculty members were considered the most

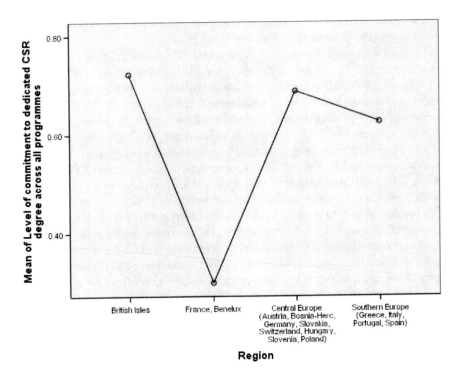

Notes: [a]Commitment scores ranged from a low of 0 (no dedicated degree/CSR course) to a high of 6 (dedicated degrees/CSR courses available in all six programs: UG/diploma, masters, FT MBA, PT MBA, generic executive education, tailored executive education). [b]All cross-region differences were statistically nonsignificant.

Figure 9.1a.   Mean plot of level of schools' commitment to dedicated CSR degree across all programs.[a, b]

important drivers of both dependent variables, which is consistent with Matten and Moon's (2004) findings. In fact, individual faculty were considered slightly more important in the second survey, increasing from 4.3 to 4.5 in perceived importance on a scale ranging from 1 (low) to 5 (high).

It is also worth noting that, according to the respondents, the other factors have generally become much more important since the first survey. In 2003, the other answers had ranged from a mean of 0.3 to 2.9. Now, the range of scores for the importance of the various other drivers extended from 2.79 to 4.00. One of the most remarkable increases can be noted for the importance of university leadership as a driver of both introduction and mainstreaming, from 1.7 to 3.87 and 3.86, respectively. This statistically significant increase may have resulted either from

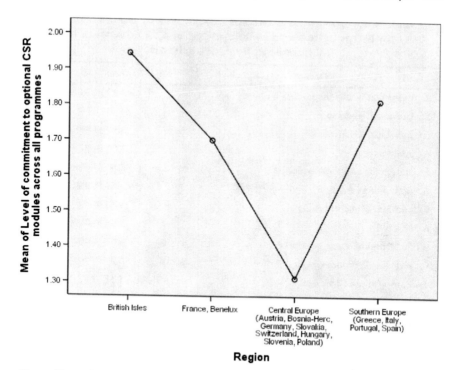

Notes: [a]Commitment scores ranged from a low of 0 (no dedicated degree/CSR course) to a high of 6 (dedicated degrees/CSR courses available in all six programs: UG/diploma, masters, FT MBA, PT MBA, generic executive education, tailored executive education). [b]All cross-region differences were statistically nonsignificant.

Figure 9.1b.   Mean plot of level of schools' commitment to optional CSR courses across all programs.[a, b]

respondents' experience during the last four years or a self-serving bias (because the 2007 respondents were more likely to consider themselves university leaders). Similarly, departments are now considered the second-most important driver of successful mainstreaming (given an average importance score of 4.00), which is consistent with the view that pedagogical innovations must be supported by a bottom-up process. These results suggest that implementation is likely to falter if educational innovations are imposed from the top in a way that does not energize faculty.

At the same time, the findings suggest that business schools are increasingly driven by forces of market demand. In the latest survey, students were accorded two standard deviations more importance than they were 4 years previously. That is, their average importance score increased from

Table 9.4.   Stakeholder Groups Considered Important Drivers for Introduction and Development of CSR Education in European Business Schools

Drivers	Mean[a] (SD)
1. Individual faculty members	4.49 (0.78)
2. University leadership	3.87 (1.14)
3. Individual departments	3.80 (0.89)
4. Students	3.67 (0.94)
5. Stakeholder network/associations	3.33 (0.94)
6. Accreditation bodies	3.31 (1.04)
7. Multinational corporations	3.30 (0.89)
8. NGOs	3.26 (0.93)
9. Small and medium enterprises	3.22 (1.02)
10. Individual/corporate donors	3.20 (1.20)
11. European policy makers	3.11 (0.92)
12. National government	3.07 (1.02)
13. Local communities	3.00 (0.98)
14. Corporate recruiters	2.98 (0.93)
15. Shareholder associations	2.79 (0.94)

Note: $N = 72$ because of missing responses. [a]Respondents scored the importance of these items, ranging from Critical (5) to Marginal (1).

1.8 to 3.7 and 3.8, respectively. This statistically significant increase is not unexpected because allowing external market forces greater sway in influencing internal university practices is consistent with broader developments in the business school sector (Kirp, 2003; Starkey & Tiratsoo, 2007).

Consistent with the findings in 2004, national governments were still judged to be relatively unimportant drivers, even though their importance score increased from 1.2 to 3.07 and 3.10, respectively (a score of 3 indicates a respondent's neutral assessment). This is perhaps surprising given the interest of governments in CSR more widely (Albareda, Lozano, & Ysa, 2007) and the continuing distinctiveness of this interest in Europe compared with that in the United States (Matten & Moon, 2008).

Interestingly, shareholder associations were considered least important as drivers of CSR teaching (i.e., of introduction/development and successful mainstreaming). These findings are very much in line with other studies that imply that relying on shareholders as agents of organizational change might be overly optimistic. Previous research shows that, in general, the impact of shareholder activism on organizations seems to be

**Table 9.5.   Stakeholder Groups Considered Important Drivers
for Successful Mainstreaming of CSR Education
in European Business Schools**

Drivers	Mean[a] (SD)
1. Individual faculty members	4.49 (0.76)
2. Individual departments	4.00 (0.88)
3. University leadership	3.86 (0.97)
4. Students	3.77 (1.02)
5. Accreditation bodies	3.56 (0.98)
6. Multinational corporations	3.41 (0.87)
7. Stakeholder networks/associations	3.37 (0.89)
8. Small and medium sized enterprises	3.30 (0.96)
9. European policy makers	3.22 (0.88)
10. NGOs	3.19 (0.89)
11. Corporate recruiters	3.12 (0.92)
12. National government	3.10 (0.98)
13. Individual/corporate donors	2.98 (1.07)
14. Local communities	2.95 (0.93)
15. Shareholder associations	2.85 (1.04)

Notes: $N = 71$ because of missing responses. [a]Respondents scored the importance of
these items, ranging from critical (5) to marginal (1).

either negligible or, in some cases, even negative (Black, 1998; David,
Bloom, & Hillman, 2007; Gillan & Starks, 2000). Hence, the expectation
that market forces may push for curricular change toward greater emphasis on ethics and social responsibility may be unrealistic (Jensen, 2002;
Shleifer, 2004).

In sum, these findings suggest that the introduction, development, and
mainstreaming of CSR in higher education depends more on the implementation of appropriate individual-level incentives within universities
rather than institution-level, national pressures. We will return to this interpretation in the next section, given that respondents' answers to the survey
question about key success factors and barriers provide further insights.

KEY SUCCESS FACTORS AND BARRIERS

An examination of the tabulated key success factors and barriers to the
mainstreaming of CSR in higher education reveals high levels of similar-

Table 9.6.   Key Success Factors (KSFs) Behind Mainstreaming of CSR in European and Worldwide Education, Research and Training Programs

European Rank and KSF	European Average[a]	SD	Average Score (Rank) in Worldwide Sample
1. Faculty interest	4.52	.60	4.44 (1)
2. Dedicated teaching and research department/center	4.26	.91	4.20 (2)
3. Collaboration with companies	4.13	.79	3.98 (5)
4. New research outputs	4.10	.78	4.04 (4)
5. Student demand	4.06	.68	4.18 (3)
6. Teaching materials	3.96	.73	3.98 (6)
7. Collaboration with stakeholders	3.94	.79	3.91 (8)
8. Research funding	3.94	.89	3.94 (7)
9. Stakeholder input	3.91	.78	3.83 (10)
10. Corporate recruitment	3.75	.91	3.77 (11)
11. Collaboration with other schools	3.63	.91	3.58 (12)
12. Individual/company sponsorship or donations	3.62	.89	3.53 (13)
13. Accreditation	3.60	.89	3.85 (9)
14. National education policy	3.15	1.11	3.27 (14)

Note: $N = 75$ in European sample because of missing responses; $N = 131$ in worldwide sample. [a]Respondents scored the importance of these items, ranging from critical (5) to marginal (1).

ity between European and worldwide schools. Tables 9.6 (key success factors) and 9.7 (key barriers) confirm the previous conclusion that CSR education is mainly driven by lower-level, decentralized forces. Faculty interest, or lack thereof, ranked at the top of respondents' perceptions of both key success factors and barriers. Dedicated research or teaching centers were ranked second in explaining the mainstreaming of CSR issues in education, research, and training programs. National education policy was considered least important both in the European and worldwide samples. As mentioned before, this finding highlights the need to target incentive structures at the appropriate micro level (i.e. individual level) where university leaders and administrators can champion further growth in CSR education. Tables 9.6 and 9.7 combined indicate that greater support for empirical research (in the form of funding, research centers, and suitable publication outlets) represents the main lever for assisting in the mainstreaming of CSR in European business schools.

Table 9.7.   Key Barriers to Mainstreaming of CSR in European and Worldwide Education, Research and Training Programs

European Rank and Key Barrier	European Average[a]	SD	Average Score (Rank) in Worldwide Sample
1. Lack of faculty interest	3.65	1.17	3.71 (1)
2. Lack of research funding	3.57	1.06	3.62 (2)
3. Lack of collaboration with companies	3.45	.97	3.43 (4)
4. Lack of individual/company sponsorship or donations	3.39	1.02	3.37 (7)
5. Lack of student demand	3.28	1.15	3.51 (3)
6. Lack of corporate recruitment	3.27	1.03	3.40 (5)
7. Lack of collaboration with stakeholders	3.22	.96	3.30 (9)
8. Lack of dedicated teaching and research department/center	3.20	1.25	3.31 (8)
9. Lack of teaching materials	3.18	1.06	3.39 (6)
10. Lack of new research outputs	3.16	.78	3.23 (10)
11. Lack of national education policy	3.07	1.19	3.14 (12)
12. Lack of collaboration with other schools	3.08	1.00	3.14 (13)
13. Lack of stakeholder input	3.00	1.09	3.11 (11)
14. Accreditation	2.71	1.07	2.73 (14)

Note: $N = 75$ in European sample because of missing responses; $N = 130$ in worldwide sample. [a]Respondents scored the importance of these items, ranging from critical (5) to marginal (1).

CORPORATE SOCIAL RESPONSIBILITY TEACHING TECHNIQUES

Table 9.8 shows the different teaching tools (listed in order of decreasing frequency) used by European universities and business schools to convey CSR content. It suggests that the use of the different teaching tools in CSR education is remarkably homogeneous in the European sample. Apart from case studies, other widely used teaching tools are guest speakers, textbooks, research papers, and seminars. Of the surveyed tools, audiovisual media and field trips exhibit the lowest level of popularity among our respondents.

Compared to the findings of Matten and Moon (2004), teachers now rely more on the case method than in the past. The use of case studies increased from 25% in 2003 to 33% in 2007. These findings suggest that the field of CSR education has become somewhat more mature during the last 4 years. Arguably, this greater maturity is partly reflected in the increased availability of high-quality case studies either from European sources or those featuring European examples. For example, at the time of this report, the European Case Clearinghouse (http://www.ecch.com) listed over 1,000 European cases related to ethics, social responsibility, or sustainability. Interestingly, in Europe case studies seem to be most popular at the undergraduate and masters levels (where they were used in 44% and 43% of these two programs, respectively) rather than in MBA programs (where case studies were used in 29% of the surveyed full-time MBA programs and in 31% of the surveyed part-time MBA programs).

The survey answers also indicated diminished reliance on guest speakers. In 2003, 32% of the European respondents indicated they had invited business speakers (Matten & Moon, 2004). The percentages reported for other speakers from nongovernmental organizations (NGOs), CSR professionals, and communications/media representatives in the 2003 study were 20%, 17%, and 5%, respectively. In other words, at a minimum, 32 percent of all surveyed institutions had invited guest speakers in 2003 (assuming maximum overlap). At a maximum, the proportion of schools inviting guest speakers may have been as high as 74% (i.e., the combined percentages) in 2003. In the second survey, speakers of all types were combined into one overall category, and in that case only 27% of the respondents indicated their use at their institutions. Although highly relevant and eminently helpful in some contexts (Metrejean, Pittman, & Zarzeski, 2002), practitioner speeches often lack the kind of intellectual or analytic rigor required in advanced disciplines of academic study. The stories they tell may consist of little more than fascinating anecdotes and 'war stories,' which may or may not advance thinking about business ethics and social responsibility (LeClair, Ferrell, Montuori, & Willems, 1999). If, as our evidence suggests, there has been some maturing of the CSR field, then we might expect schools to be able to rely on faculty to deliver a greater proportion of the modules and programs. Nonetheless, in European institutions, speakers seem to be particularly popular at the undergraduate and masters level (35% each). The respondents reported the lowest use of guest speakers (21%) in full-time MBA programs, which may be explained by instructors' greater reliance on students' own work experience in class discussions. Given other indicators of the spread of CSR in Europe, class discussions can reasonably be expected to have included more explicit reference to CSR than was the case four years prior.

Overall, textbooks were just as widely used as guest speakers—by 27% of the responding institutions. Textbooks were seen to be especially useful at the undergraduate/diploma (40%) and masters (39%) levels. Research papers (25%), seminars (21%), audiovisual media (16%), and field trips (12%) rounded out the most common teaching methods and tools used in European universities and business schools. It is worth noting that semi-

Table 9.8. CSR Teaching Tools Proportion (%) of Respondents Using the Tool

	Overall Proportion (2003)	Overall Proportion (2007)	Undergrad (Bachelor, etc.)	MSc/MA	MBA (FT)	MBA (PT)	Executive	Tailored Executive
Case studies	25%	33%[ns]	44%	43%	29%	31%	26%	25%
Guest speakers	32%[a]	27%[ns]	35	35	21	25	26	22
Text books	NA	27%	40	39	24	25	19	14
Research papers	NA	25%	36	35	22	19	19	17
Seminars	NA	21%	31	24	19	21	15	15
Audiovisual media	17%	16%[ns]	19	25	14	15	11	10
Field trips	NA	12%	14	19	8	15	6	7

Notes: $N = 72$ in 2007 (because of missing responses), and was 166 in 2003. [a]This percentage refers to business speakers. In 2003, speakers were separated into three other subcategories: 20% speakers from nongovernmental organizations, 17% CSR professional speakers, and 5% communications/media speakers. ns = statistically nonsignificant change. Based on z values ($z = \dfrac{\hat{\pi}_1 - \hat{\pi}_2}{\sqrt{\hat{\pi}(1 - \hat{\pi})\left(\dfrac{1}{n_1} + \dfrac{1}{n_2}\right)}}$, where $\hat{\pi} = \dfrac{x_1 + x_2}{n_1 + n_2}$). Where no superscripts appear, incomplete information prevented calculations regarding statistical significance.

nars were more widely used in European undergraduate (31%) than masters programs (24%).

Clearly, the relationships between particular teaching tools and learning objectives are crucial (Morrell, 2004; Ricci & Markulis, 1990; Waddock, 1997). For example, if a goal is to encourage students to consider the importance of environmental sustainability, it would be important to know how (i.e., through which teaching tools) this change can be brought about most effectively. From a broader perspective, research should also investigate the effectiveness of program structure and course content for student learning (Windsor, 2008). Often, pedagogical efforts in CSR seemingly pit business against society, whereas a more positive approach would be to convey how the complex interdependencies between business and society can be managed for mutual gain (Gentile & Samuelson, 2005; Orlitzky, 2006; Porter & Kramer, 2006). Likewise, another crucial issue is that of moral frameworks (Donaldson, 2005). For some, a multitude of ethical perspectives may hinder rather than help student learning (Locke, 2006). Conversely, paradigmatic diversity might be most useful when the goals of CSR teaching concern the testing of assumptions and critical thinking (Morrell, 2004; Treviño & Brown, 2004).

Another consideration is the emerging consensus that management teaching ought to be evidence-based (Pfeffer & Sutton, 2006; Rousseau, 2006; Rousseau & McCarthy, 2007; Rynes, Giluk, & Brown, 2007). Although not necessarily pertinent to the teaching of values (Bennis & O'Toole, 2005; Crane, 1999), the considerable empirical knowledge about business ethics in general, and CSR more specifically, that has accumulated in the organizational sciences could be shared with CSR students (see, e.g., Frederick, 1995; Messick & Tenbrunsel, 1996; Orlitzky, 2008; Orlitzky & Swanson, 2008; Treviño & Weaver, 2003).

CORPORATE SOCIAL RESPONSIBILITY RESEARCH IN EUROPE

It has been argued that one of the deficiencies of management education is rooted in the failure to teach evidence-based decision making (Rousseau, 2006). Locke (2000), Pfeffer (1993), and several other authors argue that management education without firm grounding in scientific principles and findings is of dubious value. Without such cumulative research, business knowledge will remain meager (Hilmer & Donaldson, 1996; Rousseau & McCarthy, 2007). In this sense, teaching and research are—or, better, should be—inextricably linked in any discipline of business administration, including CSR. Of course, the linkages might differ from one management discipline to another. For example, our data show that European institutions are increasingly integrating CSR content into their teaching of Entrepreneurship, with 66% of our respondents claiming to discuss CSR issues in these courses. Such findings suggest that future surveys should tap the integration of CSR with discipline-based teaching in Europe in greater depth.

As Table 9.9 shows, over half of the respondents (58%) indicated that they had a dedicated center for CSR issues. Though slightly lower than the percentage of 66% reported by Jones Christensen et al.'s (2007) respondents, our finding suggests that, at many European institutions of

Table 9.9.   CSR Research

Our school has a dedicated center for research on BiS and/or CR issues.	58%
Institution works with companies to develop tools and information that business can use to mainstream BiS and/or CR knowledge into core business practices.	65%
School's faculty members engage with business practitioners and stakeholders in collaborative learning/knowledge development around BiS and/or CR issues.	77%
Our school has a particular research focus on BiS and/or CR issues.	81%
Faculty members in our school have published literature on BiS and/or CR issues (regardless of language).	86%
School supports a PhD program dedicated to support BiS and/or CR issues.	31%
School provides faculty supervision to PhD and postdoctoral students doing research around BiS and/or CR issues.	55%
Faculty members in our school engaged in research linked to BiS and/or CR issues.	88%
Faculty members in our school have published case studies and/or teaching cases on BiS and/or CR issues (regardless of language).	58%
School dedicates resources to support faculty in BiS and/or CR research and learning (e.g., travel and conference budgets, research center and staff, scholarships, seminars, library bursaries, Department Chairs).	82%
School's faculty members engage with other centers, departments and faculties within their institution to develop new interdisciplinary projects around BiS and/or CR issues.	68%
School's faculty members engage with researchers in other schools and universities to develop new projects around BiS and/or CR issues.	72%
Institution focuses on small and medium-sized enterprises (as well as multinational companies) in its research and education activities.	84%

Note: $N = 55$ because of missing responses. BiS = business in society, CR = corporate responsibility.

higher education, faculty members have some institutional support for CSR research. Another finding from the second survey highlights the seemingly close cooperation between industry and researchers in CSR initiatives. More specifically, 65% of the respondents reported that their institution worked with industry to develop tools and information for mainstreaming CSR into core business practices (second row of Table 9.9). Similarly, 77% of respondents indicated that faculty members at their institutions were involved in collaborative learning projects with industry (third row of Table 9.9).

The other frequencies reported in Table 9.9 reaffirm this optimistic view of CSR research. For example, 81% of the respondents reported a research focus on CSR issues, while 86% indicated that their faculty members had publications in CSR. Again, without such research dissemination, the growth of evidence-based management will be stunted (Rousseau & McCarthy, 2007). As Table 9.9 shows, it appears that the schools that responded to the second survey were actively involved in CSR knowledge creation and dissemination. At the same time, the proportion of respondents that reported the existence of a PhD program dedicated to CSR issues increased by only six percentage points, that is, from 25% to 31%, in the last 4 years. However, PhD supervision of CSR projects has, remarkably, increased from 25% to 55% in the same time period (a change statistically significant at a level alpha of .05). Taken together, these findings and developments suggest that CSR research has come a long way and, in fact, has matured since the first European survey of CSR education.

As in the earlier study (Matten & Moon, 2004), the framing of CSR research continues to be extremely diverse. Table 9.10 lists the schools' CSR research topics as described by respondents. As in Matten and Moon's study, some areas were combined with others to form aggregate clusters. Though quite similar to the topics in Table 9.10, the PhD student research topics are even more heterogeneous, as shown in Table 9.11. Arguably, the most interesting trend with respect to the figures presented in those two tables concerns the dramatic percentage increase in corporate social responsibility (CSR)/performance (CSP) research topics. Four years earlier, business ethics generally predominated, with 36% of respondents indicating the existence of such a research focus at their business schools. In 2007 issues in CSR and CSP topped established and aspiring researchers' agendas (at 52% in general, as shown in Table 9.10; and used as keywords in 18% of PhD students' research, as shown in Table 9.11), with the predominance being notably greater than the predominance of business ethics four years earlier. This may indicate a shift toward CSR research becoming a more mainstream topic in management journals and business schools (see Lockett, Moon, & Visser, 2006). The way forward,

Table 9.10.   Areas of CSR Faculty Research Focus

Research Topic	Percentage (2003)	Percentage (2007)
Corporate social responsibility	20	52
Sustainability/natural environment	17	31
Business ethics	36	21
Corporate governance	17	14
Strategy	5	10
Accounting/finance	13	7
Globalization	11	7
International management	NA	7
Leadership	3	7
Organizational change	NA	7
Stakeholder management	12	7
Bottom of the pyramid	NA	3
Business and society	4	3
Climate change	NA	3
Community investment	NA	3
Corporate reputation	1	3
Diversity	NA	3
Entrepreneurship	NA	3
Environmental management	21	3
Health issues	NA	3
Human resource management	NA	3
Industrial policy	NA	3
Knowledge management	NA	3
Millennium development goals	NA	3
Privatization	NA	3
Risk	NA	3
Technology management	NA	3
Values	NA	3
Virtue ethics	NA	3

Note: $N = 61$ (in 2007) and 166 (in 2003).

though, is not obvious. While some influential researchers promote theoretical consensus (Donaldson, 1995; Pfeffer, 1993), others think research diversity will, in fact, provide the best chance of progress in the organizational sciences (Van Maanen, 1995). In other words, it may not serve theory development for CSR and CSP to subsume ethics in mainstream research.

Table 9.9.   Keywords of PhD Student Research Topics

Keywords Used in PhD Research	Percentage
Corporate (social) responsibility and performance	17.8
Business ethics/Ethics	9.3
Strategy/CSR strategy	6.8
Sustainability natural environment	6.8
Corporate governance	5.1
Environmental management	5.1
Stakeholder management/theory	5.1
Entrepreneurship/social entrepreneurship	3.4
International management/business	3.4
Organizational change	3.4
Social accounting and accountability	3.4
Globalization	2.5
Small and medium size enterprises	2.5
Leadership	2.5
Corporate citizenship	1.7
Corporate reputation	1.7
Fair trade	1.7
Nonprofit organizations	1.7
Supply chain management	1.7
Accounting/finance	0.8
Altruism	0.8
Bottom of the pyramid	0.8
Corporate philanthropy	0.8
Diversity	0.8
Economic democracy	0.8
Healthcare	0.8
Humanitarian operations	0.8
Intangible assets	0.8
Knowledge management	0.8
Marketing	0.8
NGO management	0.8
Social capital	0.8
Socially responsible investment	0.8
Trust	0.8
Virtue ethics	0.8
Values	0.8

Note: N = 77.

DISCUSSION

The second European survey of CSR education has provided a timely opportunity to consider developments in the field over the previous four years and examine regional contrasts within Europe. On the basis of this study, we can conclude that CSR education has come a long way in Europe. Earlier in this chapter we tracked European changes since 2003 and described the general increase in CSR coursework, which was most pronounced for dedicated CSR programs and optional CSR modules at the Masters level. However, we also found that, in some cases, CSR program offerings had declined, albeit only slightly, as was the case with dedicated CSR programs in MBA and Executive education. Interestingly, there was little difference in the level of CSR education among different European regions (i.e., between the British Isles, France/Benelux, Central Europe, and Southern Europe). We also noted that CSR research seems to have become more firmly embedded in European universities. In general, all these changes illustrate the maturing of CSR as a field of study. Arguably, this greater maturity might also be reflected in the greater relative use of European case studies and the decreasing use of guest speakers as teaching tools in CSR education.

In general, respondents seem to consider faculty- and university-level forces the main drivers of the introduction, development, and successful mainstreaming of CSR education. Consistent with reports in 2003 (Matten & Moon, 2004), those responding to the subsequent survey, by and large, rejected national-level policies as important determinants of CSR research and education. It is worth noting that these findings may be explained by phenomena akin to the ones invoked by Matten and Moon (2008) to explain the increase in explicit CSR initiatives in European companies: the decline of national governments in emerging systems of societal governance and the effects of new institutionalism in global management (see DiMaggio & Powell, 1983; Meyer, 2000; Meyer & Rowan, 1977). This development may have been prompted in part by the homogenization of institutional environments across national boundaries, leading to increasingly standardized and rationalized practices legitimized by three key processes: coercive, mimetic, and normative forces (DiMaggio & Powell). We tentatively suggest that organizations like the European Academy of Business in Society and the Aspen Institute contributed to similar standardization processes in CSR education, especially given the extent of European and international networking by CSR educators and the relative homogeneity of CSR educational resources,

Our findings also raise the important issue of implementing appropriate faculty-level incentives for stimulating further growth in CSR education. Examples might be case study awards for fostering new university-industry collaborations, faculty workshops, and faculty mentoring across CSR and other disciplinary boundaries.

Study Limitations

Some limitations of the study ought to be mentioned. First, the response rate was relatively low (20.1%). However, we can argue that our response rate was broadly consistent with that of the first survey (which had a response rate of 24.8%) as well as other studies (e.g., Baruch, 1999). We concluded that the data gathered might be less representative of all CSR education and, instead, might be more indicative of best practices in CSR education.

Second, our survey data, combined with the small sample size, did not allow for testing of cause-effect linkages with respect to European CSR teaching. For example, we do not currently know what factors generally lead to universities' greater commitment to CSR. However, web-based research has identified a variety of factors (e.g., a quest for distinct organizational identity) that may explain the existence of ethics teaching in business schools (Cornelius et al., 2007). Moreover, it is unknown whether greater student exposure to CSR (and related course content) will lead to more responsible decision making in organizations.

Suggestions for Future Research

Based on these study limitations, several issues could be addressed in future research. First, differences in teaching methods and techniques may not necessarily suggest the appropriateness of different teaching tools for different learning objectives. In some contexts, case studies might be the most appropriate teaching tool. In others, field trips perhaps should be used. The point is that more research is needed on the match between particular teaching tools and learning objectives. We clearly need to know more about which teaching tools best serve different learning objectives and how and why they do. The predominance of case studies only suggests that they are the most popular teaching tool, but not that they are necessarily the most effective one. From a broader perspective, we also suggest more research on the significance of program structure and course design for student learning about the complexities of business and society relations. This would include references to the most suitable moral frameworks for helping student learning in CSR education. Equally important, future research might usefully investigate the extent and effectiveness of such evidence-based learning of CSR issues.

Finally, there is increasing interest in experiential learning in business ethics and business and society programs. We need to understanding if, how, and why this approach can improve student learning – and subsequent managerial behavior.

CONCLUSION

Our chapter offers several key conclusions. First, notwithstanding patterns of decline and continuity in some areas and by some measures, and despite evidence that business school representatives may exaggerate the extent of their CSR education, we have found overall continuing growth in CSR education in Europe. This is true of enrollments and modules. The growth was most marked among dedicated Masters and undergraduate programs. Within the different forms of Executive education there has been a particular growth in tailored programs. This growth appears most marked among schools which might describe themselves as following the best practice in the field. There were no statistically different findings in levels of enrollment between schools in different European regions. Our view that this might reflect new institutional forces in the CSR teaching profession appears to be supported by our finding that teaching techniques were also relatively homogeneous.

Second, turning to drivers of European CSR education, we found that individual faculty remained the most important driver on both counts. This, along with CSR research capacity, is regarded as the key success factor in the mainstreaming of CSR education. Perhaps indicative of the growing importance with which CSR is regarded, there has been an increase in the importance of university leadership as a driver of both the introduction and mainstreaming of CSR education. Another increasingly significant driver is students, a clear sign of a market demand. Governments and shareholders alike were perceived among the least important drivers in general.

Third, our findings on the key success factors for and obstacles to CSR education echo the significance of decentralized factors noted above. Faculty interest and dedicated teaching and research centers are regarded as critical.

Fourth, our evidence suggests a maturation of CSR as an academic field within European business schools, notably in the increased use of case studies, the decline in use of guest speakers, and the consolidation of CSR research in business schools. This finding is further confirmed by the integration of CSR issues into other business school courses.

ACKNOWLEDGMENTS

The authors are grateful to the European Academy of Business in Society for providing us with the data and the financial support for the analysis and to the International Centre for Corporate Social Responsibility which administered the project.

NOTES

1. The second survey was conducted by the European Association for Business in Society (EABiS) with the support of the European Foundation for Management Development and the International Centre for Corporate Social Responsibility (ICCSR). This second survey was described as investigating *business in society and corporate responsibility research, education and other initiatives in business schools and universities*. The report on which this chapter is based was prepared by the ICCSR for EABiS.
2. The first survey was conducted by the International Centre for Corporate Social Responsibility (ICCSR) at the Nottingham University Business School in 2003 (Matten & Moon, 2004) with the support of the European Academy of Business in Society (EABiS) and the UN Global Compact. This survey invited responses about CSR or business ethics, corporate citizenship, sustainability, corporate environmental management, business and society, business and governance, business and globalization, stakeholder management, sustainability, and governance.
3. See related arguments about drawing conclusions from best case examples in Matten and Moon (2004) and Jones Christensen et al. (2007).
4. The comparisons rest on the assumption that the sampling frames and populations of Matten and Moon (2004) and this study are comparable. Nothing with respect to study design or the definition of the European population suggests that the observations in the studies are incommensurate, although the sample compositions differ. Because the sample sizes (N) were different, we report the changes and trends as proportions and not as raw numbers.
5. Masters courses (usually MA and MSc) differ from MBA courses in that they are usually (a) designed as academic rather than academic/vocational programs, (b) open to students straight from BA programs (as opposed to involving time in management prerequisites), and (c) designed to be one year in length on a full-time basis.

REFERENCES

Aaronson, S., & Reeves, J. (2002). *The European response to public demands for global corporate responsibility*. Washington, DC: National Policy Association.

Albareda, L., Lozano, J. M., & Ysa, T. (2007). Public policies on corporate social responsibility: The role of governments in Europe. *Journal of Business Ethics, 74*, 391-407.

Armstrong, J. S. (2007). Statistical significance tests are unnecessary even when properly done and properly interpreted: Reply to commentaries. *International Journal of Forecasting, 23*(2), 335-336.

Balch, O. (2007). Flexible courses and more focused teaching at Europe's schools. *Ethical Corporation, Business Education Special Report,* 8-9.

Baruch, Y. (1999). Response rate in academic studies: A comparative analysis. *Human Relations, 52*(4), 421-438.

Bennis, W., & O'Toole, J. (2005). How business schools lost their way. *Harvard Business Review, 83*(5), 96-104.

Black, B. S. (1998). Shareholder activism and corporate governance in the United States. In P. Newman (Ed.), *The new Palgrave dictionary of economics and the law* (pp. 459-465). Manchester, United Kingdom: Palgrave Macmillan.

Cohen, J. (1988). *Statistical power for the behavioral sciences* (2nd ed.). Hillsdale, NJ: Erlbaum.

Cohen, J. (1990). Things I have learned (so far). *American Psychologist, 45*, 1304-1312.

Cohen, J. (1992). A power primer. *Psychological Bulletin, 112*(1), 155-159.

Cohen, J. (1994). The Earth is round ($p < .05$). *American Psychologist, 49*, 997-1003.

Cornelius, N., Wallace, J., & Tassabehji, R. (2007). An analysis of corporate social responsibility, corporate identity and ethics teaching in business schools. *Journal of Business Ethics, 76*(1), 117-135.

Corporate social responsibility: Do it right. (2008, January 17). Corporate social responsibility: Do it right. *The Economist,* 8-14.

Crane, A. (1999). Are you ethical? Please tick Yes or No: On researching ethics in business organizations. *Journal of Business Ethics, 20*, 237-248.

David, P., Bloom, M., & Hillman, A. J. (2007). Investor activism, managerial responsiveness, and corporate social performance. *Strategic Management Journal, 28*, 91-100.

DiMaggio, P. J., & Powell, W. W. (1983). The iron cage revisited: Institutional isomorphism and collective rationality in organizational fields. *American Sociological Review, 48*, 147-160.

Donaldson, L. (1995). *American anti-management theories of organization: A critique of paradigm proliferation.* Cambridge, England: Cambridge University Press.

Donaldson, L. (2005). For positive management theories while retaining science: Reply to Ghoshal. *Academy of Management Learning & Education, 4*, 109-113.

Enderle, G. (1996). A comparison of business ethics in North America and continental Europe. *Business Ethics: A European Review, 5*(1), 33-46.

Enderle, G. (1997). A worldwide survey of business ethics in the 1990s. *Journal of Business Ethics, 16*, 1475-1483.

European Commission. (2001). *Green paper: Promoting a European framework for corporate social responsibility.* Brussels, Belgium: Author.

European Commission. (2002). *Corporate social responsibility: A business contribution to sustainable development.* Brussels, Belgium: Author.

European Commission. (2006). *Implementing the partnership for growth and jobs: Making Europe a pole of excellence on corporate social responsibility*. Brussels, Belgium: Author.

Frederick, W. C. (1995). *Values, nature, and culture in the American corporation*. New York, NY: Oxford University Press.

Gentile, M. C., & Samuelson, J. F. (2005). Keynote address to the AACSB International Deans Conference, 10 Feb. 2003: The state of affairs for management education and social responsibility. *Academy of Management Learning & Education, 4*, 496-505.

Gillan, S. L., & Starks, L. T. (2000). Corporate governance proposals and shareholder activism: The role of institutional investors. *Journal of Financial Economics, 57*, 275-305.

Golden, B. R. (1992). The past is the past--or is it? The use of retrospective accounts as indicators of past strategy. *Academy of Management Journal, 35*, 848-860.

Golden, B. R. (1997). Further remarks on retrospective accounts in organizational and strategic management research. *Academy of Management Journal, 40*(5), 1243-1252.

Habisch, A., Jonker, J., Wegner, M., & Schmidpeter, R. (Eds.). (2005). *Corporate social responsibility across Europe*. New York, NY: Springer.

Hall, P. A., & Soskice, D. (Eds.). (2001). *Varieties of capitalism*. Oxford, England: Oxford University Press.

Hambrick, D. C. (2007). The field of management's devotion to theory: Too much of a good thing? *Academy of Management Journal, 50*(6), 1346-1352.

Harlow, L. L., Mulaik, S. A., & Steiger, J. H. (1997). *What if there were no significance tests?* Mahwah, NJ: Erlbaum.

Hilmer, F. G., & Donaldson, L. (1996). *Management redeemed: Debunking the fads that undermine corporate performance*. East Roseville, Australia: Free Press Australia.

Hunter, J. E. (1997). Needed: A ban on the significance test. *Psychological Science, 8*(1), 3-7.

Jensen, M. C. (2002). Value maximization, stakeholder theory, and the corporate objective function. *Business Ethics Quarterly, 12*(2), 235-256.

Jones Christensen, L., Peirce, E., Hartman, L. P., Hoffman, W. M., & Carrier, J. (2007). Ethics, CSR, and sustainability education in the *Financial Times* top 50 global business schools: Baseline data and future research directions. *Journal of Business Ethics, 73*, 347-368.

Kirp, D. L. (2003). *Shakespeare, Einstein and the bottom line: The marketing of higher education*. Cambridge, MA: Harvard University Press.

Kline, R. B. (2004). *Beyond significance testing: Reforming data analysis methods in behavioral research*. Washington, DC: American Psychological Association.

LeClair, D. T., Ferrell, L., Montuori, L., & Willems, C. (1999). The use of a behavioral simulation to teach business ethics. *Teaching Business Ethics, 3*, 283-296.

Locke, E. A. (2006). Business ethics: A way out of the morass. *Academy of Management Learning & Education, 5*(3), 324-332.

Locke, E. A. (2007). The case for inductive theory building. *Journal of Management, 33*(6), 867-890.

Locke, E. A. (Ed.). (2000). *The Blackwell handbook of principles of organizational behavior.* Oxford, England: Blackwell.

Lockett, A., Moon, J., & Visser, W. (2006). Corporate social responsibility in management research: Focus, nature, salience and sources of influence. *Journal of Management Studies, 43*(1), 115-136.

Mahoney, J. (1990). *Teaching business ethics in the UK, Europe and the USA: A comparative study.* London, England: Athlone.

Matten, D., & Moon, J. (2004). Corporate social responsibility education in Europe. *Journal of Business Ethics, 54,* 323-337.

Matten, D., & Moon, J. (2008). Implicit and explicit CSR: A conceptual framework for understanding CSR in Europe. *Academy of Management Review, 33*(2), 404-424.

Messick, D. M., & Tenbrunsel, A. E. (Eds.). (1996). *Codes of conduct: Behavioral research into business ethics.* New York, NY: Russell Sage Foundation.

Metrejean, C., Pittman, J., & Zarzeski, M. T. (2002). Guest speakers: Reflections on the role of accountants in the classroom. *Accounting Education, 11*(4), 347-364.

Meyer, J. W. (2000). Globalization: Sources and effects on national states and societies. *International Sociology, 15,* 233-248.

Meyer, J. W., & Rowan, B. (1977). Institutionalized organizations: Formal structure as myth and ceremony. *American Journal of Sociology, 83,* 340-363.

Moratis, L., Hoff, J., & Reul, B. (2006). A dual challenge facing management education: Simulation-based learning and learning about CSR. *Journal of Management Development, 25*(3), 213-231.

Morrell, K. (2004). Socratic dialogue as a tool for teaching business ethics. *Journal of Business Ethics, 53,* 383-392.

Muijen, H. S. C. A. (2004). Corporate social responsibility starts at university. *Journal of Business Ethics, 53,* 235-246.

Nash, L. L. (1994). Why business ethics now? In J. Drummond & B. Bain (Eds.), *Managing business ethics* (pp. 7-24). Oxford, England: Butterworth-Heinemann.

Oakes, M. L. (1986). *Statistical inference: A commentary for the social and behavioral sciences.* New York, NY: Wiley.

Orlitzky, M. (2006). Links between corporate social responsibility and corporate financial performance: Theoretical and empirical determinants. In J. Allouche (Ed.), *Corporate social responsibility: Vol. 2. Performances and stakeholders* (Vol. 2, pp. 41-64). London, England: Palgrave Macmillan.

Orlitzky, M. (2008). Corporate social performance and financial performance: A research synthesis. In A. Crane, A. McWilliams, D. Matten, J. Moon & D. Siegel (Eds.), *The Oxford handbook of CSR* (pp. 113-134). Oxford, England: Oxford University Press.

Orlitzky, M., & Swanson, D. L. (2008). *Toward integrative corporate citizenship: Research advances in corporate social performance.* London, England: Palgrave Macmillan.

Pfeffer, J. (1993). Barriers to the advance of organizational science: Paradigm development as a dependent variable. *Academy of Management Review, 18*(4), 599-620.

Pfeffer, J., & Sutton, R. I. (2006). *Hard facts, dangerous half-truths, and total nonsense: Profiting from evidence-based management.* Boston, MA: Harvard Business School Press.

Porter, M. E., & Kramer, M. R. (2006). Strategy & society: The link between competitive advantage and corporate social responsibility. *Harvard Business Review, 84*(12), 78-92.

Preuss, L. (1999). Ethical theory in German business ethics research. *Journal of Business Ethics, 18*, 407-419.

Ricci, P., & Markulis, P. M. (1990). Can ethics be taught? A simulation tests a traditional ethics pedagogy. *Developments in Business Simulation & Experiential Exercises, 17*, 141-145.

Rousseau, D. M. (2006). Is there such a thing as "evidence-based management"? *Academy of Management Review, 31*(2), 256-269.

Rousseau, D. M., & McCarthy, S. (2007). Educating managers from an evidence-based perspective. *Academy of Management Learning & Education, 6*(1), 84-101.

Rozeboom, W. W. (1997). Good science is abductive, not hypothetico-deductive. In L. L. Harlow, S. A. Mulaik & J. H. Steiger (Eds.), *What if there were no significance tests?* (pp. 335-391). Hillsdale, NJ: Erlbaum.

Russell, J. (2007). Management education's big tent approach. *Ethical corporation, business education Special Report,* 19.

Rynes, S. L., Giluk, T. L., & Brown, K. G. (2007). The very separate worlds of academic and practitioner periodicals in human resource management: Implications for evidence-based management. *Academy of Management Journal, 50*(5), 987-1006.

Schmidt, F. L. (1992). What do data really mean? Research findings, meta-analysis, and cumulative knowledge in psychology. *American Psychologist, 47*, 1173-1181.

Schmidt, F. L. (1996). Statistical significance testing and cumulative knowledge in psychology: Implications for training and researchers. *Psychological Methods, 1*, 115-129.

Schmidt, F. L., & Hunter, J. E. (2002). Are there benefits from NHST? *American Psychologist, 57*(1), 65-66.

Sedlmeier, P., & Gigerenzer, G. (1989). Do studies of statistical power have an effect on the power of studies? *Psychological Bulletin, 105*, 309-316.

Shleifer, A. (2004). Does competition destroy ethical behavior? *American Economic Review, 94*(2), 414-418.

Spence, L. (2000). Teaching business ethics: Are there differences within Europe, and is there a European difference? *Business Ethics: A European Review, 9*(1), 58-64.

Starkey, K., & Tiratsoo, N. (2007). *The business school and the bottom line.* Cambridge, England: Cambridge University Press.

Treviño, L. K., & Brown, M. E. (2004). Managing to be ethical: Debunking five business ethics myths. *Academy of Management Executive, 18*, 69-81.

Treviño, L. K., & Weaver, G. R. (2003). *Managing ethics in business organizations: Social scientific perspectives.* Stanford, CA: Stanford University Press.

Tukey, J. W. (1991). The philosophy of multiple comparisons. *Statistical Science, 6*, 100-116.

Van Maanen, J. (1995). Style as theory. *Organization Science, 6*(1), 133-143.

Vogel, D. (1993). Differing national approaches to business ethics. *Business Ethics: A European Review, 2*(3), 164-171.

Vogel, D. (2005). *The market for virtue: The potential and limits of corporate social responsibility.* Washington, DC: Brookings Institution Press.

Waddock, S. (Ed.). (1997). *Research in corporate social performance and policy (Supplement 2).* Greenwich, CT: JAI.

Whitley, R. (1997). Business systems. In A. Sorge & M. Warner (Eds.), *The IEBM handbook of organizational behaviour.* London, England: International Thomson Business Press.

Windsor, D. (2008). Educating for responsible management. In A. Crane, A. McWilliams, D. Matten, J. Moon & D. Siegel (Eds.), *Oxford handbook of corporate social responsibility.* Oxford, England: Oxford University Press.

Zsolnai, L. (Ed.). (1998). *The European difference: Business ethics in the community of European management schools.* Boston, MA: Kluwer.

CHAPTER 10

ASSESSING THE INTEGRATION OF ETHICS ACROSS TWO BUSINESS SCHOOLS' CURRICULA

A Longitudinal Assessment

INTRODUCTION

While many business schools are debating the value of creating a stand-alone business ethics course versus integrating ethics across the business school curriculum, Duquesne University's Palumbo Donahue Schools of Business responded to this either-or opportunity with a resounding yes to both! However, by accepting both dimensions of the ethics education challenge, the business schools also must address the assessment of the impact of a course and the integration of business ethics. The impact of the stand-alone business ethics course at Duquesne's business schools is profiled in *Advancing Business Ethics Education* (Weber, Gerde, & Wasieleski, 2008, pp. 85-101). Therefore, this chapter seeks to report the

Toward Assessing Business Ethics Education
pp. 177–190

efforts undertaken to assess the effectiveness (or lack thereof) of integrating ethics across the business schools' curricula through a longitudinal analysis of these efforts by replicating an initial review 7 years later. The results of both assessments are provided next, with an analysis and set of recommendations presented in conclusion as a guide for others seeking to integrate ethics across the business school curriculum and wanting to assess the effectiveness of these efforts.

INITIAL ASSESSMENT: 2001

Ethics is an important component of Duquesne University's mission and vision. This was clearly indicated when the university's strategic plan described the goal of developing our national reputation for academic excellence by noting that "the university will place special emphasis on ethics" (Duquesne University, n.d.-a, p. 4). In following the university's commitment to ethics education, the John F. Donahue Graduate School of Business and the A.J. Palumbo School of Business Administration at Duquesne University similarly acknowledge the importance of ethics. A key, guiding principle for these business schools is to "espouse ethics as a winning characteristic of organizations that are successful over the long term and promote a commitment to high standards and values among the Duquesne community" (Duquesne University, n.d.-b, p. 114). This commitment is echoed in the graduate school's catalog. "Since its founding in 1878, Duquesne University has been steadfast in developing an ethical perspective within students' professional and private lives. The Donahue School strives to perpetuate that unique commitment through the required course in 'Applied Business Ethics' and the integration of ethical dimensions of decision-making throughout the curriculum" (Duquesne University, n.d.-c, p. 9).

Based on the attention afforded ethics in the university and schools' missions, the business schools' dean, James C. Stalder, directed me, because of my role as director of the Beard Center for Leadership in Ethics, to undertake a project to determine if (and, if necessary, to ensure that) ethics was emphasized across the business schools' curricula. The first effort in launching this project was to benchmark the state of ethics in the business schools' curricula. I drafted a semistructured protocol and Zuzana Hartosova, my graduate research assistant, was directed to interview the business school's full-time faculty members using this semistructured protocol.[1] These interviews were conducted during the fall 2001 term in the faculty members' offices. The semistructured interview procedure afforded each faculty member wide latitude in how they understood the questions and wished to respond. Each faculty member was promised anonymity, thus the results are presented in the statistical aggregate, preventing the identification of any single faculty member.

Interview Respondents

Hartosova attempted to contact each full-time business school faculty member over a 4-week period. Some faculty members were unavailable, despite repeated efforts at making contact or arranging a convenient interview time. In total, 37 of the 43 full-time business school faculty members were interviewed, representing an 86% response rate. The departmental breakdown of the respondents can be seen in Table 10.1. For two of the five departments, every full-time faculty member was interviewed, in two other departments only one or two faculty members were not interviewed, and, in the worst case, 3 of the 11 faculty members in one department were not interviewed despite repeated efforts to secure an interview. In total, only 6 of the 43 full-time business school faculty members were not included in this study.

As mentioned earlier, wide latitude was provided for the respondents in how they understood the questions and chose to answer them. Hartosova recorded the responses and later, along with me, identified eight different types of responses: general in-class discussion, discussion of cases from the course textbook, extensive or frequent attention to ethics, presentation of the relevant professional code of ethics, attendance at the ethics speaker program, involvement in community service, assignment of an ethics-based paper or question on an exam, and emphasis on the importance of ethics during the student's internship or job. We attempted to find similarities across the eight initial groupings and four distinctive activity groups emerged: ethics in the classroom, extracurricular ethics activities, testing on ethics, and ethics at work. These activity groups represent different approaches taken by faculty members to integrate ethics into their business school courses.

Interview Findings

The first activity group discovered from analyzing the interview material involved conducting a discussion regarding an ethical issue or situation in class. Many of the faculty members (30 of 37, 81%) reported a general or occasional discussion of ethics or a current ethical issue in their classes, as shown in Table 10.1. Nearly half of the faculty members (18 of 37, 49%) used a chapter devoted to ethical issues from their required course's textbook as the basis to frame or begin the discussion.

Table 10.1. 2001 Results

Department	Interviews/ Out of	Ethics in the Classroom			Extracurricular Ethics Activities			Testing on Ethics	Ethics at Work
		General In-Class Discussion	Case From Textbook	Extensive Attention to Ethics Cases	Professional Code Covered	Attendance at Ethics Speaker Program	Community Service	Assignment or Test on Ethics	Emphasis on Ethics During Internships or Work
A	6/7	5	5	2	2	3	0	2	0
B	8/11	4	0	0	0	0	0	0	0
C	9/9	8	6	4	0	2	0	0	1
D	7/9	7	4	4	0	2	2	5	1
E	7/7	6	3	3	1	0	1	2	0
Total	37/43	30/37	18/37	13/37	3/37	7/37	3/37	9/37	2/37
	86%	81%	49%	35%	8%	19%	8%	24%	5%

Thirteen faculty members (or 35%) described their courses as incorporating an in-depth attention to ethics by using multiple ethics cases for discussion. These cases were either provided in the course textbook or the faculty member supplemented the textbook with prepared ethics cases or current ethical issues found in the news. To place in this category, the coverage of ethics or attention to ethics must be more extensive or frequent than a general or occasional discussion of ethics or ethical issues related to the course. And, finally, three faculty members (or 8%) presented their discipline's professional code of ethics as a starter for an ethics discussion among the students.

Since some faculty members used a combination of these activities to foster an ethics discussion, the numbers for each of these activities, seen in Table 10.1, total more than the number of respondents. Overall, this was by far the most common method of emphasizing ethics in the classroom by the faculty members, accounting for 64 of the 120 activities (or 53%) mentioned in the interviews.

The second most common group of activities for introducing ethics into the curricula by the faculty members was through encouraging students to attend an ethics speaker presentation or become involved in a community service activity. More than one out of every four faculty members mentioned these activities as part of their business courses, accounting for 27% of all activities emphasizing ethics.

Each semester the Beard Center for Leadership in Ethics hosts a distinguished ethics speaker. Seven faculty members indicated that they require, assign extra credit, or simply encourage their students to attend this presentation to learn more about ethics and/or as a professional development activity. Occasionally the ethics speaker's presentation was discussed in class or students attending the presentation prepared a written report. In addition, three faculty members indicated that they emphasize ethics in their classroom by having their students engage in community service. This activity is a requirement for two of the faculty member's courses, for the other it is an extra credit opportunity.

The third activity group for emphasizing ethics across the business school curricula is testing students on their ability to recognize an ethical issue in a business case or analyze a business case using ethical principles or tools. Nine faculty members (or 24% of the activities mentioned in the interviews) described a course assignment (either an examination or essay paper) where the ability to use an ethical decision-making tool was used as part of the overall assignment's grade. In some cases it was a matter of recognizing an ethical issue embedded in a business situation or case. In other course assignments, the students were required to reason to an ethically defensible solution in resolving the ethics case or evaluate the ethical defensibility of a business manager's actions when faced with an ethical dilemma.

The fourth activity group described in the faculty members' interviews involved emphasizing the importance of ethics as students begin their business careers or internships. Although employment or an internship is often beyond the scope of the classroom, two faculty members reported a discussion in class focusing on the ethical challenges likely encountered by students during their school-sponsored internships or during the students' early work experience.

Conclusions and Recommendations

Did the business school faculty members at Duquesne University in 2001 fully emphasize ethics across the curricula? Yes and no. It is clear that ethics had a significant presence in an overwhelming number of courses taught by our full-time faculty members. But, was it present in every course? No. And we should note that part-time business school faculty members were not included in the interviews, so we are unable to assess the emphasis of ethics in their business courses. (Part-time faculty members teach only a small portion of the courses in the business schools' curricula, however.)

We can conclude that, for those wanting ethics to be integrated across the business school curriculum, they should be quite pleased with the findings from this survey. Faculty members appeared motivated by their own personal interest in ethics and ethical issues, as well as aided by the inclusion of ethics material in the required textbooks used in their courses. Additional opportunities for emphasizing ethics came from the adoption of codes of ethics by various professional associations and the ethics speakers program hosted by the Beard Center for Leadership in Ethics each semester.

The 2001 investigation suggested a number of additional supportive programs that could be launched as the business schools seek to fully integrate ethics across the curricula:

1. Develop ethics case material for each business school disciplines, especially for faculty members in Department B, as well as integrative cross-discipline ethics cases;
2. Distribute and encourage the discussion of professional codes of conduct relevant to the faculty member's particular business school discipline;
3. Sponsor programs, administered by the Beard Center for Leadership in Ethics, that emphasize ethical challenges facing specific

business disciplines, enabling students in finance or information technology, for example, to attend the presentation and then discuss the presentation when returning to class;

4. Support faculty members by placing students in community service opportunities related to their discipline, such as accounting students helping the elderly complete their tax forms, or marketing students educating at-risk consumers;

5. Conduct faculty workshops on how to introduce or analyze ethical issues in the classroom, utilizing the ethical decision-making frameworks presented in both the undergraduate and graduate required business ethics courses; and,

6. Offer professional development workshops for students, utilizing exemplary ethical leaders from the business community, to emphasize the importance of ethical behavior by employees or interns in business organizations.

In conclusion, significant progress had been made by 2001 in emphasizing ethics across the business schools' curricula at Duquesne University, but additional effort was still possible.

REPLICATION ASSESSMENT: 2008

Based on the attention afforded ethics in the university and schools' missions and at the encouragement of the new business school dean, Dr. Alan Miciak, I sought to replicate the 2001 schools of business study to assess the extent of the integration of ethics across the business schools' curricula in 2008. His quest was to uncover how ethics is integrated across the undergraduate and graduate curricula and to see if ethics continued to be emphasized across the business schools' curricula during the past decade. To achieve these goals, I drafted a semistructured protocol and trained Knut Kipper, my graduate research assistant, to interview the business school's full-time faculty members using this semistructured protocol.[2] The first round of these interviews was conducted during the fall 2008 term when Kipper visited the faculty members in their offices. The semistructured interview procedure afforded each faculty member wide latitude in how they understood the questions and responded. To complete the data collection phase of the project, Kipper resorted to an e-mailed survey of the semistructured interview in the final round of the data collection, since some faculty members were unable to meet with Kipper. Less than 10% of the information was collected through the e-mail survey technique. Each faculty member was promised anonymity, thus the results are presented in the statistical aggregate, preventing the identification of any single faculty member.

Interview Respondents

Kipper attempted to contact each full-time business school faculty member over a 4-week period. Some faculty members were unavailable, despite repeated efforts at making contact or arranging a convenient interview time. In total, 55 of the 61 full-time business school faculty members were interviewed either face to face or by e-mail, representing a 90.2% response rate. The departmental breakdown of the respondents can be seen in Table 10.2. As mentioned earlier, wide latitude was provided the respondents in how they understood the questions and chose to answer them. Kipper recorded the responses and, based on this information, Weber cataloged the responses into the activity groups created for the 2001 study. The ethics at work activity group was removed from the analysis since it was not mentioned during any of the faculty member interviews.

Interview Findings

In total, 47 of the 55 faculty members contacted reported that they integrate ethics into their courses (85.5%). No differences were mentioned regarding the level of the courses taught, undergraduate versus graduate. As noted in Table 10.2, two departments had merged since 2001. It is also noteworthy that one department—Department D—was unanimous in their integration of ethics into their courses. The remaining divisions ranged from 86% to a low of 75% of the faculty members claiming to include ethics in some way in their courses. Although there is widespread attention to ethics across the business schools' curricula, the manner that ethics is integrated into the business courses is widely divergent, with five major activity groups (or ways ethics is introduced in the courses) discovered. Since some faculty members used a combination of these activities to introduce ethics into their courses, the numbers for each of these activities, seen in Table 10.2, total more than the number of respondents.

The first activity group focused on ethics in the classroom. Within this group was the activity that involved conducting in-class discussions of ethics or conducting ethics debates using current issues drawn from business periodicals, newscasts, or the Internet. Many of the faculty members (38 of 47, 81%) reported a general or occasional discussion of ethics or the development of an ethics debate using information or issues found in business periodicals, such as *BusinessWeek* or *The Wall Street Journal*, or from national or local newscasts or from information taken off the Internet. Often the topic was one that is traditionally covered in the course but an ethical point of view or analysis was emphasized to provide students with an ethical perspective to the discipline-specific issue.

Also included in the ethics in the classroom group were instances when faculty members used a chapter devoted to ethical or social responsibility issues from their required course textbook to frame or begin the discussion or employing a case from the textbook to engage students in an ethics discussion. Many faculty members described their courses as incorporating an in-depth attention to ethics by using multiple ethics cases for discussion. In addition to cases provided in the course textbook, faculty member supplemented the textbook with prepared ethics cases based on current ethical issues found in the news. About half of the faculty members surveyed who integrate ethics into their classes (24 of 47, 52%), noted that they used these methods of ethics integration.

The second activity group involved extracurricular ethics activities. Presenting and discussing the professional code of ethics relevant for the course or discipline of study as a method used to integrate ethics into a business school course was part of this activity group. Fifteen percent of the faculty (7 of 47) incorporated this method as they sought to integrate professional development with ethics education. Faculty members also introduced ethics through extracurricular activities by encouraging (or requiring) students to attend an ethics speaker presentation or become involved in a community service. Four and three of the 47 faculty members, respectively, made use of these techniques. Typically, faculty would target the semiannual Beard Center for Leadership in Ethics Distinguished Ethics Speaker Series. Students were either required to attend and complete a written assignment based on the speaker's presentation, or they were asked to attend an in-class discussion at a subsequent class session to discuss the speaker's remarks. If not required, students often received extra credit for their attendance at the event. Or, faculty members indicated that they emphasize ethics in their classroom by having their students engage in community service. This activity is a requirement for each of these faculty member's courses.

Finally, the last activity group appearing in the 2008 study focused on testing students on their ability to recognize an ethical issue in a business case or analyze a business case using ethical principles or tools, or assigning homework that includes an ethical dimension. Thirteen faculty members (or 28% of the faculty) described a course assignment (either an examination or essay paper) where the ability to use an ethical decision-making tool was the basis of a portion of the overall assignment's grade.

In some cases it was a matter of recognizing an ethical issue embedded in a business situation or case. In other course assignments, the students were required to reason to an ethically defensible solution in resolving the ethics case or evaluate the ethical defensibility of a business manager's actions when facing an ethical dilemma. Others included ethics questions in the homework assignments for their students.

COMPARING THE 2008 AND 2001 STUDIES: CONCLUSIONS AND RECOMMENDATIONS

When comparing the results from the fall 2008 semester with the results acquired in 2001, the analysis is eerily similar. As noted earlier, 85.5% of the faculty members in 2008 reportedly integrated ethics into their courses, compared to 86% in 2001. The manner in which ethics was integrated is also very consistent.

The most common technique employed in 2008 and 2001 was the in-class ethics discussion or ethics debate, reportedly used by 81% of the faculty in each study. The second most common technique, again in each study, was the use of a chapter or case from the course textbook—51% in 2008 and 53% in 2001. The use of written assignments or homework that incorporate ethics was slightly higher in 2008—28%—compared to 2001 —24%. The presentation and discussion of professional codes of ethics doubled in 2008—used by 15% of the faculty—compared to 8% in 2001. Finally, requiring or encouraging students to attend an ethics speaker's lecture or engage in community service has dropped since 2001—27% in 2001 but only 15% in 2008.

Did the business school faculty members at Duquesne University in 2008 fully emphasize ethics across the curricula, and did this level of integration change since 2001? Yes and no. As in 2001, we have discovered that ethics has a significant presence in an overwhelming number of courses taught by our full-time faculty members. In addition, the manner used to integrate ethics into our business courses seems to be relatively consistent. But, is ethics present in every course? No. And we should note that part-time business school faculty members were not included in the study, so we were unable to assess the emphasis of ethics in their business courses, although these represent a small portion of the business schools' courses.

However, consistent with the University and business schools' missions and the desire to include ethics across the business school curricula, there were excellent confirmations found in this replication study. Faculty members appeared motivated by their own personal interest in and awareness of ethics and ethical issues in their discipline areas of study, as well as aided by the inclusion of ethics material in the required textbooks used in their courses. Additional opportunities for emphasizing ethics came from the introduction of codes of ethics developed by various professional associations and attendance at the ethics speakers program hosted by the Beard Center for Leadership in Ethics each semester. In conclusion, significant retention has occurred in emphasizing ethics across the Palumbo Donahue business schools' curricula at Duquesne University, but additional effort is possible.

Unfortunately, many of the proposed suggestions of how to more fully integrate ethics across the business schools' curricula were not implemented. There are a number of reasons why. The change is the business schools' administrative leadership caused a shift in program emphasis. Other, new programs were launched, requiring additional resources. The business ethics program was seen as a mature program, rather than an emerging program as in 2001, therefore a maintenance approach, rather than a growth approach, was assumed.

The business ethics faculty have found new challenges since 2001. With greater attention toward scholarship announced by the business schools' accreditation body, AACSB, the efforts for enhancing teaching performance diminished. This was particularly critical since two of the three full-time business ethics faculty members were untenured during this period. Also, in 2002, the business school teamed with the School of Leadership and Professional Advancement to offer a master's of science in leadership and business ethics. A series of five ethics courses were developed, staffed and assessed, diverting some attention and time from the business schools' curricula.

Yet the 2008 findings did alert the business schools to a few trends that needed attention. For example, efforts to recruit faculty members to require or strongly encourage their students to attend the Beard Center for Leadership in Ethics' ethics speakers program had waned and returned as a key focus for the center's director. Efforts to better notify and then periodically remind faculty members of these events, as well as involve faculty members in the recruitment of the speakers, are expected to bolster this approach toward integrating ethics into the business schools' curricula.

A number challenges remain that could affect the integration of ethics across the business schools' curricula: the development of cross-discipline ethics cases or other material, the involvement of faculty members in students' engagement in service-learning programs, and systematically offering faculty development workshops to enlighten or refresh the faculty members' awareness of the ethical decision framework created by the Duquesne business ethics faculty for use in all classes. It should be noted that in 2007, the university passed a requirement that all students must complete at least one course that is service-learning designated, meaning that it meets various requirements set forth by the university as approved by a universitywide committee. The required business ethics course was designated as the business schools' university-mandated, service-learning course. But, other business courses, such as statistics and marketing, also have adopted service-learning projects and the integration of ethics into these projects and courses was made easier by this new opportunity for student learning.

When compared to the 2001 survey results, the 2008 survey results indicate that there has been an institutionalization of the integration of ethics into the business schools' curricula, yet additional efforts and vigilance of the work achieved are always needed. It is clear that how a faculty member integrates business ethics into their classes is as variant as the faculty member, but whatever the approach taken for business students in Duquesne's undergraduate and graduate business schools' programs to hear about or become engaged in, it is evident that nearly seven out of every eight faculty members integrate business ethics into the business schools' curricula. Thus, as modeled at Duquesne University's schools of business, stand-alone ethics courses at the undergraduate and graduate level work in conjunction with efforts to integrate ethics across the business school's curricula to create a comprehensive and effective framework for advancing business ethics education.

NOTES

1. I asked Ms. Hartosova to conduct the interviews rather than doing so myself with the expectation that an interviewer who was not an ethics professor or director of an ethics center would be less biased in directing the interviews.
2. Mr. Kipper was asked to conduct the interviews, like my graduate research assistant before him in 2001, rather than interviewing the faculty myself with the expectation that an interviewer who was not an ethics professor would be less biased in directing the interviews.

REFERENCES

Duquesne University. (n.d.-a). *Strategic plan, 2003-2008.* Unpublished document. Available at www.duq.edu/administration/pdf/strategic-plan-2003-2008.pdf

Duquesne University. (n.d.-b). *Undergraduate catalog, Duquesne University, 2002-2003.* Unpublished document. Available at www.duq.edu/registrar/schedules/undergrad-course-catalog.cfm

CHAPTER 11

AN INTEGRATIVE APPROACH TO TEACHING AND ASSESSING ETHICS

Richard Mandel and Diane C. Chase

INTRODUCTION

In September, 2008, Babson College hosted a conference on undergraduate management education that was attended by deans of national and international schools of business. At one break-out session, the ostensible topic was assessing entrepreneurial outcomes, but the conversation soon turned to another pressing issue for these deans, that is, assessing ethics outcomes. The short, Babson-specific response was, "We assess ethics in our Coaching for Leadership and Teamwork Program [CLTP], using a rubric." Still, one dean commented, can we know from assessment whether students will carry ethics learning outcomes into the workplace? Can assessment results indicate that our graduates will be ethical people? There is no quick answer to these questions, but institution-specific examples of assessment practices can inform the discussion. Results of ethics outcomes assessment can help us understand what kinds of knowledge and competencies our students are developing, and can point to areas in which students may need more instruction or practice, all toward the

Toward Assessing Business Ethics Education
pp. 191–214
Copyright © 2011 by Information Age Publishing
All rights of reproduction in any form reserved.

long-term goal of inculcating ethical modes of professional and personal behavior.

In this chapter, we discuss the processes Babson used to articulate ethics learning objectives and infuse ethics coverage throughout an integrated curriculum. We then turn to the innovative and organic assessment method that renders findings on ethics outcomes at two points in the students' undergraduate course of study. We close with reflections on what we have learned from our assessment processes and results and ways we use this information to direct next steps and continuous program improvement in helping our students internalize ethics-based business perspectives.

ARTICULATING ETHICS LEARNING OBJECTIVES

The first step in any system of learning assessment is to have a clear set of learning goals and objectives. In the early 2000s, when the accreditation community began to emphasize direct assessment of learning outcomes in addition to more-common indirect methods, the Babson College undergraduate program was fortunate to have had a head start on the process. It had defined a set of five across-the-curriculum learning goals as early as 1993. One of these learning goals was ethics and social responsibility, defined as what we believe students should know and care about in these areas as a result of their undergraduate experiences. (More detail about this learning goal is provided later in this chapter.)

The process of articulating the ethics learning goal moved concurrently with a collegewide discussion of curriculum change and innovation. In the early 1990s, faculty and administration began to realize that the traditional undergraduate management curriculum was getting a bit stale. Enrollments were still growing, postgraduation employment figures for undergraduates were still high, and the college was still attracting high-quality faculty, but the curriculum had not undergone a complete reevaluation in many years. Faculty and administration opted to take a proactive look at the curriculum, rather than having to react in a future time of potential crisis. With a generous grant from a major financial institution, in 1993 Babson convened a 3-day, off-site conference of faculty, alumni, business leaders, and experts from other educational institutions to study the business curriculum and recommend changes to bring management education into the twenty-first century. A number of conclusions emerged from that conference and its subsequent task forces. Among them were:

- Business school graduates were generally highly skilled in their chosen fields, but were lacking in communication skills and thus had trouble relating to and conveying their knowledge and recommendations to their coworkers and clients.

- Business school graduates were generally quite knowledgeable in their major fields, but were not as likely to understand how that field related to the other functions of the firm, resulting in a time consuming and costly learning curve when they joined the workforce.

- Business schools should establish the minimum set of skills and competencies that all their students would strive for, regardless of each student's specialty.

Building from these conclusions, Babson spent the next few years radically changing its curriculum, both on the undergraduate and graduate levels. For example, regarding the perceived lack of communication skills, Babson's undergraduate program rededicated itself to its requirement that at least 50% of credits be earned in the liberal arts, even as the accrediting agencies had begun to back away from that requirement. In the most significant curricular change, to address the perceived inability to relate major fields of study to other functions of the firm, Babson made a major commitment to integration in the curriculum. Rather than delivering individual, stovepipe courses in marketing, finance, operations, and other functional areas, the revised required management curriculum integrated traditional functional areas throughout the first five semesters of an undergraduate student's studies and the first year of graduate studies. Accordingly, the first-year Babson undergraduate student would experience a year-long course (the Freshman Management Experience, since renamed Foundations of Management and Entrepreneurship or FME) in which all the management disciplines were introduced in a just-in-time manner, while students established and operated an actual business using capital supplied by the college. Building on that experience, sophomores and juniors then took intermediate-level integrated courses (currently named Organizing for Effective Management and Managing in a Competitive Environment) that delved deeper into the disciplines. All these courses required faculty to teach in an interdisciplinary manner and, in many cases, outside their core discipline. It is a tribute to the faculty and the inclusive process employed to design this curriculum that so many faculty enthusiastically embraced this teaching challenge.

Babson extended its model outside of the management disciplines and into the rest of the curriculum. Gone were traditional introductory courses in such areas as psychology, literature, political science, and philosophy, as they were replaced by Arts and Humanities Foundation and History and Society Foundation where the liberal-arts disciplines were integrated around grand themes such as immigration. These curricular changes were informed by significant study and debate within the college and by all its constituencies of five across-the-curriculum learning goals, which were embedded within the integrated model of functional disciplines. (In the course of later comprehensive reviews of the undergraduate curriculum, the number of across-the-curriculum learning goals expanded to seven.) The ethics and social responsibility learning goal was defined as follows:

- Babson graduates are prepared and willing to be responsible members of society; they are committed to continually developing intellectual, ethical, social, and professional character and abilities.

Although much time, effort, money, and planning was expended on defining, developing, and implementing the concept of integration in the curriculum and the across-the-curriculum learning goals, not as much attention was paid to the specific ethics learning objectives. Like most higher-education institutions in the 1990s, we assumed that students met the learning goal if we taught its principles and tested students on that knowledge through assignments and exams. It took Enron and its sister scandals of the early 2000s to turn the spotlight to the role of ethics in the business school curriculum.

Whether justified or not, business schools took a lot of criticism for the Enron-like scandals, as many influential commentators observed that these schools did not appear to be emphasizing ethics as part of the training of business leaders. At Babson, in reaction to such criticism, the academic vice president asked the faculty coordinator of the integrated management curriculum, a finance professor, to substantially increase the ethics content of the undergraduate management courses. This caused the faculty to take a step back and recognize that it was not clear that there was a shared understanding of what the concept of business ethics actually meant and how it (in terms of learning objectives) could be effectively taught to business students.

In response to this problem, the associate dean of the undergraduate school (a professor of law) assembled a group of faculty to address the question of ethics in the curriculum. Consistent with what had become the characteristic integrative nature of the Babson culture, and to ensure that the result of their efforts would be accessible not only to business students, but also to business faculty, the group consisted of faculty members of various rank from the disciplines of finance, philosophy, history, operations, and organizational behavior. Led by the associate dean, the group was charged with developing a shared understanding of business ethics for the undergraduate school curriculum as well as a strategy for including it in the curriculum. All faculty members served as volunteers.

The group quickly concluded that in order for their efforts to have credibility with the faculty and other college constituencies, the definition of business ethics could not appear to come out of thin air, but, instead, must have clear underpinnings in the traditional theories of ethics developed by the world's cultures over the centuries. Moreover, in order to be useful to business students, it would be best for the product of the group's efforts to be an ethical framework that amounts to a practical series of steps to take when faced with any difficult ethical problem. Thus, it was decided that the group would attempt to author an ethical decision-making framework informed by an article tying the framework to its underlying scholarly traditions.

Fortunately, the associate dean recalled having been asked more than a decade earlier to edit a book chapter by a now retired accounting professor that attempted to do just that. The author of the chapter had been concerned with the same problem now confronting this group: how to make the somewhat daunting, frequently esoteric writings of the great ethical philosophers accessible to the modern-day business student. The associate dean recalled that the author had created rough drafts of a few chapters of a planned book, and that the introductory chapter was similar in scope to the article planned by the group. A hopeless pack rat, the associate dean found the draft among his old, dusty files, and contacted the author, who was happy to allow Babson's ethics group to use it as the basis for their efforts.

Within six months, the group had produced the Babson Framework for Ethical Decision Making (see the Appendix for the most current version of this framework), along with an article that set out the philosophical underpinnings of the framework. The framework draws upon four major ethical perspectives, phrasing them as questions for students to raise in any decision-making context. It's important to note that the framework does not segregate ethical considerations from legitimate business concerns such as profitability and strategy; all of these criteria are assumed to inform an effective decision-making process. Accordingly, drawing on competencies in accounting, finance, marketing, management, and other business disciplines, students using the framework are prompted to evaluate potential decisions against these ethics-based perspectives by asking:

1. Which alternative(s) is based on a rule that could be made universal?

2. Which alternative(s) will produce the most good and the least harm?

3. Which alternative is based on a rule that would cause more good than harm in society?

4. Which alternative develops character traits you would want to encourage in yourself?

With the ethics learning goal defined and a framework in place, attention turned to articulating the learning objectives. That is, what did we want our students to know (cognitive objectives), what did we want our students to think about (affective objectives), and what did we want our students to be able to do (behavioral objectives) within the realm of ethics? In effect, the learning objectives form the basis for assessment by restating the learning goal in terms of outcomes we can reasonably measure or evaluate. The faculty retreat in the mid-1990s had produced, along with across-the-curriculum learning goals, a subset of learning objectives for each goal, and that language formed the basis for specifying ethics learning objectives, as follows:

1. Graduates have frameworks for understanding that ethics is an integral feature of all personal, social, legal, and professional considerations.
2. Graduates understand that ethics is an integral part of decision making.
3. Graduates understand their responsibilities as members of a community.
4. Graduates are accountable and accept responsibility for their actions.

This language was pared to the cognitive objectives of recognizing an ethical issue in a business context and knowing pertinent ethical theories; the affective objectives of scanning for ethical issues in business and personal contexts; and the behavioral objectives of using an ethics-based model of decision making based on seven steps (the framework) and supporting legal and ethical actions.

INFUSING ETHICS COVERAGE INTO THE INTEGRATED CURRICULUM

The other major product of the group's work grew out of Babson's commitment to curriculum integration. Although many colleges report successful learning outcomes by requiring their students to enroll in stand-alone business ethics courses, the Babson group chose a nontraditional approach of integrating ethics into the already otherwise integrated, required business curriculum. The traditional approach was criticized by faculty for encouraging students to consider business ethics only on, as one professor put it, "ethics day" and to ignore ethics when considering decision making involving other disciplines. Babson would still offer ethics courses, such as its traditional ethics course offered by its philosophy faculty, but teaching and learning about business ethics would be encountered in the context of business problems, just as they are in the business world.

This decision to integrate ethics, rather than teach it alone, raised three immediate and daunting problems. First, teaching materials would need to be developed to facilitate this approach, since very few institutions were known to excel in it. Second, professors from all different disciplines would need to become comfortable teaching and applying the framework to business problems in their classes. And third, innovative methods of assessing student-learning outcomes derived from this integrative approach to teaching ethics would need to be developed. The first two problems are addressed in the remainder of this section. The third problem of assessment is discussed later.

Development of Case Series Integrating Ethics With Business Disciplines

For some years, Babson had experimented with various forms of a freshman seminar known as the "First Year Seminar" (FYS), which acted as an extended orientation by helping students cope with time management, alcohol and drug abuse, wellness issues, and other issues common to the transition from high school to college. Among these issues was ethics, and shortly after the release of the Framework for Ethical Decision Making, the FYS faculty drafted and began to use a stand-alone ethics case to introduce and encourage use of the framework. This approach was widely criticized by both faculty and students. Although the case was somewhat compelling, in the context of FYS it was merely another example of the disjointed nature of the course syllabus, which introduced yet another topic each week that appeared unconnected with what came before and after it. Thus, the FYS faculty recently completed a redesign of the course in which all the important topics are introduced through a semester-long case series about how two students experience freshman life. At one point in the case series, the students are up against a deadline to submit a group presentation and are offered the chance to use a friend's presentation that was developed for the course in a previous year, but not actually used. Students are encouraged to use the ethics framework to suggest what these fictional students should do.

The idea of a semester-long integrating case series for FYS was actually suggested by a similar pedagogical approach, which had been adopted by the Faculty of Foundations of Management and Entrepreneurship (FME). In FME, faculty had for some time achieved year-long continuity in their course by using a home grown set of caselets that followed a small entrepreneurial business from start up to harvest, posing a series of business problems along the way. At about the time that the ethics framework had been established, the FME faculty had decided to replace the timeworn caselets with a new set that followed two fictitious business partners, Mike and Mary, through their establishment, operation, growth, and sale of a bicycle retailing business. Shortly thereafter, the associate dean who had participated in the creation of the ethics framework joined the FME faculty and became the coordinator of the course's management curriculum, leading much of the caselet development on the management side.

As a result of these efforts, students in FME follow Mike and Mary as they encounter problems such as:

- whether Mike should attempt to gather competitive intelligence by pretending to be a customer at other bicycle shops;
- whether they should terminate an employee whose poor performance may be the result of a hostile environment caused by a coworker;
- whether they should expand their sales to the Internet and indirectly compete with a friendly bicycle-store owner who gave them the loan they needed to get started, or
- whether they should recall a slightly defective product.

In addition, a significant effort to create integrative ethics teaching materials was funded by a grant from the Harold Geneen Foundation. Babson applied for and received grant money to create, over a 3-year period, a series of cases which would integrate business ethics into business cases. Under the terms of the grant:

- Each case must use the ethical framework to address the ethical question embedded in the case.
- Each case must integrate content from at least two different management disciplines in addition to business ethics.
- The cases must take place in international settings whenever possible.
- The cases must be written, in part, by current business students.

The grant was viewed as a wonderful opportunity to give students the experience of working with faculty to develop teaching materials, especially if an effective model of collaboration could be found.

In the first year, four volunteer faculty (who were paid for their involvement) were paired with 40 sophomores who were members of the honors program and enrolled in a sophomore honors seminar. The case writing project was considered part of the seminar's curriculum. Although eventually three finished cases emerged from this process, the faculty each reported that teams of 10 students were too hard to administer and that there simply was not enough work to keep all ten students busy. Thus, as an alternative in the following 2 years, the volunteer faculty were allowed to recruit up to three students as assistants, and these students were paid a stipend for their work in developing teaching materials.

Two other difficulties emerged from this process. First, it soon became clear that although the faculty were comfortable, in fact enthusiastic, about including ethical issues in their cases, they did not believe themselves capable of doing justice to the use of the ethical framework to address these issues in their teaching notes. This problem was solved by giving some of the grant money to a professor of ethics (who had been part of the framework group) to draft the ethics portion of the teaching note for most of the cases.

Second, the college failed to adequately set expectations about the ownership of the copyright of cases when they were finished. Babson had always been fairly generous in allowing faculty to own the rights to the intellectual capital they had created, but, in this case, since the grant had paid a stipend to the faculty and provided the student help, the expectations might have been different. This was especially true since the college intended these cases to be used in its curriculum and had some tentative thoughts about publishing the collection of cases itself. This issue came up late in the process when it was discovered that one of the faculty had agreed to publish her case in a journal that insisted upon its ownership of the copyright. Notwithstanding these difficulties, the Geneen grant resulted in the completion of 10 integrated cases over a 3-year period. These cases have been used in the integrated management core of the Babson curriculum, specifically on the sophomore level, with one case acting as the basis of a final examination.

In one example of the cases that have been developed, students are asked to perform an industry analysis of the health insurance industry in order to determine the strength or weakness of a particular company in that field. They are then asked to analyze the financial statements of that particular company to determine what it is about the financial performance of the company that motivated its management to resort to allegedly fraudulent financial reporting as well as to identify the areas in which the allegedly fraudulent reporting took place. In the course of that analysis, students are required to use the ethical decision-making framework to decide for themselves whether or not the identified, allegedly fraudulent practices were, in fact, fraudulent, given the inherently subjective nature of generally accepted accounting principles.

In two of the other cases, students are asked to analyze and suggest improvements to the operations, financial model, and organization of companies that import and distribute (on both the wholesale and retail levels) a variety of children's toys. In the course of this analysis, students are given facts that should lead them to understand that these toys are manufactured in a foreign country under circumstances that suggest possible exploitive child labor and the use of potentially toxic materials. Students are expected to recognize these clues and employ the ethics framework to suggest whether or not these arrangements should be continued or modified.

Enabling All Faculty to Comfortably Integrate Ethics

With all this robust materials development came the problem of effective faculty delivery. As suggested earlier, although there was no shortage of enthusiasm for the integration of ethics into the mainstream curriculum, there was widespread anxiety among the faculty about whether or not they were adequately trained to deliver such material. This problem was addressed in a number of ways. As described earlier, the very composition of the committee that drafted the framework and its accompanying justification was designed to include faculty with no particular training in ethics to ensure that the product of these efforts would be accessible to both business students and non-ethics faculty. In addition, all the new teaching materials described above were accompanied by teaching notes that described in detail the use of the framework in the course of teaching the material.

In addition to written materials, two of the faculty who had participated in the development of the framework gave a series of demonstrations of its use, conducting mock classes for faculty to observe. In one such case, these faculty members attended a meeting of the FME faculty and conducted a class using the FME faculty as students. In another approach to training, these same two faculty members conducted a mock class for a group of visiting alumni that was recorded on video media and posted on the college's internal website so that faculty could review these teaching techniques at their convenience.

AN INNOVATIVE AND ORGANIC ASSESSMENT METHOD

The third challenge mentioned earlier involves how to assess ethics when, rather than being isolated in a particular course, the subject is integrated across the curriculum. At Babson College, we were fortunate to have in place an innovative assessment technique that could be adapted to this purpose.

In the mid-1990s, two Babson professors had developed the Coaching for Leadership and Teamwork Program (CLTP), which is presently administered to all first-year and again to all third-year students enrolled at the college. At each program session, each student is assigned to a 6-hour block (along with approximately 100 of his or her peers). At the assigned time, students are divided into groups of five and sent to a room where they are greeted by five coaches, each of whom has been assigned to one of the students. These coaches are volunteer alumni, interested businesspeople from the community, and graduate students who are studying leadership. Each coach has attended a 6-hour training session prior to meeting with the students. Once in the room, the students are given a series of business cases to solve and are expected to present their solutions to the coaches. The coaches observe the interactions of the students and compare them against rubrics designed to assess such skills as leadership, teamwork, listening, and communication. When the students have completed their work, the coaches consult with each other and each coach then scores his or her student against the rubrics. Finally, the students meet one on one with their coaches to receive immediate feedback. Students and coaches are generally quite enthusiastic about this program. Students appreciate honest feedback from people who otherwise have no evaluative relationship with them (i.e., faculty may not participate in the program). Coaches appreciate the program because they learn coaching skills they can apply in their own workplaces.

Having this coaching program already in existence appeared to offer an organic solution to the problem of assessing ethics in an integrated curriculum. If the college is successfully teaching business ethics in the integrated courses, and if students had internalized the framework so as to be able to recognize ethical issues embedded in business problems and use the framework to address those issues, then they should be able to do so in the context of the coaching program. Thus, shortly after the framework was introduced into the curriculum, the coaching cases were revised to include an ethical issue within the overall business problem, and coaches were trained to apply the ethics rubric to their observations of students. The rubric incorporates the following behaviors that can be observed in the discussion and presentation: the ability to recognize an ethical issue, lead or participate in the discussion by drawing on elements of the framework, and support actions or decisions deemed ethical and legal.

For example, in one revised case, students are asked to decide whether or not to recommend postponing the introduction of a highly touted new product that is discovered at the last minute to be somewhat defective. Postponing the introduction will pose significant marketing costs, and the defect can be fixed by a patch that, it is estimated, could be developed and sent to customers within a few short weeks. Students are expected to approach this as a problem involving marketing, operations, and finance, while also considering the ethical implications of deliberately shipping a defective product. By listening to the group's discussion and observing the group's interactions, coaches assess whether or not students recognize the nature of the ethical issue, whether and how effectively they apply the ethics framework and the analyses it prompts, and whether or not they tolerate an action that could be illegal or unethical.

Linking program-level assessment of the ethics learning goal to CLTP satisfies several standards of effective assessment practice. First, the assessment is systematic, not episodic; it occurs at regular intervals and its findings are reported within the college's annual update on student-outcomes assessment sent to faculty and governing committees. Second, the assessment involves multiple stakeholders—students, faculty, administrators, alumni, and external businesspeople—who work collaboratively within a shared understanding of Babson's mission, values, and assessment methodology. Third, the assessment findings inform ongoing discussions in curriculum committees about the effectiveness of our ethics teaching approach. The assessment results are regularly used to consider whether to revise cases, the sequencing of topics or assignments within a course, discussion questions, and even the assessment process itself.

This method works particularly well in satisfying accreditation standards for assurance of learning, which is the language used by the Association to Advance Collegiate Schools of Business (AACSB), for assessment practice. It allows us to gather data on all students by using an existing program and not incurring significant additional work in the process.[1] The CLTP data from all students complements data derived from our other assessment method of scoring a random and representative sample of course-embedded assignments using a rubric developed and accepted by faculty; both approaches satisfy accreditation standards. The data we collect provides program-level outcomes broadly stated in terms of meeting or failing to meet expectations and also provides sufficiently fine grained detail so that we can identify which specific rubric elements students may be having trouble mastering. Both types of data are needed for the important step of using assessment findings for program improvement.

For faculty and administrators, the CLTP assessment exercise provides data derived from external review to supplement assessment results from faculty-scored student work, another desirable element of effective assessment practice. For students, the method provides direct and immediate feedback on how they are doing on the ethics learning goal (along with several other program-level learning goals) at each session and at two points in their academic career. Students receive, after each CLTP session, written feedback that reinforces what was discussed between coach and student in the face-to-face feedback discussion. In this way, students are meaningfully involved in the assessment activity in that they are given results they can choose to use to continue developing competency in each area. The overall curriculum and cocurricular activities, of course, prompt students to develop competency in learning objectives, but this method also allows students to own, so to speak, some responsibility for pursuing courses and opportunities that can help them focus more deliberately on what have been identified for them as individual learning objectives. We hear anecdotal evidence that indeed students do own the findings from CLTP sessions when these same students return as alumni to serve as CLTP coaches and articulate how they used the feedback they had received.

As another example of effective assessment practice, CLTP renders longitudinal data on ethics outcomes for students and College alike. In the first-year session, students receive feedback that they can use as a baseline for their third-year session, which is usually with a different coach. The third-year coach does not have information on the student's first-year session, so students can choose whether or not to discuss specific differences in observations and findings. For Babson, CLTP has now amassed longitudinal data on ethics outcomes for five years, which offers administrators a rich source to mine for analyzing results by cohort. So we can ask ourselves: By the third year of the curriculum, have students internalized the Ethics Decision-Making Framework so as to use it, without specific prompting, when confronted with a business dilemma? The findings and our analysis of longitudinal data produced some surprising results.

Situating Assessment Results within Context

To prepare for an AACSB maintenance of accreditation visit in fall 2007, we wrote up the results of our most-recent assessment findings for ethics as follows in Table 11.1.

At first glance, it might look like third-year students not only did not improve on the ethics learning goal but also may have even deteriorated.

Table 11.1.   2006-2007 Assessment Results for Ethics Learning Goal

Learning Goal	Direct Assessment Method (Scored With Rubric)	Data Source	Time	Results
Ethics and social responsi-bility	• Case analysis • Presentation	CLTP: all 1st-year students	Spring 2007	• 90% met expecta-tions • 10% did not meet expectations
		CLTP: all 3rd-year students	Fall 2006	• 79% met expecta-tions • 21% did not meet expectations

And in fact, our AACSB Visiting Team made a light-hearted reference to that quick observation. This served as a good opening for discussing with the team that assessment findings aren't necessarily best understood as stand-alone artifacts, and that these specific ethics findings were most clearly understood in the context of corresponding changes in the curriculum. Our redesigned approach, Incorporating Ethical Perspectives into a Decision-Making Framework, was formally introduced into first-year and sophomore core courses during fall 2006, when third-year students were assessed in CLTP, and our first-year students were assessed in CLTP during the subsequent semester, spring 2007. More than 20% of third-year students, who had not yet had exposure to the redesigned approach, failed to meet expectations on the ethics learning goal, whereas only 10% of first-year students failed to meet expectations. The findings suggest that first-year students were beginning to internalize the framework through exposure to it in the First Year Seminar and FME, and would likely need subsequent and consistent opportunities to use it beyond the first-year core courses. These results provided a starting point for comparing data in subsequent years.

In spring 2009, we looked at longitudinal results from several assessment points in CLTP: fall 2006/spring 2007; fall 2007/spring 2008; and fall 2008. We looked in particular at one cohort of students—those whose first-year CLTP findings were collected in spring 2007 and whose third-year CLTP session occurred in fall 2008. Findings provided in Table 11.2 point to improvement in students' scores on ethics outcomes.

Looking at findings for third-year students only, we can see a progression of improvement in scores from the fall 2006 session (21% did not meet expectations), when students had no systematic exposure to the framework, to fall 2008 (4% did not meet expectations), after which these same students had several opportunities to practice with the framework.

Table 11.2.   2007-2008 Assessment Results for Ethics Learning Goal

Learning Goal	Direct Assessment Method (Scored With Rubric)	Data Source	Time	Results
Ethics and social responsibility	• Case analysis • Presentation	CLTP: all 1st-year students	Spring 2007	• 90% met expectations • 10% did not meet expectations
		CLTP : all 3rd-year students	Fall 2008	• 96% met expectations • 4% did not meet expectations

These results are encouraging, but we do not want to overstate the meaning of these findings by extrapolating that our graduates will necessarily be ethical people in the workplace. As a method of direct assessment, CLTP helps us understand student competencies on specific measurable or observable criteria. These are: whether or not students can recognize an ethical issue in a business context; whether or not students can use the framework to inform analysis; whether or not students can recognize potentially illegal or unethical decisions. Our results suggest that our students are internalizing the framework successfully in the context of their coursework, but the higher-stakes assessment will occur in real-world, on-the-job exigencies. The indirect assessment data we collect through senior and alumni surveys indicate that the story is still unfolding. Through 2005, alumni ranked as low the impact of their College experience on understanding ethical issues—their experiences having pre-dated the significant curricular revision. On the 2008 senior survey, recent graduates who were in the Fall 2006 CLTP cohort ranked as moderate the impact of their college experience on identifying moral and ethical issues. Progress appears to be happening, and we await confirming evidence from future alumni surveys.

Ongoing Program Improvement

In academic year 2008-2009, we revised the CLTP format to give first-year students the option of participating in either the fall or spring semester. Similarly, students in their third or fourth year may do a CLTP session in either semester. We instituted these changes to give students greater scheduling flexibility, but we also benefit from having multiple streams of assessment data to inform ongoing curricular review. CLTP faculty and administrators continue to work closely in training coaches to apply the rubrics fairly and consistently; even experienced coaches, we find, appreciate the norming exercises with other team members, which allow everyone to develop a shared understanding for scoring and provide a comfortable level of confidence in using the data.

CLTP is the primary direct-assessment method Babson uses to evaluate ethics learning objectives at the undergraduate level, and we use a second direct method, course-embedded assignments, to assess how well students use the framework in a written case analysis. Although the curriculum and its demands form the largest part of students' college experience, Babson also recognizes the complementary significance of co- and extracurricular activities in helping students achieve across-the-curriculum learning goals. This conviction is inscribed in the preamble to Babson College's Undergraduate Learning Goals:

> Babson embraces the principle that students learn and develop through their experiences across their undergraduate years, both in the classroom and throughout the community. This learning-outcomes approach is focused on developing specific skills and abilities that will prepare students for their professional lives; equally important, it aims to challenge and influence students' personal growth, understanding of themselves and their responsibility to the community, and appreciation for diverse and divergent viewpoints. Through this approach Babson strives to create a learning and living environment which encourages students to become mature and well-grounded individuals and successful leaders in both business and the community.

Accordingly, we continue to look outside the formal curriculum for opportunities and assessments of all learning goals that reinforce students' learning in the classroom.

Offering students many and diverse experiences in considering ethical issues can help students bridge this learning outcome to contexts beyond the college environment. We won't have assessment results for these efforts until many years after students graduate, if ever. Our graduates leave with a framework for ethical decision making, having been given many opportunities to use it, and having received feedback at multiple points. Our assessments indicate that students can use the framework effectively. Ideally, they can carry that competency forward into personal and professional practice.

NOTE

1.   It is important to note that assessment data does not necessarily have to be collected for all students. Useful data collected from a sample of student

work can be deemed representative, valid, and reliable, according to an AACSB committee report (2007).

RESOURCES

Assessment

AACSB International Accreditation Coordinating Committee and AACSB International Accreditation Quality Committee (2007). *AACSB assurance of learning standards: An interpretation.* Retrieved from http://www.aacsb.edu/accreditation/Papers/AOLPaper-final-11-20-07.pdf

Maki, P. L. (2004). *Assessing for learning: Building a sustainable commitment across the institution.* Sterling, VA: Stylus.

Palomba, C. A., & Banta, T. W. (1999). *Assessment essentials: Planning, implementing, and improving assessment in higher education.* San Francisco, CA: Jossey-Bass.

Stassen, M. L. A., Doherty, K., & Poe, M. (2004). *Program-based review and assessment: Tools and techniques for program improvement.* Amherst, MA: Office of Academic Planning and Assessment, University of Massachusetts Amherst.

Stevens, D. D., & Levi, Antonia J. (2005). *Introduction to rubrics: An assessment tool to save grading time, convey effective feedback and promote student learning.* Sterling, VA: Stylus.

Walvoord, B. E. (2004). *Assessment clear and simple: A practical guide for institutions, departments, and general education.* San Francisco, CA: Jossey-Bass.

Ethics

Darley, J. M. (1996). How organizations socialize individuals into evildoing. In D. M. Messick & A. E. Tenbrunsel (Eds.), *Codes of conduct: Behavioral research into business ethics* (pp. 13-43). New York, NY: Russell Sage Foundation.

Romar, E. J. (2002). Virtue is good business: Confucianism as a practical business ethic. *Journal of Business Ethics, 38*(1/2), 119-131.

Wawrytko, S. A. (1982). Confucius and Kant: The ethics of respect. *Philosophy East and West, 32*(3), 237-257.

Development Coaching

Coaching for Leadership and Teamwork Program. (CLTP). Retrieved from www3.babson.edu/babson2ndgen/Ugrad/Academics/LeadershipPrograms/default.cfm.

Hunt, J. M., & Weintraub, J. (2002). *The coaching manager: Developing top talent in business.* Newbury Park, CA: Sage Publications.

Hunt, J. M., & Weintraub, J. (2004). Learning developmental coaching. *Journal of Management Education, 28*(1), 39-61.

Hunt, J. M., & Weintraub, J. (2007). *The coaching organization: A strategy for developing leaders.* Newbury Park, CA: Sage Publications.

Babson-Developed Materials

To order copies of the following materials, contact the Case Development Center, Babson College, Wellesley, MA 02457; by telephone at 781-239-6181; by e-mail at cases@babson.edu.

- Introduction to the Babson Framework for Ethical Decision-Making (2007). This essay introduces to students the ethical theories that underlie the Babson Framework for Ethical Decision-Making. It is a collective effort based on an essay originally written by Les Livingstone, with subsequent contributions from Richard Bliss, Fritz Fleischmann, Danna Greenberg, James Hoopes, Richard Mandel, Kate McKone-Sweet, Lydia Moland, and Ross Petty.
- A Framework for Ethical Decision Making (2007).
- Cases and Teaching Notes developed by Babson faculty and undergraduate students with funding provided by a Geneen Foundation grant:
  - Build-A-Bear Workshop
  - HealthSouth Corporation: The Makings of an Accounting Fraud
  - Tracy Hesitated: The Case of Marquet Consulting
  - MTN Cameroon: The Competitive Edge of Being African
  - Music-Line: To Market or Not? (A)
  - Orange Cameroon: A Global Telecommunications Company in Africa
  - Reebok: Pump 2.0
  - What Price Progress? The Case of India's Sardar Sarovar Dam Project
  - Wal-Mart Has Arrived

APPENDIX

Babson Framework for Ethical Decision Making

A Framework for Ethical Decision Making

The Decision-Making Framework[1]

The 7-step model presented here begins with 3 steps that are necessary for any effective decision-making process. Only in step 4 does the process focus specifically on ethics.

Step 4 asks you to evaluate possible decisions from the perspective of the four different ethical schools. Just as you should engage several varying business perspectives (i.e. net present value, strategic priority, time to market, feasibility, etc.) when evaluating decision alternatives, you should also engage several varying ethical perspectives such as deontological ethics, act-utilitarianism, rule-utilitarianism, and virtue ethics.

By practicing making decisions with this model you will learn to integrate ethical perspectives into your decision making. This framework will also help you learn to identify ethical issues that may not be obvious.

1. **Identify Issues**

   • Identify the issues and decisions to be considered.

2. **Gather Information**

   • Collect information and facts that are relevant to the decision.

---

1. Richard Bliss, Danna Greenberg, James Hoopes, Richard Mandel, Kathleen McKone-Sweet and Lydia Moland prepared this framework as a basis for class discussion rather than to illustrate either effective or ineffective handling of an administrative situation. Copyright 2003 © by and licensed for publication at Babson College to the Babson College Case Development Center. Updated 2007. To order copies or request permission to reproduce materials, call (781) 239-6181 or write Case Development Center, Olin Hall, Babson College, Wellesley, MA 02157. No part of this publication may be reproduced, stored in a retrieval system, used in a spreadsheet, or transmitted in any form or by any means—electronic, mechanical, photocopying, recording, or otherwise – without the permission of copyright holders

- Try to take notice of gaps or ambiguity in the available information.
- Identify the affected stakeholders and determine their interests.
- Collect relevant legal as well as business information.

3. **Brainstorm Alternatives**

   Develop as many realistic alternatives as possible.

4. **Evaluate Alternatives From Various Ethical Perspectives**

   In addition to business criteria such as profitability and strategy, one should evaluate alternatives by ethical perspectives.

   (a) **Deontological Theories:** Which alternative(s) is based on a rule that could be made universal?
   - For each decision alternative, apply Kant's universal test by determining whether you are acting on a principle that you would want to apply to all people in all situations, including yourself.
   - Also determine if each decision alternative respects stakeholders rather than treating them merely as means to an end.

   (b) **Act-Utilitarianism:** Which alternative will produce the most good and the least harm?
   - Use Table I (below) to identify the costs/benefits to the stakeholders of each decision alternative.
   - Determine if there is a solution that is Pareto-optimal—a solution that would benefit all or at least hurt none.
   - If there is no Pareto-optimal alternative, decide which alternative produces the most benefits and causes the least harm to the stakeholders.

   (c) **Rule-Utilitarianism:** Which alternative is based on a rule that would cause more good than harm in society? This differs from Act-Utilitarianism in that it considers the general rule you would be following rather than simply the particular action you are contemplating.
   - Do any of the alternatives violate a conventional moral rule?
   - Be aware that conventional moral rules—such as those about proper dress, relations between the sexes, respect for authority, and so on—need especially careful consideration when stakeholders are from different cultures.

- In evaluating alternatives, you also should consider if any of the alternatives are illegal. While it is possible for there to be an ethical argument for breaking the law—for example when a law is unjust—such situations will be extremely rare in practical business decisions. Determining that an alternative is illegal should almost always lead to its rejection.

(d) **Virtue Ethics:** Which alternative develops character traits you would want to encourage in yourself?

- Consider Aristotle's personal happiness question: Will adopting this decision allow you to be at peace with yourself and develop your character in a way that will improve your relationships with others?

- Consider Confucius' description of social virtues. Will adopting this decision cultivate social dynamics that allow everyone to carry out his/her role effectively? Will it foster an environment in which each member of the group can thrive?

- How would you feel if you shared your decision with your most respected mentors, family members, friends?

5. **Make a Decision and Examine Your Confidence in It from Different Ethical Perspectives**

- In determining which decision alternative to choose, you will have to weigh the results of the different ethical and business criteria. The challenge is for you to find the decision that produces the most value in an ethical way.

- Use Table II (below) to evaluate your decision by revisiting each of the four ethical approaches you used in Step 4 and rating your confidence in your decision.

- If you lack confidence in the decision, return to Step 1 and start the process again.

6. **Prepare to Explain Your Ethical Decision**

- Prepare an explanation which will clearly show others, especially those affected, that you have weighed the ethical issues involved and have made the most ethical decision possible.

7. **Reflect on Your Decision Making Process**

- As in business decisions, so too in ethics one should learn from experience. After you have acted on your decision, consider how well you did. Were you thorough enough in gathering information? Did you prepare an explanation that would be clear and persuasive to others? What do you need to do differently next time?

Conclusion

For many decisions you will not have the time to follow this 7-step framework in all its detail. However, if you practice this framework in your courses and when you do have time later on in your career, it will become part of the tacit knowledge you carry with you as you make quicker decisions.

As stated in the "Introduction," the basis of an ethical decision lies in your personal character. You won't do the right thing if you don't want to. Aristotle's emphasis on making virtue a habit is the best known recipe for developing the character and values enabling you to do the right thing.

But knowledge matters, too. Gathering relevant information about the situation is vital to making the right decision. And you can't do the right thing in business if you don't know how; competence in accounting, finance, marketing, management, and your general understanding of the world are essential forms of knowledge for doing the right thing.

And finally, it is important to understand ethics and to be aware of the fact that the really difficult decisions may not be between right and wrong but between right and right. There may be conflict between our understanding of *duty* (deontological ethics), our concern that our actions have good *consequences* (utilitarian ethics), and our desire to develop our *characters* (virtue ethics) so as to live peacefully with ourselves and others. That understanding points to the need to be as careful as possible in making ethical decisions.

TABLE I: Identifying Consequences to Stakeholders

If we stop and think—which this chart helps us to do—it is easier to recognize our obligations to customers, employees, owners, and the community in which we operate.

Be sure to list yourself as one of the stakeholders.

	Decision Alternative #1	Decision Alternative #2	Decision Alternative #3	Decision Alternative #4
Stakeholders	*Possible Consequences of Each Alternative on Each Stakeholder*			
1.				
2.				
3.				
4.				
5.				
6.				
7.				

TABLE II: Evaluating the Ethics of Preliminary Decision

This table will help you examine your judgment with more objectivity than you might otherwise achieve. It might be tempting to total up the score from a chart like this and decide that if you arrive at some magic number your decision is a good one. But that might make the chart a tool for escaping self-reflection rather than engaging in it. The important point is to try to be sure that you have really asked yourself each of the eight questions in the boxes below.

Ethical Decision-Making Evaluation Criteria	Confidence in Decision				
	Not Confident		Very Confident		
	1	2	3	4	5
1. Have I/we thought broadly about any ethical issues associated with the decision that has to be made?					
2. Have I/we involved as many as possible of those who have a right to have input to, or actual involvement in, making this decision and action-plan?					
3. Does this decision respect the rights and dignity of the stakeholders?					
4. Can this decision be universally applied?					
5. Does this decision produce the most good and the least harm to the relevant stakeholders?					
6. Does this decision uphold relevant conventional moral rules?					
7. Can I live with this decision alternative?					
8. Does this decision enable me to develop character traits that allow me to live with myself and others peacefully?					

CHAPTER 12

LESSONS LEARNED AS CHAIR OF A COLLEGE ASSESSMENT COMMITTEE

Implications for Assessing Ethical Reasoning

Brian P. Niehoff

We have all heard it said, whether in an all-university forum, a college faculty gathering, or a department meeting. "Assessment is not an outcome; it is a process," so the speaker will say. Our antennae go up as we have heard such triteness before. The management field is fraught with such maxims. Our academic cynicism is alerted when we catch such summative one-liners or slogans being tossed around, yet we know them to be the fabric of how real management practitioners enact our many theoretical prescriptions. They sound so meaningful, but often manifest as empty phrases. As it has turned out, in the case of assessment, I have found this maxim to hold more than a grain of truth—assessment is indeed a process and one from which I have learned a great deal. The purpose of this chapter is to convey these lessons in general in hopes that they may inform efforts to assess ethical reasoning in particular.

Toward Assessing Business Ethics Education
pp. 215–230

I first encountered assessment in the academic context after our university's 2002 visit from the Higher Learning Commission (HLC). Their positive judgment for our accreditation was tempered by a strong warning that our assessment processes across the university were lacking, and would need immediate attention if we were to seek a positive judgment on their next visit in 2012. In the college of business administration, it was as if another language was being spoken. Assessment? Yes, we assess our students. We have an entry GPA requirement to major in business, a mix of required and elective business and nonbusiness courses, and a hearty handshake at graduation for those who maintained at least the minimum GPA requirement. The faculty is entrusted with grading student work in classes. What more was needed? We found out shortly thereafter. All academic units were issued the order—each college and department must develop meaningful student learning outcomes (SLOs) and valid assessment process plans. An assessment committee was immediately created and charged with the task of developing our college's SLOs. After some time, the committee presented the faculty with nine SLOs representing our ideals with a wide range in clarity, commitment, and, most importantly, measurability. We were off and running.

My involvement in the process began as a curious onlooker, observing the assessment and curriculum committees develop this list of idealistic outcomes for our students. I was somewhat new in my position as department head at the time, yet had been a faculty member for more than 10 years. My role in the process was enhanced when each department was delegated the task of developing an assessment plan for our majors. My role was ramped up even further when, after a relaxing and rejuvenating sabbatical abroad during the fall of 2006, I was asked, and ultimately agreed, to serve in the role of chair of our college assessment committee. It must have been a weak moment. We had a short 18 months to prepare for our Association to Advance Collegiate Schools of Business (AACSB) accreditation and the dean was seeing a lack of overall progress in our assessment process. Only two of our nine SLOs were being assessed, and plans for assessing the remaining seven were still in the brainstorming stage. To cut to the chase in the story, during the next year, we developed measures and progressed on all learning outcomes, passing our accreditation with flying colors. That is the quick history, but is not the story I want to tell here.

Again, my purpose in penning this essay is to share what I learned through my involvement with assessment in hopes that the overall lessons will shed light on efforts to assess business ethics education in particular. In this context, I will discuss many of the requirements of assessing—developing effective SLOs, locating and developing good rubrics, designing valid methods for assessing, collecting the data, and closing the loop of measurement and feedback—as well as more process-oriented issues such as dealing with resistance, involving faculty, and other managerial challenges. I will also share some of the benefits our college has experienced with the process and how such benefits may apply to the assessment of business ethics education. In the process, I will address the origins and development of our assessment of ethical reasoning as a college-level learning outcome.

GUIDING THE ASSESSMENT OF STUDENT LEARNING OUTCOMES: SOME LESSONS AND CAVEATS

It is important to recognize that every college and university has its own path of discovery for its assessment journey. In hindsight, I find it very ironic that we in business—who provide instruction and research in the areas of performance appraisal, performance indicators, balanced scorecards, and other such concepts—had very little interaction with assessment of student learning prior to the policy changes from our accreditation bodies. Basically, our starting point with assessment was at ground zero. No one on the business faculty had any experience that could assist our efforts. The early assistance received came from our newly developed university office of assessment which consisted of a director (the former director of the women's studies program who had no prior experience in assessment other than training at the HLC), an administrative assistant, and a graduate assistant. Some schools might start from a very different point with much more support and experience. Our path was very self-taught, tempered with occasional discussions with the director of assessment. My guidelines on assessment, detailed later, reflect my own experiences.

I should also point out that our path toward assessment was made more complicated by differing requirements coming from our two main accreditation bodies. The HLC accredits the university and was most interested in seeing assessment plans at the major level, whereas the AACSB developed its guidelines on the assurance of learning to target the degree level. In our college, we have multiple majors (e.g., accounting, finance, management, management information systems, and marketing) but only one undergraduate degree (BS in business administration). These differing expectations lead to completely different conclusions regarding assessment, as well as accompanying workloads. Do we develop a master plan that assesses business students on the larger scale as to how they fare on the nine SLOs, or should we develop major-specific plans that identify and assess learning outcomes at the specialization level? Or do we need both? Since the university had appointed the director of assessment, and since her focus was on the requirements of the HLC, we initially veered toward assessing each major within the college. This decision created considerably more work for us in the long run, causing some duplication of efforts with departments planning assessments on the same SLOs, ignoring important college-wide learning outcomes and delaying our progress toward the AACSB assessment guidelines. Thus, although we have learned much from assessment, we were definitely not efficient in our activities. My thoughts reflect on such inefficiencies and attempt to pass on the lessons learned in decision making as well as designing assessment efforts.

Last, but not least, we started with very different opinions of how such assessments should be enacted. Each department was delegated the responsibility for assessing its majors on collegewide SLOs, and for one reason or another, all decided to work independently. Some took a very complicated and convoluted approach, with dozens of SLOs covering a broad range of content, multiple measures, and a variety of proposed methods. Others (myself included) took a more minimalistic approach, where SLOs were simplified into a short list of meaningful outcomes of course content and critical thinking, leaving the more process-oriented SLOs for a college level assessment. There was some debate and discussion across departments, but it was generally unproductive as all believed to hold the true secrets to assessment. In the end, the simplified approach proved its effectiveness, but not without much delay and a few dead ends.

Lesson 1: The Importance of Valid and Measurable Student Learning Outcomes

As mentioned earlier, our initial step was the development and finalization of SLOs for our business program. Our assessment committee, along with the college course and curriculum committee, took on the task of facilitating the early conversations to determine the ideal set of skills and knowledge expected of our business graduates. These discussions often devolve into cynical admonitions of the weaknesses in our student population. There is a tendency at this stage to brainstorm a broadly conceived wish list that borders on idealism rather than a clearly focused set of skills and knowledge one would expect all graduates to have developed in a business school. Once developed, an initial list was brought before the entire business faculty for discussion and voting. Although such a discussion among faculty in a small committee meeting can appear rational at times, a similar discussion among 50 faculty members can resemble an active trading day on the floor of the stock exchange. As one would expect, not only the definitions of the SLOs were debated, but also the identification of the best, most precise terms to use to simply name each SLO involved a variety of lectures and testimonials drawn from each faculty member's teaching and life philosophies. Yet, while the discussions were prolonged, the good news was that faculty members were clearly engaged. In the end, nine SLOs were identified and approved: (1) written communication skills, (2) oral communication skills, (3) adaptability to change, (4) computer skills, (5) ability to work on teams among diverse perspectives, (6) creative thinking skills, (7) disciplined thinking, (8) understanding of global perspectives, and (9) ethical reasoning.

The first lesson begins at this point. On the surface, each of these SLOs appears to be meaningful and quite noble, but underneath lie various meanings assigned or assumed. Similar to developing valid items for a research survey, clarity of meaning of the underlying construct is critical. For example, the SLO of oral communication skills appears very innocent, but multiple meanings stem from different contexts. Do we simply mean presentation skills? Should we include discussion skills? Would we not like our students to have debate or persuasion skills? Each of these is a legitimate interpretation of oral communication, and due to the lack of precision in our definition, we created a situation where the assessment committee members spun their wheels for months on end debating interpretations. For written communication, surely there is clarity there, right? The rules of good grammar may be slipping, but at least we know what they should be. In recent years, written communication has taken on new dimensions with email, texting, and tweeting, but in 2003 we were only at the tip of that iceberg. Were we to be responsible for assessing grammar? What about business writing? What is business writing anyway? Whether the faculty in the business school could correct grammar problems if given the charge is another question altogether. Other SLOs presented us with different challenges as we realized the vagueness of terms such as computer skills, global perspectives, creative thinking, teamwork and diversity, disciplined thinking and adaptability to change.

All of which brings us to the SLO for ethical reasoning. First, I feel very fortunate to serve on the faculty at a college where ethics is a required part of the core curriculum. We have had a course in business, government and Society on the books since the early 1970s, and that course has been a required course for all business majors since the 1980s. It has become one of our two capstone classes (business strategy being the other). Ethics is also one of our college-level strategic initiatives, as we have hired faculty across the business disciplines with an interest in ethics at the macro and micro levels. This context sets us apart from many schools and, in many ways, offers the ideal setting for assessing the ethical reasoning skills of our students.

Despite this focus on ethics in our curriculum, there was still confusion among faculty members outside the ethics area during the discussions of adding an ethics-related SLO. Does this mean we are teaching the students right and wrong? Whose ethics are we going to teach? Such questions surfaced, and were immediately laid to rest as we focused attention on process rather than content. In our estimation, it would not be practical, possible, or sensible to believe that we could develop a mechanism to assure that our graduates would always make the right decision in all situations. The multiple stakeholders perspective tells us that success in business decisions is defined through a variety of measures of performance—financial growth, profitability, revenues, production efficiency, social responsibility, sustainability, social justice, or others. The differing approaches to ethics (e.g. utilitarian, deontological, etc.) suggest that determining what is right depends on one's personal philosophy. The goal of a business ethics course is to use the existing knowledge base in theoretical and practical ethics to build students' awareness so that they can (a) recognize when they are in a situation that can be construed as containing ethical challenges, (b) develop a thought process that would allow them to understand those ethical challenges within the contexts, and (c) infer possible courses of corrective action. Thus, we determined that the focus for our SLO would be on ethical reasoning, not ethics per se. Formally stated, our entire ethical reasoning SLO is: Students should be able to demonstrate a fundamental understanding of legal and ethical situations in business and recommend practical applications for managers and public policy makers.

The first lesson, then, is that SLOs, including those crafted for ethical reasoning, need to be developed using a process similar to that of developing constructs to measure in survey research. Specificity is important—the construct can be abstract, but its definition should point toward tangible elements. Thus, the broad construct of communication skills becomes the more targeted notion of presentation skills, further defined with precise behavioral indicators. The broad category of business ethics is highly complex, so the need for narrowing the focus is critical to assessment. Our ultimate focus on ethical reasoning made sense given our course learning objectives of delivering of a body of extant knowledge aimed at facilitating the ability of students to recognize ethical challenges in business and identify possible courses of action. The existence of a required ethics course, along with having faculty members familiar with the field of business ethics, made agreement on the ethical reasoning SLO that much easier, despite some initial confusion among the nonethics faculty. In order to focus the learning outcome, one must begin with strong knowledge of the field.

Lesson 2: The Action Imperative

As I noted earlier, our assessment process was paralyzed for a few years as the committee debated interpretations and ideas, developed potential plans, and gathered information from various sources. Although I was not privy to their discussions, I sensed a fear of taking action. Assessment was a new process, and we had little understanding of what it meant for us or our accreditation. Over time, the general faculty became disengaged, moving on with their tasks of research and teaching. The assessment committee, like many faculty committees, devolved into a situation where the chair set the meetings and tried to guide discussions. Ultimately, the initiative emanated from the actions of the chair. This was tricky, since he was not a tenured or even a tenure track faculty member. His power to engage activity was limited. When he resigned, the committee floundered at best. The departments then took it upon themselves to interpret standards as best they could, with little communication across departmental lines. Activity was slow, and the motivating potential of the annual reports expected for the provost's office did not require much progress.

Upon taking the assignment as the new chair of the assessment committee, I was somewhat surprised by how little had been accomplished. I have a penchant for activity. I make lists, I determine tasks that need to be done, and I am not afraid to try new things. With our reaccreditation looming in 18 months, I felt compelled to act. In my initial meeting with the assessment committee in January of 2007, we discussed our nine SLOs and how we could assess each once within the next two semesters. I was quickly educated on the paralysis of the committee. I opened the discussion with written communication skills, the first SLO. Someone vaguely mentioned something about a class here or there that maybe had some written work assigned. Another member noted that they had also discussed having students develop a writing portfolio, followed by vague references to other undeveloped notions. I asked if anyone had located a rubric on writing skills. Someone suggested that the English language program (ELP) might be a place to look for help, but no one had ever checked with this office. I knew that faculty members who taught our capstone courses assigned short cases, so I asked if it made sense to take a small sample (less than 100) of papers from those classes and assess them according to a rubric. There were nods around the table. I said that I would talk to the instructors and have them provide written assignments with names deleted, and that I would check with the ELP for a rubric. We would do the assessment before the end of the spring semester. Off we went, with similar action-focused discussion of other SLOs.

In our discussion of assessing ethical reasoning, the same action orientation was applied. First we needed to decide on a location for assessing the SLO then determine a reasonable process for assessing it within that course's context. Our capstone course in business, government and society was clearly the appropriate location. All business majors must take the course in their senior year, and it is the course designed to deliver business ethics in the curriculum The BGS course is staffed using all ranks, from professors to an adjunct instructor. Each uses a different approach to teaching the course, some have strengths in the micro side, others on the macro side, and others excel on all fronts. Our BGS faculty members have historically operated quite independently in course design and coverage of material. Thus, our first step was to generate an agreed-upon set of learning objectives for the BGS course. How the objectives were met was left to the faculty, but it was important that all agreed to a common set of outcomes. Upon finalizing the inclusion of ethical reasoning as an SLO, faculty in the BGS courses met to have these discussions. A set of BGS course learning objectives was thus produced (as covered in the chapter by Swanson, Fisher, and Niehoff in this book).

With these course-level objectives in place, we felt more confident that while our BGS instructors might not cover all topics in the same way, their students would gain exposure to common coverage of ethical reasoning in business situations. In addition, each BGS instructor utilized case analyses in her or his classes, with the culminating experience being either a class discussion or group project and presentation.

One specific section of BGS, that of Dr. Diane Swanson, was then targeted as the location for our initial ethics assessment activity. Dr. Swanson's section utilizes comprehensive case analyses, culminating in an in-depth group presentation designed to examine all aspects of ethical issues using a wide range of applicable theoretical frameworks. Student recommendations are then generated from the diagnostic process. Our focus would be on the assessment of students' performance in these presentations, with each group being rated according to a rubric designed for this specific context. Although the entire plan was not clear initially, the direction was at least narrowed, and we could move forward on solid ground.

The point here is that the process of assessment is not perfect. It cannot and should not be treated the same as designing data collection for a top-tier journal publication. It is truly a process of discovery. In conversations with colleagues in other colleges and universities, the paralysis of perfectionism commonly stalls assessment processes because academics tend to seek the ideal. Rather than precision, the emphasis needs to be on action.

Everything begins with simply trying something. It does not have to be perfect the first time. In the case of our ethics assessment, our college's focus on ethics in the curriculum, the familiarity of many faculty members with the concept of ethical reasoning, and the willingness of one professor to offer her class for a pilot test of our rubric resulted in quick action and data to assess in an early stage of our assessment. We could now examine data to begin to understand our students' learned knowledge and application of the ethical reasoning process.

Lesson 3: The Truth about Resistance to Change

Having taught courses on resistance to change, I was fully aware of the theoretical aspects of change. Also, in my role as department head I have witnessed a number of changes in curricula, performance standards, or strategic direction over the years. I understand that people—yes, even faculty—will vary in their acceptance and adaptation to change. The assessment process gave me a much clearer perspective on dealing with resistance. I came to see six different groupings in which faculty members sorted themselves.

First, there were the *early adopters*. As soon as I had laid out our plans for assessment of the SLOs in the spring of 2007 at a faculty meeting, I had at least five faculty members visit with me afterwards, volunteering to help with either the assessment of oral communication skills or writing skills. This group consisted of some friends, some non-tenure track instructors in my department or other departments, and a couple of surprises. One full professor from another department showed his support by jumping on board quickly. This group was clearly interested in the two SLOs and truly wanted to see what the results would be.

There was a second group that I could sense. I call these the *cheerleaders*. They were generally supportive of assessment, but did not want to be in the game. This consisted of a fairly broad group across the college. They trusted me in a general sense, and felt that assessment was necessary, but had no interest in being involved at any level. I appreciated their support. In addition was a third group—call them the *broadcasters*—who did assist indirectly by making sure that our rubrics were communicated to the students. The rubrics developed for oral presentations and written work were placed on the college website, and a few broadcasters downloaded these to use as guidelines for grading in their classes. This type of activity greatly supports the assessment process, as it directly improves student learning. It felt good to have such support.

The fourth group consisted of the *expert reviewers*. These faculty members were disinterested in the early phases of the process. Once the assessment reports began to come in, or when I presented the results in a public forum, their interest was piqued. In a sense, the assessment process became like a manuscript to review. Their comments in meetings were often critical of methodology, but not so critical as to reject the study. They acted out the part of the supportive reviewer in a journal process.

They mentioned the good aspects of the study and gave helpful hints for other measures to use, other methods to implement or other populations to explore. My attempts to engage them more completely in the process—bring them onto the team—were less than successful. Like the cheerleaders, they did not want to be more involved, feeling their contribution was simply to be helpful.

The fifth group can be termed the *late adopters*. This group sat on the sidelines in the early phases of the assessment, but they were supportive. As the assessment gained strength and data, it became clear to them that they could directly contribute to the process. Providing classroom time for assessing their students, assisting in revamping a rubric, or learning from watching, this group provided, and still provides, great assistance in assessing students. They have even taken some of the original rubrics (e.g., computer skills, ethical reasoning), and made significant improvements.

The sixth and final group is the *resistors*. For whatever reason—lack of belief in the utility of assessment, lack of understanding of the purpose of assessment, lack of motivation in general or simply arrogance—there are those who have never made an effort to provide support in any way. No cheerleading, no broadcasting, not even an expert opinion. At every instance possible, they express their doubts about the process or make statements indicating that they have never bought into the purpose from the start. The lucky thing for me has been that there are only a few people who seem to be in this group. It offended them that their grading of students was not good enough to serve as an assessment. They distrust others who seek less than perfect means for assessing student performance, and they doubt all assessment results that they themselves did not design. Basically this group is not helpful, but appears to be a fact of life in the world of assessment. It disturbs me that scholars at an academic institution are not curious about student learning, but I recognize that 100% agreement is probably never a possible outcome.

Change reveals people—their perceptions, their opinions, their emotions. It is important, as in all managerial tasks, to keep your own feelings in check during the assessment process. Getting too high on those who are supportive, or too low on those who are negative, only creates dysfunctional sidetracks for a leader. Keeping focused on the goal and providing opportunities for those who want to be involved, combined with accurate reporting and constructive discussion of the findings, provide credibility to the assessment process that the majority should be able to support. It is neither a steady state nor a destination—assessment is a constant process of improvement. People invariably choose their level of acceptance of, commitment to, and participation in the process.

This lesson applies to the entire gamut of possible SLOs, including ethical reasoning. As we moved forward in the assessment of ethical reasoning, more faculty members expressed an interest in the process. Having a critical mass of faculty in areas related to ethics—corporate social responsibility, organization citizenship, workplace justice, and accounting ethics to name a few—helped lower the general resistance to the assessment of ethical reasoning. As always, there seems to be a Resistor or two who doubt the validity of any assessment process, but that has not deterred our progress toward a better understanding of where our students stand in their understanding of ethical reasoning.

Lesson 4: The Impact of Data

In academia, we often refer to various puzzles as "an empirical question." Assessment provides data that can directly inform our discussions of students and their learning in our programs. Rather than stating "I think our students are all great communicators," we can now state more precisely that "55% of our students gave satisfactory or better presentations." Rants claiming that "none of our students can write," can be addressed with the data "83% of seniors in the sample were rated at the satisfactory or above level on their writing skills."

Data are critical to the process of assessment. There are two general models used in academic assessment data gathering methodology. The first is to assess every student on every SLO. This requires much testing and the development of a portfolio for each student. Although this method is thorough and provides much data, most large university business programs with thousands of students make such a method impractical. The second strategy is that of sampling. We all understand the notion of statistical sampling. As long as we truly sample in a random fashion, not gearing our samples toward the high or low end of the distribution, we should be able to determine a good estimate of the "true score" on assessments. We used sampling in three of our four assessments completed in my first semester as chair, and learned a great deal from the data.

Once data are gathered, most academicians begin to take interest. I found plenty of interested parties once we had data. Some commented on the weaknesses of my design, some suggested different measures, and others were drawn into the process by their own curiosity and have become valuable members of the assessment team. In my view, that is the impact of gathering data—getting faculty engaged.

Regarding the assessment of ethical reasoning, the data from the initial assessment showed students to be achieving the learning objectives of the course at a very high rate. A second round of data revealed consistency with the first. Given these results, we will now expand the assessment to other sections of the BGS course in order to gain a more generalized sample under the instruction of other faculty members. The challenge will be that other instructors of the course do not utilize such an in-depth case methodology as the present one. The rubric will be offered as a means to assess an applicable activity from the other classes, and the faculty members will determine where in their class the use of the rubric would make the most sense.

One methodological issue that applies relative to our data on ethical reasoning is that the assessment is based on a group presentation, not individual students. Each student in a group speaks to a fairly substantial application of theoretical models to understand the ethical issues in the case, but each student addresses a different set of frameworks. The ratings on the rubric assess the perceived performance of the group as a whole. Although not perfect, this level of data still informs us as to the achievement of our students' performance on the ethical reasoning SLO. We will continue to seek ways to improve our assessment process.

Notably, I believe that teaching ethics in a stand-alone class contributed to the successful achievement of learning objectives and our ability to assess ethical reasoning, since the focus on ethics is concentrated in this class. When ethics is integrated across the curriculum, it might be more difficult to assess the process of ethical reasoning, since it is more difficult to establish adequate depth of coverage. The stand-alone course also provided a clear location for the assessment to occur, and allowed for all aspects of ethical reasoning to be assessed in one place. The alternative distributed model of teaching ethics across an integrated curriculum may not provide the depth that a stand-alone course provides, nor does it offer a clear place in the curriculum to assess the learning of ethical reasoning. Since there would be no clear point in the curriculum where students are provided a deepened exposure to the many frameworks necessary for diagnosing ethical dilemmas and cases, one could question what is being assessed. Also, in integrated ethics programs, the coverage of ethics is often defined by its appearance on the syllabus, which is no guarantee that a quality level of coverage results. If we find that ethical reasoning is not being learned, the integrated model does not offer a clear location to correct the problem. It makes sense to all involved with the assessment of ethical reasoning that it be under the supervision of the ethics faculty. (Again, see the Swanson-Fisher-Niehoff chapter for more discussion of this issue).

Lesson 5: Simple Ideas and Seamless Processes

As noted earlier, our initial assessment planning consisted of each department devising its own learning outcomes for the different majors, and designing accompanying strategies for assessing students. As can often be the case, when faculty members become very engaged in a committee or planning process, every possible detail is likely to emerge due to the nature of the inquisitive faculty mind. On the one hand, it is good to have such engagement. On the other, the result can be pedantic and overly complex. The probability of the latter is increased when there is some disagreement or ambiguity regarding the purpose, end product, or objective of the exercise. Faculty will generally gravitate toward more complexity rather than less.

The complexity of the assessment process is affected by the area of study. In some areas, there is a relatively large common body of knowledge due to the number of required courses. A large common body of knowledge can create a much wider degree of content knowledge subject to assessment. Keeping assessment simple depends on what information will be assessed.

In addition to simplicity is seamlessness. It is important to balance thoroughness with the reality of needing an assessment process that is repeatable and efficiently executed. For example, if a department embeds specific questions on tests across a variety of courses or in a capstone course, then it becomes relatively easy to collect the assessment data each year. If, instead, the different SLOs require many different methods and processes for assessment, assessment becomes more complex and less institutionalized.

For ethical reasoning, once we decided on a location and developed our rubric, the process became quite simple and seamless. The rubric was tailored to fit the student case presentations, identifying four general skills in analyzing ethical situations—(a) identify the social or ethical dilemma, (b) consider the range of stakeholders in terms of ethical perspectives, (c) analyze the moral reasoning of the main decision makers, and (d) make recommendations for corrective action. These would be rated as unacceptable, acceptable, or exemplary. A complex process became relatively simple and seamless for the instructor of the course.

Simplification of SLOs does not mean that we trivialize program objectives or fail to specify what we believe to be important knowledge to be gained by students. Nor should the process boil down to a few general learning outcomes that we can assure our students understand upon graduation. One aspect of assessment should be clear—it is not intended to replace education. Our purpose in higher education is that of creating educated people who can apply critical reasoning skills to a wide range of topics and experiences. This is especially true in the case of ethical reasoning, since graduates of business schools typically become managers who can affect social outcomes. Assessment is not an exercise in setting low goals then assuring students can reach them each year—that is, teaching to the test. Instead, student learning outcomes should have meaning, reflect depth of knowledge, skills, or attitudes, and receive an adequate amount of attention in the curriculum. They should not dominate the curriculum, but if we truly believe they are important, then they should be a focus of what we do in our classrooms.

The more seamless we can make the process, the easier it will be to repeat in future years. The ethics rubric for the BGS course, described earlier, is just one example. The rubric provides a very simple mechanism for the BGS faculty to determine the level of learning of ethical reasoning. It is simple and repeatable, yet informative.

Lesson 6: Developing, Locating and Refining Applicable Rubrics

I know I heard the term rubrics before our initial discussions of assessment in our college, but I believe the word has become a part of my weekly vocabulary since my involvement in assessment implementation. Rubrics are the fabric of many assessments, similar to surveys in the research process. Similar to surveys, it is critical to assure that the rubrics selected reflect a valid model of assessing the intended learning objective. Not all assessment processes require the use of rubrics. Some assessments consist of using targeted questions embedded in exams, while others utilize standardized test scores. Rubrics enter into the process when the need arises to determine students' progress or performance on less concrete indicators such as presentation skills, critical thinking, or ethical reasoning. Rubrics are generally used as a means for rating students on specific objectives or outcomes. They are behaviorally anchored rating scales, where three or more levels of performance (e.g., unsatisfactory, satisfactory, and exceptional) are defined clearly in terms of the behaviors or characteristics visible at each level.

Our program uses rubrics in the assessments of both oral and written communication, ethical reasoning, computer skills, critical thinking, and teamwork. We are working on potential rubrics for diversity and global understanding.

For ethical reasoning, a web search resulted in the location of a rubric assessing the concept at the Open Source Portfolio, featured as "a robust, non-proprietary, open-source electronic portfolio application, developed by a community of individuals and organizations from around the world" (http://www.theospi.org/resource/ethical-consideration-rubric). The rubric was tested in the selected BGS course by observing group presentations and assessing students' ability to reason through the various ethics models and frameworks. After the pilot test, I met with Dr. Swanson to discuss needed changes in the rubric. After the discussion, she revised the rubric and utilized it to assess the student group case presentations in the following semester. The final rubric consisted of the four skills discussed in the previous section. The ethics assessment data derived from this rubric supplements the assessment data now collected from a 24-item survey given to students before and after they take the BGS course. This survey, still in the pilot stage, is designed to tap four of the BGS course-level objectives. (These four objectives and the data derived from the pilot survey are detailed in the Swanson-Fisher-Niehoff chapter.)

As schools move further into the assessment process, there is no reason to use the lack of a good rubric as an excuse for not assessing ethical reasoning or any SLO, for that matter. A simple online search will locate more than enough rubrics, assessing a variety of outcomes for business schools. The main difficulty in their construction is the assurance that the behaviors described for each level of performance are clearly distinguishable from other levels of performance, and that such behaviors are visible in the work being assessed. After the initial construction, some piloting is important, particularly having others use the rubric and getting feedback on its performance in the process. What I have learned is that the accreditation bodies are not so concerned about the exact rubrics being used, but that assessment is being performed. What matters to me, as the chair of the assessment committee, is that we are assessing what we believe to be important, and good rubrics help us more clearly define what we believe to be important aspects of our students' progression toward our predefined outcomes.

CONCLUSION

Like most learning opportunities, I thought I understood assessment going into the process, but was quickly educated on different methods, nuances, and terminology through my ensuing experiences. I have learned that accreditation bodies, from the HLC to the AACSB, are interested in two questions: (1) what do you believe your students should know or be able to do when they graduate, and (2) how do you know that they know or can do these things? To these bodies, it is not the content of the assessment that matters most. Instead, it is the process being assessed.

Consequently, the schools themselves must decide upon the ethics content to deliver. It is our responsibility for educating the next generation of business leaders and demonstrating that we are doing what we can to try to improve the ethical climate in business environments. The public trust in business schools will wane if we veer away from this responsibility. We must decide on appropriate ethics content and personalize the delivery of it as much as possible, through discussions, case studies, simulations, or other teaching methods, so that students can see beyond the theoretical into the applicable. Inherent in that responsibility is also the imperative that we assess what students have learned from such personalized assignments. Given the ongoing debates about the murkiness of what is right and wrong in business decisions, it makes sense to focus on teaching students to recognize when they find themselves in situations requiring critical thinking about ethics and provide guidance for using the tools and methods that ethics education can provide. In the College of Business Administration at Kansas State University, we approach this task with a required stand-alone course for delivering ethics in the curriculum and, therefore, a critical mass of faculty already committed to this enterprise or receptive to it. In my view, I cannot imagine a more supportive and efficient environment in which to assess ethical reasoning.

Although business ethics is a complex construct, so are organizational behavior, leadership, and any number of business disciplines. Such complexity should not deter us from assessing students' learning of our educational objectives. If we can improve the ethical reasoning of the next generation of business leaders sufficiently, more conscientious decisions may ensue, with more focus on socially responsible business practices in general. It is our hope that effective assessment of ethical reasoning will move us closer to that ideal.

CHAPTER 13

PLANNING AND PERSONALIZING COURSE ASSESSMENT

Steve Payne

Many factors influence personal choices of assessment strategies and techniques for faculty teaching business ethics and social issues courses. This chapter encourages faculty to consider many external and cultural factors influencing assessment choices, yet not to neglect in these choices their own evolving personal philosophy of teaching and student learning. Somewhat different student learning goals for ethics and social issues courses, in contrast to many other courses in business schools, suggest that faculty focus more assessment concern on student learning or acquisition of certain skills, dispositions, and values. A few additional assessment approaches and tools, beyond those typically found and broadly applied within most business programs, are explored.

INTRODUCTION

I appreciate this opportunity to share personal perspectives concerning assessment of student learning for business ethics and social issues courses. Having long taught these courses, I have experimented with a

Toward Assessing Business Ethics Education
pp. 231–240

number of different assessment-related alternatives. My comments in this chapter have been shaped by several distinct experiences related to assessment concerns. Cochairing and helping develop a faculty development program on course assessment potentials at my own institution was certainly such an experience. This program extended over several years and involved many groups of four to 10 faculty meeting for about 3 hours a week over 7 weeks of an academic semester. The coordinator for this faculty development program, Autumn Grubb, had a very strong background related to course assessment and provided participants with remarkable forms of structure, possibilities, and reinforcement for their own individual learning. Likewise, I am indebted to Jim Weber at Duquesne University for several long conversations concerning our similar and contrasting perspectives related to assessment potentials for business ethics and social issues courses. Along with Jamie Hendry, we organized and led a learning assessment workshop at the 2005 meeting of the International Association of Business and Society in Sonoma, California.

Obtaining informative feedback concerning aspects of actual student learning in our courses seems so critical, particularly given the many challenges for moral and socially sensitive conduct within business cultures and the continuing and strong criticisms of misconduct by many in corporate management. Yet Kraft (2000) describes deficiencies in assessment efforts by faculty and traces these to certain cognitive and relational characteristics found in academic cultures. Existing norms and attitudes toward learning assessment found in many business schools often can be significant barriers for the reflexivity and creativity needed to explore means for increased student learning. In over three decades of college teaching, and until the last decade, seldom did I observe much actual interest among business faculty in discussing forms of student learning assessment or developing anything like a systematic approach for course assessment. Usually I noted quite limited faculty responses to outside pressures or unexpected events, even in cases when reports on assessment approaches/results for institutional or professional accreditation were required, such as those requested by the Association to Advance Collegiate Schools of Business (AACSB). Business faculty often appeared to me to be in a largely reactive or defensive mode of response to these dictates or requirements.

I believe that faculty teaching ethics-related courses can assume a special leadership role in the assessment of student learning by encouraging other business faculty to go beyond a largely passive role. More than other faculty, ethics faculty should recognize a need to assume responsibility or forms of control for their teaching plans and consequences. We counsel students and those in business organizations to take responsibility through various performance-related, social or ethics audits, and we should have a corresponding concern for well-developed, transparent, and effectively communicated assessments of student learning. We stress moral values such as promise keeping, so should we not at least ask students to assess the degree to which they perceive that we have helped them accomplish learning goals or objectives that we place in our own course syllabus?

QUESTIONS AND POTENTIALS

Too often outside or top-down demands for already-determined categories of assessment reporting can seem to discourage faculty from perceiving course assessment as a very personal responsibility that starts first with taking the time for serious exploration of one's own teaching philosophy. Such effort initially to describe a teaching philosophy and anticipated student learning outcomes can help support faculty buy-in and follow-through in developing teaching plans and activities and related student learning assessments. Individual thought and peer discussion concerning teaching philosophies can lead faculty to transform implicit impressions or vague goals into more explicit objectives for student learning. A course portfolio as a next step, and in contrast to a traditional teaching portfolio, might contain a statement of course objectives, a plan for accomplishing these objectives, information demonstrating extent of recent student achievement of these objectives, and personal reflections on these interacting objectives, plans, and assessments (Course Portfolio Initiative, 2001). Within such a course portfolio might be a document presented in tabular form called a "course assessment matrix" that would list the various assessments chosen for and undertaken during the course, including upon which learning outcomes these assessments individually or collectively focused (A. Grubb, personal communication, 2004). Periodically developing a course portfolio containing one's emerging teaching philosophy and related planning and assessment approaches provides an input that can be shared in dialogues with faculty colleagues and allows faculty to contrast their personal commitments, strategies, and learning choices.

Although developing a basic description of what one is attempting to accomplish through student learning objectives is vital for developing a course assessment approach, it is also important for faculty in ethics-related courses to recognize the much broader context for student learning and assessment into which their individual efforts fit. This broader context includes understanding what many scholars and teachers in the field of business ethics and social issues in business are attempting related to their own learning goals/competencies and assessment activities. Scholarly or professional reviews of articles and conference papers on assessment topics can offer some guidance for possible learning of assessment potentials and can promote refinement or expansion of initial personal commitments. The Scholarship of Teaching and Learning (SOTL) movement and its literature over the last two decades certainly provide background knowledge on specific possibilities for course learning assessments. Specific authors and books describe many different course assessment concerns and techniques, some of which are well suited for learning goals in business ethics and social issues courses. Two useful resources are books by Angelo and Cross (1993) and Huba and Freed (2000), but a quick scan of faculty development pages on various university websites can result in the discovery of many additional resources on course assessment.

It is obviously necessary to consider university assessment goals and the extent to which these can significantly influence an individual faculty member's choices for student learning assessment. Of equal or greater concern, however, are the learning goals and assessment approaches of particular academic programs within a business school. Similar to the institutional context, the program or school context can influence, and also be impacted by, individual faculty assessment in particular courses. Given expectations for student learning about ethics and social issues in business schools, it is important for faculty teaching a required or elective course in business ethics and/or social issues to recognize what faculty in core courses in functional business fields and in other courses, such as information systems or business communications, for example, are planning, doing, and assessing in ethics and socially-related areas. The time allowed within most business curricula for focusing on ethics and socially-related student learning and related assessment is limited, so such opportunities should be time effective, and not unnecessarily repetitive of assessment that other faculty have already completed. Often neglected is "closing the assessment loop" or communicating to others the results or learning implications that faculty have gained from assessment activities.

Closing the assessment loop by communicating assessment approaches and results in business ethics courses seems particularly important for the evolving area of business ethics. Over recent decades, there has been considerable debate whether ethics-related topics in business programs should be addressed in a stand-alone course, through integration in all core business courses, or by both of these approaches. Proponents for increased ethics and social issues learning in business schools need to offer more and better evidence through assessment activities showing relative deficiencies or merits of stand-alone courses and/or integration of learning across the curriculum. Business ethics scholars, particularly Jim Weber (1990), have long raised questions concerning the short- and long-range learning impact of business ethics courses, and better assessment activities done by more faculty teaching these courses could provide more evidence to help convince business deans and faculty of the need for increased emphasis on ethics in undergraduate and graduate business programs (Swanson, 2004).

A more thorough or systemic approach by faculty teaching ethics and social issues courses would seem to me to include serious faculty consideration of the following major questions:

1. Should the assessment approach focus on assessing student learning as the acquisition of certain knowledge, skills, and dispositions from course activities, or just the possession of such knowledge, skills, or dispositions at the conclusion of the course?

    Conducting early or precourse assessments seems as important for determining the acquisition of learning as a result of activities in a particular course as doing end-of-course learning assessments. Assessment can also include student testing and feedback at the end of academic programs. This form of assessment, and also contacts with alumni and/or employers, can provide at least some limited evidence concerning the extent of longer-term learning by students versus the erosion of certain knowledge, skills, or dispositions.

2. How might the assessment approach include the three types of controls described in management theory as (a) feed-forward, (b) process, and (c) feedback?

    If early or precourse assessment can be viewed as a type of feed-forward control, then assessment of many aspects of on-going learning (specific classroom activities or techniques) can be viewed as a form of process control. Creating assignment-specific rubrics can assist the instructor in determining the effectiveness of individual learning assignments and the relative effectiveness of contrasting learning approaches (lectures, experiential experiences, cases, etc.) as parts of the learning mix. For both process and feedback controls, faculty can use a variety of assessment techniques, especially short or micro surveys that gauge the actual learning associated with specific course assignments. Such techniques can take very little classroom time to provide useful student feedback, and these can counter initial faculty objections that course assessment activities can subtract from the limited classroom time available for student learning. Some assessment methods also can be assigned for student thought and completion outside of class meeting time for their written submission at the start of the next class period. Angelo and Cross (1993) identify a huge number of assessment exercises for different learning objectives along with estimates of the amount of preparation time required for faculty to create these exercises and the time required for students to complete these inside or outside of class.

3. What are students' responsibilities for active learning in business ethics courses, and what degree of skills or dispositions related to these courses do students bring at the beginning of these courses, during these courses, and at their conclusion?

A consideration of this question might shed some light on why faculty who teach a course or course component similarly from one semester to the next receive quite different student feedback on their learning. Such differences could involve classes of students having contrasting learning skills, strategies, and/or dispositions. An early or precourse assessment tool, such as the Motivated Strategies for Learning Questionnaire (MSLQ) (Pintrich, McKeachie, & Smith, 1989), allows instructors to gain partial knowledge of certain existing student skills, strategies, and dispositions related to a particular course. The motivational scales in this tool are intrinsic goal orientation, extrinsic goal orientation, task value, control of learning beliefs, self-efficacy for learning and performance, and test anxiety. Strategies scales include learning rehearsal, elaboration, organization, critical thinking, and metacognitive self-regulation. A third set of scales in the full 81-item questionnaire consist of time and study environment, effort regulation, peer learning and help seeking. Shorter (with fewer scales) and free online versions of the MSLQ that students can complete and obtain instant feedback are available. The University of Arizona's 40-item MSLQ version (at http://www.ulc.arizona.edu/mslq.php) is one that I have requested students to complete. Duncan and McKeachie (2005) report that the MSLQ is a reliable and useful tool for academic researchers, instructors, and students. Survey feedback to students of overall class responses on instruments such as the MSLQ, can offer students comparative information and communicate to them the instructor's expectation of learning as a shared responsibility for which students have a critical role.

4. To what extent does the assessment approach involve individualized student learning and assessment rather than obtaining mere class or overall levels of student learning?

Certain assessment tools and activities can allow faculty to obtain feedback on individual differences among students, such as their expectations of the course or their possession of contrasting learning strategies and abilities. This feedback can provide faculty with knowledge of individual student challenges, so that the faculty member might try to assist certain individuals who are confronting particular learning obstacles. What particularly worrying or disturbing barriers to potential learning do these students experience? Following a path-goal motivational approach, to what extent and how might faculty reduce significant obstacles in the path of learning for them? Opening more and diverse paths for individualized learning by students can be important for some faculty in their evolving teaching philosophies, and assessment activities can provide potential guidance. However, issues of individual anonymity on surveys or through feedback, as well as means for possibly identifying and communicating with those students experiencing difficulties, need to be considered.

5. Do the assessment activities include feedback from faculty peers at other institutions and from key stakeholders impacted by student knowledge, skills, and dispositions?

   What are the areas of knowledge, skill, and disposition related to ethics and social issues that stakeholders, such as employers and those in the local business community, actually expect or demand, especially given recent debates about and criticisms of business ethics? Have such stakeholders been contacted and might a few of them be willing to review faculty learning objectives, methods, and assessments? What additions or modifications might these employers or business leaders suggest as worth exploration? Who are some of the more experienced or knowledgeable faculty in related academic fields, and what might they suggest in this regard? Assessment activities might include these concerns and seek to answer these types of questions.

6. To what extent and how does the choice of learning objectives and assessments go beyond learning outcomes in the cognitive domain —such as Bloom's (1956) concern for knowledge, comprehension, application, analysis, synthesis, and evaluation—to consider affective or dispositional outcomes for student learning?

   Although not widely known, Bloom and others (Krathwohl, Bloom, & Masia, 1973) examined aspects of student learning in both the domains of psychomotor or skill development and affective or feeling development. Particularly the affective or dispositional domain for student learning seems very relevant to faculty teaching ethics and social issues courses. The developmental steps in this affective domain include (a) receiving (or being aware of something in the environment), (b) responding (or displaying certain new behavior as a result of such an experience), (c) valuing (or demonstrating some actual commitment or involvement related to the experience), (d) organizing (or integrating a new value somehow into the individual's overall values set, and (e) internalizing such values (acting consistently in response to these values). Students can be assessed as to their awareness of certain moral or social issues in various contexts (local, national, or global). For these levels of student awareness, it is possible as well to survey the extent to which students express any concern, commitment to actions, or actual responses related to a particular issue. For example, students might rank or prioritize certain sets of values, such as the terminal value in Rokeach's (1973) Value Survey of a "world of beauty" or global environmental concerns relative to many other personal values. Beyond the use of the Rokeach instrument, student valuing can be investigated through the administration of other common values inventories or ethics surveys (Payne, 1988).

7. How might the approach for assessment of student learning in an ethics or social issues course be influenced by theories and models of learning/conduct that are accepted by ethics or social science scholars?

The moral psychologist James Rest (1986) stresses the processes of perceiving a moral dilemma/issue (component one), reasoning concerning this situation (component two), and intending to act or respond (component three) as leading to actual behavioral choices or conduct (component four). Much attention within ethics courses is obviously placed on moral/ethical reasoning processes, and there are assessment tools/techniques that could provide faculty with feedback concerning the development of student reasoning, particularly in regard to handling provocative cases or potential ethical challenges in business environments posed by experiential exercises. Some of these learning and assessment tools seem closely associated with critical thinking models. However, there does not appear to be nearly as much attention directed to student learning and assessment opportunities associated with Rest's first, third, and fourth components in his process model. If one's teaching and learning philosophy is influenced by a concern for how individuals actually perceive that an ethical dilemma exists and how they move beyond mere vague intentions or plans for an ethical response, then one should develop associated teaching plans and learning assessment activities for students. In my case, this led to more focus on teaching and assessment activities for cognitive and affective biases that affect perception, intention to respond, and behavioral choice (Payne, 2006).

CONCLUDING REMARKS

The title of this chapter includes the term "personalizing." The norms and routines that are experienced and often implicitly accepted within academic cultures in business schools need to be questioned or tested periodically. Also subject to testing are our personal and professional commitments, as well as our related assumptions influencing our teaching and learning choices. Teaching business ethics and social issues courses demands that choices be made, such as which social values and issues to include and/or emphasize and how to do this. These plans, the process toward their potential accomplishment, and the impact of actual student learning from these choices are obviously important. These plans, activities, and outcomes certainly deserve significant faculty attention and better communication with and transparency for our primary and secondary stakeholders. Faculty can benefit from thoughtful and careful assessment, and the primary issue becomes how best to manage this process of student learning assessment and personal/professional faculty learning.

REFERENCES

Angelo, T. A., & Cross, K. P. (1993). *Classroom assessment techniques: A handbook for college teachers* (2nd ed.). San Francisco, CA: Jossey-Bass.

Bloom B. S. (1956). *Taxonomy of educational objectives: Handbook I. The cognitive domain*. New York, NY: David McKay.

Course Portfolio Initiative. (2001). *Peer review of teaching, Indiana University.* Retrieved from http://www.indiana.edu/~deanfac/portfolio

Duncan, T. G., & McKeachie, W. (2005). Making of the motivated strategies for learning questionnaire. *Educational Psychologist, 40*(2), 117-128.

Huba, M. E., & Freed, J. E. (2000). *Learner-centered assessment on college campuses: Shifting the focus from teaching to learning*. Needham Heights, MA: Allyn & Bacon.

Kraft, R. G. (2000). Teaching excellence and the inner life of faculty. *Change, 32*(3), 48-52.

Krathwohl, D. R., Bloom, B. S., & Masia, B. B. (1973). *Taxonomy of educational objective: Handbook II. Affective domain*. New York, NY: David McKay.

Payne, S. L. (1988). Values and ethics-related measures for management education. *Journal of Business Ethics, 7*, 273-276.

Payne, S. L. (2006). The ethical intention and prediction matrix: Reducing perceptual and cognitive biases for learning. *Journal of Management Education, 30*, 177-194.

Pintrich, P. R., McKeachie, W. J., & Smith, D. (1989). *The motivated strategies for learning questionnaire*. Ann Arbor, MI: National Center for Research to Improve Postsecondary Teaching and Learning, University of Michigan.

Rest, J. R. (1986). *Moral development: Advances in research and theory.* New York, NY: Praeger.

Rokeach, M. (1973). *The nature of human values.* New York, NY: The Free Press.

Swanson, D. L. (2004). The buck stops here: Why universities must reclaim business ethics education. *Journal of Academic Ethics, 2,* 43-61.

Weber, J. (1990). Measuring the impact of teaching ethics to future managers: A review, assessment, and recommendations. *Journal of Business Ethics, 9,* 183-190.

CHAPTER 14

A HOLISTIC METHOD FOR ASSESSING STUDENT PERFORMANCE IN A BUSINESS ETHICS AND SOCIETY COURSE

Denis Collins

My primary teaching goal is to engage students in creating ethical organizations whose managers take into consideration individual and community well-being. This chapter summarizes my assumptions about the course and student motivation, and provides justifications for 12 student performance assessments. Students earn points for (1) attending class, (2) speaking in class, (3) submitting daily homeworks, (4) journaling on a weekly basis, (5) taking quizzes prior to discussing assigned chapters, (6) facilitating the discussion of an ethical dilemma experienced at work, (7) working on a service-learning team project, (8) writing a report about the project, (9) sharing a meal with those needing the services of a community meal program, (10) composing a purpose-of-life essay, (11) sharing important class concepts with a boss, coworker, or subordinate, and (12) submitting extra credit assignments.

Toward Assessing Business Ethics Education
pp. 241–261
Copyright © 2011 by Information Age Publishing
All rights of reproduction in any form reserved.

INTRODUCTION

Millions of Americans have died in wars so that we could be free. With freedom comes responsibility. My primary teaching goal is to engage students in creating ethical organizations whose managers take into consideration individual and community well-being. I want them to gain the critical thinking skills necessary to be first-class managers and communicators, as well as informed citizens contributing to the ethical evolution of a democratic society (Dewey, 1916).

I have been teaching business ethics and society courses to students for more than 20 years. Currently, I teach a social responsibility in business class to traditional undergraduates and returning adult students at a small liberal arts college. Previously, I taught the course to MBA students at a research university.

My interdisciplinary class integrates ethical analysis from philosophy, persuasion from communication arts, and management principles from business (Collins, 2006a). Students explore and implement the critical thinking, communication, and managerial skills necessary for developing socially responsible organizations and ethical citizenry through lectures, debates, experiential exercises, class participation, and service-learning projects.

This is a learning-by-doing course. A Chinese proverb is "What I hear, I forget. What I see, I remember. What I do, I know." I provide opportunities for students to see and do things, in addition to hearing. Students are challenged to become a partner in this educational process and step through the learning doors I open. The purpose of education is to transfer knowledge and develop ethical citizenry, and hopefully both are achieved.

Such lofty goals require a holistic assessment of student performance. Students are measured on three different levels: individual and group performance, speaking and writing skills, and along Bloom's learning taxonomy—beginning with remembering information and progressing through understanding, applying, analyzing, evaluating, and creating new ideas (Anderson & Krathwohl, 2001).

This chapter summarizes my assumptions about the course and student motivation, and provides justifications for 12 student performance assessments. Students earn points for (1) attending class, (2) speaking in class, (3) submitting daily homeworks, (4) journaling on a weekly basis, (5) taking quizzes prior to discussing assigned chapters, (6) facilitating the discussion of an ethical dilemma experienced at work, (7) working on a service-learning team project, (8) writing a report about the project, (9) sharing a meal with those needing the services of a community meal program, (10) composing a purpose-of-life essay, (11) sharing important class

Table 14.1. Performance Measures

Assignment	Point Value
Nonquiz class attendance	8% (80 points)
Verbal class participation	10% (100 points)
Homework submissions	8% (80 points)
Weekly journaling	3% (30 points)
Readiness quizzes	22% (216 points)
Critical incident group facilitation	2% (20 points)
Service-learning project team work sessions	7% (70 points)
Service-learning project report	8% (84 points)
Community meal program essay	7% (70 points)
Purposes-of-life essay	4% (40 points)
Final exam	21% (210 points)
Potential extra credit	2% (20 points)
Total potential points:	1,020

concepts with a boss, coworker, or subordinate, and (12) submitting extra credit assignments.

Table 14.1 lists the 12 assessments, the point total assigned to each assessment, and the percentage of the total grade for a typical semester. The class operates on a 1,000 point system, with another 20 points available for extra credit. To earn an A the student must accumulate 950 points (95%), 890 points for an AB, 840 for a B, 780 for a BC, 700 for a C, 650 for a CD, and 600 for a D. Due to the very fluid classroom discussions we have, if a student has earned 1,000 points, the student cannot receive higher than a C if he or she missed 20% of the class sessions. The class meets for 75 minutes twice a week for 15 weeks, a total of 30 class meetings. After five missed classes the student is warned that another missed class will result in the enforcement of the attendance rule. In extremely rare circumstances, I may deviate from these grading guidelines.

PHILOSOPHICAL AND THEOLOGICAL ASSUMPTIONS

Teaching is a spiritual calling that requires an emotional and heart-felt experience by both the professor and student (Palmer, 1997). Students and professor should become better people, and make the world a better place, as a result of their interactive journey in class.

The philosophical foundation for such a claim rests with the nature of life on earth. The earth is a rock that has been orbiting the sun for at least 4.5 billion years. This floating spaceship continuously, and simultaneously, moves in two directions—approximately 66,000 miles an hour on an elliptical path around the sun and 1,000 miles an hour on its axis.

There are many potential explanations for the earth's existence. Most religions have a creation story that begins with an earthly paradise. In the Judeo-Christian version, the metaphorical Adam and Eve frolicked in paradise in direct communion with God. They were to achieve spiritual perfection, unconditionally love each other, populate the world, and live happily ever after. Then something happened that distanced humans from God, and the world has been an ethical mess ever since. Rather than heaven on earth, the world is a floating purgatory where people have free will to do good or bad, and where enlightened citizens practice kindness and try valiantly to achieve a just society.

If humans do have a common lineage then we are all related to each other. Therefore, I treat students sitting in my classroom as my siblings. The class is a large family gathering and I, as the educationally eldest sibling, create activities to enhance the transfer of wisdom. I have much to teach them based on more than half a century of experiencing, reflecting, reading, and writing about business ethics topics.

The students also have much to teach me. In a traditional undergraduate class, assuming 25 enrollees and an average age of 21, the students have an accumulated 525 years of life experiences. A similar sized returning adult or MBA class has even more life experiences, approximately 750 years. Although few students have thought as deeply as I have about business ethics topics, their life experiences serve as a validity test for issues raised in class.

I have one semester to provide students with tools to help them recognize they are ethical beings who impact the well-being of others on a daily basis, including while at work. This is a difficult task because most students fear failure, and they have been habituated to be educationally passive. I must push them out of their comfort zones and encourage critical reflection. On the other hand, the job is made easier because, deep-down, students are idealistic beings who want to make the world a better place. To verify this, just ask students to raise their hands if they want to make the world a better place. In addition, I possess a powerful leverage, the distribution of grades.

Of the earth's 6.8 billion inhabitants, I assume that there is a small core of imperfectly good people who are actively and conscientiously trying to create a more ethical world. These are the ethical go-getters. I assume that there is a parallel small core of imperfectly good people who intentionally harm others. These are the ethical adversarials. I also assume that there is a huge group of imperfectly good people sitting on the fence, observing this battle of wills between the ethical go-getters and adversarials from the sidelines. Individuals in this group of ethical fence-sitters switch back and forth between assisting those trying to create a better world and those who intentionally harm others. The social change challenge is to link the ethical fence-sitters with the ethical go-getters and raise their expectations about life's possibilities.

I apply the same social change theory to my class. In my traditional undergraduate class, I assume a bell-shaped continuum of student motivation. A small group of students are go-getters. They will actively engage in class activities because the go-getters strongly desire to be ethical managers who create ethical organizations. A small group is likely to be adversarials. They prefer the banking system of education where professors deposit information into their minds which the student withdraws at test time to determine if any interest has been earned on the stored knowledge (Friere, 1971). Most students are likely fence-sitters, willing to do what is required by the professor to receive a good grade. In my MBA and returning adult classes, I assume a larger number of go-getters and fewer fence-sitters and adversarials because they are paying a premium price for their education and can benefit from the immediate application of the skills and knowledge they gain in class.

In either case, I teach to the ethical go-getters, expect that the excitement they exhibit in class and during group activities will inspire the fence-sitters, and closely monitor the behavior of adversarial students. I kindly engage adversarial students the very first moment adversarial behaviors are exhibited and ask them to express their views to the entire class. If necessary, we also speak in private regarding my expectations and, applying management-by-objectives techniques, we jointly develop goals that would enable them to get the most out of the class.

CLASS ATTENDANCE

Students earn points for attending class. I cannot converse with students who are not physically present. Attendance at each class session is expected because in-class activities and discussions complement, but do not duplicate, textbook information. Many issues raised in class are not addressed by the textbook. There are no excused absences except to participate in a preapproved collegiate sporting event, which is college policy.

There are always many reasons to miss a class, including work obligations and other activities. Most of my traditional undergraduate students work 20 to 30 hours a week and take 18 credits per semester. I emphasize that they are only undergraduate students once in their lives and will be working the rest of their lives. Together the students and I create a learning organization, and we are all responsible for the learning that takes place in this organization.

The student's first responsibility in this relationship is to show up. I also warn the traditional undergraduates to be very careful about missing classes at the beginning of the semester because personal emergencies might happen later in the semester. If they miss six of the 30 classes then they can receive no higher than a C for the class, no matter how well they performed on everything else. I email students who miss two consecutive class sessions, noting that we learned less than we could have because he or she was not available to share information. After the third and fifth missed classes, I send an email reminding them about the six missed classes rule. Approximately 120 students enroll annually in the course and only one or two of them miss six classes.

I do not take attendance. Submitting the short homework assignment due most class sessions, and receiving the returned homework submitted the previous class session, verifies attendance. Students who miss a homework assignment are responsible for submitting a note verifying their attendance that day.

Daily attendance is even more important in the returning adult class, which meets 4 hours, once a week, for 7 weeks. Missing one night is equivalent to missing approximately 15% of a semester. As a result, students who miss an entire night cannot earn an A unless they do a make-up assignment.

Returning adults are allowed one, and only one, make-up assignment for missing an entire night of classes. The three-part assignment must be submitted prior to the final class session. For the first part of the make-up assignment, the student must interview a classmate and compose a paragraph about two things the classmate learned during the class the student missed.

Next, the student must watch a C-SPAN Senate or House session and observe politicians at work. Watching academics or pundits talk about politicians is not acceptable. The student must watch actual politicians in action. Sessions are available on the internet at www.cspan.org or www.c-span.org/Politics. The student must compose one paragraph describing the issues the politicians explored and another paragraph agreeing or disagreeing with the politicians.

For part three of the make-up assignment, the student must create a one-page handout summarizing work-related expert knowledge he or she possessed that would benefit classmates. Each student is an expert about something because of the type of work he or she performs. Accountants know the latest accounting rule changes, information technology specialists know how to avoid getting spammed, receptionists know how to get people on the boss' busy agenda, writers know how to get published, and so on. The student is then provided a few minutes to distribute and discuss the handout during the next class session.

Verbal Class Participation

As suggested by the class format, the course requires a great deal of verbal participation. Students have a responsibility to share their understandings and experiences with the class to advance the group's collective skills and knowledge, and are expected to come to class prepared to make relevant points and ask relevant questions. The ability to engage in productive dialogues with others is an essential part of being an effective manager, and this entails being an excellent active listener too. All students are encouraged to become more verbally assertive, even if they think they are already assertive, to fully appreciate all that life has to offer.

Many students fear speaking in front of others or sharing personal information. They must overcome these communication fears to become ethical managers.

Students develop a habit for speaking in class during our very first meeting by sharing information three separate times in front of the classroom under the guise of community building. One row at a time, students line up and tell everyone their name and hometown. This superficial information is quickly conveyed to the relief of the speakers. Relieved that they got that over with, students begin over again by responding to a different set of questions. One row at a time students tell everyone their parents' occupations. This information reveals more about who they are in a supportive environment that helps them constructively expose their vulnerabilities (Lencioni, 2005).

After we discuss the syllabus, students do a third public speaking iteration. One row at a time, students share their childhood dream job and what they now consider to be an ideal job. All this information helps students quickly connect with each other. By the end of the first class meeting some students are now much more comfortable speaking in front of others. We have begun to create a circle of trust, where students and the professor are provided the freedom to express who they are (Palmer, 2004).

Table 14.2 provides the grading scale used to assess verbal class participation. At midterm, students submit a paragraph stating how many points they have earned using the scale, and why they believe they have earned this amount. They can choose any number from 0 to 100, such as 85 or 93, it does not have to be a multiple of 10. I reply in agreement or

Table 14.2.   Verbal Participation Grading Scale

Each student is graded at the end of the semester using the following scale:

- 100 points: You verbally contribute very informative and insightful comments in every class; if not a member of this class, the quality of our daily discussions would diminish significantly.

- 80 points: You verbally contribute informative and insightful comments in most classes; if not a member of this class, the quality of discussion would diminish considerable.

- 60 points: You verbally contribute informative and insightful comments occasionally; you contribute in small groups but rarely in the large class discussions; if not a member of this class, the quality of discussion would diminish somewhat.

- 40 points: You verbally contribute very little in large or small group discussions; if not a member of this class, the quality of discussion would change very little.

- 0 points: Contributions in class reflect inadequate preparation and are seldom informative, insightful, or constructive; if not a member of this class, the quality of discussion would not change or valuable air time would be saved!

note that the student's self-assessment is either too harsh or lenient. These self-assessments are rather accurate because students know in advance that I'll be commenting on them. We do the same activity at the end of the semester, at which point I either accept their verbal participation grade recommendation or modify it. I usually modify less than 10% of their recommendations, primarily because they undervalued their class participation.

The point total assigned to class participation is large enough to result in an entire grade reduction if a student has not been an active verbal participant. Students whose native language is not English, or those who are shy, occasionally claim that they are at a disadvantage because participation does not come as naturally to them as it does to others. I express empathy and inform them that I will measure whether or not they demonstrated sincere effort at continuous verbal improvement during the semester.

HOMEWORK SUBMISSIONS

I want students to not only show up and speak out in every class, but also reflect on class concepts prior to discussing them. Most class sessions have short homework assignments, such as one paragraph reflections about experiencing course concepts at work, responses to ethical dilemmas, impressions of reading assignments, and self-assessment surveys. The submissions must be typed to receive full credit. I grade them on a one to five scale based on a demonstration of thorough analysis. Most students earn full credit for most homework assignments. Managers must meet deadlines, so homework submissions are penalized 20% for each class period that they are late.

The returning adult class has more applied homework assignments than the traditional undergraduate class because these students have more in-depth work experience. The applied homeworks are based on how concepts in the textbook are experienced at work (Collins, 2009). For instance, a returning adult class session on ethics training is preceded by homework reflections on the extent and effectiveness of ethics training at their current employer. Similarly, a discussion on how to differentiate job candidates according to their ethics is preceded by homework reflections on whether or not their organization screens job candidates for ethics and how they, their boss, or a human resource manager determines the ethics of job candidates.

The traditional undergraduate students read a book on a contemporary issue. Topics have included the flow of undocumented immigrants into the United States (Nazario, 2006) and best practices in environmental management (McDonough & Braungart, 2002). For the Spring 2009 semester, students were assigned President Barack Obama's autobiography (Obama, 1995). Chapters are staggered throughout the semester, usually one chapter per week, and students write one or two paragraphs about something in the chapter they found interesting and worthwhile sharing.

Also for homework, both classes read *Behaving Badly: Ethical Lessons Learned from Enron* (Collins, 2006b). The book puts the reader in the shoes of Enron executives through the journey of the once prominent and now infamous company. Enron's problems are treated as complex ethical issues managers may face daily—often without recognizing them as such. Key decisions are presented in real-time from several perspectives, including those of Ken Lay, Jeff Skilling, Andy Fastow, board members, auditors, lawyers, and investment bankers. Enron was at the forefront of the new economy, but human nature hadn't changed. The ethical dilemmas Enron experienced have existed for centuries and will exist for centuries to come. For many of the book's dilemmas, the reader must choose between two undesirable options. Students write a justification for the decision option they would have chosen, and debate them in class.

WEEKLY JOURNALING

The purpose of journaling is to deepen student awareness of events that take place in their lives on a daily basis (Dennehy, Sims, & Collins, 1998). Events they currently experience at work or school will influence their attitudes and behaviors throughout life. Students are very busy people and for that very reason need to find some quiet time to reflect on their daily experiences.

Students make dated journal entries in a computer file once a week in response to work-related ethical issues experienced or observed as an employee or customer, and explore their reactions to them. These journal entries highlight situations where values such as honesty, promise keeping, respect for people or respect for property were either supported or violated. All information in the journal is considered confidential. I occasionally provide advice during office hours to a specific student experiencing a work-related situation. With the student's permission, I will share the situation with the entire class for their awareness and input.

The journals are collected three times during the semester and graded on a ten-point scale based on the thoroughness of the reflections. Each successive submission requires an extra layer of analysis. For the first four weeks of class, students describe behaviors experienced or observed at work that were either praiseworthy or blameworthy. For the next four weeks, students also examine why the reported praiseworthy or blameworthy behavior excited them in a positive or negative manner, and what this says about them. For the final four weeks, students also write about what could be changed to foster more repetition of the praiseworthy behavior or less repetition of the blameworthy behavior.

INDIVIDUAL AND GROUP READINESS QUIZZES

Twelve class sessions require textbook reading assignments (Collins, 2009). In order to maximize classroom learning, it is important for students to have a basic understanding of the reading assignments prior to class discussion.

We begin each textbook class session with a six-question multiple-choice readiness quiz highlighting the main points of the reading. The quiz serves as an outline for the class session. Quiz performance demonstrates how prepared students are for the class discussion. To reduce quiz anxiety, a list of key concepts from each chapter, ones that they will likely be quizzed on, appears in the syllabus.

The quizzes are distributed the first minute of class, thus encouraging all students to arrive on time. Each individual readiness quiz is worth 12 points, or two points per question. The individual quiz takes only five to seven minutes to complete. Students may take the quiz prior to class if they plan on being absent. If they are late, or miss the class, they get a zero for the quiz because the answers are discussed shortly after the quizzes are collected.

Immediately after I collect the individual readiness quiz, students complete the same quiz in groups of two or three. Within the small group, students share their knowledge and understanding of the subject matter with peers and must reach consensus. Students who have not studied the assigned material typically opt out of the discussion, which creates some public embarrassment for them. Each correct team answer is worth one point, for a combined individual and group quiz value of 18 points. I inform students who score higher on the individual quiz than the group quiz that they must become more assertive during the group decision making process.

We discuss the quiz questions during the class session. This process provides students with immediate feedback on incorrect questions during the group or class discussions. Typically, students become more vocal when they realize the group chose an incorrect answer, requesting further clarification from the professor. This deepens the learning process.

CRITICAL INCIDENT GROUP FACILITATION

Employees are often tempted to hide ethical dilemmas from each other, or to make decisions that have significant ethical ramifications without input from effected stakeholders. I want my students to take a leadership role in organizations by facilitating the discussion of work-related ethical issues as they arise.

Given this goal, early in the semester we discuss a series of ethical dilemmas I encountered at work when the age of my students. These include misleading customers about product quality, ignoring customer complaints, overestimating the value of damaged products to buffer inventory calculations, and suspecting or hearing about sexual relationships between managers and nonmanagement employees.

As a homework assignment, students compose one short paragraph describing a real-life incident they encountered or experienced at work (including a part-time job or student organization) that represented an ethical dilemma, i.e., something that troubled their conscience. They also compose a paragraph describing an incident at work that was either (1) contrary to the organization's interest, (2) contrary to industry or professional standards, (3) contrary to local or national laws, (4) not to the greatest good of the greatest number affected by it, or (5) disrespectful toward other human beings. In order to preserve anonymity, references to specific people and places are changed. These incidents are then shared in small group discussions.

Next, I choose a handful of incidents that represent a range of ethical dilemmas, such as employee theft, unsafe products, and lying to the boss.

In groups of three, including the person who originally submitted the incident, the students further develop the written dilemma for class presentation. The first sentence begins from the perspective of the key decision maker, i.e. "You work part-time in a grocery store." Both sides of the issue are described in detail so classmates can understand why the unethical option seemed reasonable for the decision-maker to pursue in the first place. Changes are made in the dilemma wherein the decision maker has only two or three options, and each option appeals to an equal proportion of student respondents. The student team ends the written dilemma at the key decision point, asking the reader which option he or she should would pursue and why.

Each team has approximately ten minutes to facilitate a discussion about the critical incident. The team distributes a written copy of the dilemma to everyone in class and briefly acts out the dilemma, stopping at the key decision point. The team then reads the dilemma and addresses clarifying questions. Classmates must choose an option and write one sentence justifying the choice. A vote is taken, with the tally written on the board. Next, a team member asks someone with the minority perspective to persuade others in the class that his or her chosen option is the right thing to do in this situation. The team must then choose someone from a different perspective to respond to the justification just provided and facilitate a discussion between people holding opposing viewpoints. At the end of the discussion the team informs the class what really happened in this situation.

As noted in Table 14.3, the assignment is graded based on the written dilemma and the facilitation process. The written dilemma should be informative, interesting, understandable, grammatically correct, and follow the appropriate format. Each decision option should attract an equal number of classmates. All team members should participate in the facilitation, and, most importantly, they must connect conversations so that all issues raised are addressed.

SERVICE-LEARNING PROJECT TEAM WORK SESSION

Students will serve on work teams throughout their professional careers. Well functioning team experiences can greatly enhance the quality of work life. Ethical issues common to teams include being prepared for meetings, being constructive members during meetings, and sharing the workload.

Approximately 20 to 30% of the course is dedicated to a service-learning team project (Collins 1996, 2006a). I teach my students project management skills, which they immediately apply. Every fall the class works on management projects that benefit local nonprofit organizations. Since

Table 14.3. Critical Incident Facilitation Grading Rubric

TEAM MEMBERS:

	Unacceptable: C-F	Good: B; Nice Effort but Needs a Major Change	Very Good: AB; Needs a Minor Change	Superior: A; No change
Written Dilemma: Informative, interesting, understandable, grammar, follows format, even vote [50%]	0-18 points	19-21 points	22-24 points	25 points
Discussion Facilitation: All team members involved, empowered minority, challenged majority, connected conversations [50%]	0-18 points	19-21 points	22-24 points	25 points

Professor Denis Collins' Grade Summary: Using a standardized 100 point scale—Superior (A), 95-100 points: Could facilitate discussion at company. Very Good (AB), 85-94 points: Need to make a few minor changes before facilitating. Good (B), 72-84 points: Need to make a few major changes before facilitating. Unacceptable (C-F), Below 72 points: Need a lot more practice before facilitating.

many nonprofits are understaffed and underfunded, I offer my students to nonprofit organizations as free laborers who have expertise across business fields, including marketing, accounting, finance, information technology, communications, and general management. Recent organizations served include the Vilas Zoo, the Dane County Boys and Girls Club, the Chamber of Commerce, and the Madison-Arcatao (El Salvador) Sister City Project.

I work closely with the organizations' staff to design projects that are meaningful, yet can be completed by a team working 75 minutes once a week for 7 weeks. The student team work sessions are held during regularly scheduled class time to minimize the problem of arranging busy student schedules. These are called work sessions rather than meetings because the students must work on something during the allocated time period. Students also tend to assume that most meetings are a waste of time, whereas work sessions must be taken seriously. Typical projects include developing a marketing plan, designing brochures, updating web pages, and other items on the executive directors' to-do list. In the spring term, the teams manage an annual eco-olympics competition among residence halls (Collins, 2008).

Team members assess their performance at the conclusion of every team work session. As shown in Table 14.4, team members evaluate each other in terms of being prepared for the work session, attendance, and being constructive during the work session. They summarize on an evaluation form what was accomplished during the work session, assignments due prior to the next work session, and the agenda for the next team work session. The team submits a signed copy of the assessment at the end of the work session.

Table 14.4. Team Work Session Assessment

The team project is worth **154 points – 70 points** for your performance during team work sessions and **84 points** for the quality of the final product.

Team Work Session Performance Evaluation

You must meet as a team an equivalent of 7 class sessions to work on your team project. Each work session is worth 10 points. After each team work session please Xerox this page, insert the points representing each team member's effort for the work session, have each person in attendance sign the sheet, and then give it to me at my office or slide it under my door. Please be honest in your assessments.

Class:	Date:			
Team Members	Name	Name	Name	Name
1. Work session preparation: Fulfilled expected work tasks due—Point Scale: 0 (none), 1 (little), 2 (half), 3 (a lot), or 4 (all)				
2. Work session attendance—Point Scale: 0 (missed it), 1 (some); 2 (most), 3 (attended all of it)				
3. Was a constructive participant during work session—Point Scale: 0 (no), 1 (a little), 2 (most of the time), 3 (all the time)				
Total points earned by each team member				

- What did team members do during the 75 minutes set aside to work on the project?
- What will team members do before the next team work session?
- What will team members do during the next 75 minutes set aside to work on the project?

Just as often happens at work, individuals are sometimes placed on teams with people who are disruptive influences or do not do their fair share of work. In such circumstances, the teams are expected to try to work out their differences prior to appealing to a higher authority. At the very first team working session, norms of behavior are established for sharing the work, dealing with conflict, and attending working sessions. If someone does not contribute sufficiently, team members are told to assume that he or she wants to become more involved but is shy or doesn't know how to contribute (particularly if language problems exist). The team must speak directly to the person, and hopefully misperceptions are corrected and a more productive role is undertaken. However, if there is no change in performance, then the team informs me and I provide advice on how to manage the person.

SERVICE-LEARNING PROJECT REPORT

Students will also compose reports throughout their careers, some of which will be jointly written. Ethical issues related to project reports include the fair distribution of writing tasks, gathering information in a timely manner, and meeting deadlines. The quality of the finished product can either enhance, or detract from, a team member's reputation.

In addition to a cover page, table of contents, executive summary and issue definition, the final report includes the team's initial project management plan and anticipated obstacles. This is followed by a documentation and discussion of the implementation experience and the results achieved. Unrealistic deadlines and any changes in task assignments are examined. Each team member summarizes his or her primary lessons learned about project management and themselves. The grading rubric used to assess the project report appears in Table 14.5.

Rewarding team performance at work, and assessing each other's performance, can be an ethical minefield. Not every person has the same talent or motivation. A grade is assigned to the submitted paper, and can be modified based on individual performance. A student earns the paper grade if all team members perform equally. The student earns a higher or lower grade based on superior or inferior performance relative to other team members.

We discuss these issues at the beginning of the project. The class reviews the seven characteristics of an excellent team member that appears in Table 14.6. Upon submitting the final report, team members evaluate the performance of each team member, including themselves, according to these criteria. They also rate individual performance relative to each other.

Table 14.5.   Service-Learning Project Paper Grading Rubric

Human Issues Project Grading Rubric	Unacceptable: C-F	Good: B; Nice Effort but Needs a Major Change	Very Good: AB; Needs a Minor Change	Superior: A; No Change
Class Presentation: Informative, interesting, within time constraints, all members involved [10%]	0-4 points	8 points	9 points	10 points
Report Appearance and Writing Quality: Format, neatness, grammar [10%]	0-4 points	8 points	9 points	10 points
Executive Summary and Action Plan: Thorough and logical [30%]	0-12 points	24 points	27 points	30 points
Implementation Experience and Results: Thorough and reasonable; data supporting your statements [20%]	0-8 points	16 points	18 points	20 points
Newspaper Article: Thorough and appropriate [10%]	0-4 points	8 points	9 points	10 points
Task Activity Team Log (Appendix A): Thorough and understandable [10%]	0-4 points	8 points	9 points	10 points
Personal Reflections (Appendix B): Thorough and appropriate [10%]	0-4 points	8 points	9 points	10 points

Professor Denis Collins' Grade Summary: Excellent (A), 95-100 points: Could hand in report to the boss. Very Good (AB), 85-94 points: Need to make a few minor changes before giving to the boss. Good (B), 72-84 points: Need to make a few major changes before giving to boss. Unacceptable (C-F), Below 72 points: Need to start over again.

These evaluations are then shared among the team members and consensus achieved. This can be a very difficult process, particularly if one student did not perform well. Team members might grade each other equally to avoid a confrontation with the underperformer or free-rider. I strongly suggest that team performance assessment anxiety can be reduced if the problematic member takes a courageous step by admitting the obvious. Also, given the weekly team work session assessments, most performance problems have already been addressed, minimizing the likelihood of any last minute surprises. On rare occasions there may remain some conflict on the team, and I intervene to help the team achieve grading consensus.

Table 14.6.   Peer Evaluation Form

Your Name: _____

Please evaluate yourself and each group member in a fair and accurate manner. Your ratings will be kept *anonymous*. Take your time and provide a useful and complete evaluation.

1. Point Allocation – below, rate yourself and your team members using a zero to four point scale (4 = superior, 3 = adequate, 2 = average, 1 = poor, and 0 = no contribution).

Team Member Names (Include Yourself):				
Organizational ability				
Cooperativeness				
Originality or creativity of ideas contributed				
Functional contribution—analysis and recommendations				
Dependability				
Quantity of work contributed				
Quality of work contributed				
Total points				

2. Percent Allocation—below, rate yourself and your team members using the following 80% to 120% scale:

120%: This team member performed **a lot more** than everyone else
100%: This team member performed **the same** as everyone else
80% (or less): This team member performed **a lot less** than everyone else

Your and Team Member Names	*120%, 100% or 80% using scale above*

PLEASE PROVIDE COMMENTS ON BACK
EXPLAINING YOUR EVALUATION

FREE COMMUNITY MEAL PROGRAM

Adam Smith conceived of capitalism in the 1700s as an economic system that would eradicate poverty (Collins, 1988). This hasn't happened yet. As future leaders, and people who have already benefitted from capitalism, students need to deepen their understanding of the nature of poverty. People find themselves in the need of a free meal for a variety of reasons, including a low-wage job, sustained job loss without sufficient economic savings, a loss of savings due to an accident or expensive family situation, mental illness, and alcohol and drug addictions.

Some businesses and nonprofits give back to the community by encouraging groups of employees to serve food at free-meal locations.

This is a very nice offering, but sometimes serving food solidifies the power imbalance between the haves and have nots rather than leveling the playing field. The executive director of a free community meal program and I have created an immersion experience where students experience a free community meal from the perspective of the meal recipient. Students are encouraged to experience this on their own. They may go in pairs, particularly if English is not their native language or if concerned about safety issues, but then they must sit at different tables so as not to overwhelm the usual guests.

This experience pushes most students out of their comfort zone. We discuss in class that it is natural for students to feel nervous, anxious or even scared if they have never shared a dinner at a free community meal center. The meal experience only takes about 30 minutes.

Many ethical issues may arise during this experience. These include the student's fear of the unknown, prejudices about this population, determining the type of clothing that would enable the student to fit in, waiting in line outside a free community meal location where a passersby might observe them, observing clients in an intimate setting, engaging clients in a conversation, and new prejudices students might develop as a result of this experience. If questioned by a client, students are encouraged to tell them that this is a class assignment designed by the executive director. The students meet with the executive director after the meal to discuss their experiences, and they are also debriefed in class toward the end of the semester. Some students are concerned about taking food away from clients, but there is always food left over and any client needing extra food can get some.

Students submit a two-page essay after the experience that details their preconceptions about free community meal recipients prior to their visit, what they did and learned during their visit, whether their expectations were confirmed or disconfirmed, and new preconceptions they may have developed regarding free community meal recipients. The value of the assignment is calculated at a level where a student who does not complete it loses an entire grade.

PURPOSES-IN-LIFE ESSAY

My traditional undergraduate students are on the verge of more fully entering adulthood. Many returning adult students are in a transitional period between promotions or changing careers. For both student groups, this is a good time to take account of who they are and where their lives are heading. To that end, students compose a six to nine page essay articulating their values and purposes in life based on life experiences. The essay also prepares them for job interviews, where they must express their values and ethics to strangers in a very short time period.

First, students discuss three characteristics that best describe who they are. Next they discuss their work organization in terms of the five values in Edgewood College's mission statement—truth, justice, compassion, partnership, and community. For instance, are employees where they work truthful and compassionate, do they pursue fairness, develop partnerships and engage others in the spirit of community? Students also explore their reactions to an injustice and ethical dilemmas discussed in class, and categorize their ethics, and those of society, in terms of being egoists, social group relativists, cultural relativists, deontologists, and utilitarians.

The second part of the essay is a direct answer to the question: What are your purposes in life and how will these purposes be fulfilled through your work, career and family? These essays are assessed based on how well the student demonstrates self-exploration and systematic analysis.

FINAL EXAM

The traditional undergraduate class final exam consists of eight short essays based on material contained in the textbook. The exam is designed as a conversation between the student and his or her boss about basic information I want my students to share with others. Ethically, the fictitious organization is like many others. Most employees are very conscientious and have good intentions, although a few don't. Upper management has assumed that everyone has been behaving ethically, but a few anonymous comments placed in the employee suggestion box indicate otherwise. The boss is very impressed by my student's energy, experience, intellect and ethics and asks for clarification about some key business ethics concepts, such as how being ethical impacts profitability, a perspective on the major ethical theories, whether or not he or she recommends that a poor performer be fired, and an explanation of the Sarbanes-Oxley Act of 2002 and the Federal Sentencing Guidelines.

The returning adult final exam is very different. Given their work-related responsibilities, it is important that they actually educate their boss and peers based on what they have learned in class. I also want the returning adult students to impact organizational performance by initiating some ethics-based change during the semester. If not employed, they can do so for a nonprofit or community organization.

And so, for their final exam, returning adults write about their efforts to share class information, and attempts to initiate or inspire workplace change. The information shared may be about how ethics improves organizational performance, lessons learned from Enron, public policy issues, qualities of an ethical employee or environmental management, to name a few. Changes students have initiated include modifying the code of conduct, providing ethical dilemmas to be used when interviewing job candidates or conducting ethics training workshops, and revising performance appraisals to reward ethical behavior.

In terms of grading, the returning adults earn all available points if they continually shared class information at work and initiated and inspired one change to improve the organization's ethical performance.

EXTRA CREDITS

Students can earn points for two extra credit assignments. These assignments are designed to expand the student's knowledge base or personal experiences. One-page extra credit essay possibilities include:

- Watch 60 minutes of C-SPAN and write a reaction to the discussion.
- Attend a political or business talk and discuss an ethical issue associated with it.
- Attend a religious service not of your tradition and write about your experience.
- Watch a movie that dramatizes an ethical dilemma that might be experienced at work and write a reaction to it.
- Do something that you've always wanted to do but have not yet had the time to do, such as attending an opera or visiting the local zoo, and write a reaction to it.

CONCLUDING COMMENTS

Business ethics professors can provide students the experience of making the world a better place, particularly through the organizations that employ them. This chapter discusses twelve different assessments I use to help my students lead well-integrated lives based on self-understanding and creative action. By the end of the semester, students are better public speakers and much more fully aware of the ethical issues they experience, or will experience, on a daily basis. They experience improving the management of a nonprofit organization or campus activity, and have personal interactions with people needing the services of a free community meal program.

All of these activities are aimed at creating ethical managers who practice kindness on a daily basis in ways that benefit those with whom they interact as well as bottom-line profitability.

REFERENCES

Anderson, L. W., & Krathwohl, D. R. (Eds.). (2001). *A taxonomy for learning, teaching, and assessing: A revision of Bloom's taxonomy of educational objectives.* New York, NY: Longman.

Collins, D. (1988). Adam Smith's social contract. *Business and Professional Ethics, 7*(3/4), 119-146.

Collins, D. (1996). Serving the homeless and low-income communities through business & society/business ethics class projects: The University of Wisconsin-Madison plan. *Journal of Business Ethics, 15,* 67-85.

Collins, D. (2006a). Taking business ethics seriously: Best practices in teaching and integrating business ethics within a business program. In R. DeFillippi & C. Wankel (Eds.), *New visions of graduate management education* (pp. 319-349). Greenwich, CT: Information Age.

Collins, D. (2006b). *Behaving badly: Lessons learned from Enron.* Indianapolis, IN: Dog Ear.

Collins, D. (2008). Creating environmental change through business ethics and society courses. In D. Swanson & D. Fisher (Eds.), *Advancing business ethics education in the 21st century* (pp. 243-263). Charlotte, NC: Information Age.

Collins, D. (2009). *Essentials of business ethics: How to create organizations of high integrity and superior Performance.* Hoboken, NJ: John Wiley & Sons.

Dennehy, R. F., Sims, R. R., & Collins, H. E. (1998). Debriefing experiential learning exercises theoretical and practical guide for success. *Journal of Management Education, 22*(1), 9-25.

Dewey, J. (1916). *Democracy and education.* New York, NY: The Macmillan Company.

Friere, P. (1971). *Pedagogy of the oppressed.* New York: Herder and Herder.

Lencioni, P. (2005). *Overcoming the five dysfunctions of a team.* San Francisco, CA: Jossey-Bass.

McDonough, W., & Braungart, M. (2002). *Cradle to cradle: Remaking the way we make things.* New York, NY: North Point Press.

Nazario, S. (2006). *Enrique's journey.* New York, NY: Random House.

Obama, B. (1995). *Dreams from my father.* New York, NY: Three Rivers Press.

Palmer, P. J. (1997). *The courage to teach: Exploring the inner landscape of a teacher's life.* San Francisco, CA: Jossey-Bass.

Palmer, P. J. (2004). *A hidden wholeness: The journey toward an undivided life.* San Francisco, CA: Jossey-Bass.

CHAPTER 15

ASSESSING ETHICS EDUCATION IN A BUSINESS, GOVERNMENT, AND SOCIETY COURSE CONTEXT

Archie Carroll and Ann Buchholtz

Business, government, and society courses have been offered in colleges and universities for approximately 35 to 40 years. Today, they are variously called business, government, and society (BGS) or, more frequently, business and society (B&S). Other titles given to such courses include business and its environment, business and public policy, or corporate social responsibility. Some schools now cover the topic in a business ethics course. Very few colleges and universities have formal programs or majors in these topics; therefore, the coverage of this material is typically left to a single course or, at most, a small set of interrelated courses.

Beginning in the 1980s, new courses in business ethics began appearing in business school curricula. As these courses became more prevalent, two trends seemed to occur. First, the traditional business and society courses began incorporating more business ethics subject matter. Second, the business and society courses had to stand side-by-side and compete with the newly established business ethics courses and, since they often

Toward Assessing Business Ethics Education
pp. 263–276
Copyright © 2011 by Information Age Publishing
All rights of reproduction in any form reserved.

shared some-to-much of the same material, or overlapped in their content, some of the business and society courses were no longer offered or were offered on a less frequent basis. The more common occurrence was that the business and society courses adapted to include more business ethics content and many of these courses became almost indistinguishable from business ethics courses.

When business and society courses, or any of the others using the titles suggested above, first began, they had a distinctive issues orientation. In other words, there was not much formal structure or theory to the courses but rather they covered various categories of social issues in which businesses' role and responsibilities were discussed. With the passage of time, these courses took on more of a managerial, public policy, stakeholder, or business ethics framework, and this occurred in parallel to the time that theory and concept development and research in the field began. By the 1990s and early 2000s, textbooks in the business and society field were strongly oriented toward business ethics and stakeholder management, as these became two of the most enduring themes.

Since this chapter is on the topic of assessing ethics education in a BGS or business and society context, it only seemed logical that we use our own textbook as a framework or context for this discussion. Therefore, we will develop our discussion around the seventh edition of our textbook, *Business and Society: Ethics and Stakeholder Management* (Carroll & Buchholtz, 2009), and use its framework and organization for purposes of exposition. This comprehensive textbook covers all of the mainstream topics in the field, and the topics chosen for discussion also will be common to other major textbooks in this field.

In this discussion, we will first identify some of the learning objectives that are important in a business and society course. Next, we will discuss the accrediting agency's expectations about business ethics teaching, followed by a major study conducted to ascertain what students learned about business ethics. Finally, we will propose some learning areas that students need to take away from business ethics coverage. In the process, we will emphasize the importance of students developing higher order thinking skills that facilitate success in terms of the learning objectives identified earlier.

In the final analysis, we must be careful what we assume and extrapolate about the measurement of business ethics learning. We are reminded of a *Wall Street Journal* comic strip several years ago in which a business executive had his hand on the shoulder of a recent business school graduate as he says to his colleague: "If we run into any tricky problems, we now can turn to young Mitchell, here. He got an A in business ethics." Though business executives would like to think this way, it's not that simple, is it? Someone could get an A in a business ethics class and still have questionable values or ethics, couldn't they? Would an ethics course have saved Bernie Madoff? We doubt it. By the same token, someone could end up with a C in a business ethics class and be the most ethical person you ever met. The problem, of course, is the potential and likely gap between knowing business ethics and doing business ethics. There can be a huge chasm between these two, and it is not easy to measure or predict what the outcomes will be. And, of course, all this is amplified when business ethics teaching is just one part of broader courses, such as business and society.

LEARNING OBJECTIVES IN THE BUSINESS AND SOCIETY COURSE

To appreciate ethics learning within the context of the business and society course, it must be understood that this coverage is a legitimate and expected part of these courses. Such is the case and is evident when an examination is made of the learning objectives in business and society courses. One way to see that business ethics is a legitimate part of these courses is to examine the typical textbooks used in this area. The Carroll and Buchholtz (2009) textbook is representative of these and, in fact, it probably provides more business ethics coverage than most business and society books. It has four specific chapters devoted to business ethics topics, and business ethics is intertwined with the discussions in most other chapters. Depending on the placement of the course in the curriculum or the individual instructor's philosophy or strategy, the course could be used for a variety of objectives. The typical business and society course and textbook include several essential learning objectives, such as the following:

1. Students should gain an understanding of the expectations and demands that emanate from stakeholders that are placed on business firms.

2. As prospective managers, students should gain an understanding of appropriate business responses and management approaches for dealing with social, political, environmental, technological, and global issues and stakeholders.

3. Students should gain an appreciation of ethical issues and the influence these issues have on society, management decision making, behavior, policies, and practices.

4. Students should gain an understanding of business' legitimacy as an institution in a global society from both a business and societal perspective, including the importance of building trust with society and all stakeholders.

5. Students should gain an understanding of the critical importance of social, ethical, public, and global issues from a strategic perspective.

All five of these typical course objectives touch upon ethical issues, but objectives 3 and 5, in particular, pertain to the business ethics objective within the context of the course. Later in the chapter, we will cover learning areas that facilitate the achievement of these learning objectives.

THE ACCREDITING AGENCY'S EXPECTATIONS ABOUT BUSINESS ETHICS LEARNING

Most business and society courses seek to meet the accrediting standards (revised January 31, 2007) of the Association to Advance Collegiate Schools of Business (AACSB International) with respect to the business ethics topic. Though the AACSB does not mandate any specific courses, its standards indicate that the school's curriculum should result in undergraduate and master's degree programs that contain business ethics coverage. For an undergraduate degree program, the AACSB holds that learning experiences should be provided in such general knowledge and skill areas as ethical understanding and reasoning abilities and multicultural and diversity understanding. For both undergraduate and master's degree programs, learning experiences should be provided in such general knowledge and skill areas as ethical and legal responsibilities in organizations and society and domestic and global environments of business. Most business schools seek to comply with these standards through the offering of business and society or business ethics courses, or striving to integrate or infuse this material into other required business courses. It is clear that business ethics and related topics are expected to be a part of business and society courses and textbooks.

Most business and society texts have at least one chapter on business ethics and often two. In the Carroll and Buchholtz (2009) text, we have an entire section dedicated to business ethics and management and four specific ethics chapters: "Business Ethics Fundamentals," "Personal and Organizational Ethics," "Business Ethics and Technology," and "Ethical Issues in the Global Arena." In addition, the subject of business ethics is addressed in the coverage of such topics as stakeholder management, corporate social responsibility, corporate governance, and businesses' relationships with both internal (shareholders, employees) and external (consumers, community, environment) stakeholders.

Most major business schools are accredited by AACSB International. Other schools aspire to be accredited by the AACSB, as it is the prominent accrediting agency for business schools. In recent years, the AACSB has paid close attention to ethics education in business schools (AACSB, 2004).

AACSB's current learning standard with respect to the topic of ethics is contained in its Section 2: Assurance of Learning Standards, Standard 15 (AACSB, 2004). Under a heading entitled "Management of Curricula," AACSB states the topic areas in which business students are expected to possess general knowledge and skills. Those that relate uniquely to ethics are given below:

- Normally, the curriculum management process will result in an undergraduate degree program that includes learning experiences in such general knowledge and skill areas as ethical understanding and reasoning abilities.
- Normally, the curriculum management process will result in undergraduate and master's level general management degree programs that will include learning experiences in such management-specific knowledge and skills areas as ethical and legal responsibilities in organizations and society.

Other topics, such as communication abilities, analytic skills, use of information technology, are also in the standards, but the above two general knowledge and skill areas represent those that most closely resemble the unique coverage of ethics topics that might appear in a business and society course. The AACSB does not mandate that specific courses exist in its various standards areas and gives schools wide latitude in terms of how they may meet the standards. It has been quite common for the above stated ethics standards to be covered in business and society type courses, addressed later in terms of specific topics.

STUDENT LEARNING IN BUSINESS ETHICS

Before examining the business ethics dimensions of typical business and society topics, it is useful to review one major study about what students actually learn while taking a business ethics course. The logic here is that there is a relationship between what students learn in business ethics courses and what they learn about ethics in business and society courses. The study reported here was conducted by one of the authors of this chapter and it involved the gathering of student responses about what students learned and how they learned in a stand-alone business ethics course (Carroll, 2005). Data were gathered by two different professors over a three year period in undergraduate business ethics courses offered through a management department. One professor had a management background and the other professor had a philosophy and management background, but the results from both classes of students were almost identical. The students were given a questionnaire with three questions: What were they learning in the business ethics course? How were they learning; that is, what teaching/learning approaches were most effective? How valuable was their business ethics course relative to other courses in the business curriculum? We will only discuss the first two questions here.

To discover what students were learning from their business ethics course, they were asked at the end of the semester to rank order seven possible outcomes of their classroom experience. These seven possible outcomes were gleaned from several open-ended questions asked in earlier classes. In terms of results, students indicated they were learning the following, in order of importance:

1. Greater awareness of the ethical aspects of a business situation;
2. Ethical concepts that will help me analyze decisions;
3. Ethical principles that can help me make better decisions;
4. Ways to be a more ethical person;
5. Reasons my classmates see things so differently;
6. Reasons my classmates see things so similarly; and
7. I'm not sure what I learned in this class.

Since a key goal of ethics education is to help students perceive ethical issues that might not be readily apparent, it seemed logical that awareness would rank high. In fact, even awareness sometimes requires moral imagination—the ability to perceive that a web of competing economic relationships is also a web of moral relationships (Werhane, 1999). Potential ethical issues and dilemmas are not always immediately obvious. Often they must be searched out by someone attuned to complex situations. An ethics education is successful if it teaches students to develop sensitivity to such situations and a willingness to explore them (Carroll, 2005, p. 37).

The fact that ethical concepts ranked second indicated that students generally appreciated their importance. Concepts are descriptive. In an ethics class, they might include such ideas as integrity strategy, descriptive versus normative ethics, stakeholder management, enterprise strategy, and moral development. These concepts can be especially useful to students later in life, since they often act as frameworks or models that help managers in decision making and analysis. Third, principles were ranked as important. By contrast with concepts, principles often are more abstract and students sometimes find it difficult to apply them in practical situations. Ethics textbooks typically explore at least three key principles—rights, justice, and utilitarianism—and many ethics educators also discuss the Golden Rule. It was encouraging that "how to be a more ethical person" was ranked fourth. Quite often, students seem to resist this as a goal or result in an ethics class. It sounds neither academic nor fashionable to say that a course is teaching one to be more ethical, as this may imply some deficiency that must be overcome. This ranking suggests that students may not be totally resistant to this idea (Carroll, 2005).

Students also learned that some of their classmates view topics much differently than they do, and that similarities also exist, both of which are essential understandings for managers attempting to resolve ethical issues in the workplace. Typically, students come to this realization through case study discussions when they discover that not everyone else had responded to a particular set of circumstances in the same way they had. Realizing that the world is full of people (prospective managers and colleagues) with different viewpoints is an essential learning goal for classroom education. Finally, it was a huge relief to discover that the lowest ranked item on the list was "I'm not sure what I learned in this class." It was a gamble even to include this item. However, since the questionnaires were completed anonymously, this ranking has some credibility.

The second purpose of the research study was to determine how students thought they best learned business ethics. Students were asked which teaching and learning methods were most effective as they studied business ethics, and they ranked the alternatives in the following sequence:

1. Lectures/presentations by the instructor;
2. Instructor-led discussions after student case presentations;
3. My own reading of texts/articles prior to class;
4. Studying for and taking the exams;
5. Case presentations by student groups; and
6. My own reading and studying of cases prior to class (see Carroll, 2005, pp. 38-39)

There were some surprising results in this ranking of teaching/learning approaches. Though modern educational theory often holds that hands-on learning is best for students, these students obviously thought more highly of professor-directed approaches. This might have been because they had little formal knowledge about ethics before entering the course, so they were willing to defer to their instructor's knowledge on this particular subject. The students also seemed skeptical of their fellow students' ability to present worthwhile case analyses and unsure of their own ability to read and study on the topic outside of class. The guidance of an experienced instructor seemed to be welcomed. In any case, students seemed to value case studies and discussions, since they gave these high marks in end-of-course evaluations. It is likely they find case studies valuable (and interesting) both because they see the importance of the team-building experience and because case discussions give them a chance to explore current topics and others' points of view.

A primary takeaway from this discussion is that when it comes to business ethics, students see the most value in awareness, concepts, and principles. In addition, the students rank highly instructor-led lectures, presentations, and discussions. And, they see good value in their own reading and preparation for exams. Student-led case analyses and their own advance preparation came in last place in relative terms, although case studies were assigned absolute value in separate end-of-course evaluations. These findings are helpful when we think about business ethics learning and measurement of learning in business and society courses, which we will discuss later.

BUSINESS ETHICS TOPICS CENTRAL TO BUSINESS AND SOCIETY COURSES

Virtually every topic covered in a business and society course has an ethical dimension to it. For purposes of our discussion here, however, we will identify the typical topics in which business ethics is central or essential to the subject matter. Though these specific topics are not specified by the AACSB for purposes of content coverage, each of them requires ethical understanding and reasoning as a basis for learning about business' ethical and legal responsibilities in organizations and societies, which is consistent with the agency's two learning standards described earlier. Using this guideline, the following topics typically covered in a business and society course would have a clearly defined ethics component:

- Corporate social responsibility/performance/citizenship;
- Stakeholder management;
- Corporate governance (see Carroll & Buchholtz, 2008);
- Business ethics fundamentals, personal and organizational ethics, global ethics;
- Business and government relations;
- Consumer stakeholder issues;
- Natural environment issues;
- Business and the community; and
- Employee stakeholders and employment discrimination.

The specific topic areas listed above contain strong coverage of the ethics aspects in a business and society course or curriculum. Certainly, other topics could have been chosen as well.

LEARNING AREAS AND ASSESSMENT EXERCISES

Earlier, we established that the areas of learning that students ranked most highly were awareness, concepts, and principles. As professors, we find that these areas of learning can facilitate the business and society course learning objectives that we identified earlier. We believe that effective ethics instruction should provide students with skills that will enable them to address complex ethical challenges more effectively, and so we focus on the development and assessment of students' ethics-oriented higher order thinking skills as a means of attaining the learning objectives discussed earlier.

Higher order thinking skills are those found at the top levels of Bloom's (1956) taxonomy, specifically, analysis, synthesis, and evaluation. Each of these comes into play in a consideration of awareness, concepts, and principles. We will organize our discussion of assessment around these three learning areas, presenting them in alphabetical order below, as they are of equal importance for this exercise.

Our suggested exercises do not represent an exhaustive list. A variety of different pedagogical techniques can be used in teaching a business and society course. These include structured lectures, analysis of cases (both long and short), student presentations of case analyses, written papers (both long and short), role playing, discussion of short videos, simulations, and so on. In most of these, business ethics topics and issues can be discussed. In our discussion of awareness, concepts, and principles that follow, we focus on two particular types of exercises that we have found especially useful in dealing with business and society topics—a personal dilemma exercise and a current issue exercise

Awareness

Awareness of the ethical aspects of situations, both in business and otherwise, is an essential component of moral judgment that often requires moral imagination (Werhane, 1999). As Powers and Vogel (1980) show, moral judgment involves multiple elements, and awareness is an aspect of two of those elements. For one, moral imagination is the ability to see the interconnectedness of economic and ethical relationships and considerations. Moral imagination entails being aware of the ethical elements of situations even as the daily stresses and strains of life compete for attention. The other element that entails moral imagination is moral identification, which is the ability to recognize ethical issues as issues which can and should be factored into the decision making process.

Assessing student awareness requires an open-ended type of exercise that calls for students to scan their larger environments for ethical issues. We have utilized two classroom assignments that not only provide the student with an opportunity to develop his or her awareness but also provide the instructor with an opportunity to assess that student's level of awareness. One is at the individual level of analysis and the other is at the organization/industry level of analysis.

Personal Dilemma Exercise

In this exercise, we ask students to identify an ethical dilemma they faced in their lives. We remind them that a dilemma, by definition, involves a difficult choice between two or more options and, therefore, something that is obviously right or obviously wrong is not a dilemma. Ideally, the chosen dilemma would involve their work experiences, but sometimes we need to relax that restriction when students are having difficulty coming up with a decision to analyze. Sometimes the issue might be an experience they had as a consumer, because all students are consumers. We have even had to allow some students to interview family and friends to identify an ethical dilemma when they could think of no dilemma in their own lives. From a pedagogical perspective, our interaction with students as they struggle to identify an ethical dilemma provides us with an excellent opportunity to instill in them a greater awareness of the ethical aspects of everyday decisions. At the same time, the exercise provides us with an opportunity to assess their levels of awareness and adjust instruction accordingly.

We often use this as a paper assignment for students to complete by the end of the course. This works well because students are generally thinking of what will serve as their dilemma throughout the semester. On other occasions, we require the dilemmas to be presented earlier so that some of the more interesting of them can be discussed in class. When a dilemma is particularly compelling, we ask students for permission to include them in future editions of our textbook (with anonymity being an option for the student). Their participation is completely voluntary and we give them full authorship, unless they request to remain anonymous. These ethics in practice segments have proven very effective in the classroom. Of course, student confidentiality is paramount. We encourage students to disguise cases that are sensitive in any way, and all information is confidential, unless the student opts to make it public.

Current Issue Exercise

This exercise is similar to the personal dilemma exercise described above, except that it is at the organizational and/or industry level of analysis. In this exercise, students are expected to scan the news looking for current events that have an analyzable ethics component. The topic might be found in a number of different business and society relationships—business and employees, consumers, competitors, government, community, environment, and so on. This exercise also differs from the personal dilemma because it lends itself more readily to group analysis. The final deliverable could be an individual or group paper and/or presentation. The benefits of these presentations are that they update all the students in the class on the most current ethical issues in the world of business.

Concepts

Concepts in ethics instruction are comparable to concepts in other fields of inquiry in that they can be assessed with a variety of formats, from the specificity of true/false and multiple choice test formats to the more open-ended short and long answer essays. In addition, the above personal dilemma and current issue exercises can provide insight into students' understanding of concepts by their choices of which concepts to apply and the skill with which they apply them in either written or verbal analyses.

We find it useful to use a variety of formats for assessment of students' understanding of concepts. Students tend to vary as to which question format works best for them and, hence, the choice of options gives them more opportunities to succeed. As business ethics is an applied discipline, our ultimate goal is that students apply the concepts in their future worlds of work and make ethics a part of their business practices. Accordingly, it is important to assess their higher order thinking, described earlier. This can be accomplished using any of the question formats.

Student assessment is a field in and of itself with a wealth of advice on course objectives, test construction, and other areas of general interest. While it is beyond the scope of this chapter to address this literature, we encourage the reader to turn to it for specific advice on the general assessment of students' learning of concepts.

Principles

Principles are general guidelines for decision making and action. Principles are normative or prescriptive, in contrast to the more descriptive/

analytical concepts. As such, the depth of students' understanding of principles takes on added importance because understanding of principles enables students to hone their moral compasses through developing their moral judgment. Moral ordering and moral evaluation are key elements of moral judgment (Powers & Vogel, 1980). Principles provide students with a variety of perspectives for ranking ethical issues in terms of their importance, as well as evaluating ethical issues against a clear criterion. Some of the more well-known principles that we emphasize include the principles of rights, justice, utilitarianism and the Golden Rule. If time allows in the business and society course, we also address the ethic of care, virtue ethics, and servant leadership.

An understanding of ethical principles can also enable students to understand the views of others who approach ethical issues from a different perspective. Known as tolerance of moral disagreement and ambiguity (Powers & Vogel, 1980), the ability to abide different points of view is an essential life skill for students to develop. Learning the logic that underlies various principles can make it possible to understand a different perspective, even if one never shares it. Students can come to understand that their differences in opinions may be traceable to using or emphasizing different principles from their classmates.

The previously discussed personal dilemma exercise provides an opportunity for students to determine which principle(s) most closely reflect their personal values, while also noting how principles relate to each other. Students who analyze each decision option in the dilemma through the lens of an ethical principle will gain practice drawing on the logic and underlying arguments of ethical principles. This expectation can be an explicit requirement of the exercise, thus providing instructors with an opportunity to assess students' abilities to draw on ethical principles to evaluate ethical dilemmas.

Similarly, drawing on ethical principles can be made an explicit requirement of the aforementioned current issue exercise. The more practice students have applying principles to events in their environment, the more likely they are to think of ethical principles as tools they can use to live a better life. The most straightforward way for instructors to assess students' abilities to understand and apply ethical principles is to have students apply ethical principles to real situations and assess their ability to do so directly. The key to effective assessment is to make sure the instructor is evaluating the effective application of the principle and not whether the student's final opinion is consistent with the instructor's opinion or expectation.

Of course, varieties of other assessment techniques are useful for assessing students' understanding of ethical principles. Essay questions are well suited to assessing student's higher order understanding of ethical principles. In an essay exam question, students can be asked to compare and contrast two principles that either overlap or differ completely. In addition, instructors can ask students to apply select ethical principles to the resolution of given situations.

While the open-ended nature of essay questions lends itself readily to higher order reasoning, a well-designed multiple-choice, matching, or true-false question can also assess higher order thinking skills. For example, students could be given an example of a person's way of thinking through a challenge and then be asked to choose from a selection of principles that person appears to be using. Similarly, with the matching format, students could match ethical principles to actions that reflect them.

SUMMARY AND CONCLUSION

Most business and society courses and textbooks provide fairly extensive coverage of business ethics. Many business and society topics have ethics issues embedded within them. This is especially evident in topics such as corporate social responsibility, corporate governance, and businesses relationships with both internal and external stakeholders. In addition, many such courses and books dedicate several chapters to the business ethics topic. With that being the case, considerable teaching and assessing of students' ethics education is a vital component of the course. A complete and accurate understanding of the relationship between business and society requires moral judgment, which includes moral imagination, moral identification and ordering, moral evaluation, and tolerance of moral ambiguity. Ethics education can enable students to develop these skills which may allow them to respond effectively to the ethical challenges that arise from the interaction of business and society.

In our experience, the three key areas of student learning that stand out include awareness, concepts, and principles. Therefore, assessment has to be targeted toward the achievement of these areas which, in turn, can facilitate the course learning objectives proposed herein. If students can learn to identify ethical issues and bring them to their consciousness, they will become aware of the ethics issues, problems, challenges, and dilemmas embedded in business and society relationships. To paraphrase the late philosopher and educational reformer, John Dewey, a problem well defined is a problem half solved (Dewey, Hickman, & Alexander, 1998). Awareness is what enables students to get on the right track towards understanding course content as a basis for effectively addressing and resolving ethics issues.

Concepts and principles are also essential because they contain the analytical and prescriptive power that can facilitate course objectives and make more effective management decisions and recommendations possible. By understanding descriptive and analytical concepts related to business ethics and the principles that can guide decision making, students are in a position to recommend courses of action that managers might make or should make in actual business and society applications. It can be seen that concepts and principles are not just theoretical constructs. They must be learned and applied. The aforementioned personal dilemma and current issues exercises can help the instructor to determine whether that learning is taking place.

Teaching and assessing business ethics within a business and society course context is a subject that is broad and deep. The ideas presented here are some that we have found to be useful in our teaching. As suggested earlier, there is a wealth of literature on this and related topics, and we view the ideas presented here as one modest addition to that body of knowledge.

REFERENCES

Association to Advance Collegiate Schools of Business International. (2004). *Ethics education in business schools*. St. Louis, MO: Association to Advance Collegiate Schools of Business.

Bloom, B. S. (Ed.). (1956). *Taxonomy of educational objectives: The classification of educational goals; Handbook I. Cognitive domain*. New York, NY: David McKay.

Carroll, A. B. (2005, January/February). An ethical education. *BizEd*, 36-40.

Carroll, A. B., & Buchholtz, A. K. (2008). Educating students in corporate governance and ethics. In D. L. Swanson & D. G. Fisher (Eds.). *Advancing business ethics education* (pp. 285-304). Charlotte, NC: Information Age.

Carroll, A. B., & Buchholtz, A. K. (2009). *Business and society: Ethics and stakeholder management* (7th ed.). Mason, OH: South-Western CENGAGE Learning.

Dewey, J., Hickman, L. & Alexander, T. M. (1998). *The essential Dewey: Ethics, logic, psychology*, Bloomington, IN: Indiana University Press.

Powers, C. W. & Vogel, D. (1980). *Ethics in the education of business managers* (pp. 40-45). Hastings-on-Hudson, NY: The Hastings Center.

Werhane, P. H. (1999). *Moral imagination and management decision-making*. New York, NY: Oxford University Press.

CHAPTER 16

THE CASE FOR ASSESSING ETHICS IN A STANDALONE COURSE AND RESULTS FROM A PILOT STUDY

Diane L. Swanson, Dann G. Fisher, and Brian P. Niehoff

In this chapter we argue that assessing business ethics education is best accomplished by requiring a course in the curriculum designed to deliver ethics concepts cohesively. We describe our experience with this approach at Kansas State University, including results from a pilot study designed to assess certain learning outcomes in a standalone undergraduate ethics class.

THE ASSESSMENT DILEMMA

Calls for more socially responsible business education go back to independent reports issued in 1959 by the Ford Foundation and Carnegie Corporation, both scathing indictments of the mediocrity of short-sighted, narrowly focused, and inward-looking business degree programs (Frederick, 2006). The call then was for business education that could produce visionary leaders capable of understanding the dynamic complexities of

Toward Assessing Business Ethics Education
pp. 277–305
Copyright © 2011 by Information Age Publishing
All rights of reproduction in any form reserved.

the social environment instead of vocational trade school graduates with circumscribed world views. Similar views have been echoed more recently by scholars who assert that business education is out of touch with the realities of management (Bennis & O'Toole, 2005; Mintzberg, 2004; Pfeffer & Fong, 2002) and fails to expose future managers to their moral responsibilities as key stewards of society's scarce resources (Giacalone & Thompson, 2006; Ghoshal, 2005; Khurana, 2007; Swanson, 2004; Waddock, 2003). In reaction to recurring outbreaks of business scandals, the popular press has also criticized business schools, even to the point of finding them complicit in fostering a narrow view of management that inevitably contributes to ethical lapses (Smith & Van Wassenhove, 2010). In an article in the *Financial Times*, Gladwin and Berdish (2010) bluntly state that business schools are not preparing MBAs for a morally complex future.

A campaign spearheaded in 2002 by Diane Swanson, William Frederick, and Duane Windsor sought to address these concerns.[1] Endorsed by hundreds of business professors and practitioners, the campaign called for at least one ethics course to be required in the business school curriculum (Benner, 2002; Swanson & Frederick, 2005; Windsor, 2002), a position the accrediting agency, the Association for the Advancement of Collegiate Schools of Business (AACSB) rejected in favor of allowing ethics to be distributed across the curriculum, a policy referred to as integration. In the aftermath, many business schools have scrambled to understand how to assess ethics absent a required course, as evidenced from discussions posted to various academic lists. In our view, this scrambling indicates an assessment dilemma brought about because ethics coursework is not required as a condition of accreditation. If it were, schools could simply assess how ethics material is covered in a course dedicated to delivering it, just as other courses in the curriculum exist for precisely such purpose. Absent this requirement, many schools appear to be trying to prove that they deliver ethics coherently across other courses when no such plan was in place to assure this outcome in the first place.

Not that this is the case for all schools. There is the stellar example of Babson College where efforts to integrate ethics across the curriculum changed that curriculum qualitatively, due to the sustained efforts of college leaders to develop ethics course material, train faculty on how to use it, and assess the effectiveness of the integrated ethics curriculum over time. It can be seen from the case of Babson College, detailed in chapter 11 in this book, that truly integrating ethics across the curriculum is a daunting, time consuming project that must have the sustained commitment of the faculty and key administrators. For those schools not engaged in such a monumental change process, the first step toward assuring that ethics material is delivered cohesively is to require that at least one course in the curriculum be dedicated to delivering it whole cloth. In this chapter, we detail the reasons for doing so. We also describe how such coursework was embedded decades ago in the undergraduate and graduate curricula in our host institution, the College of Business Administration at Kansas State University. Finally, we report some preliminary data from a pilot assessment study conducted in three sections of the required undergraduate course designed to deliver ethics content in a business and society context.

THE CASE FOR REQUIRING STANDALONE ETHICS COURSEWORK

There are at least four interrelated reasons for requiring that ethics be delivered in a freestanding course, the avoidance of assessment errors being one that goes directly to the theme of this book. We discuss these reasons next, starting with the need for business schools to be aligned with the university's core mission.

Aligning With the University's Core Mission

Acknowledging Appropriate Goals for Business Ethics Education

A claim that gets in the way of advancing ethics education is that ethics cannot be taught and learned (Swanson & Fisher, 2008, 2009). Yet endorsers of the Swanson-Frederick-Windsor campaign did not assert that one ethics course would resolve ethical lapses or alter the personal behavior and beliefs of students. Instead, campaign advocates proffered that business schools should simply insure that students are exposed to road maps for making sound moral judgments that are self-regulated instead of externally coerced. Ethics education in this context is inextricably bound up with the mission of the university. From its Greek origins, this institution has promoted the pursuit of knowledge for its own sake as well as the practical development of personal intellect and character. The medieval university extended this mission by preparing students for certain professions, most notably the clerical, medical, and legal, while emphasizing public service to the community or state (Reed, 2004). Business schools, shaped both by Greek and medieval traditions, typically require that students take liberal arts courses as preparation for the more technical, professional education delivered in business degree programs. Given this tradition, it can be seen that business ethics education should have three interrelated goals: imparting knowledge that explains the moral dimensions of the business and society relationship, striving to develop the personal intellect and character of students, and encouraging graduates of business schools to become socially useful practitioners (Swanson, 2008).

Given these goals, the claim that ethics cannot be taught amounts to a reframing of the issue that obscures the responsibility that business schools have to expose students to useful knowledge and ideals (see Neubaum, Pagell, Drexler, Mckee-Ryan, & Larson, 2009). This claim also smacks of anti-intellectualism and antiprofessionalism. Ethics, as a branch of philosophy that is more than 2,000 years old, influences many fields, including the law, medicine, journalism, engineering, psychology, and biology. Exempting business from this intellectual tradition means excluding it from the legitimacy enjoyed by the broader academic community. Few business school deans would openly agree to such exclusion and even fewer highly paid chief executive officers would want their MBA degrees viewed as narrowly vocational and nonacademic (Swanson, 2004). This was the gist of the Ford Foundation and Carnegie Corporation reports issued decades ago. It is also a sentiment echoed today by business school deans themselves. A majority of them polled by Evans and Weiss (2008, p. 54) around the time of the Swanson-Frederick-Windsor campaign agreed with the statement: "A business ethics course should be required of all undergraduate or MBA students." Despite this consensus, the current accreditation policy means that business schools do not have to require such a course, a situation that fuels ongoing criticism of their degree programs (Thomas, 2009; Willen, 2004). Because of this lapse, business schools fail to convey that business practitioners, like doctors and lawyers, are part of a profession that includes a code of conduct and ideology about business' responsibilities to society (see Khurana, 2007; see also chapter 3 by Buchholz). This is perhaps the most glaring sign that business schools have broken faith with the core mission of the university.

Putting Behavioral Arguments in Perspective

To repeat, business ethics education involves three interrelated goals: imparting knowledge that explains the moral dimensions of the business and society relationship, striving to develop the intellect and character of students, and encouraging graduates of business schools to become socially useful practitioners (Swanson, 2008). The key words are "imparting," "striving," and "encouraging." That is, it is hoped that ethics courses will have positive spillover benefits for society, just as education in general is expected to. But there are no guarantees, just as there are no warranties that students who take organizational behavior, leadership, conflict management, human resource management, and other behaviorally based courses will alter their beliefs and conduct as a result. Similarly, it is irrational to insist that ethics courses are invalid unless it can be shown that they alter the personal philosophies that students bring with them or the behaviors that they will exhibit in the future. Indeed, we know of no other course held to such burden of proof. After all, one could just as well profess that students should not be exposed to other courses for the same reason. An accounting professor puts the situation in perspective by asking: "And do we say that financial, auditing, and accounting courses are utter failures when over 500 companies had to restate their financial reports in 2005? Therefore do we stop teaching these courses?" Another professor, formerly a business school dean, observes: "To say that ethics education has no influence is equivalent to saying that education has no influence. If we give up on ethics education we might as well give up on all education. Is that what the cynics advocate?" (cited in Swanson & Fisher, 2008, p. 9).

Putting the burden of altered behavior on an ethics course is even more absurd when one considers that ethics is typically housed in the management departments of business schools. Management theorists, including ethicists, understand quite well that behavior in organizations is contextualized by a complex chain of inputs, including organizational policies and procedures, formal command and control structures, group pressure, cultural mechanisms, decision making discretion, professional norms, stakeholder interests, and regulation or lack of it. As Petrick (2008, p. 104) states, "It is unreasonable to expect that one single link in this chain of inputs can control behavior by itself." The issue then is simply how business ethics education can be a strong link in the chain, rather than asserting that it alone can eradicate unethical behavior (Williams & Dewett, 2006, cited in Petrick, 2008). Bluntly put, requiring one ethics course is the very least that business schools can do as members of the broader university community.

Ironically, while critics keep proffering that ethics cannot be taught and learned, evidence suggests that a questionable form of narrow self interest is being taught to and imbibed by business students. According to one study, what Swanson (1999) calls "normative myopia," or the tendency to ignore or downplay ethics and values in decision making, worsens as exposure to economics and financial coursework increases (Orlitzky, Swanson, & Quartermaine, 2006). Another study found that self-oriented values become more important than other-oriented values as students progress in their MBA coursework (Krishnan, 2007). This finding is troubling, since other evidence suggests that prospective MBA students already value ethics less than other subjects (CarringtonCrisp 2010). An equally troubling discovery is that MBA students cheat more than their nonbusiness graduate peers, a finding attributed largely to observed peer behavior (McCabe, Butterfield, & Treviño, 2006; see also chapter 19 by Wright). Some worry that business education contributes to or reinforces these bad habits by emphasizing maximization of shareholder wealth as the primary barometer of success to the exclusion of broader measures. In the process, the role of managers as economic stewards of society's scarce resources gets downplayed or ignored (Smith & Van Wassenhove, 2010). This does not have to be the case, since evidence suggests that formal education can be designed to improve attitudes and moral reasoning instead of reinforcing narrow mindsets (see Rest, 1986,1994; Rest & Narvaez, 1991), a prospect we will broach in the next two sections.

Offering an Alternative to Myopic Self-Interest

Why not require at least one ethics course as an alternative to the myopically dangerous form of self-interest that has dominated business education? Although advocates of ethics coursework do not claim that such coursework will resolve ethical lapses, there is convincing evidence that social and behavioral skills can be learned and improved upon through exposure to educational programs that blend theoretical principles and practice (Rynes, Trank, Lawson, & Ilies, 2003). In this vein, consider the evidence offered in chapter 5 where McGaw draws on a recent Aspen Institute survey of MBAs to report that educational experience appears to have some impact on student attitudes regarding the social responsibilities of companies. Indeed, most of the accrediting deans polled in 2003 go further to indicate their belief that ethics education and business practice are linked. Specifically, these deans agreed to some extent with the statement, "A concerted effort by business schools to improve the ethical awareness of students eventually will raise the ethical level of actual business practice" (Evans & Weiss, 2008, p. 51). This belief, reported by business school deans themselves, is a stark contrast to the recurring mantra that ethics cannot be taught, a statement designed to put ethics education continually on the defensive and thwart its advancement in education and practice. Such diversion obscures the real issue, which is that business degree programs need a rehaul so that narrow self interest does not crowd out concern for community (Frederick, 2006; Gladwin & Berdish, 2010; Waddock, 2003).[2]

We do not see any such rehaul happening soon. As long as business schools provide universities with extra revenue that is easy to come by, a critical analysis of their programs will probably not occur (see Holland, 2009). Meanwhile, requiring one ethics course is the very least that business schools can do to demonstrate good faith with the university's core mission while conveying an alternative to the myopic form of self interest promulgated in their programs.

Practicing Sound Pedagogy

The practice of scattering ethics topics across the curriculum may satisfy weak accreditation standards, but it flies in the face of sound pedagogy. The main problem with the distribution method is that, in most cases, it fails to insure that ethics material can be grasped cohesively. Without such cohesion, a sole reliance on distribution easily defaults to the application of a few simple rules that denies the complexities of decision making that occur in distinct organizational cultures and chain-of-command structures in a variety of business environments. Courses designed to address such contingencies are often labeled "business, government, and society," "business ethics," "corporate citizenship," "management of legal, ethical, and public policy issues," and equivalent nomenclatures. In these courses, decision making is analyzed in terms of well-developed ethics perspectives (e.g., rights, justice, deontology, and utilitarianism) and moral reasoning relevant to the complexities of business and society interactions.

In contrast, the policy of scattering ethics across the curriculum takes for granted that a firm grasp of ethics material already exists. This approach is entirely inconsistent with Bloom's (1956) taxonomy of learning objectives because it bypasses or assumes prior knowledge and comprehension (the first levels in the taxonomy). Instead, the process moves directly to class discussions that require students to be capable of application, analysis, synthesis, and evaluation (the remaining sequential levels of the taxonomy) before they are prepared. Rather than being analytically sound, this approach easily becomes superficially naïve and encourages empty, uninformed discussions to count as ethics coverage for the purposes of accreditation (Swanson & Fisher, 2008). The sound alternative to this piecemeal approach is to deliver a body of ethics material whole cloth in a required course.

The bottom line is that it is a false dichotomy to pitch ethics education as either a standalone course or distribution across the curriculum. Sound pedagogy involves doing both (Adler, 2002), with the standalone course serving as a fulcrum for integrating ethics into other courses. For example, the requirement of a standalone course would mean that students engaged in writing assignments and group projects in other courses would have the background to apply ethics to these assignments and in-house faculty specialists to consult. Potentially everyone gains from the cross-fertilization of knowledge that a standalone ethics course can provide. Moreover, students are more likely to take ethics seriously when it is taught as foundational to a variety of business applications. The scattershot approach of relying on distribution across the curriculum prevents ethics from reaching this plane so that it can be viewed as having the same legitimacy as other courses. Before ethics can serve as one of the pillars for business applications, ethics concepts must be introduced at an appropriate time in the curriculum and delivered whole cloth by knowledgeable faculty in keeping with the mission of the university (Swanson & Fisher, 2008, 2009).

Providing Building Blocks for Continuing Education

Rest (1983, 1986) found that formal education is the most powerful predictor of moral reasoning abilities and that moral reasoning skills continue to increase as long as formal education is pursued. His 56-study meta-analysis (Rest, 1986,1994; Rest & Narvaez, 1991) shows that ethics education programs are especially effective in promoting the moral reasoning abilities of graduate and professional students, which suggests that improving students' ethical reasoning skills through foundational ethics coursework is both relevant and doable (Fisher, Swanson, & Schmidt, 2007) . This is an important consideration for continuing education programs that assume prior knowledge of ethics as prerequisite for on-site ethics training programs. These programs have increased dramatically in recent years since the passage of the U.S. Federal Sentencing Guidelines for Organizations and Sarbanes Oxley, the first designed to encourage on-the-job ethics training, the latter formulated to prompt disclosure of ethics codes for senior financial officers (see Holland, 2009).

The dramatic increase in the number of states requiring ethics coursework in continuing education as a condition for CPA license renewal also raises the stakes for ethics coverage in degree programs. Specifically, a survey conducted in 2005 revealed that thirty-four of the 54 State Boards of Accountancy had implemented an ethics continuing education requirement, a dramatic increase from earlier years (Fisher et al., 2007). Other state-level organizations have not waited for universities to realize their responsibility to deliver ethics education. For instance, the Texas Commission on Real Estate (TREC) recommended mandating coursework in law and ethics, similar to requirements in New Mexico where complaints against practitioners have steadily declined since such courses were established (TREC, 2003). In 2004, the National Association of Credit Management mandated a standalone course called "Business Ethics in Society" in its 2-year executive education program in the wake of Enron and other business scandals (NACM, 2010).

This data suggests a troubling trend. On the one hand, standalone ethics coursework in the business school curriculum has declined, especially since accrediting standards were changed in the early 1990s (see Collins & Wartick, 1995; Willen, 2004), with some courses axed even in the immediate aftermath of scandals like Enron (Kelly, 2002). On the other hand, ethics coursework in continuing education is moving in the opposite direction (Fisher et al., 2007). The problem is obvious. It is like putting the cart before the horse. That is, practitioners taking continuing education ethics courses will be expected to handle material they never saw in the first place, undermining the intent of continuing education to build upon previously acquired knowledge. This is the opposite of what happens in other areas. Consider, for instance, the fact that most business schools require students to take freestanding economics courses, presumably because students need the building blocks for other courses, notably finance and strategic management. The logic is that economic analysis would be too difficult or cumbersome unless students have received a solid theoretical foundation to guide analysis. Economic theory and principles are required so that business education can be placed systematically within an economic paradigm. Economics is the theory; business is the application. Yet, at the same time, many of these schools send their graduates into the business world without the building blocks for ethical analysis and application. That these graduates see ethics material whole cloth for the first time in continuing education simply contributes to the tarnished reputations of business schools (see Vidaver-Cohen, 2008) and fuels the recurring criticism that business degree programs are out of touch with the needs of practitioners.

Avoiding Assessment Errors

Despite the support from business deans for standalone ethics coursework, reported above, the response to the Swanson-Frederick-Windsor campaign by the accrediting agency, AACSB, at the time in the process of reviewing its standards, was to reject the modest proposal of mandating a standalone ethics course in favor of allowing the distribution of ethics across the curriculum. This policy flies in the face of the collective wisdom of campaign endorsers, many of whom went on record to indicate that the distribution policy typically amounts to a listing of ethics on various syllabi that does not add up to any particular standard (see Swanson, 2004). Instead, it implies that superficial, often uninformed coverage can be judged equivalent to a standalone ethics course designed to deliver a body of knowledge by faculty members trained in the area. In many, if not most, schools, this ad hoc approach will fail to yield sound coverage of ethics, a state of affairs that sets the stage for inadequate business education for decades to come. For when ethics is scattered across the curriculum, assessing learning outcomes becomes difficult if not impossible.

According to Swanson and Frederick, two assessment errors are inevitable:

1. Ethics coverage will be assessed as being sufficient when it is woefully inadequate or even missing in action.
2. Ethics content can be distorted, diluted, or trivialized but still pass inspection (Swanson & Frederick, 2005, pp. 229-230).

When ethics is scattered across the curriculum, it is difficult to know if the topics become meaningfully integrated in the minds of students, which is one of the higher order objectives in Bloom's (1956) taxonomy of learning domains. To be fair, AACSB has now included ethics at the top of a list of content areas for accreditation. They also added certain ethics material to AACSB's website, but only after the flood of petitions, mentioned previously, prompted media coverage and heated debate on scholarly discussion lists. In reality, however, AACSB holds fast to the claim that ethics can be integrated across the curriculum, absent foundational coursework. When asked if ethics can be adequately covered this way, Ray Hilgert, emeritus professor of management and industrial relations at Washington University's Olin School of Business, said: "If you believe it's integrated in all the courses, then I'm willing to offer you the Brooklyn Bridge" (Nicklaus, 2002, p. C10).

As a result of the distribution policy, academic lists are replete with queries, usually sent in advance of a visit by the AACSB accrediting team, on how to assess business ethics absent ethics coursework. These queries often convey a note of panic, which goes to our earlier observation that the assessment dilemma is created by the failure to mandate ethics coursework. Many who place these queries on the lists do not seem to know what they are supposed to be assessing. This is especially true in cases where business ethics professors are not on the faculty, which is usually the case, given that most business schools do not require ethics coursework (Thomas, 2009; Willen, 2004). This panic and the search to recreate the wheel could easily be avoided. Although it is beyond the scope of this chapter to go into the resource implications of staffing ethics faculty, we note that business PhD programs specializing in ethics and corporate social responsibility have existed for decades. That there is a supply of trained ethics educators is evidenced by the existence of certain academic associations, including the Society for Business Ethics, International Association of Business and Society, and Social Issues in Management division of the Academy of Management. Conferences and symposia devoted to ethics abound. In terms of other resources, there is no dearth of ethics textbooks and academic journals devoted to ethics. Moreover, corporate resources aimed at ethics practices have grown rapidly (Hyatt, 2005) The problem is that most business schools do not take advantage of the resources that the ethics field has spawned since being recognized as a legitimate area of the academy several decades ago.

As first set for the by Swanson and Frederick, the three-part benchmark standard for assessing business ethic education is quite straightforward.

1. A required foundational ethics course is necessary.
2. Efforts to integrate ethics across curriculum should be a goal.
3. Other initiatives, such as hosting guest speakers, offering service learning projects, and establishing endowed chairs in ethics, are highly desirable (Swanson & Frederick, 2005, p. 235).

Potentially everyone gains by keeping the material on ethics intact as a required foundational course. By design, this approach encourages cross-fertilization of ideas within other business courses, rendering integration across coursework meaningful. Moreover, it can serve as a countermeasure to narrowly amoral business education in three ways. First, a standalone course sends the proper signal to students: ethics matters. Second, it mitigates amoral business education by providing students with the conceptual building blocks that will allow advanced learning to occur throughout the curriculum and beyond. Third, a standalone ethics course moves business schools away from the habit of promulgating amorality by providing a built-in opportunity for sound assessment of ethics in the curriculum (Swanson & Fisher, 2008). This last point goes directly to resolving the assessment dilemma that, in our view, is artificially created by the lack of required ethics coursework.

REQUIRED BUSINESS ETHICS COURSEWORK
AT KANSAS STATE UNIVERSITY

Because many if not most business schools do not have a history of requiring a standalone course for delivering ethics, they are at a disadvantage when asked to assess ethics education. As far as we can tell, the most recent statistic acknowledged publicly by the accrediting agency is that only one third of accredited business schools offer a standalone ethics course (Derocher, 2004; Willen, 2004), and presumably fewer require one. Hence, it appears that most schools are being asked to assess something they do not deliver whole cloth, meaning that they lack in-house ethics specialists on faculty to weigh in on the very area in need of assessment. Those schools in the minority with a history of a standalone ethics courses are simply in a better position to assess something that they have had experience delivering. This is the case at Kansas State University, where we recently conducted a pilot study for assessing ethics education. Before describing this study, we will give a brief accounting of how ethics coursework became required in our college.

A Brief History

Two formers deans, Clyde Jones and Robert Lynn, were instrumental in embedding standalone ethics coursework in the undergraduate and MBA curriculum decades ago. Jones explains:

> The social unrest of the 1960s brought with it a realization that business schools were doing little to prepare their students to live and work in such a rapidly changing society. We did a good job of teaching the functional areas of business and required elective courses in the social sciences and humanities. At Kansas State, we saw a need to integrate these liberal arts subjects into the business curriculum. We did that with a new required course, business, government, and society, introduced under the leadership of our new dean, Robert Lynn, in 1967. While serving as a vice president of the university, I taught a section of the new course in the fall of 1969. After returning to full time teaching in 1970, I became the lead professor for the undergraduate course and also developed a graduate course, the legal and social environment of business, required of all our MBA students. (Personal correspondence, October 15, 2002)

These two required courses, business, government, society and the MBA equivalent (now called "management of legal, ethical, and public policy issues") became the vehicles for delivering ethics in the curriculum in a focused, cohesive manner.[3] Delivering ethics in these required courses provides assurance that students get whole cloth exposure to the ethical issues stemming from business interactions with various stakeholders. Eventually, ethics became a targeted area for excellence in our college, largely due to the required coursework that guarantees a critical mass of in-house faculty conducting research in the area.[4] Along the way, ethics and corporate social responsibility topics were integrated into other courses. Notably, undergraduate students are now exposed to three class periods dedicated to ethics and corporate social responsibility in management concepts, their first required course in the business curriculum. This sets the stage for more comprehensive coverage of ethics in their required business, government, and society course.

This brief history illustrates two points. First, standalone ethics courses typically require internal faculty champions and support from top administrators (Swanson, 2004; see also in this volume, chapter 9 by Orlitzky and Moon). Indeed, without such champions, ethics courses are often the first ones axed when faculty compete for the inclusion of other courses in the curriculum (Kelly, 2002; Windsor, 2002). Second, the existence of ethics courses can function as a magnet for faculty recognition of ethics education as an important area in the curriculum. Indeed, faculty collaboration was leveraged to create the college's standards for ethics education, discussed next.

Faculty-Driven Standard for Ethics Education

Building upon past leadership, the current standard for ethics education in the college is as follows.

Students should be able to demonstrate a fundamental understanding of legal and ethical situations in business and recommend practical applications for managers and public policy makers.

This student learning outcome was initially formulated in 2003 by the college's course and curriculum committee (which Diane Swanson chaired at the time) in consultation with the assessment committee. Approved by faculty in 2004, this statement represents an expectation of what students should be able to do when they have finished the program. Consistent with our earlier point that ethics education cannot be held hostage to proving that behavior changes as a result of taking one ethics course, this expected outcome is the same as for other courses. That is, the goal quite simply is a demonstration of knowledge.

According to Nichols (1995, p. 30), one of the most difficult aspects of the assessment process on campuses is the identification of intended educational outcomes by faculty. In our experience, however, the approval of the student learning outcome for ethics was relatively easy due to the existence of the required business, government, and society course in the curriculum. This situation helped create ethics champions among key faculty members and receptivity to their goals among others.

Faculty-Driven Course Objectives

In addition to the college standard, the three full-time faculty members teaching business, government, and society were asked to identify learning objectives for this required course.[5] These management professors formulated the following five learning objectives.

In taking the business, government, and society course, students should:

1. Gain a working knowledge of the terminology of business, government, and society.

2. Demonstrate a comprehension of the major theoretical perspectives and concepts in the field, including business ethics, corporate social responsibility, and the stakeholder model of the firm.

3. Recognize the national and international forces that impact the business environment, using an interdisciplinary perspective shaped by economics, law, political science, philosophy, psychology, sociology, science, and technology.

4. Recognize organizational elements that impact the business and society relationship, such as corporate governance, leadership, corporate culture, ethical climates, and the social contract between employers and employees.

5. Demonstrate an ability to diagnose and analyze legal and ethical situations in business and recommend solutions for managers and public policy makers.

The first course objective goes directly to the foundational level of Bloom's (1956) taxonomy of educational objectives, mentioned earlier, which indicates that before students can develop higher order thinking skills they must first be able to demonstrate knowledge of the subject, which includes the ability to identify and classify key terms. Consequently, the first course objective is aimed at exposing students to the language of business, government, and society, particularly those terms that signal the value laden content conveyed by objectives two, four, and five. The third and fourth course objectives are similar in their aims of knowledge recognition whereas the second objective is geared to the next level in Bloom's taxonomy, which is comprehension or understanding. Finally, the fifth course objective matches the final four sequential levels in Bloom's taxonomy of application, analysis, synthesis, and evaluation.

ASSESSING ETHICS IN THE REQUIRED UNDERGRADUATE COURSE: A PILOT STUDY

Methodology

We used three sections of the business, government, and society (BGS) undergraduate course as the basis for our pilot study. Notably, the very existence of this required course indicates that ethics assessment has been conducted for decades in our college. That is, the students in this course are routinely tested and graded for ethics knowledge, just as students in other courses are routinely tested and graded for other course-specific knowledge. Even so, we were interested in obtaining longitudinal data to help us assess the transfer of knowledge that occurs in the BGS course. As a starting point, we developed a pretest survey of 24 multiple-choice items selected for content validity and designed to assess the first four course objectives, discussed above. The fifth course objective was not part of this study. It is assessed separately by assigning business cases to students who give comprehensive oral presentations that involve the higher order thinking skills of applying, analyzing and synthesizing material as a basis for evaluating problems and recommending solutions. Another aspect of this case project is that students are required to provide a written critique of each group's presentation, an assignment also designed to promote higher order thinking skills.

Students were asked to complete the 24 questions as a quiz on the first day of the course, prior to instruction. This served two purposes. First, this pretest was designed to sample the knowledge of ethics that the students brought to the course, knowledge that may have been developed in other courses or through life experiences. Second, the pretest established a baseline from which to assess the learning that took place during the semester. The students completed the same 24 questions again at the end of the semester, embedded as part of the final exam. This allowed for measuring the acquisition of knowledge during the semester. The pretest and posttest were completed by students in Diane Swanson's section of the BGS course during three consecutive semesters—fall 2008, spring 2009, and fall 2009. During fall 2008, 36 students completed the pretest. Two were eliminated from the sample because they did not complete the course and thus did not take the posttest. This resulted in 34 usable responses. During spring 2009, 15 students completed the pretest. One student added the course after the first day, but because this student did not complete the pretest, her responses on the final exam were excluded. During fall 2009, 23 students completed both the pretest and the posttest. In total, we obtained 72 usable responses. Although a more complete assessment will eventually require that we test all students in all BGS class sections, consistency of instruction allowed us to control for this variable in our pilot study. Another variable we controlled for was that the same textbook was used for all three sections.

Because the 24 pretest items will continue to be embedded as a posttest in future final examinations, we do not replicate them here. Instead, we briefly describe their content in terms of their relevance to the first four course objectives and the knowledge or comprehension that they were designed to tap in each case.

Assessing the First Learning Objective

The first course objective is for students to gain a working knowledge of the terminology of business, government, and society. Arguably, all survey items tap this objective. However, after items related to theory (objective two), national and international forces (objective three), and organizational elements (objective four) were eliminated, we were able to sample terms that specifically point to the value laden nature of the business and society relationship conveyed by objectives two, four, and five. The content of these items is as follows.

- **Item #1: Corporate philanthropy.** Philanthropy is widely practiced in the business sector as a form of giving back to community and buttressing corporate reputations.
- **Item #2: Enterprise-level strategy.** Enterprise-level strategy reflects a corporation's posture toward society. This posture, which ideally should be constructive, is often codified in a firm's mission statement, credo, or statement of values.
- **Item #3: Immoral, moral, and amoral management.** Managers can have various approaches to ethical considerations. In the case of immoral management, there is active opposition to considering ethical dimensions in decision making. Moral management, on the other hand, denotes a conscious striving to include such dimensions. Finally, amoral management is based on a premise that ethics lies outside the realm of business and is therefore not relevant to decision making.
- **Item #4: Voluntary management responses.** A response by managers to social issues based on their personal values and beliefs is defined as voluntary, which is distinct from those responses prompted by the law and government regulation (involuntary) or stakeholder pressure (forced).

Assessing the Second Learning Objective

The second course objective is for students to demonstrate a comprehension of the major theoretical perspectives and concepts in the field, including business ethics, corporate social responsibility, and the stakeholder model of the firm. The main criterion for selecting these items was that they tap an understanding of theoretical perspectives of business and society. We included more items for this objective (13 in all), since comprehending theory indicates a higher order thinking skill than merely recognizing definitions. Moreover, several of the items were designed to assess the students' ability to differentiate among theories. For instance, virtue ethics (item #17) emphasizes the internal character traits of a decision maker whereas utilitarianism (items #7 and #10) focuses on the outcomes of managerial decisions.

- **Item #5: Corporate social responsibility.** Theories of corporate social responsibility distinguish between economic, legal, ethical, and philanthropic duties in terms of what society requires as law or expects as customary practice.
- **Item #6: Corporate citizenship**. Research on corporate citizenship distinguishes between corporate social responsibility (duties to society), corporate social responsiveness (managerial actions), and corporate social performance (outcomes of business conduct).
- **Item #7: Utilitarian decision making.** The use of utilitarianism in decision making means focusing on outcomes, using cost-benefit analysis.
- **Item #8: Conventional moral reasoning.** According to research in this area, people who reason at the conventional level are conforming to peer and family expectations as well as social norms that have been codified into law.
- **Item #9: Justice ethics.** The principle of justice can be distinguished from other ethics perspectives by an emphasis on the fair treatment of each person.
- **Item #10: The broad form of utilitarianism.** This formulation is typically understood in terms of a rule for picking the action that provides the greatest good for the greatest number of people.
- **Item #11: Utilitarianism, rights, and justice.** As a decision rule, the weakness of utilitarianism is that it does not handle individual rights and justice particularly well.
- **Item #12: Secondary social stakeholders.** In contrast to primary stakeholders, secondary stakeholders have an interest in the firm that is public in nature. These stakeholders include regulators, social activists, and the media.
- **Item #13: The ethics of care.** This ethic focuses on the moral quality of relationships instead of predetermined principles.
- **Item #14: The Categorical Imperative.** In contrast to the focus on outcomes of utilitarianism, The Categorical Imperative is deontological in its emphasis on duty to others.
- **Item #15: Primary social stakeholders.** In contrast to a firm's secondary stakeholders, primary stakeholders have a direct, influential stake in a firm's success. These stakeholders include owners, suppliers, customers, and employees.

- **Item #16: Procedural justice.** This form of justice emphasizes the fairness of due process instead of outcomes.
- **Item #17: Virtue ethics.** In contrast to action-oriented ethics, virtue ethics focuses on the internal character traits of the decision maker.

Assessing the Third Learning Objective

The third course objective is for students to recognize the national and international forces that impact the business environment, using an interdisciplinary perspective shaped by economics, law, political science, philosophy, psychology, sociology, science, and technology.

- **Item #18: The macro environment of business.** Political-legal, economic, sociocultural, and technological forces all impact and shape the general environment for business.
- **Item #19: The ethics of globalization.** Globalization, a force that tends to erase or minimize national boundaries, poses certain justice and rights issues for stakeholders.
- **Item #20: The interactions between business, government, and the public.** The interactions between business, government, and the public include lobbying, regulating, and advertising.
- **Item #21: The national and international forces shaping the new workplace environment.** The new environment for work is shaped by the forces of globalization, deregulation, stockholder activism, and technological advances.

Assessing the Fourth Learning Objective

Finally, the fourth course objective is for students to recognize organizational elements that impact the business and society relationship, such as corporate governance, leadership, corporate culture, ethical climates, and the social contract between employers and employees. We originally had four items in this section, consistent with the number of items used to tap the first and third course objectives, which focus on recognizing terms instead of comprehending theories of business and society vis-à-vis the second course objective. However, right before giving the survey to the first class in fall 2008, we noticed an unnecessary redundancy in two questions for the fourth learning objective and therefore eliminated one.

- **Item #22: Organizational dispute resolution methods.** Organizational methods of due process for employees are a form of procedural justice that include an open door policy on the part of management and use of ombudsmen and peer review panels.

- **Item #23: Corporate governance.** The major groups involved with corporate governance or the oversight of a firm's operations are the owners, board of directors, managers, and employees.
- **Item #24: Corporate culture and leadership.** Executive leaders can shape corporate cultures by several means, including how they react to crisis, who and what they reward, and the systems and procedures they put in place.

Analysis

Individual change patterns are used to evaluate the results of each question. Individual change patterns can take one of four forms—a negative difference, an unfavorable tie, a favorable tie, or a positive difference.

A negative difference occurs when a student answers the question correctly in the pretest and incorrectly in the posttest. A negative difference, especially if they are few, suggests that the student merely guessed correctly during the pretest since he or she could not replicate this success during the posttest. An unfavorable tie results when the student answers the question incorrectly in both the pretest and posttest. Taken together, these two change patterns reveal the percentage of students who cannot demonstrate the desired knowledge at the end of the semester (i.e., percent negative). This implies that the student may have failed to gain an understanding of this topic during either this course or other courses in the curriculum.

A favorable tie occurs when the student answers the question correctly both during the pretest and the posttest. Answering the question correctly during the pretest implies one of two results. One possibility is that the student guessed correctly. A second possibility is that the student came to the course with knowledge of the question content acquired either from a previous course or through life experiences. This possibility is enhanced because, as mentioned earlier, the management concepts course that all undergraduate business majors are required to take prior to BGS delivers three class periods devoted to ethics and corporate social responsibility. Given a survey that Diane Swanson conducted in 2003, we also know that ethics topics are covered in other courses taken before BGS. Each of the multiple-choice questions has five item-choices creating at least a 20% chance of guessing correctly during the pretest. Thus, 14 responses (20% of 72 total responses) or less in the favorable tie category most likely indicates random guessing during the pretest. Greater than 14 responses in the favorable tie category suggests that at least some of the students came to course with an understanding of the question content.

A positive difference results when the student answers the question incorrectly in the pretest and correctly in the posttest. Although guessing successfully during the posttest is a possibility, the positive difference provides reasonable assurance of a successful transfer of learning during the course. Taken together, these two change patterns reveal the percentage of students who are able to demonstrate the desired knowledge at the end of the semester (i.e., percent positive). Whereas the positive difference provides an assessment of the transfer of learning taking place in the BGS course (i.e., course assessment), the percent positive provides an assessment of the transfer of learning that has taken place in the curriculum (i.e., program assessment).

Results

The results for the first learning objective are presented in Table 16.1. The results provide reasonable assurance that our students are obtaining a working knowledge of critical BGS terminology. The average percent positive for this learning objective is 88%. More than 80% to as much as 95% of the students are able to correctly define the terms presented. Given the substantial number of favorable ties for three of the four questions, we conclude that earlier course work, especially the class periods in

Table 16.1. Learning Objective 1: Gain a Working Knowledge of the Terminology of Business, Government, and Society

Questions	Neg. Diff.	Unfavor. Tie	% Neg.	Favor. Tie	Posit. Diff.	% Posit.
1. Corporate philanthropy	2	1	4.17	33	36	95.83
2. Enterprise-level strategy	0	7	9.72	7	58	90.28
3. Immoral, moral, and amoral management	6	5	15.28	37	24	84.72
4. Voluntary management responses	6	7	18.06	21	38	81.94
		Avg. Neg. = 11.81%			Avg. Posit. = 88.19%	

Note: Neg. Diff. = negative differences (pretest correct and posttest incorrect); Unfavor. Tie = unfavorable tie (both pretest and posttest incorrect); % Neg. = percent negative (percentage who answered posttest incorrectly); Favor. Tie = favorable tie (both pretest and posttest correct); Posit. Diff = positive difference (pretest incorrect and posttest correct); % Posit = percent positive (percentage who answered the posttest correct).

management concepts dedicated to corporate social responsibility, provided a strong foundation. Because three of the four questions had positive differences for 50% or more of the students, we believe that the BGS course has played a significant role in our students gaining this knowledge.

The results for the second learning objective are presented in Table 16.2. Taken as a whole, the results for the second learning objective also are positive. The average percent positive for this learning objective is

Table 16.2. Learning Objective 2: Demonstrate a Comprehension of the Major Theoretical Perspectives and Concepts in the Field, Including Business Ethics, Corporate Social Responsibility, and the Stakeholder Model of the Firm

Questions	Neg. Diff.	Unfavor. Tie	% Neg.	Favor. Tie	Posit. Diff.	% Posit.
5. Corporate social responsibility	0	6	8.33	10	56	91.67
6. Corporate citizenship	4	16	27.78	19	33	72.22
7. Utilitarian decision making	4	3	9.72	38	27	90.28
8. Conventional moral reasoning	1	8	12.50	19	44	87.50
9. Justice ethics	10	8	25.00	34	20	75.00
10. The broad form of utilitarianism	1	5	8.33	23	43	91.67
11. Utilitarianism, rights, and justice	11	18	40.28	20	23	59.72
12. Secondary social stakeholders	3	15	25.00	8	46	75.00
13. The ethics of care	4	13	23.61	28	27	76.39
14. Categorical imperative	2	7	12.50	20	43	87.50
15. Primary social stakeholders.	2	3	6.94	46	21	93.06
16. Procedural justice	3	10	18.06	30	29	81.94
17. Virtue ethics	1	2	4.17	38	31	95.83
			Avg. Neg. = 17.09%			Avg. Posit. = 82.91%

Note: Neg. Diff. = negative differences (pretest correct and posttest incorrect); Unfavor. Tie = unfavorable tie (both pretest and posttest incorrect); % Neg. = percent negative (percentage who answered posttest incorrectly); Favor. Tie = favorable tie (both pretest and posttest correct); Posit. Diff = positive difference (pretest incorrect and posttest correct); % Posit = percent positive (percentage who answered the posttest correct).

almost 83%. The percent positive for 8 of the 13 questions is 80% or better, and the substantial number of positive differences for each question provides assurance that the students are gaining an understanding of the major theoretical perspectives and concepts during the BGS course.

The results for the third learning objective are presented in Table 16.3. Again the results are very positive. The average percent positive for this learning objective is nearly 88%. More than 81% to as much as 97% of the students are able to correctly recognize the national and international forces that impact the business environment. Because this learning objective requires an interdisciplinary perspective, we would expect a significant number of favorable ties because the students should come to the course with a reasonable understanding of economics, law, political science, philosophy, psychology, sociology, science, and technology acquired from courses taken prior to enrolling in BGS. Moreover, we expect many of these issues to be addressed in other business courses, such as management concepts. Nevertheless, three of the four questions had more positive differences than favorable ties suggesting that student understanding in this area has been advanced in the BGS course.

Table 16.3. Learning Objective 3: Recognize the National and International Forces That Impact the Business Environment, Using an Interdisciplinary Perspective Shaped by Economics, Law, Political Science, Philosophy, Psychology, Sociology, Science and Technology

Questions	Neg. Diff.	Unfavor. Tie	% Neg.	Favor. Tie	Posit. Diff.	% Posit.
18. The macro environment of business.	1	1	2.78	33	37	97.22
19. The ethics of globalization	2	8	13.89	30	32	86.11
20. The interactions between business, government, and the public	7	6	18.06	40	19	81.94
21. The national and international forces shaping the new workplace environment	2	9	15.28	25	36	84.72
			Avg. Neg. = 12.50%		Avg. Posit. = 87.50%	

Note: Neg. Diff. = negative differences (pretest correct and posttest incorrect); Unfavor. Tie = unfavorable tie (both pretest and posttest incorrect); % Neg. = percent negative (percentage who answered posttest incorrectly); Favor. Tie = favorable tie (both pretest and posttest correct); Posit. Diff = positive difference (pretest incorrect and posttest correct); % Posit = percent positive (percentage who answered the posttest correct).

Table 16.4.   Learning Objective 4: Recognize Organizational Elements That Impact the Business and Society Relationship, Such as Corporate Governance, Leadership, Corporate Culture, Ethical Climates, and the Social Contract Between Employers and Employees

Questions	Neg. Diff.	Unfavor. Tie	% Neg.	Favor. Tie	Posit. Diff.	% Posit.
22. Organizational dispute resolution methods	4	4	11.11	21	43	88.89
23. Corporate governance	7	13	27.78	16	36	72.22
24. Corporate culture and leadership	5	36	56.94	4	27	43.06
		Avg. Neg. = 31.94%			Avg. Posit. = 68.06%	

Note: Neg. Diff. = negative differences (pretest correct and posttest incorrect); Unfavor. Tie = unfavorable tie (both pretest and posttest incorrect); % Neg. = percent negative (percentage who answered posttest incorrectly); Favor. Tie = favorable tie (both pretest and posttest correct); Posit. Diff = positive difference (pretest incorrect and posttest correct); % Posit = percent positive (percentage who answered the posttest correct).

The results for the fourth learning objective are presented in Table 16.4. For this objective, the results reveal some weakness. The average percent positive is only 68%. Because we have only three questions for this objective, the results are skewed by student performance on question 24 regarding corporate culture and leadership. We discuss some implications of these results next.

Implications

From the results of our pilot study, we have evidence that a substantial number of students can demonstrate the desired knowledge of business ethics. Moreover, the results indicate that much of this transfer is taking place in the standalone BGS course. But because of the brevity of our instrument, in most cases offering only one question per topic, we must be careful not to overstate the results. Although the reliability and validity of our instrument would benefit from additional questions, we have to weigh the need for assessment with the time constraints within a course that assessment may cause. Although student assessment is important, a fine line must be walked between evaluating student learning and taking away from student opportunities for learning. A lengthier assessment instrument becomes more important when a standalone course is not used, and program administrators must rely on the instrument as the primary source, if not the only source, of evidence that business ethics knowledge is being acquired by their students. That is not to say that our instrument would not benefit from additional analysis and testing. The fourth learning objective, which we inadvertently limited to three questions, could undoubtedly benefit from another question or two.

At any rate, the results from our instrument are best combined with other evidence from the course, such as exams, written case analysis, and presentations, to provide a richer interpretation of the strengths and weakness of our students, our course, and our program. From an assessment standpoint, this additional input goes to the obvious advantage of having a standalone course. In other words, the results of a short instrument, such as ours, is best used merely as a guide for the faculty who teach the course to better understand what seems to be working, what might be concerns, and what might be potential avenues for improvement, given the totality of assignments in the course. Mentioned earlier, the BGS students are required to give comprehensive oral presentations of business cases as a basis for assessing the higher order thinking skills of applying, analyzing, and synthesizing material and evaluating problems and recommending solutions. As part of this assignment, students are also required to provide a written critique of each group's presentation. These case-based assignments are designed to assess the fifth course learning objective, which is to demonstrate an ability to diagnose and analyze legal and ethical situations in business and recommend solutions for managers and public policy makers. The students are assessed individually within their group for this ability, and the group as a whole is also assessed.

We can also use these case assignments to shed light on the results of the test items designed to tap the first four course objectives. Specifically, given the relative weakness of results for the two items in the areas of corporate governance, culture, and leadership, we can examine future case presentations to see if the same weaknesses manifests in those assignments too. The same can be said for the other test items with percentages under 80%, For instance, an examination of the results for Questions 10 and 11 suggests that students are better at defining utilitarianism than they are at addressing its relative disadvantages. Since understanding these disadvantages goes to a higher level of critical thinking, this result is not surprising. Even so, the lower score presents an opportunity to assess case presentations in this area, as well as emphasize the material in class lectures.

In the final analysis, given the results of our pilot study, we see the need to improve learning outcomes in the areas corporate citizenship (Question 6), justice ethics (Question 9), utilitarianism (Question 11), secondary social stakeholders (Question 12), the ethics of care (Question 13), corporate governance (Question 23), and leadership and culture (Question 24). Although the results for these items indicate that a transfer of learning is taking place (and the results of the case-based assignments may buttress this conclusion), the scores for the other 18 items are higher (i.e., greater than 80% positive difference). Hence, the data presents an opportunity for educational improvement, which is the whole point of assessment (Banta, Lund, Black, & Oblander, 1996).[6]

So far, we have limited our analysis to whether or not the student answered the question correctly. For all items, but particularly those with less success, our questions would benefit from an analysis of item distracters (Haladyna, 1994). If students are not choosing the correct answers, what are they choosing and why? This not only has implications for the questions being employed, but also may suggest issues that need to be addressed in the course delivery. As with any survey instrument, our quiz can benefit from statistical reliability and validity testing. Nevertheless, we believe that our instrument meets our purpose, which is to supplement the assessment evidence that comes from requiring a standalone ethics course in the curriculum.

CONCLUDING REMARKS

Again, ethics champions have never claimed that one required ethics course will resolve all ills. Obviously, students will find themselves in workplace situations where organizational complexities and other factors shape the nature of ethical challenges and opportunities. Given these complexities, it is modest to propose that at least one course in the curriculum be focused on arming students with the ability to recognize ethical dilemmas and possible solutions. Importantly, this approach can help align the business school curriculum with the mission of the university. A standalone course also resolves the two assessment problems identified earlier. First, ethics coverage will not be assessed as being sufficient when it is woefully inadequate or even missing in action. Second, ethics content will not be distorted, diluted, or trivialized but still pass inspection.

In contrast, those schools that rely upon the approach of distributing ethics across the curriculum necessarily take on an additional burden of proof. That is, they need to develop and administer a valid survey instrument that measures ethics knowledge before students enter their degree programs and upon completion of coursework. Such instrument must be extensive, far more so than our 24-item quiz, if designed to tap the knowledge routinely delivered whole cloth in a required ethics course. Given the complexity of such an instrument and the time it would take to administer it and track results, it would clearly be easier to encourage the coverage of ethics in all courses while requiring a standalone ethics course and diligently assessing the transfer of knowledge that takes place in it. To do otherwise risks sound pedagogy.

NOTES

1. For a detailed account of the Swanson-Frederick-Windsor campaign that called for better business ethics education, see Swanson (2004).
2. For criticism of business education from business professors, see Frederick (2006).
3. Besides delivering ethics on the undergraduate and graduate levels vis-à-vis required coursework, an elective in professional ethics is offered for MBAs and master of accountancy students.
4. The strength of business ethics education at Kansas State University has been recognized publicly by the Association to Advance Collegiate Schools of Business, the accrediting agency (AACSB Ethics Education Resource Center, 2010).
5. See chapter 15 by Carroll and Buchholtz for another discussion of assessing ethics in a business, government, and society course.
6. See chapter 1 for a discussion of using summative and formative assessment to improve student learning and instruction.

ACKNOWLEDGMENT

We thank Professors Clyde Jones and Robert Lynn for their pivotal administrative leadership in embedding stand-alone ethics coursework in the curriculum of the College of Business Administration at Kansas State University decades ago.

REFERENCES

Adler, P. S. (2002) Corporate scandals: It's time for reflection in business schools, *Academy of Management Executive, 16*, 148-149.
Association to Advance Collegiate Schools of Business Ethics Education Resource Center. (2010). Retrieved from http://www.aacsb.edu/resource_centers/EthicsEdu/practices.asp
Banta, T. W., Lund, J. P., Black, K. E., & Oblander, F. W. (1996). *Assessment in practice: Putting principles to work on college campuses.* San Francisco, CA: Jossey-Bass.
Benner, J. (2002, November 14). MBA accreditation body resists professors' call for required ethics course. *AFX Global Ethics Monitor Online.* Retrieved from www.globalethicmonitor.com/afx-eth/homepage_summary.html

Bennis, W. G., & O'Toole, J. (2005, May). How business schools lost their way. *Harvard Business Review, 83*, 96-104.

Bloom, B. (Ed.). (1956) *Taxonomy of education objectives.* New York, NY: David McKay.

CarringtonCrisp. (2010). What do tomorrow's MBAs Want? *Executive Summary.* London, England: Author.

Collins, D., & Wartick, S. L. (1995). Business and society/business ethics courses: Twenty years at the crossroads. *Business & Society, 34*, 51-89.

Derocher, R. (2004, January/February). Knowing right from wrong. *INSIGHT Magazine Online.* Retrieved from www.insight-mag.com/insight

Evans, F. J., & Weiss, E. J. (2008). Views on the importance of ethics in business education: Survey results from AACSB deans, CEOs, and faculty. In D. L. Swanson & D. G. Fisher (Eds.), *Advancing business ethics education* (pp. 43-66). Charlotte, NC: Information Age.

Fisher, D. G., Swanson, D. L., & Schmidt J. J. (2007). Accounting education lags CPE requirements: Implications for the profession and a call to action. *Accounting Education, 16*, 345-363.

Frederick, W. C. (2006). *Corporation, be good! The story of corporate social responsibility.* Indianapolis, IN: Dog Ear.

Giacalone, R., & Thompson, K. (2006). Business ethics and social responsibility education: Shifting the worldview. *Academy of Management Learning & Education, 5*, 266-277.

Ghoshal, S. (2005). Bad management theories are destroying good management practices. *Academy of Management Learning and Education, 4*, 75-91.

Gladwin, T. N., & Berdish, D. (2010, February 10). MBAs unprepared for a morally complex future. *Financial Times.* Retrieved from www.ft.com/cms/s/0/df5c80e2-1452-11df-8847-00144feab49a.html

Haladyna, T. M. (1994). *Developing and validating multiple-choice test items.* Hillsdale, NJ: Erlbaum.

Holland, K. (2009, March 15). Is it time to retrain b-schools? *New York Times.* Retrieved from http://www.nytimes.com/2009/03/15/business/15school.html?ref=business

Hyatt, J. C. (2005, Summer). Birth of the ethics industry. *Business Ethics.* Accessed August 5, 2005, http://www.business-ethics.com/current_issue/summer_2005_birth.html.

Jones, C. C. (2002). *Statement on the history and philosophy of business ethics coursework at Kansas State University.* Retrieved from http://www.cba.k-state.edu/DocumentView.asp?DID=124.

Kelly, M. (2002, Fall) It's a heckuva time to be dropping business ethics courses. *Business Ethics,* 17-18.

Khurana, R. (2007). *From higher aims to hired hands: The social transformation of American business schools and the unfulfilled promise of management as a profession.* Princeton, NJ: Princeton University Press.

Krishnan, V. R. (2007). Impact of MBA education on students' values: Two longitudinal studies. *Journal of Business Ethics, 83*, 233-246.

McCabe, D. L., Butterfield, K. D., & Treviño, L. K. (2006). Academic dishonesty in graduate business programs: Prevalence, causes, and proposed action. *Academy of Management Learning & Education, 5*, 294-305.

Mintzberg, H. (2004). *Managers not MBAs: A hard look at the soft practice of managing and management development.* San Francisco, CA: Barrett-Koehler.

Neubaum, D. O., Pagell, M., Drexler, J. A., Jr., Mckee-Ryan F. M., & Larson, E. (2009). Business education and its relationship to student personal moral philosophies and attitudes toward profits: An empirical response to critics. *Academy of Management Learning & Education, 8*, 9-24.

National Association of Credit Management. (2010). Retrieved from http://www.nacm.org

Nichols, J. O. (1995). *Assessment case studies: Common issues in implementation with various campus approaches to resolution.* New York, NY: Agathon Press.

Nicklaus, D. (2002, December 18). Is a bigger dose of ethics needed in business schools? *St. Louis Post Dispatch*, p. C10.

Orlitzky, M., Swanson, D. L., & Quartermaine, L. -K. (2006). Normative myopia, executives' personality, and preference for pay dispersion: Toward implications for corporate social performance. *Business & Society, 45*, 149-177.

Petrick, J. (2008). Using the business integrity model to advance business ethics education. In D. L. Swanson & D. G. Fisher (Eds.), *Advancing business ethics education* (pp. 103-124). Charlotte, NC: Information Age.

Pfeffer, J., & Fong, C. (2002). The end of business schools? Less success than meets the eye. *Academy of Management Learning and Education, 1*, 78–95.

Reed, D. (2004). Universities and the promotion of corporate responsibility: Reinterpreting the liberal arts tradition. *Journal of Academic Ethics, 2*, 3-41.

Rest, J. (1986). *Moral development: Advances in research and theory.* New York, NY: Prager Press.

Rest, J., & Narvaez, D. (1991). The college experience and moral development. In W. M. Kurtines & J. L. Gerwitz (Eds.), *Handbook of moral development and behavior: Vol. 2. Research* (pp. 229-245). Hillsdale, NJ: Erlbaum.

Rest, J. R. (1983). Morality. In J. Flavell & E. Markman (Vol. Ed.) and P. Mussen (Gen. Ed.), *Manual of child psychology: Vol. 3. Cognitive development* (pp. 556-629). New York, NY: John Wiley and Sons.

Rest, J. R. (1994) Background: Theory and research. In J. Rest & D. Narvaez (Eds.), *Moral development in the Professions* (pp. 1-26). Hillsdale, NJ: Erlbaum.

Rynes, S. L., Trank, C. Q., Lawson, A. M., & Ilies, R. (2003). Behavioral coursework in business education: Growing evidence of a legitimacy crisis. *Academy of Management Learning & Education, 2*, 269-283.

Smith, N. C., & Van Wassenhove, L. (2010, January 11). How business schools lost their way. *BusinessWeek.* Retrieved from www.businessweek.com/bschools/content/jan2010/bs20100111_383186.htm

Swanson, D. L. (1999). Toward an integrative theory of business and society: A research strategy for corporate social performance. *Academy of Management Review 24*, 506-521.

Swanson, D. L. (2004). The buck stops here: Why universities must reclaim business ethics education [Special issue]. *Journal of Academic Ethics, 2*, 43-61.

Swanson, D. L. (2008). Moral education. In R. Kolb (Ed.), *The business ethics and society encyclopedia* (pp. 1414-1416). Thousand Oaks, CA: Sage.

Swanson, D. L., & Fisher, D. G. (Eds.). (2008). Business ethics education: If we don't know where we are going, any road will take us there. In *Advancing business ethics education* (pp. 1-23). Charlotte, NC: Information Age.

Swanson, D. L., & Fisher, D. G. (2009). Business ethics education: If we don't know where we are going, any road will take us there. *Decision Line, 40,* 10-13.

Swanson, D. L., & W. C. Frederick. (2005). Denial and leadership in business ethics education. In O. C. Ferrell & R. A. Peterson (Eds.), *Business ethics: The new challenge for business schools and corporate leaders* (pp. 222-240). Armonk, NY: M.E. Sharpe.

Texas Real Estate Commission. (2003). *Final report of the Education Task Force.* Retrieved from http://www.trec.state.tx.us/pdf/education/EducationTaskForce _FinalReport.pdf

Thomas, C. (2009, January 7). Corporate ethics, missing in action; The Wall Street mess reflects badly on America's business schools. *Pittsburgh Post-Gazette.* Retrieved from http://www.post-gazette.com/pg/09007/939959-109.stm

Vidaver-Cohen, D. (2008). Architectures of excellence: Building business school reputation by meeting the ethics challenge. In D. L. Swanson & D. G. Fisher (Eds.), *Advancing business ethics education* (pp. 67-84). Charlotte, NC: Information Age.

Waddock, S. (2003, August). *A radical agenda for business in society education.* Paper presented at the Academy of Management, Social Issues in Management Division, Seattle.

Willen, L. (2004, March 8). Kellogg denies guilt as B-Schools evade alumni lapses. *Bloomberg News Wire.* Retrieved from http://www.cba.k-state.edu/departments/ ethics/docs/bloombergpress.htm.

Williams, S. D., & Dewett, T. C. (2006). Yes, you can teach business ethics: A review and research agenda. *Journal of Leadership and Organizational Studies, 12,* 109-120.

Windsor, D. (2002, October 8). An open letter on business school responsibility. Retrieved from http://info.cba.ksu.edu/swanson/Call/Call.pdf

CHAPTER 17

CORE KNOWLEDGE LEARNING OBJECTIVES FOR ACCOUNTING ETHICS EDUCATION BASED ON BLOOM'S TAXONOMY

**Linda A. Kidwell, Dann G. Fisher,
Robert L. Braun, and Diane L. Swanson**

INTRODUCTION

"We have a learning objective for ethics. Do you know of a measure we can use to assess this?"

We have heard this question on numerous occasions from accounting colleagues desperately searching the listserv in vain for an easily administered measure. Why are so many schools struggling with the assessment of ethics education?

We assert that, in accounting, the problem has two interrelated causes. First, effort among accounting educators toward effective integration of ethics across the curriculum has been weak, completely absent, or, in some cases, directed toward its undoing. Seemingly more effort has gone

Toward Assessing Business Ethics Education
pp. 307–333

into writing justifications in support of integration than has gone into the act of integration itself. If indeed ethics is not being adequately, effectively, and meaningfully integrated into the accounting curriculum, then measuring student competency will be difficult, if not impossible. The bottom line is that it is hard to find a measure that will produce results reflecting a positive student learning outcome for a topic that many faculty half-heartedly teach, may refuse to teach, or signal both implicitly and explicitly has no place in the curriculum. These educators are content to search for simplistic measures that could be used to signal to the accrediting bodies and other external constituencies that ethics is being covered adequately. This will allow them to return to teaching their technical material with the least amount of disruption.

The second cause of the struggle to assess ethics education in accounting is that, despite a proliferation of articles over the past 2 decades examining this issue, we are not aware of a coherent, widely accepted set of learning objectives for the area. If we don't know what we wish our students to learn, and if we leave to each faculty member the responsibility to weave ethics coverage into his or her course, then we should not be surprised that we are having trouble figuring out whether or not we have been successful. In comparison to a standalone ethics course, integration across the curriculum requires significant coordination for learning objectives to be developed and implemented. Given the lack of expertise in and commitment to ethics education in accounting, this seems a tall order.

Rather than succumbing to the demand for superficial assessment measures, we should use this opportunity to move accounting ethics education forward. In this chapter, we propose core knowledge learning objectives for accounting ethics education that can become the subject of meaningful assessment tool development. We wish to disclose that we are biased in favor of a standalone accounting ethics course that would serve as the foundation for meaningful integration in other courses. Part of this bias is a concern that the integration approach assumes that students have the knowledge and theoretical background needed to channel analysis of and dialogue about ethics issues toward constructive results, but does not provide the means for students to develop these tools. If students do not have this background, then class discussions and case analyses become superficially naïve, rather than meaningful and instructive. Because very few accounting programs offer a standalone course (Blanthorne, Kovar, & Fisher, 2007)—the method that we use to ensure that our students receive the necessary background for our technical areas—we should not assume that accounting students receive or even have been exposed to this body of knowledge. Rather this is an empirical question in need of testing.

Assessment, in this case, provides the critical means, perhaps the only means, to determine if accounting students possess these fundamentals.

The remainder of the chapter is organized as follows. The next section traces the deterioration of ethics education in the curriculum. Following this candid analysis that offers stern criticism of the academy's efforts thus far, the chapter offers a perspective that encourages thoughtful consideration as to whether or not ethics education in accounting is a worthy goal. This section makes the contention that perhaps our lack of will is traceable, in part, to the absence of a set of learning objectives in the field. The third section describes Bloom's taxonomy upon which the learning objectives for accounting ethics education will be constructed. The fourth section proposes a pedagogically sound set of learning objectives for ethics education in accounting. The fifth section critiques arguments for integration of ethics coverage, particularly with regard to assessment issues, thus making the case for a standalone ethics course.

THE DETERIORATION OF ETHICS EDUCATION IN ACCOUNTING

Zeff (2003), in analyzing the troubled state of the accounting profession after the accounting scandals at the turn of this century, asserts that the profession reached its peak in reputation and influence in the 1960s and has been in decline ever since. An important characteristic of this decline, according to Zeff, is the deterioration of professional values. Paralleling the corrosion of professional values is the repeated call over the past four decades for inclusion of ethics in the accounting curriculum.

In 1968, the call for ethics in the curriculum was made by the American Institute of Certified Public Accountants' (AICPA) Beamer Committee as part of their suggested model curriculum ("Academic Preparation," 1968; AICPA, 1969). Unlike other subjects in the model curriculum, ethics was not given a credit-hour requirement. The model curriculum was widely embraced and adopted because it "was a business school dean's dream, with large dollops of all the latest fads" (Van Whye, 1994, p. 119). But by failing to recommend hours for ethics coverage, the Beamer Committee, perhaps inadvertently, relegated ethics to inferior status in the accounting curriculum, an outcome that would be consistently repeated until it became ingrained.

During the 1970s, the AICPA pushed for the creation of 5-year, professional schools of accountancy meant to be independent from business schools (Van Wyhe, 2007). The AICPA believed that a professional program should involve 2 years of liberal arts education tailored toward professional study and 3 years of professional study that "would include the traditional accounting subjects as well as organization of the profession, ethics, and the environment of accounting" (Van Whye, 2007, p. 486).

In 1978, the Association to Advance Collegiate Schools of Business (AACSB)[1] announced intentions to accredit accounting programs. Although the AICPA had intended to form its own accreditation agency, the Accounting Accreditation Council (AAC), they reluctantly yielded control over accreditation of accounting programs to the AACSB. In return, the AICPA asked the AACSB to promise that the accreditation standards would contain at least a few key issues, including greater emphasis in the curriculum on "the environment and organization of the profession, its ethics and responsibilities" ("AACSB Council," 1980, p. 13). The goals of AACSB differed markedly, however, from those of the AICPA. Emphasis was placed on quantitative research by faculty, while focus on practice and professionalism was downplayed (Van Wyhe, 2007). Rather than supporting the needs and demands of the profession, the resulting research emphasis resulted in a documented chasm between practice and academia (Bloom, Heymann, Fuglister, & Collins, 1994; Bricker & Previts, 1990). Moreover, the emphasis on quantitative research, much of it grounded in the amoral precepts of agency theory, made classroom instruction in ethics an anathema (Shaub & Fisher, 2008).

The savings and loan crisis, which resulted from massive accounting failures and allegations of auditor fraud, characterized the 1980s, bringing embarrassment to the accounting profession. In response to the fraud crisis, the Treadway Commission (National Commission on Fraudulent Financial Reporting, 1987) recommended that ethics be incorporated into every business and accounting course. Around the same time, the American Accounting Association (AAA) created the Project on Professionalism and Ethics, because "the urgency of current ethics issues ... precipitate(s) much needed additions to the accounting curriculum" (Langenderfer & Rockness, 1989, p. 59). Unwittingly, this advisory committee dealt another blow to the incorporation of ethics into the accounting curriculum by again failing to call for a standalone course in accounting ethics. Influenced by the Treadway Commission's recommendation that ethics be assimilated into all business courses, the AAA Professionalism and Ethics Committee recommended that ethics be integrated into existing accounting courses as "the quickest way to expose the maximum number of accounting students to ethics" (Loeb & Rockness, 1992, p. 487). In the end, the integration approach was endorsed not for its perceived effectiveness, but rather for its expediency. Reinforcing this dynamic, the Big Eight White Paper ("Big Eight," 1989) and the Accounting Education Change Commission (AECC, 1990) were very critical of the silo approach to accounting education and called for better integration of accounting topics. Equally telling, the AECC, in offering grants for the improvement of the quality of accounting education, did not fund any attempts to improve accounting ethics education (Mintz, 1993). Against this backdrop, the creation of a standalone course in accounting ethics stood little chance.

Ample opportunity to add ethics coverage to the accounting curriculum was created in the 1990s, when a growing number of states implemented the 150-hour rule as a requirement to sit for the CPA exam. Despite the expansion of the curriculum, ethics coverage never arrived.

In 2003, the National Association of State Boards of Accountancy (NASBA), in conjunction with the AAA, surveyed accounting educators, finding that 46% of schools offered a separate course in business or accounting ethics and 51% of schools required an ethics course for accounting majors (Mastracchio, 2008). Once NASBA officials obtained syllabi, however, they determined that most of the courses designated as ethics were, in reality, business law courses and that these courses "with a few exceptions, did not provide adequate coverage of ethics, values, and appropriate professional conduct" (Mastracchio, 2008, p. 67).

Based on this observation, NASBA (2005) concluded that ethics and professionalism was not being covered sufficiently in the accounting curriculum, resulting in that organization proposing that a candidate for the CPA exam should be required to complete 3 hours of university coursework in business ethics and 3 hours of university coursework in accounting ethics and professional responsibility. The AACSB (2005) expressed disfavor with NASBA's proposal, citing its implementation as a potential challenge to the agency's own flexible, mission-driven accreditation standards. The AAA (2005) harshly criticized NASBA for taking a policy position on curricular issues.

Those opposed to the NASBA proposal hypothesized that adding ethics content to the CPA exam would encourage accounting educators to include ethics coverage in the curriculum, thereby rendering mandated ethics coverage unnecessary. In order to explore this conjecture, NASBA conducted a survey of 980 accounting educators. The results indicated that a significant number of educators were not aware of CPA exam content, and most believed that state boards of accountancy requiring specific courses as a condition to be met to sit for the CPA exam was far more likely than CPA exam content to influence ethics coverage in the curriculum. Based on the survey results, NASBA concluded that the CPA exam content cannot be relied upon to drive course content (Mastracchio, 2008).

In response to the criticisms leveled at the initial proposal, NASBA formed a task force of representatives from the AACSB, AAA, and NASBA. The revised proposal (Mastracchio, 2008; NASBA, 2009), with a few exceptions, no longer has credit-hour requirements. The new proposal, however, still requires a minimum of three credit hours in accounting ethics, but states that the requirement may be met through integration into the curriculum rather than through a standalone course. The proposal also asserts that in determining whether or not a candidate to sit for the CPA exam has met the stated requirements, state boards may rely on transcripts from accredited accounting programs. Given that the accreditation standards allow and, frankly, encourage integration of ethics across the curriculum rather than a standalone course, we would expect that any new directive from state boards of accountancy, should it ever come to pass, would do little more than encourage ethics to be integrated into accounting courses. Later in this chapter, we address the problems that this reliance on integration poses for assessment.

Given the calls for more and better coverage of ethics in the accounting curriculum, why did meaningful change fail to occur? Since the 1970s, accounting academia has been dominated by quantitative researchers, most of whom do not believe that normative discourse has any place in accounting thought and literature, much less in the classroom (Shaub & Fisher, 2008). The vast majority of these educators simply do not support inclusion of ethics in the curriculum. Most believe that either ethics cannot be taught or is better left to philosophers (Van Whye, 2007), clear signals that they believe that ethics has no place in accounting programs.

The AACSB, in developing the standards that were passed in 1991, moved to a flexible, mission-driven standard that allowed for integration of ethical coverage into other courses, rather than requiring a standalone course. The primary outcome of this standard has been the documented deterioration of required business ethics coursework in the curriculum (Willen, 2004). Some observers proffer that, in looking for more and more programs to recognize and sanction with these flexible, mission-based standards, the AACSB is allowing business schools to erode professionalism and the stable knowledge base from which it derives (Gioia & Corley, 2002; Schmotter, 2000; Trank & Rynes, 2003; Yunker, 2000). In other words, the decline of ethics courses may be seen as a symptom of the larger degeneration in the overall quality of business school education and a rather dramatic failure of academic self-regulation and self-correction. In an environment where business ethics coverage, with a longstanding tradition that once enjoyed a critical mass of dedicated faculty, has been allowed to wither, accounting ethics coverage seems unlikely to spring to life.

The next section shifts the focus of the discussion to the questions that accounting educators should be asking. We believe that despite the salience of the ethics issue over the last 40 years, many in accounting have not given thoughtful and objective consideration as to whether or not the current state of ethics education is in the best interest of our students or the profession. In the next section, we ask that accounting educators cast aside preconceived notions about ethics education in accounting in the interest of arriving at a reasoned conclusion.

IS ETHICS EDUCATION IN ACCOUNTING A WORTHY GOAL?

These are difficult times for accounting education. Accounting standard setters are producing authoritative guidance at a dizzying pace. The uncertainty surrounding convergence and/or conversion to International Financial Reporting Standards (IFRS) adds further complexity to the educator's task of curriculum management. Tightening budgets seriously constrain curriculum innovation, and the emphasis that accreditation standards place on measurable learning outcomes further adds an element of risk to innovation in the curriculum, especially with no clear mandate for improved ethics coverage. Adding ethics and professionalism requirements to the increasing technical burden may seem like the last item to be squeezed into or, more likely, out of the curriculum. Apathy and institutional forces have made ethics education in accounting the stepchild of the curriculum.

Does It Matter If Accountants in Practice Behave Ethically or Unethically?

If, as accounting educators, we can't all agree that ethics matters, there is little point in proceeding. An important distinction needs to be made here, however. This is not the same question as: does it matter if accountants in practice behave legally or illegally? Clearly, the economic devastation caused when accounting is performed illegally exacts a severe toll on society. Although the blatantly illegal actions of Bernard Madoff, Andrew Fastow, Scot Sullivan, and others help to make this point, we run the risk of losing sight of what ethics is as a discipline if we define it only in terms of what is legal.

Ethics has to do with what is right and wrong and how we make that determination. Questions about legality occupy an important space in the field of ethics. The field, however, is much broader. We take the position that the study of ethics in accounting programs should extend beyond the study of the laws and rules governing accountants into the principles that have shaped the profession and the perspectives from which they derive. This leads us to our next question.

Should We Examine Issues Beyond
Rules of Conduct and Applicable Laws?

There are many accounting educators who believe that any discussion of ethics outside of the rules of conduct and applicable laws is the stuff of pseudointellectualism at best and dangerous, subversive thinking at worst. But consider those financial scandals with which we have been bombarded. Do they start with a corporate villain bent on ripping off unsuspecting investors through accounting manipulations (all the while laughing maniacally), or do they start with judgments that focus on short-term self-interest or a too-narrow set of perceived stakeholders? Do the accountants who process questionable journal entries do so because they carefully weigh all of the alternatives and the effects that each entry would have on all parties involved, or do they book these entries simply because their bosses tell them to, and they think that doing so is just part of their jobs? And what of the auditors who figuratively climb into bed with their clients? Is doing so a conscious decision to forgo professional responsibilities to the public interest, or is doing so the result of a series of smaller decisions that make that next step toward bias easier or even inevitable? Belief in the latter alternatives to each of these questions indicates that ethics education should extend beyond rules and laws. For if we reduce ethics education in accounting to memorization of the rules of conduct and familiarity with applicable laws, then we miss out on the opportunity to consider the role of sensitization to different perspectives, the importance of moral reasoning in accounting judgment, and the impact that organizational culture and client pressure plays in decision making and subsequent implementation. This leads us into the next question.

Can Ethics Be Taught to Accounting Students?

We suspect that this question separates many in accounting on the issue of ethics in the curriculum. The division, we hope, results from an ill-defined question rather than fundamental differences. Of the four words in the question, two are poorly defined in the context of this debate: "ethics" and "taught."

We contend that, as a discipline, we in accounting have not exerted enough effort to define what professional ethics is as a field of study. For this reason, we suspect that most accounting educators, if asked to teach an accounting ethics class, would have little to no idea of the topics to be taught and may never have even given it much thought. Certainly the grasp of what this course should entail would be nowhere near the understanding that these educators would have for what should be taught in a technical course, such as intermediate accounting. Why is this? Most of our technical courses, such as intermediate accounting, have an established, agreed-upon core body of knowledge. This allows anyone who must teach this course to have a basic idea of what needs to be taught and provides external constituents of our programs with an expectation for the knowledge of our graduates. Because there has never been a clear mandate for ethics in the accounting curriculum like there has been for the coverage of technical topics, accounting educators have never been pressed to consider, let alone define, the existence of a core body of knowledge for ethics. Is it any wonder then that most accounting educators believe that ethics, if it must be addressed at all, can be limited to a superficial integration across the curriculum?

The second point of contention surrounds the word "taught." Many naysayers among accounting educators think that if a student exposed to ethics education behaves unethically in the future (which, undoubtedly, some will), then ethics has not been or cannot be taught. Those who speak disparagingly of ethics education tend to set standards that are beyond the reach of instruction for any topic of substance. Ethics education cannot provide indemnification of the profession from future misdeeds. We can no sooner guarantee that an accountant having taken an ethics class will never commit a fraud than we can guarantee that an accountant having taken a tax class will prepare flawless tax returns. The tax class can lay the foundation for understanding the principles that underlie the tax code, the language of taxation, the rules that have broad applicability, the theory behind tax law, and the resources available to address matters not covered specifically in the class. Some students will avail themselves of the content of the course. Some will not. Some will learn the material well enough to pass the test and then forget most of it. When we teach taxation, we seek to develop course content that reflects the common body of knowledge available for the course and implement assignments and tests that measure achievement of learning objectives. Why do we insist on taking a different approach to teaching ethics than we do for teaching technical material? A primary reason appears to be a lack of understanding that there is a body of knowledge that needs to be delivered. In the next section of this chapter, we attempt to advance the dialogue toward establishing a common body of knowledge and learning objectives for accounting ethics education that we hope will help accounting educators to view ethics education on a similar plane with technical content areas.

BLOOM'S TAXONOMY

Much of the discourse of accounting ethics education gets caught in the trap of discussing whether or not we can somehow force our students to become better people, thus ending accounting-related business corruption as we know it. This is patently impossible, and the trap prevents us from evaluating what we actually can accomplish in trying to advance accounting ethics education. Therefore, let us consider the development of ethics learning in the same way that we consider the development of learning in technical matters such as lease accounting. We cannot take a beginning accounting student with little or no personal experience with leases and no knowledge of double entry accounting and teach him or her lease accounting without first developing the knowledge base. We must begin by teaching this student the basic elements of accrual accounting, the definitions of assets, liabilities, and expenses, the present value of money, and the fundamental conceptual differences between owning and renting. Only after the student has learned this terminology, understood the concept of accrual, and learned to analyze the characteristics of a particular lease is that student prepared to understand lease accounting and apply it appropriately, usually only after at least three semesters of accounting instruction. Why then do we expect accounting professors to produce perfectly ethical beings through occasional cases peppered in end-of-chapter materials in accounting textbooks? More importantly, why do we set the impossible as a goal and then throw up our hands when we fail to achieve it? Like lease accounting, ethics must be taught with an understanding that learning is sequential and hierarchical in nature. We must take the time to build the foundation for critical thinking on ethical matters rather than assuming all of the tools are present when college freshmen walk in the door and use a few token ethics cases in various courses to comply with accreditation standards that demand ethics education.

Bloom's taxonomy (Bloom, Engelhart, Furst, Hill, & Krathwohl, 1956) has been used for over 50 years to help educators develop curricula in numerous domains, and we propose a similar approach for developing learning objectives in accounting ethics. (For another discussion of Bloom's taxonomy and learning objectives, see chapter 16 of this book by Swanson, Fisher, and Niehoff.) We will briefly explain Bloom's taxonomy, followed by a discussion of some specific accounting ethics learning objectives built using the taxonomy. Bloom et al. (1956, p. 10) wrote that, "If we view statements of educational objectives as intended behaviors which the student will display at the end of some period of education, we can then view the process as one of change." The taxonomy is based on the idea that complex behaviors are made up of simpler components. Therefore, the educational process is one whereby simpler components must be taught first, which then may "develop and become integrated with other behaviors to form more complex behavior which is classified in a different way" (Bloom et al., 1956, p. 10).

Bloom's taxonomy consists of six major classes of learning: knowledge, comprehension, application, analysis, synthesis, and evaluation. Figure

17.1 provides a graphic representation of Bloom's taxonomy; Panel A presents the taxonomy as originally advanced by Bloom et al. in 1956, and Panel B presents the taxonomy as revised by Anderson et al. (2001).

PANEL A: Original Taxonomy by Bloom, Engelhart, Furst, Hill, and Krathwohl (1956)

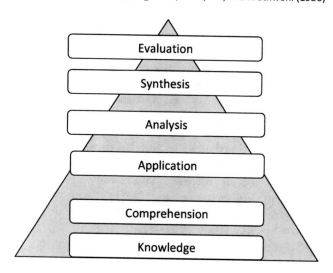

PANEL B: Revised Taxonomy by Anderson, Krathwohl, Airasian, Cruikshank, Mayer, Pintrich, et al. (2001)

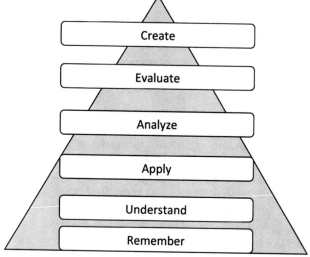

Figure 17.1.   Bloom's Taxonomy.

Knowledge, the basic foundation of learning, involves the recall of specifics and universals, methods of inquiry and processes, patterns, and structures. In their revision of the taxonomy, Anderson et al. (2001) relabeled this first level of learning as remembering, including both recognizing and recalling knowledge or facts, concepts, and procedures. With knowledge, the student can bring to mind appropriate material. Knowledge is often assessed through questions of when and what, definitions, lists, identification, and matching (Davidson & Baldwin, 2005).

Remembering itself does not imply understanding; the next level in the taxonomy is comprehension (Bloom et al., 1956) or understanding (Anderson et al., 2001). Comprehension occurs when the learner understands what is being communicated and can make use of the material, without necessarily relating it to other information or understanding its full implications (Bloom et al., 1956). Comprehension is demonstrated when the learner can translate ideas into his or her own words, interpret them, or extrapolate ideas into expanded domains. Understanding includes the ability to interpret, exemplify, classify, summarize, infer, compare, and explain (Anderson et al., 2001). Comprehension may be assessed by asking students to compare, differentiate, discuss, explain, or answer why (Davidson & Baldwin, 2005).

The third level in Bloom's taxonomy is application. Application involves the use of abstractions in specific and concrete situations. This can include application of an idea learned in one topic area to another or the ability to predict probable effects of changing one or more components of a problem (Bloom et al., 1956). Applying knowledge can include both executing known processes in a familiar task or implementing them in new tasks (Anderson et al., 2001). Assessing application skills requires the use of a new setting or sufficient change to the details of the present setting for the situation to be truly new to the learner. Minor tinkering with details merely requires the learner to remember facts depending on how they understood the problem, reflecting knowledge, and perhaps comprehension levels of learning.

The fourth level of the taxonomy is analysis. Analyzing involves the breakdown of communications into their constituent elements, understanding the relations among ideas, recognizing unstated assumptions, and distinguishing between facts and hypotheses or opinion (Bloom et al., 1956). Analysis demonstrates the hierarchical nature of learning. For a learner to conduct analysis, he or she must first have knowledge of basic facts, patterns, and settings, must comprehend what information is being communicated, and must be able to apply abstractions to specific situations. Students who have reached the analyzing level of learning should be able to differentiate among alternatives and organize their knowledge in meaningful ways (Anderson et al., 2001).

In the original taxonomy, Bloom et al. labeled the fifth level of learning as synthesis. This entails putting disparate pieces together to form a whole, combining them into a pattern or structure not previously evident. Synthesis can be demonstrated through the production of unique communications, such as prose, plans, or sets of operations, or it can be demonstrated through proposing a set of abstract relations (Bloom et al., 1956). The highest level of learning described in Bloom's taxonomy is evaluation. Judgments about the value of material and methods for given purposes, the ability to identify or check for logical fallacies, the determination of whether a process is internally consistent, and the capacity to compare with the highest known standards are all manifestations of evaluation skills (Anderson et al., 2001; Bloom et al.)).

In their revision of Bloom's taxonomy, Anderson et al. (2001) relabeled and reordered the highest two levels of learning. Evaluate moved down the hierarchy to fifth. Synthesis became create and is presented at the highest level of learning. Creating was moved to the highest level in part because research had not supported the hierarchical delineation between synthesis and evaluation. Further, by clarifying that creating included Bloom's synthesis but also hypothesis generation, planning, and producing, Anderson et al. maintained that evaluation is a necessary skill for the development of unique contributions.

CORE KNOWLEDGE AND LEARNING OBJECTIVES FOR ACCOUNTING ETHICS EDUCATION

One of the challenges to teaching ethics to accounting students, already mentioned in this chapter, is the lack of clarity as to what they should actually learn. There is no set core of knowledge prescribed by the AACSB, NASBA, AICPA, or AAA. The one thing most of these organizational members seem to agree upon is that accounting ethics education should emphasize what matters to future professional accountants, rather than being a broad-brush philosophy course. Therefore, we propose a set of core knowledge learning objectives for accounting ethics education. We do not insist that this is an all-inclusive list; rather, we intend to shift the discussion from a debate about whether ethics can or should be taught in accounting to a discussion about the body of ethics knowledge to which accounting students should be exposed. In order for this discussion to be productive, we believe that it needs to start with a comprehensive, objectives-based framework that can be modified through scholarship and can be used to build a common body of knowledge for the profession.

Codes of Conduct

One of the least contentious items in any set of learning objectives for accounting ethics education is learning the various codes of conduct or ethics applicable to accountants. Professional expectations are clearly spelled out in the AICPA Code of Professional Conduct, (AICPA, 2010) and most auditing classes already cover this subject in at least some detail. On the other hand, accounting students should know that accounting careers outside of public accounting also have applicable codes of conduct. The Institute of Management Accountants' (IMA) Statement of Ethical Professional Practice (IMA, 2008) provides guidance to practitioners, but also can be used to teach students that ethical conduct should be expected even where independence is not relevant and licenses to practice are not at stake. Likewise, the Association of Government Accountants (AGA) has a code of ethics for government accountants generally and Certified Government Financial Managers specifically (AGA, 2003).

One of the codes that may be less familiar to many accounting faculty is the Code of Ethics for Professional Accountants, promulgated by the International Ethics Standards Board for Accountants (IESBA, 2008), an arm of the International Federation of Accountants (IFAC). This code has a conceptual approach similar to that of the IMA and the AGA and unlike the rules-based emphasis of the AICPA. The IESBA code spells out fundamental principles, including integrity, objectivity, professional competence and due care, confidentiality, and professional behavior. In addition, Section 290 and 291 of the IESBA code address independence in audit and review engagements and independence in other assurance engagements, respectively. The IESBA code also has separate sections that pertain to professional accountants in public practice and professional accountants in business. Throughout this code, threats to the accountant's ability to comply with fundamental principles are described (self-interest, self-review, advocacy, familiarity, and intimidation threats), approaches to mitigating threats are suggested, and accountants are reminded of the necessity of either reducing threats to an acceptable level or declining engagements. This general framework can be very useful in teaching students to analyze ethical issues without having to memorize detailed ethical rulings from the AICPA.

Recall that the idea behind Bloom's taxonomy is that in order to reach the higher levels of learning, students need to build a solid foundation at the lower levels. As such, the current educational process, in which students are exposed to cases without core knowledge of fundamental ideas regarding ethics, is not likely to stimulate meaningful discussion beyond platitudes regarding right and wrong. The learning objectives that we propose in this area and those that follow are comprehensive in nature.

We encourage instructors to give careful attention to lower-level objectives with the goal of developing core knowledge that can be used to analyze more complex cases.

Following Bloom's hierarchical taxonomy, we propose learning objectives related to codes of ethics are as follows:

- Remember principles and rules of conduct governing the profession (e.g., various codes of conduct, practice standards, SEC regulations, and Sarbanes-Oxley provisions).
- Understand the purpose of codes of conduct. Understand the meaning of terms and associations between them. Compare the guidance in different codes. Understand the role of integrity in the profession.
- Apply understanding of concepts associated with codes of conduct by describing a situation and identifying relevant sections of the codes of conduct that could provide guidance.
- Analyze behavior of accountants with respect to codes of conduct. Determine whether described actions violate the codes. Identify what the accountant could have done differently to avoid violations.
- Evaluate the effectiveness of codes of conduct. Consider various enforcement mechanisms in contributing to the efficacy of codes. Link ideas advanced in codes of conduct with classical ethics theories.
- Create plans for improving compliance with rules and adherence to principles. Design a code of conduct or training session based on the code for a firm, business, or educational setting.

The various codes discussed above are an important part of ethics education for accountants, but there are other ethics-related pronouncements and regulations of which accounting students should be aware. Clearly, students need to be knowledgeable about the Sarbanes-Oxley Act of 2002. They should also know about the Federal Sentencing Guidelines, though the specifics may be less important than a general awareness that such guidelines do exist and will apply to them as accountants in the future. They should also be aware of the role the Securities and Exchange Commission plays in the rules governing accountants' behavior.

To this point, the core knowledge we have proposed is uncontroversial and is likely part of the standard accounting curriculum at many schools, most likely addressed in the audit course. We assert that more general knowledge of the role of accounting in society is necessary, including general corporate governance components, the concept of public trust, and the role of accounting and auditing in a western economy.

Corporate Governance

Corporate governance education should include a firm grasp on the terminology of governance and an understanding of many of the components of governance. This can include a more detailed study of the Sarbanes-Oxley Act, but it can also extend to various roles an accounting student can foresee in the future. For example, the governance roles of cost accountants, internal auditors, audit committees, and members of the board of directors are important for students to understand. Corporate codes of ethics and proper whistle-blower processes and protections also fall in this category. Learning objectives associated with corporate governance, Sarbanes-Oxley, and Federal Sentencing Guidelines at the different levels of Bloom's taxonomy are as follows:

- Remember components of the Sarbanes-Oxley Act and Federal Sentencing Guidelines. Remember the terminology of corporate governance and corporate social responsibility.
- Understand the role accountants play in corporate governance. Understand how compliance programs can affect sentencing. Summarize the guidance in Sarbanes-Oxley. Understand the ideas of stakeholder theory.
- Apply concepts of stakeholder theory and Sarbanes-Oxley to cases. List stakeholders involved in cases. Identify harms and benefits associated with alternative courses of action.
- Analyze stakeholder theory by contrasting it to the theory of the firm. Analyze historical cases to determine how losses might have been decreased if Sarbanes-Oxley had been in place.
- Evaluate the effectiveness of Sarbanes-Oxley with regard to its effect on stakeholders since its enactment. Evaluate the role of enforcement on the effectiveness of the act.
- Create a plan for implementing Sarbanes-Oxley within an organization. Create a plan for impacting corporate culture in professional life.

All of the subjects above can be treated at a basic level, and rules related to codes and regulations might be treated no differently than Financial Accounting Standards Board (FASB) standards or International Accounting Standards Board (IASB) standards for financial accounting. However, to really delve into the subjects that resulted in many of the scandals over the years, as well as the rules promulgated as a result, students need to learn to probe more deeply, and this is where we believe that the potential for meaningful ethics education begins.

The Accounting Profession

In order to make the transition from the study of rules and regulations governing the profession into a richer context, students need to gain a deeper understanding of accounting as a profession. This involves an understanding of the history and traditions of the profession and an awareness of the effect that accounting decisions have on stakeholders and the economy. We propose the following list of potential learning objectives about the accounting profession:

- Remember the chronology of events associated with the development of the accounting profession.
- Understand the effect that accounting decisions can have on stakeholders. Understand the role of accounting in the economy and society.
- Apply characteristics of professions to the accounting profession.
- Analyze how the accounting profession compares to other professions.
- Evaluate how changes in the profession have impacted the functioning of the economy (e.g., changes in advertising rules, private securities litigation reform, Sarbanes-Oxley).
- Create a strategic plan for an accounting firm to effectively respond to changes in the economic and regulatory environment in the years ahead.

Studying the profession itself may provide the opportunity to discuss how accounting is unique among professions with respect to the central role that the third party plays in the demand for true and fair accounting and the essential role that trust plays in these relationships. Understanding these relationships provides an opportunity to transition into a discussion of the level of moral development that is required of accountants in order to honor that trust.

Moral Development

According to moral development theory, differences exist among individuals in the complex cognitive processes used to make ethical judgments. Moral development is the result of the "progressive understanding of the purpose, function, and nature of social cooperation" (Rest, 1983, p. 562). Experience is believed to increase understanding of the need for social arrangements, the types of social arrangements that are possible, and the benefits and obligations that may result from each arrangement (Rest, 1983, 1986; Rest, Narvaez, Bebeau, & Thoma, 1999). The lasting effects of social experiences are stored in long-term memory in the form of moral schema or schemes of cooperation (Rest et al., 1999). The various moral schema are referred to as stages. The stage model, as developed by Kohlberg (1969), revised by Rest (1979), and modified by Rest et al. (1999), asserts the existence of six stages or schema, each characterized by distinct notions of fairness and justice. A full explanation of the stage theory is beyond the scope of this chapter. A thorough explanation and suggestions for implementation can be found in Kohlberg and Hersh (1977), Rest et al. (1999), and Thomas (2004).

Learning the stage theory will help the students recognize their current state of moral development and expose them to higher levels to which they should aspire. Moreover, exposure to moral development theory may be the earliest and easiest exposure that accounting students will have to a moral perspective beyond simply what rules tell them to do, and this type of thinking should equip them for future issues where there are no rules to guide them or where strictly following the rules may mislead others.

In addition to understanding stages of moral reasoning, students should be exposed to the four-component model of moral behavior (Rest, 1983, 1986; Rest & Narvaez, 1991; Rest et al., 1999), a model that both Armstrong, Ketz, and Owsen (2003) and the International Accounting Education Standards Board (IAESB, 2006) recommend for use in accounting ethics education. In contrast to moral reasoning, the other three components—the moral sensitivity required to recognize a moral issue before moral reasoning can be applied, the moral decision making that is required to forsake self-interest in favor of a moral alternative, and the moral action which draws upon the courage of the actor in following an ethical path—are more closely associated with skill and character development than the more content-laden moral reasoning material. The four-component model demonstrates to students the complex nature of ethical behavior and is useful in explaining how external factors, such as workplace culture and client pressure, can make the moral ideal difficult to attain. We propose the following list of potential learning objectives for moral development:

- Remember Kohlberg's stages of moral development. List the steps in Rest's four-component model of moral behavior.
- Understand the changes in perspective associated with different levels of moral reasoning.
- Apply understanding of moral reasoning to predict how accountants at different levels would respond to different situations. Dis-

cuss moral dimensions of current events and everyday decisions to help develop moral reasoning.

- Analyze the level of moral reasoning involved in accounting decisions described in cases. Analyze personal characteristics of individuals making unethical and ethical decisions.

- Evaluate the relationship between levels of moral reasoning and elements of classical ethics theories. Evaluate how personal values and reasoning skills affect what one does and for what one stands.

- Create a hypothetical continuing professional education seminar to help individuals in a CPA firm improve their moral sensitivity, reasoning, decision making, and actions.

Classical Ethics Theories

Disagreement exists among those who teach accounting ethics regarding whether or not the classic ethics theories should be taught (see Blanthorne et al., 2007) and whether or not they belong in the set of core knowledge. We believe that these theories should be part of an ethics education. Where philosophy is part of the general education requirements for all students, then discussion of ethical theories in an accounting ethics course may be unnecessary. When this is not the case, students should be exposed to these important classical ways of thinking about ethical issues. At a minimum, we believe that students should be exposed to egoism, utilitarianism, deontology, rights theory, justice theory, and virtue ethics. We propose the following learning objectives associated with classical ethics theories:

- Remember ideas, terminology, and philosophers associated with classical ethics theories (e.g., egoism, utilitarianism, deontology, rights, justice, and virtue).

- Understand the strengths and weaknesses of each of the theories. Understand which theory best corresponds to one's own initial attitudes toward resolving ethical dilemmas.

- Apply classical theories to address current issues and questions in business and accounting.

- Analyze contemporary perspectives and current events within the context of classical ethics theories. Analyze whether behavior of individuals involved in cases reflected classical theories.

- Evaluate whether theories provide practical guidance for current issues. Evaluate ethical perspectives demonstrated by characters in popular movies.

- Create persuasive arguments in support of ethical choices using the language and reasoning of classical ethics theories.

Decision-Making Models

Ethical decision making is a complex, multifaceted process. Students need help to organize their analysis. As a result, an important part of ethics education is to provide students with a structure for ethical decision making.

One possibility that, because of its inherent limitations, should be used only as a starting point, is an ethics decision tree developed by the AICPA (AICPA, 2002). The decision tree recommends that the accountant work through the organization to resolve concerns, starting with an examination of the firm's ethics policy and then taking questions further up the chain of command until a satisfactory resolution is reached. A weakness of the decision tree is its failure to offer guidance on how to weigh either the consequences to various parties or questions of right and wrong; it is a bureaucratic approach targeted squarely at the conventional (rule-oriented) level of moral development (Kohlberg & Hersch, 1977).

The weaknesses of the AICPA decision tree—its inability to deal with ethical issues where asking a superior is not a viable approach, where the organizational director is the source of the dilemma, or where the person with the dilemma is in fact the final decision maker—can be exploited to help students understand why a richer model is needed and can channel discussion of the considerations that should go into that model. Students should recognize key components in a good decision model: recognize the issues, identify the stakeholders, determine possible alternatives and consider how they impact others, analyze the alternatives, make a decision, implement the decision, and monitor the outcomes (Hartman & Desjardins, 2008; Mintz & Morris, 2008). Students should learn to consider applicable laws, standards for professional conduct, and ethical principles learned from the study of ethics theory as they analyze potential benefits and consequences of alternatives.

Decision models help students learn how to make decisions systematically, rather than by gut reaction. A systematic approach teaches students to adequately address ethical considerations before taking action and prepares students to be ready to account for and be able to articulate their decisions when questions arise. A firm grasp of a decision model will allow students to apply higher-level analysis to the cases and issues integrated into the technical courses in the accounting curriculum. We propose the following learning objectives related to decision-making models:

- Remember steps in a decision model for handling ethical issues.
- Understand situations in which decision models may be useful.
- Apply decision-model frameworks to situations involving moral choice.
- Analyze the effectiveness of decisions made using decision models.
- Evaluate the decisions of others made with decision models and determine whether they used the models appropriately and correctly.
- Create a decision-making model incorporating classical ethics theories.

INTEGRATION POSES ASSESSMENT ISSUES FOR ACCOUNTING ETHICS EDUCATION

We believe that a standalone ethics course provides the best means for attaining the learning objectives that we have proposed. Assessing learning outcomes is difficult when ethics coverage is scattered across the curriculum. According to Swanson and Frederick (2005), two assessment errors are inevitable. First, ethics coverage may be deemed sufficient when the coverage is weak or nonexistent. The proposed NASBA (2005) changes to Rules 5-1 and 5-2 of the Uniform Accountancy Act state that, "Compliance with these [ethics] requirements may be evidenced by course syllabi and/or a letter from the institution." Simply listing topics on course syllabi does not guarantee that the topics have been covered meaningfully or even addressed at all. NASBA expressed concerns that state boards of accountancy might struggle to determine whether or not ethics subject matter had actually been integrated into courses (Mastracchio, 2008). As a result, NASBA specified that state boards may assume that CPA exam candidates from AACSB-accredited accounting programs meet the ethics credit-hour requirement. But this assumption is unfounded unless AACSB visitation teams scrutinize the means and depth of integration occurring in accounting programs. If accreditation teams are willing to allow programs to merely point to syllabi and superficial assessment measurements as proof that ethics has been effectively integrated, then the intent of the NASBA proposal will be easily circumvented.

The second assessment error identified by Swanson and Frederick (2005) is that ethics in the hands of untrained faculty may pass inspection when, in reality, the material has been trivialized, diluted, or distorted past recognition. Integration assumes that educators will systematically intertwine ethics with technical coverage. Preferring to focus first and foremost on the delivery of technical expertise, many accounting educators consider the need to integrate ethics into their courses overly burdensome. To make matters worse, some accounting professors are markedly hostile toward ethics, which is not surprising given that most are themselves products of amoral business education (Shaub & Fisher, 2008). Predictably, many perceive that making room for ethics requires cutting material they assign greater priority; thus, ethics coverage in many technical accounting courses is superficial at best.

In weighing the merits of a stand-alone course versus integration, NASBA concluded that a standalone course delivered by an educator trained in ethics would make it easier for state boards to verify compliance with the credit-hour requirement and "might be easier than having the faculty as a whole teach the subject" (Mastracchio, 2008, p. 67). The American Accounting Association Education Committee (AAA, 2005), questioning who would be capable of teaching a standalone course, claimed, "Few, if any, [accounting faculty] are trained for this in our doctoral programs." This statement, although offered in support of integration, is not only an indictment of our doctoral programs, but also suggestive of the potential fallacy of integration. If accounting educators have little or no training in ethics, then what leads one to believe that these educators are capable of, or even interested in, adequately weaving ethics coverage across their technical courses, especially when they and their students lack the knowledge and theoretical background necessary for integration to be effective? In this environment, programs may be able to document that ethics has been included in these courses, but the coverage, if it exists at all, may be so distorted as to be unrecognizable. Moreover, this attitude toward doctoral education supports the status quo, making the problem persistent and self-fulfilling.

The (AAA, 2005) claims that, "Many schools have chosen ethics for their accounting and/or business programs as a learning goal against which they assess outcomes. If these work, then why do they need to change?" But does this indeed work? Although the AACSB's flexible standards have the benefit of allowing a broad spectrum of schools to be accredited, their vagueness on ethics allows for weak, meaningless ethics objectives and assessment. Allowing each program to create its own learning objective for ethics while developing an assessment measure to be used as justification for success does not ensure that students have learned what they need, merely that they have learned what that program promised to superficially assess. It denies that a common body of knowledge in ethics exists and needs to be delivered. More than a half century ago, Gordon and Howell (1959, p. 449) proclaimed, "At present, it [AACSB] seems to be content to act primarily as the guardian of a respectable kind of academic mediocrity." With regard to accounting ethics education, this statement continues to be true, and is perhaps an understatement.

Whether or not significant time is being committed to the integration of ethics into the curriculum, we are concerned that this approach generally fails to provide students with a conceptual foundation, making meaningful application difficult. Without exposure to conceptual building blocks, students lack the theory and principles necessary to channel the analysis and dialogue toward constructive results. Inconsistent with Bloom's taxonomy, the integration approach bypasses or assumes the existence of knowledge (remember), comprehension (understand), and application (apply), instead moving directly to class discussions and case analysis. This requires students to be capable of reasoning at the taxonomy's higher levels of analysis (analyze), synthesis (evaluate), and evaluation (create), before they have the capacity to do so. Lacking solid theoretical underpinnings, the process of integrating ethics across the curriculum cannot help but be superficial and naive.

We assert that the starting point for eliminating the risk of assessment errors is to affirm a common body of knowledge for accounting ethics education and then deliver it, whole cloth, in a standalone ethics course that can then be used as the foundation for the integration of ethics coverage across the accounting curriculum.

CONCLUSION

This chapter described the 40-year debate resulting in the failure of the accounting academy to embrace ethics education, advanced a carefully conceived set of learning objectives for ethics in accounting, and raised the assessment issues associated with the current academic environment. The case is augmented by the following quote from Cynthia Cooper (2008), the director of internal audit at WorldCom, who is widely regarded as having played the key role in exposing billions of dollars of misstatements at that company:

> Some argue you can't teach ethics at the ... college level because values are primarily instilled at a young age. But character is not static. People can and do change throughout their lives, and by incorporating ethics into the curriculum, we can challenge students to think and help make sure they have the tools to recognize an ethical dilemma, think it through, and make the right decision. (p. 364)

We understand the concerns that ethics coverage raises among accounting educators who have been told to do more with less. We are faced with an ever-expanding body of technical knowledge in addition to requirements to develop communication, judgment, and ethics skills. Something has to give. Should it be ethics? We have made every attempt to follow that path for 40 years. As Waddock (2005, p. 147) points out, "The accounting profession seems to have failed to acknowledge that accounting is fundamentally an ethical, rather than a technical, discourse." The results of this failure for the profession have been catastrophic.

Should professional ethics education be viewed then as just another burden for accounting students and faculty or should it be considered fundamental to the preservation, fulfillment, and enhancement of the profession and protection of the public interest? Why does accounting exist? What qualities does the public expect accountants and auditors to possess? These are questions that we need to address so that our students can, in turn, reach their own understanding of the important social role that they will play as accountants. Consider the admonition of Gandhi (1999/1925) as he enumerated seven sins of society: "Politics without principles; wealth without work; pleasure without conscience; knowledge without character; commerce without morality; science without humanity; and worship without sacrifice" (p. 135). Can we dispute this wisdom? Can we continue to justify giving our students the power that comes with the knowledge of accounting while giving only a cursory wave to helping them understand the importance of character in application of this knowledge? Why are we not uncomfortable with sending generations of accounting students into the world armed with an amoral education?

We must embrace our responsibility to provide meaningful, assessable ethics education to our accounting students. Our lamentable history of well-intentioned impotence in effecting meaningful change can be reversed. Change requires a critical mass of accounting educators who have given thoughtful consideration to the importance of ethics education. Change requires a common body of knowledge in order to establish an ethics course as a universally viable and accepted part of the curriculum. Change requires the development of meaningful assessment of learning once the common body of knowledge is established. Change requires a commitment from educators to do what is right, just, and fair to make it happen—the same kind of commitment we expect our students to demonstrate as professionals.

NOTE

1.   At that time, AACSB was known as the American Association of Collegiate Schools of Business.

REFERENCES

AACSB council adopts rules to accredit accounting programs. (1980, August). *Journal of Accountancy, 150*(2), 10-13.

Academic preparation for professional accounting careers. (1968, December). *Journal of Accountancy, 126*(6), 57-63.

Accounting Education Change Commission. (1990). Objectives of education for accountants: Position statement number one. *Issues in Accounting Education, 5*(2), 307-312.

American Accounting Association. (2005). *AAA task force position statement on the NASBA exposure draft.* Retrieved from http://aaahq.org/temp/NASBA/index.cfm

American Institute of Certified Public Accountants. (1969). *Report of the committee on education and experience requirements for CPAs.* New York, NY: Author.

American Institute of Certified Public Accountants. (2002) *Ethics decision tree: A guide for CPAs in business and industry.* Retrieved from http://www.aicpa.org/InterestAreas/ForensicAndValuation/Resources/PractAidsGuidance/DownloadableDocuments/decision_tree_bai.pdf

American Institute of Certified Public Accountants. (2010). *AICPA professional standards.* New York, NY: Author.

Anderson, L. W., & Krathwohl, D. R. (Eds.), Airasian, P. W., Cruikshank, K. A., Mayer, R. E., Pintrich, P. R., et al. (2001). *A taxonomy for learning, teaching, and assessing: A revision of Bloom's taxonomy of educational objectives.* New York, NY: Longman.

Armstrong, M. B., Ketz, J. E., & Owsen, D. (2003). Ethics education in accounting: Moving toward ethical motivation and ethical behavior. *Journal of Accounting Education, 21*(1), 1-16.

Association of Government Accountants. (2003). *AGA ethics handbook.* Retrieved from http://www.agacgfm.org/about/2003EthicsHandbook.pdf

Association to Advance Collegiate Schools of Business. (2005). *AACSB comment letter to NASBA.* St. Louis, MO: Author. Retrieved from http://www.aacsb.edu/wxyz/aacsbcommentletter-nasba05.pdf.

Big Eight Accounting Firms Sponsoring Partners. (1989). *Perspectives on education: Capabilities of success in the accounting profession.* New York, NY: Big Eight Accounting Firms.

Blanthorne, C., Kovar, S. E., & Fisher, D. G. (2007). Accounting educators' opinions about ethics in the curriculum: An extensive view. *Issues in Accounting Education, 22*(3), 355-390.

Bloom, B. S. (Ed.), Engelhart, M. D., Furst, E. J., Hill, W. H., & Krathwohl, D. R. (1956). *Taxonomy of educational objectives: The classification of educational goals. Handbook 1: Cognitive domain.* New York, NY: David McKay.

Bloom, R., Heymann, H. G., Fuglister, J., & Collins, M. (1994). *The schism in accounting.* Quorum Books: Westport, CT.

Bricker, R. J., & Previts, G. J. (1990). The sociology of accountancy: A study of academic practice community schism. *Accounting Horizons, 4*(1), 1-14.

Cooper, C. (2008). *Extraordinary circumstances.* Hoboken, NJ: John Wiley & Sons.

Davidson, R. A., & Baldwin, B. A. (2005). Cognitive skills objectives in intermediate accounting textbooks: Evidence from end-of-chapter materials. *Journal of Accounting Education, 23*(2), 79-95.

Gandhi, M. K. (1999). *The collected works of Mahatma Gandhi (electronic book)*. New Delhi: Publications Division Government of India. (Original work published 1925). Retrieved from http://www.gandhiserve.org/cwmg/VOL033.PDF

Gioia, D. A., & Corley, K. G. (2002). Being good versus looking good: Business school rankings and the Circean transformation from substance to image. *Academy of Management Learning and Education, 1*, 107-120.

Gordon, R. A., & Howell, J.E. (1959). *Higher education for business*. New York, NY: Columbia University Press.

Hartman, L. P., & Desjardins, J. (2008). *Business ethics: Decision-making for personal integrity & social responsibility*. New York, NY: McGraw-Hill/Irwin.

Institute of Management Accountants. (2008). *Statement of ethical professional practice*. Retrieved from http://www.imanet.org/about_ethics_statement.asp

International Accounting Education Standards Board. (2006). *International education practice statement IEPS 1: Approaches to developing and maintaining professional values, ethics and attitudes*. Retrieved from http://web.ifac.org/publications/international-accounting-education-standards-board

International Ethics Standards Board for Accountants. (2008). *Code of ethics for professional accountants*. International Federation of Accountants. Retrieved from http://www.ifac.org/ethics

Kohlberg, L. (1969). State and sequence: The cognitive development approach to socialization. In D. Goslin (Ed.), *Handbook of socialization theory and research* (pp. 347-480). Chicago, IL: Rand McNally.

Kohlberg, L., & Hersh, R. H. (1977). Moral development: A review of the theory. *Theory into Practice, 16*(2), 53–59.

Langenderfer, H. Q., & Rockness, J. W. (1989). Integrating ethics into the accounting curriculum: Issues, problems, and solutions. *Issues in Accounting Education, 4*(1), 58-69.

Loeb, S. E. & Rockness, J. (1992). Accounting ethics and education: A response. *Journal of Business Ethics, 11*, 485-490.

Mastracchio, N. J. (2008). The role of NASBA and state boards in accounting education: How should an accounting curriculum be determined? *The CPA Journal, 78*(3), 64-69.

Mintz, S. M. (1993). Concerns about the generalizability of results of the AECC grant program. *Journal of Accounting Education, 11*(1), 93–100.

Mintz, S. M., & Morris, R. E. (2008). *Ethical obligations and decision making in accounting: Text and cases*. New York, NY: McGraw-Hill/Irwin.

National Association of State Boards of Accountancy. (2005). *Proposed revisions to the uniform accountancy rules 5-1 and 5-2*. Retrieved from http://www.nasba.org/NASBAfiles.nsf/Lookup/UAAEducationRulesExposureDraft/$file/UAAEducationRulesExposureDraft.pdf.

National Association of State Boards of Accountancy. (2009). *Uniform accountancy act model rules*. Retrieved from http://www.nasba.org/862571B900737CED/F3458557E80CD8CA862575C3005DBD36/$file/UAA_Model_Rules_April24_2009.pdf

National Commission on Fraudulent Financial Reporting (The Treadway Commission). (1987). *Report of the national commission on fraudulent financial reporting*. Washington, DC: Author.

Rest, J. R. (1979). *Development in judging moral issues*. Minneapolis, MN: University of Minnesota Press.

Rest, J. R. (1983). Morality. In J. Flavell & E. Markman (Vol. Eds.) & P. Mussen (Gen. Ed.), *Manual of child psychology: Vol. 3. Cognitive development* (pp. 556-629). New York, NY: John Wiley and Sons.

Rest, J. R. (1986). *Moral development: Advances in research and theory*. New York: Prager Press.

Rest, J. & Narvaez, D. (1991). The college experience and moral development. In W. M. Kurtines & J. L. Gerwitz (Eds.), *Handbook of moral development and behavior, Vol. 2: Research* (pp. 229-245). Hillsdale, NJ: Erlbaum.

Rest, J. R., Narvaez, D., Bebeau, M. J. & Thoma, S. J. (1999). *Postconventional moral thinking: A neo-Kohlbergian approach*. Mahwah, NJ: Erlbaum.

Schmotter, J. W. (2000). An assignment for the new century. *Selections, 16*, 36-39.

Shaub, M. K., & Fisher, D. G. (2008). Beyond agency theory: Common values for accounting ethics education. In D. L. Swanson & D. G. Fisher (Eds.), *Advancing business ethics education* (pp. 305-328). Charlotte, N.C.: Information Age.

Swanson, D. L., & Frederick, W. C. (2005). Denial and leadership in business ethics education. In O.C. Ferrell & R. A. Peterson (Eds.), *Business ethics: The new challenge for business schools and corporate leaders* (pp. 222-240). Armonk, NY: M.E. Sharpe.

Thomas, C. W. (2004). An inventory of support materials for teaching ethics in the post-Enron era. *Issues in Accounting Education, 19*(1), 27-52.

Trank, C. Q., & Rynes, S. L. (2003). Who moved our cheese? Reclaiming professionalism in business education. *Academy of Management Learning and Education, 2*, 189-205.

Van Whye, G. (1994). *The struggle for status: A history of accounting education*. New York: Garland.

Van Whye, G. (2007). A history of U.S. higher education in accounting, Part II: Reforming accounting within the academy. *Issues in Accounting Education, 22*(3), 481-501.

Waddock, S. (2005). Hollow men and women at the helm...hollow accounting ethics? *Issues in Accounting Education, 20*(2), 145-150.

Willen, L. (2004, March 8). Kellogg denies guilt as B-Schools evade alumni lapses. *Bloomberg News Wire*. Retrieved from http://www.cba.k-state.edu/departments/ethics/docs/bloombergpress.htm

Yunker, J. A. (2000). Doing things the hard way—Problems with mission-linked AACSB accreditation standards and suggestions for improvement. *Journal of Education for Business, 75*, 348-353.

Zeff, S. A. (2003). How the U.S. accounting profession got where it is today: Part I. *Accounting Horizons, 17*(3), 189-205.

CHAPTER 18

THE MEASURED IMPACT OF THE TRANSTHEORETICAL MODEL OF EDUCATIONAL CHANGE ON ADVANCING BUSINESS ETHICS EDUCATION

Joseph A. Petrick

INTRODUCTION

The general pattern of irresponsible financial risk management that originated in the United States and caused the Great Global Recession of 2008 has provoked a global demand for more reputable business leadership and business ethics education (Greider, 2009; Kansas, 2009; Korten, 2009; Petrick, 2009). Specifically, in light of the educational pedigrees of convicted U.S. business criminals like Bernard Madoff and others who have defrauded millions of stakeholders, the record of U.S. undergraduate business student cheating (Smith, Davy, & Easterling, 2004), and the published study documenting that MBA students are the biggest cheats among U.S. graduate students (McCabe, Butterfield, & Trevino, 2006), multiple stakeholders are demanding to know what else U.S. business

Toward Assessing Business Ethics Education
pp. 335–360

schools are doing besides credentialing more future white-collar business criminals (Swanson & Frederick, 2005; Trank & Rynes, 2003). Successfully addressing this domestic and global public challenge and empirically documenting it are front burner concerns of responsible business educators (Sims & Felton, 2006; Swanson, 2004; True, Ferrell, & Ferrell, 2006), business professional associations (AACSB Ethics Education Task Force, 2004; Hinings & Greenwood, 2002; Pritchard, 2006) and business practitioners (Carroll, 2004; Giacolone & Thompson, 2006; Trevino & Brown, 2004).

In addition, many business ethics educators implicitly assent to the modified Socratic claim that the unexamined business life is not worth living. Some business ethics students are more ready than others to engage in this inquiry. Business ethics educators who are aware of the transformation model of educational change (Tyler & Tyler, 2006) can both provide structure and facilitate the constructive contributions of peer student educational catalysts to accelerate the advance of business ethics education. Yet, this process is usually underutilized due to the lack of educational change literacy and the absence of a tested tool to identify "high ethical readiness" students. That is why measuring the effective teaching of business ethics in a stand-alone, undergraduate, foundational course for future business leaders (Bowie, 2004; Windsor, 2004), along with the structured, accelerating, peer impact of students who are ready for business ethics inquiry, is worth sharing (Beggs, Dean, Gillespie, & Weiner, 2006; Whittier, Williams, & Dewett, 2006). The focus of this chapter, therefore, will be on empirically measuring *what* was successfully taught and, more importantly, *how* it was successfully taught with the structured aid of selected student catalysts to provide useful guidance to future business ethics educators.

The structure of this chapter consists of the following areas: (1) selected competency goals of business ethics teaching; (2) the transtheoretical model of educational change; (3) method and findings; (4) discussion; and (5) limits of research and directions for future research.

SELECTED COMPETENCY GOALS OF BUSINESS ETHICS TEACHING

Nearly every business ethics educator wants to prevent unethical conduct, but preventing any and all unethical behavior is an unrealistic goal for either an ethics training program or for a business ethics course (Petrick, 2008; Williams & Dewett, 2006). Ethical behavior is a function of a variety of personal and situational factors, including but not limited to moral development, enforced norms, opportunity for and punishment of violations, rewards for moral conduct, self-control, and ethics training (Arnold, 2009; Trevino, 1986). It is unreasonable to expect that one single link in this chain of inputs can control behavior by itself. The issue becomes how business ethics education can be a strong link in the chain, rather than searching in vain for ways in which business ethics education alone can eradicate unethical behavior (Williams & Dewett, 2006).

A survey of literature on goals of teaching business ethics reveals at least three targeted competency goals: (1) cognitive decision-making competence; (2) affective prebehavioral disposition competence; and (3) context management competence (Felton & Sims, 2005; Liszka, 2002; O'Fallon & Butterfield, 2005; Rossouw, 2002).

Cognitive Decision-Making Competence

The goal of cognitive decision making competence in business ethics teaching is to demonstrate the abilities to recognize, understand, analyze, and make responsible judgments about moral matters in business (Rossouw, 2002; Sims, 2002a, 2002b). Although there are a variety of ethical decision-making models (Ford & Richardson, 1994; Kelley & Elm, 2003; Loe, Ferrell, & Mansfield, 2000), the following cognitive competencies are essential to them.

1. *Moral awareness:* Demonstrating the ability to perceive and discern the ethical dimensions of a business issue as distinct from its economic, legal, or cultural dimensions. This entails an awareness of the multiple stakeholders inside and outside of the firm that may be adversely impacted by business decisions and the commensurate moral responsibilities associated with those impacts (Anderson, 1997; Rossouw, 2002).

2. *Moral understanding:* Acquiring the conceptual foundation to understand the moral roots of business ethics conflicts and dilemmas. Moral understanding permits the process of cognitive decision making in business ethics to move forward with the use of all the relevant theoretical resources necessary for initial moral discourse and preliminary moral judgment formation (Mahoney, 1999; Trevino & Brown, 2004).

3. *Moral reasoning and dialogue:* Engaging in moral argumentation and dialogue rather than relying exclusively on legal precedent, emotional intensity, or politico-economic expediency to justify resolutions of business ethics issues. Taking a reasoned stance on an ethical issue develops intellectual independence and allows individuals to actively participate in sustained, respectful, critical moral discourse (Brown, 2005; Trevino, 1992).

4. *Moral complexity resolution:* Analyzing challenging ethical issues by acknowledging moral tradeoffs by inclusively balancing arguments for moral results, rules, character, and context, and engaging in moral dialogue about the factual observations, value priorities, evaluation assumptions, and reasonable responses to opposing views before arriving at sound moral resolutions and enacting them (Brown, 2005; Petrick & Quinn, 1997).

Affective Prebehavioral Disposition Competence

The goal of developing affective prebehavioral dispositions in business ethics teaching is to shape and internalize the inclinations, motivations, and expectations to be ready to act ethically at individual and collective levels (Hartman, 1996; Hill & Stewart, 1999; Paine, 1991). A person with superior cognitive decision-making competence does not automatically demonstrate a strong character disposed and ready to behave ethically in a business setting. What is needed besides cognitive competence is attention to the internalized affective, volitional, relational, and imaginative dimensions of character development (Brown, 2005; Chen & Wang, 2002; Solomon, 1993, 2006; Whetstone, 1998). Strengthening character presupposes the possibility of intrapersonal improvement and increasing degrees of internalized congruence between words and deeds, so that virtue cultivation at the emotional, moral, social, political, and intellectual levels can enhance the repeated readiness to act ethically and to spontaneously demonstrate behavioral disposition competence (Doris, 2005; Paine, 1991; Petrick & Quinn, 1997; Solomon, 2006). The following competencies are essential to achieving this goal.

1. *Moral sensitivity/emotional virtue:* Empathizing, caring about, and sympathizing with past, current, and future victims (or potential victims) of business actions while intuiting the appropriate category of moral concern (Paine, 1991; Solomon, 1993, 1999b). Along with cultivating other emotional virtues (e.g., honesty and love) that consist of feeling and expressing joy when acting ethically or experiencing moral passions (as opposed to immoral passions such as arrogance, greed, envy, apathy, gluttony, lust, jealousy, sloth, or hate), morally sensitive business leaders restore humane caring to the emotional standards of expected rapport in business stakeholder relationships (Gilligan, Ward, & Taylor, 1989; Goleman, Boyatzis, & McKee, 2004; Noddings, 1984; Solomon, 1992, 2006).

2. *Moral courage/moral virtue:* Exhibiting the strength of one's convictions which enables individuals and collectives to venture, persevere, and withstand moral danger, fear, or difficulty firmly and resolutely for a higher purpose (Chaleff, 1998; Keyes, 1998; Mahoney, 1999). Along with cultivating other moral virtues (e.g., trustworthiness and resilience) that consist of resolutely heeding the call of an examined conscience, morally courageous business leaders are determined to persevere in continually improving the morality of business practices and challenging others to do likewise (Brown, Trevino & Harrison, 2005; Chaleff, 1998; Solomon, 1992, 2006).

3. *Moral tolerance/socio-political virtue:* Exhibiting the willingness to allow others to express views and lead lives based on a set of beliefs contrary to one's own as long as mutuality of respect and restraint from violence prevail (Heyd, 1996). Along with other social and political virtues (e.g., respect and justice) that consist of the spontaneous fondness for the company of good people and the responsible use of power, morally tolerant business leaders instill respect for diversity and dialogue in business decision making (Brown, 2005; Walzer, 1997).

4. *Moral imagination/intellectual virtue:* Disengaging from and mentally critiquing the situation at hand, projecting preferred alternatives, and evaluating newly formulated possibilities in terms of their moral worth (Ciulla & Burns, 2004; Johnson, 1993; Kekes, 1993). Along with cultivating other intellectual virtues (e.g., wisdom and prudence) that consist of knowing and appreciating what is ethically desirable, morally imaginative business leaders do not callously settle for narrowly manipulative work environments. Instead, they stimulate themselves and others by imagined, yet actualizable visions of more morally worthy work settings (Kupperman, 1989; Werhane, 1999).

Context Management Competence

The goal of developing context management competence in business ethics teaching is to enable individuals to acknowledge responsibility for skills in designing, building, and/or shaping supportive moral environments within and outside organizations that sustain cognitive and behavioral moral competence (Petrick & Quinn, 1997; Trevino, Hartman, & Brown, 2000; Trevino & Weaver, 2003). Context management competence focuses on improving the "moral barrels" (organizations and other environments) into which the "moral apples" (good people) are placed organizationally and extraorganizationally, domestically and globally (Arnold, 2009). If fully implemented, context management competence should create or enhance a morally supportive environment that facilitates stakeholder ethical actions (Fudge & Schlacter, 1999; Petrick & Quinn, 2000; Wood, Logsdon, Lewellyn, & Davenport, 2006).

The following context management competencies are essential to achieving this goal:

1. *Responsible management of the organizational compliance and ethics context:* Knowing how to design, implement, control, and continually improve the organizational compliance and ethics system to ensure an ethically supportive environment in the workplace (Trevino & Weaver, 2003). The moral manager must understand and be able to use the formal and informal systems within the organization to construct a network of processes to rapidly control and justly punish immoral conduct, as well as to recognize and reward morally commendable conduct in the firm (Paine, 1994; Trevino et al., 2000). While the organizational compliance orientation prevents criminal activity (e.g., the U.S. Federal Sentencing Guidelines and the Sarbanes-Oxley Act of 2002), the organizational ethics orientation enables responsible moral conduct based on moral culture development, moral infrastructure processes, and transparent moral accountability (Brown, 2005; Cameron, Bright, & Caza, 2004).

2. *Responsible management of the corporate governance context:* Knowing how the system by which corporations are strategically directed and controlled through the distribution of rights and responsibilities among the board, managers, investors, and other stakeholders so that accountability for managing business integrity capacity as a strategic asset is assumed and the system continually improved (Colley, Doyle, Logan, & Stettinius, 2003; Monks & Minnow, 2004). Exposure to different types of corporate governance systems and how they handle chief executive officer compensation, audit engagements, level of investor activism, and level of stakeholder voting and non-voting participation enlarges the framework of choice to responsibly enact an ethically supportive corporate governance context (Cameron, Quinn, Degraff, & Thakor, 2006; Luo, 2007; Waddock, Bodwell, & Leigh, 2006).

3. *Exercising business citizenship to influence the institutionalization of ethically supportive, extraorganizational contexts in the domestic and global environments:* Knowing how to exercise domestic and global business citizenship in a systematic manner that demonstrates and institutionalizes commitment to triple bottom line accountability

and intergenerational sustainability (Fort & Schipani, 2004; Wood et al., 2006). Business citizenship context management competence goes beyond domestic and global compliance to proactively partnering with private, public, and nonprofit institutions to strengthen the network of human and natural sustainability agreements and standards that advance the national and international external moral contexts of business (DesJardins, 2007; Dunphy, Benveniste, Griffiths, & Sutton, 2000).

Now that *what* to teach in a stand-alone undergraduate business ethics course has been treated, *how* to effectively teach it is the next topic. The use of the transtheoretical model of educational change, the Indicator of Readiness for Business Ethics Inquiry (IRBEI), and stage-appropriate activities are now discussed to demonstrate one way to accelerate effective business ethics education.

TRANSTHEORETICAL MODEL OF EDUCATIONAL CHANGE

The transtheoretical model of change has been applied in varied transformational contexts and used to understand student-learning motivation and change (Cole, Harris, & Field, 2004; Prochaska, DiClemente, & Norcross, 1992). Originally designed for clinical assessment and treatment, the model can be modified to advance and assess business ethics education. Once modified, the transtheoretical model is one useful framework for identifying student readiness for ethical change and then sequencing business ethics instructional interventions (activities) to leverage the impact on student business ethics' competencies (Tyler & Tyler, 2006). The model explains why some students recognize the distinctive challenge of ethical issues and are willing to actively engage in thorough analysis and resolution, while other students are seemingly unable to grasp or act on the ethical dimensions present in a business event or decision.

As indicated in Table 18.1, the modified four stages of readiness-to-change include precontemplation, contemplation and preparation, action, and maintenance/ongoing improvement (DiClemente & Prochaska, 1982). Their parallel modified stages of intervention treatments include engagement, persuasion, active treatment, and relapse prevention/sustainable performance (Mueser, Noordsy, Drake, & Fox, 2003). Only the last change and intervention stages of the transtheoretical model have been modified to include "ongoing improvement" and "sustainable performance" respectively. By introducing stage-appropriate business ethics activities, the model predicts that business ethics instructors who interject "activating events" at each appropriate stage can foster

Table 18.1. Modified Transtheoretical Model of Change and Sequenced Business Ethics Activities

Stages of Change	Stages of Treatment	Selective Stage-Appropriate Business Ethics Activities
Precontemplation This is the stage at which there is no intention to change behavior in the foreseeable future.	**Engagement** 1. Activities that attempt to help students identify concerns and become aware of moral relevance in business and in life. 2. Activities that focus on recognition or understanding of negative consequences of immoral behavior.	• Indicator of Readiness for Business Ethics Inquiry (IRBEI) • *Journal of Critical Incidents in Academic Ethics* and other student-anchored experiential contexts (e.g., cheating) • Classic and contemporary film clips on business ethics scandals (e.g., *Enron: The Smartest Guys in the Room*) • Visits from ex-white collar criminals convicted of business ethics and business law violations
Contemplation & Preparation During the contemplative stage, people become aware that a problem exists and begin thinking seriously about overcoming it, but have not yet made a commitment to take action. During the preparation stage, people create meaningful intentions to take action.	**Persuasion** 1. Activities that increase awareness of positive personal and business moral responses. 2. Students are more receptive to learning opportunities, and more experimental activities can be used to illustrate and reinforce concepts and attitudes toward moral progress.	• Introduction to business integrity capacity model and its practical uses (e.g., *Enron Case Analysis*) • Use of structured ethical-decision making framework (R^2C^2) in business ethics cases based on a pluralistic view of human nature • Classic and contemporary film clips on positive business ethics practices (e.g., *The Ethical Marketplace*) • Exercise: business virtues & improving stakeholder relations (e.g., What emotional/moral difference would it make to you and other internal and external stakeholders if you and/or your coworkers were more caring?) • Readings: Positive organizational scholarship

Action	Active Treatment
This is the stage in which people modify their behavior, experiences, or environment in order to overcome their problems.	1. Activities that support the student's determination to change behavior and willingness to take specific steps to engage in ethical behavior.
	• Intercollegiate ethics bowl participation • Business citizenship service learning projects • Business college ethical culture/climate development projects (e.g., business college code of ethics, statement of values & ethics processes, business college ethics audit) • Business College community-building activities (e.g., business integrity capacity day)
Maintenance & Ongoing Improvement This is the stage in which people work to prevent relapse to prior behaviors and attitudes, and focus on continued developmental progress.	Relapse Prevention & Sustainable Performance 1. Activities that consolidate and advance moral commitments 2. Activities that proactively work to maintain and further develop ethical decision-making processes among multiple stakeholders
	• Institute for Business Integrity: Ongoing outreach as an institutional resource for sustaining business integrity capacity on-campus and off-campus. • Electronic ethics newsletter for business students, alums, and practitioners focusing on business ethics best practices and new research • Business integrity breakfasts that host business ethics experts to sustain business and civic engagement in advancing workplace ethics • Business integrity capacity awards to honor local individual and collective ethical leadership

a process of student learning in relation to ethical understanding and likely future behavior that will ignite and sustain personal moral transformation (Cranton, 2002; Tyler & Tyler, 2006).

In the first change stage of precontemplation, business students are engaged by prearranging themselves into teams on the basis of their scores on the Indicator of Readiness for Business Ethics Inquiry (IRBEI). (See the Appendix for a copy of the IRBEI and its interpretive scoring.) Those teams that are completely or partially composed of students with a heightened readiness for business ethics' inquiry and openness to change can serve as peer catalysts for morally challenging conventional business beliefs and/or taking action on justified moral beliefs. Too often traditional business ethics pedagogy assumes that the instructor alone must function as the agent of change and that there is no need for an educational process of structured change that engages and leverages high ethical readiness students to collaboratively partner with the instructor to advance business ethics education. The adoption of the transtheoretical model of change for business ethics teaching challenges both of these assumptions and actively engages peer catalysts in a structured set of stage-appropriate activities to accelerate and sustain the class momentum toward improved business ethics competency.

In the first change stage of precontemplation, requiring entries into a student journal providing detailed accounts of critical incidents that students have experienced in academic ethics or other student-anchored experiential moral contexts (e.g., observed cheating on tests) is helpful. Showing classic and contemporary film clips relating to business ethics scandals and/or challenges, and specifically featuring the Enron case, can stimulate moral awareness of the harmful consequences of unethical business practices. Any visits from former white collar offenders who can realistically shock students into recognizing the adverse personal and career impacts of unethical conduct can also be helpful at this stage.

In the second change stage of contemplation and preparation, persuading engaged business students to consider positive personal and business moral practices and providing them with effective, conceptual tools to enable meaningful moral intentions to form around a growing sense of moral self-efficacy is essential. At this stage, since the Enron case was introduced in the first stage, it is important to provide a comprehensive moral analysis and resolution of the Enron case stressing the lessons to be learned and positive proactive steps to take in order to prevent a recurrence (Petrick & Scherer, 2003). The use of classic and contemporary film clips that focus on positive business ethics practices is appropriate for this stage of moral persuasion. Exercises that require student teams to make presentations that select three business virtues and describe how each would improve internal and external stakeholder relations can sharpen students' expectations of themselves and others to be ready to act ethically and concretely realize how character should count in the business environment (Solomon, 1999a). Reserve readings from positive organizational scholarship can provide examples of constructive ways that individuals, groups, and organizations are successfully building and strengthening business integrity capacity (Cameron, Dutton, & Quinn, 2003).

In the third change stage of action, activities that support the student's determination to change behavior and willingness to take specific steps to engage in ethical behavior are appropriate. Carefully structured business citizenship service-learning projects, delivered both on campus and off, can develop habits in future business leaders that help them make a positive difference in the communities of which they are a part (Zlotkowski, 1996). Furthermore, including students or their representatives as voting stakeholders on committees that engage in the ongoing assessment and development of the business college ethical culture and climate provides another immediate, incentivized avenue for constructively applying integrity capacity concepts to improve the students' own educational environment. Sponsoring a day each year (e.g., business integrity capacity day) dedicated to business community-building activities, run primarily by business ethics students, and including special guest lecturers on business ethics, as well as sporting and social events that involve faculty, administrators, students, and staff mixing outside the classroom is another action that empowers students to constructively build a more caring academic community for themselves.

In the fourth stage of maintenance and ongoing improvement, moral relapse (into addictive moral drifting) prevention and sustainable moral performance are enabled through institutionalized reinforcement and continual creativity relating to new business moral challenges. One form of institutionalized moral sustainability is through ancillary ethics centers or institutes, such as the Institute for Business Integrity (IBI). Through service, teaching, and research activities, the IBI can fulfill the mission of the business college to develop successful and ethical business leaders, while initiating business integrity capacity projects on-campus and off-campus. Through this institutionalized form of business ethics education, current business students and practitioners, as well as alumni, can always replenish and refresh their business integrity capacity resources through reading about the latest business ethics research and organizational ethics best practices in the *Business Integrity E-Newsletter*. They can focus their attention on positive individual and organizational role models during events such as the Business Integrity Capacity Awards Day, which publicly honors individual and/or collective business integrity capacity award winners that meet exemplary moral standards. Alumni can contact the IBI for confidential analysis and resolution of work ethics issues or can contract with the IBI to conduct objective, professional organizational ethical climate/culture assessments or ethics audits.

Ultimately, these four stages of educational change, when correlated with the four phases of sequential business ethics activities and leveraged with contributions from high ethical readiness students, can have a profound accelerating effect on improving targeted moral competencies, as the following research findings demonstrate.

METHOD AND FINDINGS

To assess the effectiveness of applying the transtheoretical model of change to business ethics teaching and the use of the IRBEI, I conducted a five-year study at an AACSB accredited business school in a Midwestern public university. Undergraduate business students who were enrolled in 18 sections of required undergraduate courses titled "business integrity" and "ethical and legal issues in global business" were given pretests on the first class meeting and posttests on the last class meeting in an academic quarter system. This was done to measure any moral competency improvements by using (a) the business integrity capacity theoretical model as the content structure for analyzing and resolving business ethics' issues (Petrick, 2008), (b) the transtheoretical model of educational change as the foundational structure for course process coverage, and (c) the IRBEI to identify and leverage the contributions of high ethical readiness students to accelerate group development of targeted business ethics competencies. The tests were numbered so that each student's progress could be tracked with anonymity. Five sections ($n = 125$) used the IRBEI and adhered to the transtheoretical model of educational change in the sequencing of stage-appropriate business ethics activities and using "high ethical readiness" students at the outset in teams and thirteen sections did not ($n = 400$). The aggregate difference in mean improvement in moral competencies between the posttest and pretest results of the IRBEI-sections and the non-IRBEI sections is recorded in Table 18.2.

The research sample ($n = 525$) consisted of 268 (51%) females and 257 (49%) males. The mean age of the sample was 21.4 years ($SD = 4.1$), with a mode of 20.1 years. The ages ranged from 17 years to 47 years. In terms of academic majors, the sample included 105 (20%) for accountancy, 89 (17%) for management of information systems, 95 (18%) for marketing, 100 (19%) for finance/financial services, and 125 (24%) for management/human resource management. The remainder of the sample consisted of

Table 18.2. IRBEI and Non-IRBEI Differential Improvements in Business Ethics Competencies

Ethics Statements	Ethics Competencies	Mean Improvement of IRBEI- Sections n =125	Mean Improvement of Non-IRBEI Sections n =400	Percentage Increase in Mean Improvement
1. I recognize (perceive) ethical issues (as distinct from economic and legal issues) in business that affect multiple stakeholders inside & outside the firm.	Cognitive	1.798	1.445	24.4%
2. I understand how regularly engaging in ethical business practices strengthens my character (readiness to act ethically) & sustains my humanity	Cognitive	1.622	1.304	24.3%
3. It is important to tolerate diverse & even opposing moral perspectives & to creatively imagine ways to morally improve situations at work.	Affective prebe-havioral	0.897	.717	25.1%
4. I care about the impact of business actions on those affected by it & I am determined to continually improve the morality of business practices.	Affective prebe-havioral	0.994	.777	27.9%
5. I understand the multiple factors (results, rules, character & context) to be considered in making responsible ethical judgments through moral reasoning.	Cognitive	2.956	2.342	26.2%
6. I understand how my business philosophy & management/work style influence and reflect my value priorities with regard to expected business behavior.	Cognitive	3.325	2.694	23.4%

(Table continues on next page)

Table 18.2. (Continued)

Ethics Statements	Ethics Competencies	Mean Improvement of IRBEI- Sections n =125	Mean Improvement of Non-IRBEI Sections n =400	Percentage Increase in Mean Improvement
7. Ethical business leaders are expected to elevate the moral development of their Followers and their work culture/climate.	Affective prebehavioral	1.563	1.224	27.6%
8. Corporate governance leaders are morally accountable for managing business integrity capacity as a strategic asset to enhance or protect organizational reputation.	Managerial	1.826	1.477	23.6%
9. Business should be held to triple bottom line accountability (for economic, social and ecological performance) to respect current & future generations of multiple stakeholders.	Managerial	1.902	1.449	31.2%
10. Ethical business leaders should develop their organizational compliance & ethics systems to sustain a morally supportive work context.	Managerial	1.198	.893	34.1%
11. Ethical business leaders should exercise positive influence in their firms' external sociopolitical-legal-ecological environments, both domestically & globally, to sustain a morally supportive external context for responsible business citizenship.	Managerial	1.104	.879	25.5%

Note: The mean difference for all 11 statements is significant at $p < .0001$.

11 (2%) individuals with various other business-related majors (operations management, economics, and organizational leadership).

The improvements were calculated for each student and for each statement. The means were calculated for each statement, and t tests were run to see if any of these means were significantly different from zero. All 11 of the statements in Table 18.1 showed significant improvement, at $p <$ .0001 between the pretest and posttest survey responses. After using a Bonferroni correction for multiple tests (see Tabachnick & Fidell, 1996), the results remained significant for all of the eleven statements.

With regard to the cognitive ethics competencies, IRBEI-section students were better able to recognize ethical issues in business that affect multiple stakeholders inside and outside the firm than non-IRBEI section students. They also improved their understanding of how their business philosophy and management style influenced and reflected their moral value priorities more than non-IRBEI section students. Furthermore, IRBEI-section students increased their understanding of how regularly engaging in ethical business practices strengthens their character and sustains their sense of humanity more than non-IRBEI-section students. Finally, IRBEI-section students increased their understanding of the multiple factors (moral results, rules, character, and context) that are to be considered in making responsible ethical judgments through moral reasoning more than non-IRBEI-section students.

With regard to the affective prebehavioral ethics competencies, IRBEI-section students raised their expectations that ethical business leaders should elevate the moral development of their followers and their work culture and climate higher than non-IRBEI section students. Again, IRBEI-section students indicated that they care more about the impact of business actions on those affected by it and are more determined to continually improve the morality of business practices than non-IRBEI-section students. Finally, the results showed that the IRBEI-section students value the importance of diverse, even opposing, moral perspectives, while creatively imagining ways to morally improve situations at work more than non-IRBEI-section students.

With regard to ethics competencies in managing moral contexts, IRBEI-section students increased their moral context management competencies more effectively than non-IRBEI section students by increasingly specifying triple bottom line accountability and multiple stakeholder respect for current and future generations, the necessity to implement an organizational compliance and ethics system to institutionalize a morally supportive work context, and the importance of exercising responsible business citizenship, domestically and globally, to positively influence the extraorganizational context in terms of morally supportive dimensions. In addition, IRBEI-section students raised their organizational context moral expectations regarding the accountability of corporate governance leaders to manage business integrity capacity as a strategic asset in order to embrace or protect organizational reputational capital more than non-IRBEI-section students.

In effect, the findings of the pretests and posttests demonstrate that it is possible to accelerate significant improvements in business ethics competencies by using the transtheoretical model of educational change and leveraging contributions from high ethical readiness students within stand-alone, required foundational business ethics courses.

DISCUSSION OF FINDINGS

There are at least two interpretive explanations of the findings and a cautionary note. The first interpretation is that the deliberately modified application of the transtheoretical model of change from the clinical realm of addiction treatment, where it has proven to be so effective, to the educational realm of assessing and improving business ethics competencies is a creative adaptation of a health care process modality that appears to be promisingly effective. Why might this be so? One possible explanation is embedded in the factual profile of students who self-select formal business education. Numerous studies have depicted business students as being more motivated by the love of money than other types of students (some being much more motivated) (Cunningham, Frauman, Ivy, & Perry, 2004; Tang & Chen, 2008; Tang, Luna-Arocas, & Sutarso, 2005). If this hyper-acquisitive predilection for money is regarded as a form of "mental addiction" prevalent among business students that may demand fulfillment at any cost, one way to treat that addiction would be to offer business ethics education in a way that it becomes a structured process as an educational intervention. Indeed, since the obscene, acquisitive love of money has been such a key motivational factor for numerous business-degreed white-collar criminals, there is some basis for adapting a clinical process modality to business ethics education, delivered at regular intervals during business careers as an antidote to the temptation of excessive love of money. In any event, this "therapeutic process structure" is rarely used by business ethics educators to deliberately overlay and guide historical, topical, theoretical or latest-business-scandal approaches to teaching business ethics.

The second interpretation of the findings is that the IRBEI may well be another useful but underutilized tool for business ethics educators to accelerate group development of ethics competencies by leveraging the peer impact of high ethical readiness students. Too often business ethics educators deny or ignore the collaborative opportunity of partnering with select students who want to serve as catalysts in advancing ethical transformations in business education. The early and systematic identification of these students through the IRBEI, administered in class on the first day affords the instructor the option of forming an entire team at the outset composed of high ethical readiness students or deliberately having at least one or more of them in each of the teams at the beginning of the course. Either method of distribution can accelerate the collective readiness of students through peer dynamics to move from a state of precontemplation of business ethics beliefs onto persuasive engagement, active commitment, and/or eventual sustained moral performance. Too often business ethics educators feel that they are or ought to be the sole agents of change, or these educators find out halfway through the course that a number of students who ardently support the advancement of business ethics competencies are so haphazardly distributed that they have little strategic impact on class dynamics. The use of the IRBEI can remedy those conditions and, if properly used, can provide a win-win-win scenario for the instructor, the high ethical readiness students, and the class as a whole.

The cautionary note to consider in this research is that business ethics education is not and should not be a form of forced propagandizing of students, therapeutic or not. Respect for the dignity and intellectual freedom of each student remains paramount. Some business students may not be able, ready, or willing to move through the educational transformation changes as the model forecasts. However, the seasoned and respectful business ethics educator has the academic freedom to create a classroom atmosphere of group dynamics not held hostage to the most recalcitrant student(s). Even if some business students choose not to move beyond the first two stages, they can at least witness other business students who benefit from doing so and perhaps at a later time the positive examples of their peers will impact their future choices (Giacalone, 2004).

LIMITS OF RESEARCH AND FUTURE RESEARCH DIRECTIONS

There are a number of research limitations that need to be acknowledged. First, some pretest and posttest ethics statements contain two variables (e.g.,question 3 contains both moral tolerance and moral imagination variables; question 4 contains both moral caring and moral resolution variables). Therefore, the extent of statistically measured improvement on each factor cannot be determined, whereas separating the factors would have diminished that issue. Second, the face validity of the survey items administered in a business ethics course may well have generated social desirability biases on both pretests and posttests. Students may well have wanted to "put their best foot forward" on the pretests in an ethics course and then rationalize their investment of time and energy in the course by doing the same on the posttests. To some extent, it is important to acknowledge that this cannot be completely controlled, given the type of survey method employed. Third, since the total number of reported IRBEI subjects and sections were less than the non-IRBEI subjects and sections, the extent of generalization is limited and awaits future confirmatory studies. Fourth, the business ethics survey items did not measure actual moral behavior during the course or on the job subsequent to the course, but only cognitive, affective prebehavioral, and managerial moral competencies. The caveat, of course, is that students may "talk a good game" but not actually "walk the talk" in college or later at work. This limitation in scope must be acknowledged. Fifth, there may be other factors in addition to the three factors employed in this study (i.e., business integrity capacity theory, transformational model of educational change, and the IRBEI) that contributed to the differential improvements in business ethics competencies. For instance some of the non-IRBEI-section students were taught by adjunct business faculty whereas the IRBEI-section students were taught only by full-time business faculty.

In terms of assessing business ethics education, there are a number of future research directions that could be taken. Future research could include: (a) confirmatory studies conducted by other business ethics educators domestically or globally on the relative impact of the use of the transformational model of educational change as a successful process guide in stand-alone foundational courses in business ethics; (b) confirmatory studies conducted by other business ethics educators domestically or globally on the relative impact of the use of the IRBEI along with the transformational model of educational change as a successful tool and process guide in stand-alone foundation courses in business ethics; and (c) longitudinal follow-up research on all the business ethics students in all the sections over a 2-, 5-, or 10-year period to determine any changes in belief and/or behavior over time.

APPENDIX

Indicator of Readiness for Business Ethics Inquiry (IRBEI)

PURPOSE: This precourse survey is designed to assess preliminary readiness to address current business ethics beliefs. Each statement describes how a student might feel when starting a course.

DIRECTIONS: Please indicate the extent to which you tend to agree with each statement. In each case, make your choice in terms of how you feel **right now**, not what you have felt in the past or would like to feel. There are **FIVE** possible responses to each of the items in the questionnaire:

strongly disagree, disagree, undecided, agree, and strongly agree. Circle the number that best describes how much you agree or disagree with each statement.

	Strongly Disagree	Disagree	Undecided	Agree	Strongly Agree
1. It might be worthwhile to examine my business ethics beliefs.	1	2	3	4	5
2. I think I might be ready for some moral self-improvement.	1	2	3	4	5
3. I am doing something about my business ethics beliefs that had been bothering me.	1	2	3	4	5
4. As far as I'm concerned, I don't have any business ethics beliefs that need changing.	1	2	3	4	5
5. I'm not aware of any issues with my business ethics beliefs. I don't see the relevance of this to my business education.	1	2	3	4	5
6. It concerns me that I might slip back into negative business ethics beliefs I have already changed, so I am here to sustain positive business ethics beliefs.	1	2	3	4	5
7. I am finally taking some action based on my business ethics beliefs.	1	2	3	4	5
8. I've been thinking that I might want to change some of my business ethics beliefs.	1	2	3	4	5
9. I have been successful in building sound business ethics beliefs, but I'm not sure I can keep up the effort on my own.	1	2	3	4	5
10. At times changing my business ethics beliefs is difficult, but I'm trying.	1	2	3	4	5
11. Being here is pretty much of a waste of time for me because business ethics has nothing to do with me or my future career.	1	2	3	4	5
12. I'm hoping this class will help me to better understand my business ethics beliefs.	1	2	3	4	5
13. I guess I have faulty business ethics beliefs, but they're nothing that I really need to change.	1	2	3	4	5

	Strongly Disagree	Disagree	Undecided	Agree	Strongly Agree
	1	2	3	4	5
14. I am really working hard to change my business ethics beliefs.	1	2	3	4	5
15. I have unexamined business ethics beliefs and I really think I should change them.	1	2	3	4	5
16. I'm not sustaining the positive business ethics beliefs for which I have already changed as well as I had hoped, and I'm here to stop this.	1	2	3	4	5
17. Even though I am not always successful in changing my business ethics beliefs, I am at least critically examining them.	1	2	3	4	5
18. I thought once I had changed my business ethics beliefs they would remain stable, but sometimes I still find myself reverting to my old views.	1	2	3	4	5
19. I wish I had more ideas on how to view business ethics.	1	2	3	4	5
20. I have started working on my personal ethics beliefs but I would like help.	1	2	3	4	5
21. Maybe this class will be able to open my mind about the value of business ethics beliefs.	1	2	3	4	5
22. I may need a boost right now to help me maintain the business ethics' belief changes I've already made.	1	2	3	4	5
23. I may have faulty business ethics beliefs, but I don't really think I do.	1	2	3	4	5
24. I hope that this class will have some good business ethics advice for me.	1	2	3	4	5
25. Anyone can talk about changing business ethics beliefs; I'm actually doing something about them.	1	2	3	4	5
26. All this talk about business ethics is boring & irrelevant. Why can't people just believe whatever they want?	1	2	3	4	5

	Strongly Disagree	Disagree	Undecided	Agree	Strongly Agree
27. I'm here to prevent myself from going back to my old business ethics' views.	1	2	3	4	5
28. It is frustrating, but I feel I might be having a recurrence of unethical business beliefs I thought I had already resolved.	1	2	3	4	5
29. I have some concerns about business ethics, but so does everyone. Why spend time thinking about the topic?	1	2	3	4	5
30. I am actively examining my business ethics beliefs.	1	2	3	4	5
31. I would rather cope with my faulty business ethics beliefs than try to change them.	1	2	3	4	5
32. After all I had done to try and change my former business ethics beliefs, every now and again they come back to haunt me.	1	2	3	4	5

Scoring Key

Precontemplation items	4, 5, 11, 13, 23, 26, 29, 31
Contemplation items	1, 2, 8, 12, 15, 19, 21, 24
Action items	3, 7, 10, 14, 17, 20, 25, 30
Maintenance items	6, 9, 16, 18, 22, 27, 28, 32

Description

The scale is designed to be a continuous measure. Thus, subjects can score high on more than one of the four stages. To score, add up the total number for each item corresponding to the correct color for each of the four subscales. Higher scores indicate a greater likelihood to be currently in that stage of change regarding business ethics beliefs.

Source

Adapted from McConnaughy, E., Prochaska, J., & Velicer, W. (1983). Stages of change in psychotherapy: Measurement and sample profiles. *Psychotherapy: Theory, Research and Practice, 20,* 368-375.

REFERENCES

AACSB Ethics Education Task Force. (2004). Ethics education in business schools. *Ethics Education Task Force of AACSB International, 1*(1), 1-8.

Anderson, J. (1997). What cognitive science tells us about ethics and the teaching of ethics. *Journal of Business Ethics, 16*(3), 279-291.

Arnold, D. (2009). *Essentials of business ethics.* New York, NY: Wiley.

Beggs, J., Dean, K., Gillespie, J., & Weiner, J. (2006). The unique challenges of ethics instruction. *Journal of Management Education, 30*(1), 5-10.

Bowie, N. (2004). Special Issue: The stand alone course in business ethics. *Journal of Business Ethics Education, 1*(2), 3-9.

Brown, M. (2005). *Corporate integrity: Rethinking organizational ethics and leadership.* New York, NY: Cambridge University Press.

Brown, M., Trevino, L., & Harrison, D. (2005). Ethical leadership: A social learning perspective for construct development and testing. *Organizational Behavior and Human Decision Processes, 97*, 117-134.

Cameron, K., Bright, D., & Caza, A. (2004). Exploring the relatedness between organizational virtuousness and performance. *American Behavioral Scientist, 47*, 766-790.

Cameron, K., Dutton, J., & Quinn, R. (2003). *Positive organizational scholarship.* San Francisco, CA: Berrett-Koehler.

Cameron, K., Quinn, R., Degraff, J., & Thakor, A. (2006). *Competing values leadership: Creating value in organization.* Northampton, MA: Edward Elgar.

Carroll, A. (2004). Managing ethically with global stakeholders: A present and future challenge. *Academy of Management Executive, 18*, 114-120.

Chaleff, I. (1998). *The courageous follower: Standing up to and for our leaders.* San Francisco, CA: Berrett-Koehler.

Chen, L., & Wang, C. (2002). The concept of integrity in China and Western countries: Its difference and implications. *Journal of Philosophy Research, 8*, 35-40.

Cole, M., Harris, S., & Field, H. (2004). Stages of learning motivation: development and validation of a measure. *Journal of Applied Social Psychology, 34*(7), 1421-1456.

Colley, J., Doyle, J., Logan, G., & Stettinius, W. (2003). *Corporate governance.* New York, NY: McGraw-Hill.

Cranton, P. (2002). *Professional development as transformative learning.* San Francisco, CA: Jossey-Bass.

Ciulla, J., & Burns, J. (2004). *Ethics—The heart of leadership* (2nd ed.). Westport, CT: Greenwood.

Cunningham, P., Frauman E., Ivy, M., & Perry, T. (2004). The value of money and leisure and college student's choice of major. *SCHOLE: A Journal of Leisure Studies and Recreation Education, 19*, 65-72.

DesJardins, J. (2007). *Business, ethics, and the environment: Imagining a sustainable future.* Upper Saddle River, NJ: Pearson-Prentice Hall.

DiClemente, C., & Prochaska, J. (1982). Self-change and therapy change of smoking behavior: A comparison of processes of change in cessation and maintenance. *Addictive Behaviors, 7*, 133-142.

Doris, J. (2005). *Lack of character: Personality and moral behavior.* New York, NY: Cambridge University Press.

Dunphy, D., Benveniste, J., Griffiths, A., & Sutton, P. (2000). *Sustainability: The corporate challenge of the 21st century.* Sydney, Australia: Allen & Unwin.

Felton, E., Jr., & Sims, R. (2005). Teaching business ethics: Targeted outputs. *Journal of Business Ethics, 60,* 377-391.

Ford, R., & Richardson, W. (1994). Ethical decision making: A review of the empirical literature. *Journal of Business Ethics, 13,* 205-221.

Fort, T. & Schipani, C. (2004). *The role of business in fostering peaceful societies.* Cambridge, England: Cambridge University Press.

Fudge, R., & Schlacter, J. (1999). Motivating employees to act ethically: An expectancy theory approach. *Journal of Business Ethics, 18,* 295-304.

Giacalone, R. (2004). A transcendant business education for the 21st century. *Academy of Management Journal, 3*(4), 415-420.

Giacalone, R., & Thompson, K. (2006). Business ethics and social responsibility education: Shifting the worldview. *Academy of Management Learning & Education, 5,* 266-277.

Gilligan, C., Ward, J. & Taylor, J. (Eds.) (1989). *Mapping the moral domain.* Cambridge, MA: Harvard University Press.

Goleman, D., Boyatzis, R., & McKee, A. (2004). *Primal leadership: Learning to lead with emotional intelligence.* Boston, MA: Harvard University Press.

Greider, W. (2009). *Come home America: The rise and fall (and redeeming promise) of our country.* New York, NY: Rodale.

Hartman, E. (1996). *Organizational ethics and the good life.* New York, NY: Oxford University Press.

Heyd, D. (1996). *Toleration: An elusive virtue.* Princeton, NJ: Princeton University Press.

Hill, A., & Stewart, I. (1999). Character education in business schools: Pedagogical strategies. *Teaching Business Ethics, 3,* 179-193.

Hinings, C., & Greenwood, R. (2002). Disconnects and consequences in organization theory. *Administrative Science Quarterly, 47,* 411-421.

Johnson, M. (1993). *Moral imagination.* Chicago, IL: University of Chicago Press.

Kansas, D. (2009). *The Wall Street Journal guide to the end of Wall Street as we know it.* New York, NY: Collins Business.

Kekes, J. (1993). *The morality of pluralism.* Princeton, NJ: Princeton University Press.

Kelley, P., & Elm, D. (2003). The effect of context on moral intensity of ethical issues: Revising Jones's issue-contingent model. *Journal of Business Ethics, 48,* 139-154.

Keyes, C. (1998). Social well-being. *Social Psychology Quarterly, 61,* 121-140.

Korten, D. (2009). *Agenda for a new economy: From phantom wealth to real wealth.* San Francisco, CA: Berrett-Koehler.

Kupperman, J. (1989). Character and ethical theory. *Midwest Studies in Philosophy, 13,* 98-111.

Liszka, J. (2002). *Moral competence: An integrated approach to the study of ethics.* Upper Saddle River, NJ: Prentice Hall.

Loe, T. W., Ferrell, L., & Mansfield, P. (2000). A review of empirical studies assessing ethical decision making in business. *Journal of Business Ethics, 25*, 185-204.

Luo, Y. (2007). *Global dimensions of corporate governance*. Malden, MA: Blackwell Publishing.

Mahoney, J. (1999). Cultivating moral courage in business. In G. Enderle (Ed.), *International business ethics: Challenges and approaches* (pp. 249-259). Notre Dame: University of Notre Dame Press.

McCabe, D., Butterfield, K., & Trevino, L. (2006). Academic dishonesty in graduate business programs: Prevalence, causes, and proposed action. *Academy of Management Learning and Education, 5*(3), 294-306.

Monks, A., & Minow, N. (2004). *Corporate governance* (3rd ed.). Malden, MA: Blackwell.

Mueser, K., Noordsy, D., Drake, R., & Fox, L. (2003). *Integrated treatment for dual disorders: A guide to effective practice*. New York, NY: Guilford Press.

Noddings, N. (1984). *Caring*. Los Angeles, CA: University of California Press.

O'Fallon, M., & Butterfield, K. (2005). A review of the empirical ethical decision-making literature: 1996-2003. *Journal of Business Ethics, 59*(4), 375-413.

Paine, L. (1991). Ethics as character development: Reflections on the objective of ethics education. In R. Edward Freeman (Ed.), *Business ethics: The state of the art* (pp. 78-90). New York, Ny: Oxford University Press.

Paine, L. (1994, March/April). Managing for organizational integrity. *Harvard Business Review*, 106-117.

Petrick, J. (2008). Using the business integrity capacity model to advance business ethics education. In D. Swanson & D. Fisher (Eds.), *Advancing business ethics education* (pp. 103-124). Charlotte, NC: Information Age.

Petrick, J. (2009). Toward responsible global financial risk management: The reckoning and reform recommendations. *Journal of Asia-Pacific Business, 10,*1-33.

Petrick, J., & Quinn, J. (1997). *Management ethics: Integrity at work*. Thousand Oaks, CA: Sage Publications.

Petrick, J., & Quinn, J. (2000). The integrity capacity construct and moral progress in business. *Journal of Business Ethics, 23*, 3-18.

Petrick, J., & Scherer, R. (2003). The Enron scandal and the neglect of management integrity capacity. *Mid-American Journal of Business, 18*(1), 37-50.

Pritchard, M. (2006). *Professional integrity: Thinking ethically*. Lawrence, KS: University Press of Kansas.

Prochaska, J., DiClemente, C. & Norcross, J. (1992). In search of how people change. *American Psychologist, 47*(9), 1102-1114.

Rossouw, G. (2002). Three approaches to teaching business ethics. *Teaching Business Ethics, 6*, 411-433.

Sims, R. (2002a). Business ethics teaching for effective learning. *Teaching Business Ethics, 6*, 393-410.

Sims, R. (2002b). *Teaching business ethics for effective learning*. Westport, CT: Quorum Books.

Sims, R., & Felton, E. (2006). Designing and delivering business ethics teaching and learning, *Journal of Business Ethics, 63*(3), 297-312.

Smith, K., Davy, J., & Eastering, D. (2004). An examination of cheating and its antecedents among marketing and management majors. *Journal of Business Ethics, 50,* 63-80.

Solomon, R. (1992). *Ethics and excellence: Cooperation and integrity in business.* New York, NY: Oxford University Press.

Solomon, R. (1993). *The passions: Emotions and the meaning of life.* Indianapolis, IN: Hackett.

Solomon, R. (1999a). *A better way to think about business: How personal integrity leads to corporate success.* New York, NY: Oxford University Press.

Solomon, R. (1999b). Business ethics and virtue. In R. E. Frederick (Ed.), *A companion to business ethics* (pp. 30-37). Malden, MA: Blackwell.

Solomon, R. (2006). *True to our feelings: What our emotions are really telling us.* New York, NY: Oxford University Press.

Swanson, D. (2004). The buck stops here: Why universities must reclaim business ethics education. *Journal of Academic Ethics, 1,* 43-61.

Swanson, D., & Frederick, W. (2005). Denial and leadership in business ethics education. In O. Ferrell & R. Peterson (Eds.), *Business ethics: The new challenge for business schools and corporate leaders* (pp. 222-240). Armonk, NY: M.E. Sharpe

Tabachnick, B., & Fidell, L. (1996). *Using multivariate statistics* (3rd ed.). New York, NY: HarperCollins.

Tang, T., & Chen, Y. (2008). Intelligence vs. wisdom: The love of money, Machiavellianism, and unethical behavior across college major and gender. *Journal of Business Ethics, 82,* 1-26.

Tang, T., Luna-Arocas, R., & Sutarso, T. (2005). From income to pay satisfaction: The love of money and pay equity comparison as mediators and culture (the U.S. and Spain) and gender as moderators. *Management Research: The Journal of the Iberoamerican Academy of Management, 3*(1), 7-26.

Trank, C., & Rynes, S. (2003). Who moved our cheese? Reclaiming professionalism in business education. *Academy of Management Learning and Education, 2*(2), 189-205.

Trevino, L. (1986). Ethical decision making in organizations: A person-situation interactionist model. *Academy of Management Review, 11,* 601-617.

Trevino, L. (1992). Moral reasoning and business ethics. *Journal of Business Ethics, 11,* 445-459.

Trevino, L., & Brown, M. (2004). Managing to be ethical: Debunking five business ethics myths. *Academy of Management Executive, 18*(2), 69-81.

Trevino, L., Hartman, L., & Brown, M. (2000). Moral person and moral manager: How executives develop a reputation for ethical leadership. *California Management Review, 42*(4), 128-142.

Trevino, L., & Weaver, G. (2003). *Managing ethics in business organizations.* Stanford, CA: Stanford University Press.

True, S. L., Ferrell, L. & Ferrell, O.C. (2005). *Fulfilling our obligation: Perspectives on teaching business ethics.* Kennesaw, GA: Kennesaw University Press.

Tyler, C., & Tyler, J. (2006). Applying the transtheoretical model of change to the sequencing of ethics instruction in business education. *Journal of Management Education, 30*(1), 45-64.

Waddock, S., Bodwell, C., & Leigh, J. (2006). *Total responsibility management.* Sheffield, England: Greenleaf.

Walzer, M. (1997). *On toleration.* New Haven, CT: Yale University Press.

Werhane, P. (1999). *Moral imagination and management decision-making.* New York, NY: Oxford University Press.

Whetstone, J. (1998). Teaching ethics to managers: Contemporary problems and a traditional solution. In C. Cowton & R. Crisp (Eds.), *Business ethics: Perspectives on the practice of theory* (pp. 177-206). Oxford, England: Oxford University Press.

Whittier, N., Williams, S., & Dewett, T. (2006). Evaluating ethical decision making models: A review and application. *Society and Business Review, 4,* 94-112.

Williams, S., & Dewett, T. (2006). Yes, you can teach business ethics: A review and research agenda. *Journal of Leadership and Organizational Studies, 12,* 109-120.

Windsor, D. (2004). A required foundation course for moral, legal and political education. *Journal of Business Ethics Education, 1*(2), 10-26.

Wood, D., Logsdon, J., Lewellyn, P., & Davenport, K. (2006). *Global business citizenship: A transformative framework for ethics and sustainable capitalism.* Armonk, NY: M.E. Sharp.

Zlotkowski, E. (1996). Opportunity for all: Linking service-learning and business education. *Journal of Business Ethics, 15,* 5-19.

CHAPTER 19

CHARACTER ASSESSMENT IN BUSINESS ETHICS EDUCATION

Thomas A. Wright

Character (ethos) refers to those interpenetrable habitual qualities within individuals and applicable to organizations that both constrain and lead them to desire and pursue personal and societal good. Five objectives are undertaken in this chapter on the importance of assessment of character in business education. First, a discussion of why character is relevant to business education assessment is introduced, with an emphasis on the epidemic of student cheating. Second, a conceptualization of what is character is provided. Third, an overview of how character can be assessed in business education is presented. Fourth, research is used to propose that a lack of positive role models constitutes one reason why we are today faced with moral challenges in business education, particularly the increase in student cheating. This chapter closes with a discussion of how we can best address these student challenges in the classroom.

Toward Assessing Business Ethics Education
pp. 361–380
Copyright © 2011 by Information Age Publishing

Education has for its object the formation of character.

—Herbert Spencer (1851, pt. II, p. 17)

INTRODUCTION

As evidenced by the opening quote from the nineteenth century social philosopher, Herbert Spencer, recognition of the important role of character is longstanding in nature. It did not simply commence with the recent financial collapse of AIG, Countrywide, Bear Sterns, Merrill Lynch, Enron, and Lehman Brothers, among all too many others. Many citizens are increasingly seeing the potentially grave consequences of these dishonest and fraudulent actions by our business and political leaders. Considered together, they threaten not only the financial well-being of American workers, but also the very moral fiber of our nation (Callahan, 2004; Wright, 2006). Unfortunately, and especially so in these trying times, a number of social commentators have eulogized the possibility that character, if not dead is dying (Hunter, 2000; Wright & Huang, 2008).

More germane to those interested in management education, many of these unethical and illegal actions are being committed by the students that we teach. This awareness moved Beatty (2004, p. 187) to wonder, "how we as professors may have contributed to it." Certainly, as business professors in an increasingly "just show me the money" business school environment, we share responsibility for this moral decline. Labeled the consumer metaphor (Zell, 2001), this approach represents an attempt to reduce the wide spectrum of human endeavor to the mere status of an economic good or commodity. In the present case, this is clearly demonstrated with the ever-increasing tendency by all too many to reduce the pursuit of knowledge or virtuous behavior to a cost-benefit analysis (Wright, 2006). Fortunately, all is not lost. There is reason to be hopeful. This hope is predicated on a better understanding of how one's strengths of character can impact our everyday behaviors (Wright & Huang, 2008).

While still relatively unknown in our schools of business, a particularly promising approach to the assessment of character was developed by the positive psychologists, Christopher Peterson and Martin E. P. Seligman (2004). As we will see, their assessment approach draws its theoretical impetus from the field of virtue ethics (Velasquez, 2002; Yearley, 1990). Certainly this virtue ethics influence can be readily seen in the work of Herbert Spencer and many of his contemporaries. Spencer (1970) considered character in the context of explicit moral standards or codes of conduct oriented toward work, building, and sacrifice designed for the benefit of the common good. In other words, the so-called producer values which are so central to Weber's *Protestant Work Ethic* (Weber, 1947; Wright & Huang, 2008)

Starting after World War I, there has been a gradual shifting in Western society away from this production-based orientation to an emphasis on such mass consumption-based values as material good accumulation, leisure, and the cultivation of personal preferences (Hunter, 2000; Wright & Huang, 2008). Distressingly, there have been a number of disturbing consequences of this consumption based values (over) emphasis. One has been the ever-increasing belief by all too many today that good or acceptable character is evidenced if we do not lie, cheat or steal too much. That is, as long as our behavior is seen as being instrumental in our pursuit of material wealth, while not hindering our personal choice preferences, we are willing to accept a modicum of lying, cheating, and stealing behavior from both ourselves and our leaders as a cost of doing business. There is perhaps no better venue for highlighting the widespread acceptance of this approach in today's society than the current proliferation of student cheating.

SCOPE OF STUDENT CHEATING

While academic dishonesty has long been recognized as a problem in education and research (Brown, 1995; Wright, 2004), there is widespread evidence clearly demonstrating that more and more students are currently engaging in cheating and other academically dishonest behaviors (Whitley & Keith-Spiegel, 2001; Wright, 2006). As a case in point, almost 70 years ago Drake (1941) reported a student cheating rate of 23%. Over time, this percentage has continuously increased, so that today, a number of studies have assessed student cheating at rates of up to 90% (cf. Whitley & Keith-Spiegel, 2001). Unfortunately, these statistics mirror those reported to me by my own students, with roughly 88% of junior/senior level undergraduate management major students assessed admitting that they cheat (Wright, 2004, 2006). More troubling, the modal response for how often they cheat is 100-plus times. These figures are consistent across any number of demographic and cultural variables.

Considered together, neither student marital status, level of financial independence, living arrangements, year in school, gender and country of origin appears to be related to the propensity to cheat (Whitley & Keith-Spiegel, 2001; Wright, 2006). Hitting closer to the current business ethics readership, business and economic students admit to cheating more frequently than other majors (for further discussion, see Brown, 1995; Wright, 2006). Even more telling, as previously reported (Wright, 2004, 2006), the vast majority of students that I have assessed readily acknowledge that it solely depends on the situation whether a person should lie, cheat or steal. Highly germane to our current discussion of student character assessment, this cavalier acceptance of cheating by our students has a number of serious consequences, both short-and long-term in nature (Callahan, 2004; Wright, 2006).

Students who cheat early on in school are not only more likely to cheat in graduate and professional school, but are also more likely to engage in unethical business practices (see Baldwin, Daugherty, Rowley, & Schwartz, 1996; Whitley & Keith-Spiegel, 2001). Academic dishonesty has been linked to such dysfunctional behaviors as petty theft and lying (Wright, 2006). There is perhaps no better example of this problematic, character-challenged behavior than the increasingly widespread willingness of many job applicants to misrepresent accomplishments on their resume. Callahan (2004) reported the results of a pre-employment screening study in which 95% of college-age respondents reported a willingness to lie to get a job. An amazing 41% admitted to have already lied. As a further sign of these cheating times, Dalrymple (2004) reported that the number of Americans willing to cheat on their taxes has significantly increased. In 2009, nowhere is this willingness to cheat on taxes more evident than in the public disclosures that multiple Obama cabinet nominees have failed to properly report and pay their taxes. Considered together, substantial evidence exists that students who cheat in college are also more likely to cheat in other aspects of their lives (Whitley & Keith-Spiegel, 2001; Wright, 2004). Alternatively, and highly relevant to our topic of character strength assessment, ethically acting students are less likely to engage in unethical workplace behavior (McCabe, Treviño, & Butterfield, 1996; Wright, 2006).

CHARACTER DEFINED

Defining what character is remains a challenge that has perplexed generations of industrial and organizational scholars (Wright & Goodstein, 2007; Wright & Huang, 2008). Highlighting this seeming paradox regarding the meaning of character is the work of Filter (1921, p. 297), who was so moved to note in an article published in the *Journal of Applied Psychology* that, "The looseness of meanings attached to names of character traits demands first consideration. A trait must be defined in order to be studied intelligently." Unfortunately, and even after this glowing testament by Filter regarding the need for definitional rigor, the author then failed to provide an even rudimentary definition of character. Filter was not alone in this failure. This conceptual ambiguity was plainly apparent in the work of a number of early organizational scholars (cf. Schwesinger,

1926; Slawson, 1922). Fortunately, a more well-articulated view of what constitutes character, along with how it can be best assessed, can be found in a number of philosophical and religious sources (Peterson & Seligman, 2004; Wright & Goodstein, 2007).

As expressed in the quote by Herbert Spencer, the traditional views of character were influenced by any number of sources. These sources include Aristotelian thought as evidenced in the *Nicomachean Ethics*, Judeo-Christian beliefs (well expressed in Saint Paul's faith, hope, and charity), such Eastern philosophies as Confucianism, as well as by the more modern, secular approaches proposed by utilitarian, justice and social contract models (Hunter, 2000; Peterson & Seligman, 2004; Wright & Goodstein, 2007). Benjamin Franklin's (1790/1961) well-known classification of strengths of character and virtue extolling the merits of leading well-ordered, humble, industrious, sincere, clean, and just lives has been highly influential on subsequent traditional thought. More specifically, these traditional definitions of character contained both moral and social dimensions. In other words, character is best assessed as a multidimensional construct (Peterson & Park, 2006; Wright & Huang, 2008).

The first, and most basic, component of this traditional approach to character is moral discipline (for a further discussion of the components of character, see Hunter, 2000; Wright & Goodstein, 2007). In particular, a core component of any classic definition of character is one identifying an individual's ability to constrain their personal appetites on behalf of the supposed needs of a greater societal good (Wright & Huang, 2008). Consistent with this communitarian idea of a greater societal good is the second element of character, moral attachment. This moral attachment component clearly reflects the affirmation of our commitments to someone or something greater than us (Wright & Goodstein, 2007). Hunter (2000, p. 16) refers to this as "the embrace of an ideal that attracts us, draws us, animates us, and inspires us." Lastly, inherent in more traditional definitions of character is an element composed of the moral autonomy of the individual in his or her capacity to freely make ethical decisions (Hunter, 2000; Wright & Huang, 2008). In this context, autonomy means that a person has both the necessary discretion and the skills of judgment at their disposal to freely act morally. More to the point, moral autonomy suggests the dual notions of individual responsibility and free will (cf. Hunter, 2000; Wright & Goodstein, 2007). Incorporating aspects of each of these three components, Thomas A. Wright and his colleagues (Wright & Goodstein, 2007; Wright & Huang, 2008), defined character as those interpenetrable and habitual qualities within individuals and applicable to organizations that both constrain and lead them to desire and pursue personal and societal good.

ASSESSMENT OF CHARACTER

As noted, the assessment of business student strength of character is quite limited at present. One especially promising avenue to assessing character may be found in the framework proposed by Peterson and his colleagues (Dahlsgaard, Peterson, & Seligman, 2005; Peterson & Seligman, 2004). Typically, past research on character and the formation of character has concentrated on one component of character at a time, leaving unaddressed issues about the underlying structure of character within an individual. For example, while some individuals may be prudent and persistent, they might lack in vitality and hope. Likewise, while other individuals may be fair and demonstrate integrity, they may be challenged in their love of learning and creativity (Park, 2004). In addition, assessing a full range of strengths of character may help alleviate concerns about participants responding with what they perceive to be socially desirous answers by allowing individual respondents the opportunity to report something positive about themselves (Peterson & Seligman, 2004).

In a systematic attempt to address these longstanding conceptual and empirical ambiguities in the assessment of character, Katherine Dahlsgaard conducted a comprehensive literature review of the world's influential religions and philosophical traditions. In the case of Judaism, the books of Exodus and Proverbs were reviewed, as regards Confucianism, the Analects, for the Taoist tradition, the Tao Te Ching, among other sources (Dahlsgaard et al., 2005). The virtues mentioned in these classic works were systematically identified by Peterson and Seligman (2004) and a core set of virtues common to all works was identified. Some of the criteria used (for a further discussion, see Peterson & Seligman, 2004; Peterson & Park, 2006; Peterson, Park, & Seligman, 2005) to identify whether a potential strength of character belonged in the classification framework include:

- ubiquity—the strength is widely recognized across time and culture;
- morally valued—the strength is valued in its own right and not only as a means to an end;
- measurable—the strength has been successfully measured;
- distinctiveness—the strength is not redundant;
- does not diminish others—the strength elevates others;
- paragon—the strength is strongly demonstrated in some individuals;
- selective absence—the strength is totally missing in some individuals; and

- trait-like—the strength is an individual difference with measurable temporal stability.

More specifically, Peterson and Seligman (2004) identified six core virtues (with the strengths of character common to each virtue listed in parentheses): wisdom and knowledge (creativity, curiosity, open-mindedness, love of learning, perspective); courage (bravery, integrity, persistence, vitality); humanity (kindness, love, social intelligence); justice (fairness, leadership, citizenship); temperance (forgiveness, modesty, prudence, self-regulation); and transcendence (appreciation of beauty, gratitude, hope, humor, spirituality). This classification framework provides an excellent starting point for a rigorous investigation of character assessment.

Peterson and Seligman's classification is measured by the Values in Action Inventory of Strengths (VIA-IS) (Peterson, Park, & Seligman, 2005). The VIA-IS is a 240-item self-report questionnaire that uses 5-point Likert-scales to measure the degree to which respondents endorse strength-relevant statements about themselves (1 = *very much unlike me* through 5 = *very much like me*). Each of the 24 strengths of character assessed by the VIA-IS is measured with 10 items. For example, sample items of the character strength perseverance include "I always finish what I start" and "I get sidetracked when I work" (reverse scored); sample items for the character strength creativity include "I like to think of new ways to do things" and "Most of my friends are more imaginative than I am" (reverse scored); sample items for the character strength prudence include "I avoid activities that are physically dangerous" and "I sometimes make poor choices in friendships and relationships" (reverse scored). Responses are averaged within scales, with higher numbers reflecting more of the strength. All 24 scales have been shown to have satisfactory internal consistency (Cronbach alpha coefficients > .70), along with substantial test-retest correlations over a four month period (Peterson, Park, Hall, & Seligman, 2009). As discussed next, I have taken the initial steps to systematically assess the strengths of character of business students at Kansas State University.

Over the past two years, I have assigned my MBA graduate level courses in Organizational Behavior and Positive Organizational Behavior the task of filling out the 240-item VIA-IS questionnaire. This questionnaire can be accessed at: http://www.viastrengths.org. After completing the questionnaire online, the students receive immediate feedback detailing their scores. Responses are averaged within scales, so that a respondent learns the relative (within subject) ranking of the 24 strengths of character. After completing the questionnaire, we have a class discussion about character and its role in helping to develop more ethical individuals and a more ethical society. We concentrate our discussion on the students' reported top five strengths of character or signature strengths. To date, the most commonly self-reported strengths of character for Kansas State University MBA students are: fairness, integrity, persistence, open-mindedness and hope. The least commonly self-reported are: social intelligence, self-regulation, perspective, vitality and love of learning.

Using focus groups composed of four to five students, I assign the groups the task of identifying the signature strengths they consider to be most necessary (their ideal top five character strength profiles) to be an effective MBA student and an effective manager, among other categories. Interestingly, the students assess social intelligence as being one of the top two strengths necessary to be an effective manager, while love of learning is assessed as the top strength necessary to be a successful MBA student. Interestingly, both of these strengths are among the least common self-reported by the students. Germane to our present discussion, many students self-rate the strength of character, honesty, as a top five signature strength. Yet, in reality, student cheating behavior is at an all-time high. This disconnect is especially troubling since the business students of today become the corporate executives of tomorrow. I next visit social exchange research to pose one reason why we are today faced with such a moral challenge in our schools of business.

TOWARD A "NEW" MODEL OF SOCIAL EXCHANGE

As defined by Cropanzano, Rupp, Mohler, and Schminke (2001, p. 27), "a social exchange theory is one that emphasizes the exchange of resources, among individuals or other social entity (e.g., a work organization)." These authors also note that a myriad number of perspectives to viewing social exchange have been proposed in the social and organizational sciences. For example, Gouldner (1960) suggested three primary views of social exchange, what I term here as instrumental, interpersonal and moral approaches. However, and irrespective of the particular approach, a basic consideration to any model of social exchange is what constitutes a just or fair exchange. A core assertion of this chapter is that over time our students have increasingly come to dramatically reassess what constitutes a just or equitable social exchange, resulting in a collective view that is increasingly different from that of past generations (Wright, 2006). Emphasizing both the prevailing student evolution in thought and its proposed consequences, I next examine each of these approaches to social exchange.

The instrumental approach, or as it is known to many, utilitarianism, is widely acknowledged to be the prevailing exchange perspective taught in our schools of business (Wright & Wright, 2000). According to utilitarianism, exchange-based actions and policies should be primarily assessed on the basis of the costs and benefits they impose on the organization or society at large (Velasquez, 2002). In fact, our business students are highly familiar with the Francis Hutcheson quote, later made more famous by Joseph Priestly and Jeremy Bentham (Rawls, 1971, p. 22, note 9), "That action is best which procures the greatest happiness for the greatest numbers."

Consistent with this belief that the end justifies the means, traditional or rule utilitarianism in theory focuses on the anticipated consequences of a particular action. In addition, and over time, this exchange focus has evolved from one emphasizing the overall effectiveness of the group or organization, to one with an emphasis on more individual-based gratification (Wright & Wright, 2002). At the extreme, this is exemplified by the classical economic notion that the organization's core stakeholders should be the prime, if not sole, beneficiaries of corporate actions, if need be to the exclusion of the interests of all other parties (e.g., Friedman, 1970; Wright, 2006). Likewise, for many students today and highly consistent with the consumer metaphor in management education, the greatest good for the greatest number mantra has been supplanted with the greatest good for me. From this self-indulgent, revised utilitarian perspective, it has become all too easy for many students to simply rationalize away the basis for their cheating behavior (for a further discussion of this topic, see Wright, 2004, 2006). In other words, students increasingly have come to assess themselves as customers who are purchasing a service or commodity from a business, in this case, their university (Gross & Holger, 2005). Thus, the question whether cheating is morally wrong has been supplanted by the readily apparent, highly tangible, and totally self-interest-based benefit of cheating to improve one's grade. In like manner, the perceived cost to the student simply reduces to one of whether they will get caught.

Providing additional support for this revised, special case utilitarian values perspective, are the results from many studies conducted over the years to assess why students engage in academic dishonesty, in particular, why they cheat (Brown, 1995; McCabe & Trevino, 1995). As summarized by Whitley and Keith-Spiegel (2001), the primary factors motivating student consideration of cheating and other forms of academic dishonesty are self-interest dominated. More specifically, they focus on individual performance concerns (e.g., I will flunk this course), external self-focused academic pressures (e.g., the course workload is way too heavy), nonacademic self-focused external pressures (e.g., I work too many hours at work) and rationalizations for their lack of effort (e.g., I didn't have the time or energy to adequately study for the exam). As one can readily assess, each of these rationalizations is highly consistent with the underlying basis of the consumer or commodification metaphor. That is, all share the fundamental need to put a specific economic value on the attainment of course credit (Wright, 2004, 2006).

The second approach to assessing a just or fair social exchange is an interpersonal one, emphasizing not only one's possible economic or instrumental benefits, but also the social nature of relationships among stakeholders. Based upon the notion that issues of fairness or justice are among the most social of psychological processes, this stream of research treats exchanges as types of relationships (Cropanzano et al., 2001). The interpersonal approach has been extensively used in organizational research on a wide range of topics, including organizational citizenship behavior (Eisenberger, Armeli, Rexwinkel, Lynch, & Rhoades, 2001) and psychological contracts (Rousseau, 1995). Whitley and Keith-Spiegel (2001) provide such interpersonal-based student rationalizations for cheating as those involving professors who are seen as being unfair to the student (e.g., the grading is harsh and unfair), to one focusing on the need to help fellow classmates cheat (e.g., I need to help my best friend find a way to pass this course).

The final social exchange perspective is a moral or deontological principles approach. This approach focuses on the commitment to a set of ethical standards that, while also containing a social component, are not solely predicated on only fulfilling one's vested self-interest, whether that is instrumental or interpersonal in nature (Wright, 2006). Greatly influenced by the classic work of Kant (1964) and such modern justice proponents as Rawls (1971), the deontological approach suggests that individuals make fair decisions based upon the application of universalistic standards, that is, standards that are not just focused on self-interest (Cropanzano et al., 2001). Of particular note to the present discussion and providing support for the notion that moral virtue and strength of character share a universalistic, even culturally transcendent nature, is the work of Peterson and Seligman (2004).

As noted earlier, these scholars assess twenty-four strengths of character shown to have consistently emerged over time and across history in philosophical and religious discussions on human goodness and worth. What distinguishes this deontological assessment approach is the belief that people are fair and just, persistent, kind, forgiving, grateful (and so on), not only because it is in their best self-interest (either economically or interpersonally), but because it is the right or even selfless thing to do (cf. Folger, 2001). Unfortunately, many students are quite candid in expressing almost a disdain for the supposed benefits of virtuous behavior and other forms of traditional behavior (Wright, 2004). In fact, cynicism appears to be a dominant way of perceiving life for many as we further navigate the twenty-first century (Dean, Brandes, & Dharwadker, 1998).

A vivid case in point of this widespread disdain is readily apparent in the following example. In two class discussions on various ethics-related topics in my senior undergraduate management and MBA course in organizations, no student present (a total of 54 students) disagreed (in fact, many very proactively agreed) with the assessment that it solely depends on the situation whether a person should lie or cheat. The most common rationale for this assessment is: If everyone else is doing it, why shouldn't I? So much for the importance of character as traditionally defined. My extensive conversations with many students over the years provide a clear-cut explanation for this troubling cynical attitude of all too many of today's students: the lack of positive role models.

CYNICISM AND THE LACK OF POSITIVE ROLE MODELS

As a prime example of this current dearth of positive role models, consider the realm of sports. For generations, prominent sports figures, deservedly or not, have been enthusiastically assessed as positive role models for a number of our young (and not so young) For many, this dramatically changed in 1989 when a track and field coach, known to some as "Charlie the Chemist" Francis, testified under oath before a high profile Canadian government panel. Francis testified that his protégé, Olympic gold and world record holder in the 100 meters at the Seoul 1988 Olympics, Ben Johnson, used banned performance-enhancing drugs. Charlie the Chemist's response was: So what? After all, in his view essentially all other elite Olympic athletes were cheaters (Fainaru-Wada, 2004). Twenty years later the drug cheating scandal has overrun major league baseball, involving such prominent athletes as Barry Bonds, Gary Sheffield, Roger Clemens, Sammy Sosa, Alex Rodriquez and Mark McGuire (among many others) certainly making Charlie the Chemist's words ring true. When faced with the choice to break the rules or lose it is obvious that many of these elite athletes, considered as role models by many of our students, choose to break the rules and cheat in order to win, often in a highly public manner.

It is not only the athletes who break the rules, but another group of potential positive role models, college coaches. Highly similar to the grades-as-money metaphor, many college coaches appear to be caught up in the seemingly ever-spiraling commodification process. Top major sports coaches (read: football and basketball) at large Division I schools probably have the most ethically challenging jobs in America today (Callahan, 2004). They are typically the most visible, and highly paid, members of the university community. Coaches are considered heroes, even celebrities (witness the public's fascination with such controversial coaches as Bob Knight), as long as they are winners. However, lose and you are history, or in the words of University of Texas athletic director, DeLoss Dodds, "If you don't win, you're not doing your job ... and you don't survive" (Callahan, 2004, p. 234). So much for the development of character as traditionally defined.

Closer to the author personally, a scenario that has become all too prevalent nationwide happened in the spring of 2004 at the University of Nevada, Reno, the author's employer at the time. After leading the basketball team to the Sweet 16 round of the NCAA tournament for the very first time in school history, the coach parlayed the team's success, and his role in it, into a 5-year contract renewal reported to be worth in the neighborhood of $500,000 per year, at the time, more than five times the average salary of a full professor at the Division 1 university. At a press conference held on March 30, 2004 to announce the contract renewal, the coach was quoted as saying, "The easiest thing to do in the coaching profession is to take off and take the next highest paycheck." The coach was also quoted as follows, "My first priority is to take care of the kids I've been associated with at (this) university." According to the University president at the press conference, "He (the coach) is an extraordinary individual who epitomizes our values of integrity, leadership and excellence." However, less than two months later, a different song was being sung on campus. On May 25, 2004, the university's director of athletics announced that the coach was leaving his job. In fact, he had skipped out on his less than 2 month-old contract and signed another contract at a higher profile basketball program at Stanford University for much more money. In the view of many students (among others), honesty and integrity lost out once more.

I offer a final example of the systemic commercialization of values that has permeated academics and is also endemic of our society at large: The increasingly blatant commodification of the PhD degree. Several years ago, the *Chronicle of Higher Education* provided a truly fascinating assessment of the multimillion dollar world of diploma mills (Bartlett & Smallwood, 2004, pp. A17-19). Briefly defined, a diploma mill is typically an unaccredited institution that sells degrees for cash, with the explicit expectation of only very minimal work being done to obtain the degree. According to this *Chronicle* special report, diploma mills have become a very significant problem in higher education. As a case in point, the article focused on the suspect credentials of an assistant professor of management from a school accredited by the Association to Advance Collegiate Schools of Business (AACSB). Even more disturbing are the quotes attributed to the faculty member's business school dean. According to the article, the professor's dean acknowledged that he knew before hiring that the assistant professor had a fake PhD. The dean is further quoted as stating, "Hell, we knew it was worthless." According to the dean, it's not that uncommon for professors, or even top administrators, to have bogus credentials. To confirm this, the dean noted that "I've dealt with provosts with degrees from mail order institutions here in the United States," although he declined to name names. Finally, the dean acknowledged the scope of this type of cheating by stating, "I guess, you know, we're guilty of institutionalizing a fraud."

This can not be solely dismissed as the misplaced values, or lack of character, of an isolated college administrator. This particular dean had previously served as a prominent member of the prestigious AACSB site visit accrediting team. In that position, along with his fellow members, he was highly instrumental in assessing which business schools would be (re)accredited by the AACSB. In other words, he was a designated role model for those schools wishing to be AACSB accredited. Sadly, as is evident from these examples, it appears cheating at the university level is equally served by a number of university stakeholders. That is, not only students, but also professors and high-ranking university administrators must share in the blame. Given this apparent dearth of positive role models, is it any wonder that cheating by our students has reached epidemic proportions, with no end in sight? Ironically, while academic dishonesty and the apparent lack of integrity has seemingly reached epidemic proportions in American education, many educators report that they know very little about either its causes or how to prevent its occurrence (Whitley & Keith-Spiegel, 2001). Apparently, it is not just our students who feel the need to practice denial or dissonance reduction (cf. Festinger, 1957). However, all is not lost. A personal experience involving one of my students provides uplifting support for the role of strength of character and positive role models in reducing student cheating behavior.

COUNTERPOINT: AN ACADEMIC EXAMPLE OF "DELAYED" CHARACTER

Over the years, similar to many of my management colleagues, I have had all too many encounters with students cheating. The present example was highly different. This example involved a student who turned himself in to me after he had successfully cheated (i.e., he was not caught cheating) on the class final exam (for a further, more detailed assessment of this experience, see Wright, 2004). As is typical in many cases, the student cheated because he was not confident in his ability to perform well on the final exam. Although he knew that cheating was wrong, these doubts as to his ability ultimately led him to cheat. However, after the exam, he experienced another, different kind of doubt. He had a very difficult time emotionally after leaving the test. In fact, he reported to me that he was an emotional wreck. Because of tightness in his chest, he had trouble eating later that day and even the next morning. His new self-doubt was the result of his failure to do what, according to him, he knew to be the right thing, that is, to not cheat on the exam.

In addition, and consistent with the second or interpersonal approach to justice, the student considered me to be a positive role model (cf. Bandura, 1977). As a result, he did not want to disappoint and embarrass me. In the end, the student's moral mandate (see Skitka, 2000) to do the right thing, coupled with his personal assessment of me as a positive role model, led him to turn himself in to me and tell the truth. An increasing number of studies, taken from various research venues, provide increasing empirical support that people will often forsake self-interest and do the moral, right thing. For example, Kahneman, Knetsch, and Thaler (1986) demonstrated that people will forego economic gain in order to try and correct for past injustice. I propose that through positive social modeling, we as business professors can help address the truly epidemic nature of student cheating behavior in our schools of business.

USING THE CLASSROOM TO ENCOURAGE POSITIVE CHARACTER DEVELOPMENT

Bandura and his colleagues (Bandura, 1977; Bandura & Walters, 1963) provide consistent testimony to the important role of social learning or modeling in human behavior. In an interesting program of study, Bandura and Walters (1963) found that boys from intact, affluent homes modeled the negative, aggressive attitudes of their parents. Other research by Bandura and his colleagues (Bandura, Ross, & Ross, 1963), involving the famous Bobo doll, extended the scope of social learning by demonstrating that learning could occur in the absence of immediate reinforcement, leading Bandura et al. to conclude that social modeling was a powerful, but undeveloped, learning tool. Unfortunately, more than 40 years later, it still appears that positive social modeling is an underdeveloped learning tool in secondary and higher education. Nowhere is this more evident than in the collective, lethargic response of academics to the problem of student cheating.

While most academics will agree that student cheating is wrong (Wright, 2004), many are far from proactive in their approach to dealing with cheating behavior in their classes (Whitley & Keith-Spiegel, 2001). In fact, many do not even formally address the topic in class, implying that

"If we don't talk about it, it doesn't exist." For instance, while employed at the University of Nevada, Reno, I conducted a short survey assessment and found that roughly 50% of the full-time faculty in the College of Business Administration's Department of Managerial Sciences made absolutely no reference to academic dishonesty in their most recent syllabus (Wright, 2006). I am currently a professor of organizational behavior at Kansas State University. Unfortunately, and based solely upon my experience, expressions of faculty concern regarding student cheating appear to be similarly apathetic. Providing at least partial affirmation to my assertion, Kansas State University MBA students have consistently told me that student cheating is rarely discussed in their classes. Obviously, the first step in any successful intervention must be to make all parties concerned both acutely aware and willing to take the initiative to both assess and address the problem of cheating. Using insights derived from Bandura's social learning or modeling approach (Bandura, 1989, 1997) and personal experience-based examples, I next discuss class-based interventions I have undertaken to help commit both myself and my students to a course of action to end the epidemic of student cheating.

Salancik (1977) noted that a key determinant in establishing commitment is to get individuals to undertake a particular course of action on their own volition. As an initial step, an awareness of the evils of cheating must be fully comprehended by the students themselves. I have undertaken several methods to assess this awareness in my classes. First, I provide specific definitional assessments of what constitutes cheating in the class syllabus. At the University of Nevada, Reno, roughly 75% of my department colleagues failed to provide specific definitions of cheating. Anecdotal evidence indicates that this figure appears to be consistent with the percentages found at many departments of management across the country. Second, from the very beginning of the semester (and throughout the semester when appropriate), I engage the class in an assessment of what constitutes cheating and other forms of academic dishonesty. I note that I consider cheating to be wrong. Equally important, I then ask students if they agree with my assessment that cheating is wrong.

Interestingly, while the majority will admit to cheating, the vast majority will acknowledge that cheating is wrong, at least in the abstract. Therein lies our hope. I then undertake to assess why they believe that cheating is inappropriate. Once there is a class consensus that cheating is wrong, I introduce the topic of character strengths and virtues (e.g., Peterson & Seligman, 2004). In this discussion, I emphasize that various forms of academic dishonesty, including cheating, are of serious concern. For one thing, they demonstrate a lack of personal integrity (Johnston, 1996; Wright, 2006), one of Peterson and Seligman's (2004) 24 strengths of character. Finally, I engage the class in a discussion that if cheating is wrong, what should be appropriate negative consequences, and why, for those who cheat.

In other words, and consistent with another of Salancik's (1977) determinants of commitment, the assessment of what constitutes an act of cheating is made highly explicit in our class discussion. Incorporating aspects of the psychological contract (Rousseau, 1995), all students are asked to sign and turn in to me a psychological contract agreement (which includes the pitfalls/penalties of academic dishonesty) stating that "By my signature, I confirm that I have read, understand and agree to abide by the terms and conditions of our class contract." When each student has turned in their signed agreement (required by the second week of class), I make this consensus agreement public to the class, further building student commitment to the actual terms of the class contract (see Salancik, 1977).

Once the class is underway, there are a number of ways for faculty to further demonstrate positive modeling behavior. For example, Wright (2004) noted that students assess the apparent reluctance of professors to proactively address instances of academic dishonesty as a form of instructor ethical misconduct. One student outside the classroom setting told me that he felt this reluctance demonstrates a lack of courage, one of Peterson and Seligman's (2004) six universal virtues. In fact, students assess several of the 24 strengths of character as being especially relevant to the present discussion on cheating. More specifically, the character strengths of perspective, integrity, fairness and self-regulation have proven to be especially instrumental in stimulating spirited class dialogue on the subject of cheating. In addition, our class discussions on character strengths have personally helped me to revisit how I am assessed as a role model by my students. As a result of this self-reflection, I was forced to carefully scrutinize how I previously monitored in-class exams, and the possible role that my previous approach had on student cheating behavior.

In the past, I would either have my graduate assistant proctor the exam or I would passively proctor the exam myself. By passively proctoring an exam, I mean that I would show up, pass out the exam, briefly walk around the room to let everybody know that I was there and meant business, and then sit down and bury my nose in a book or grade my class assignments. According to a number of students, this type of passive approach to exam proctoring tells students that cheating really doesn't matter to many professors. After all, if it really mattered and was important to the professor that students not cheat, the professor would expend the necessary effort to help make sure that cheating didn't occur during their class test time. By the way, these student perspectives appear to have merit. Research is quite clear that a diligent, thoughtful and proactive approach to exam proctoring can serve as an effective deterrent to student cheating (Genereaux & McLeod, 1995; Stern & Havlicek, 1986; Whitley & Keith-Spiegel, 2001; Wright, 2004, 2006). As a result, I now make my physical presence very conspicuous throughout the entire length of my exams. In addition, I often have my graduate assistant help me in proctoring exams, especially in larger class sections. In these larger classes, we position ourselves in different parts of the room and actively move around throughout the entire exam.

The interested reader will note that not only are my actions designed for students to assess me as a positive role model, but also to encourage students to become more proactive and self-regulatory regarding monitoring their own behavior. According to Bandura (1991), I am attempting to help students develop an agentic motivational perspective. The basic premise of an agentic approach is that students come to view themselves as self-regulatory and self-reflective organisms, not just as passive beings reacting to influences from their environment. The format and class discussion on cheating is constructed to help students personally reflect on and individually assess why cheating is harmful and what they can do to self-regulate the temptation to engage in acts of academic dishonesty. Of course, our students do not live in a vacuum. To that end, Bandura's (1997) view of human agency is considered to be a collective one. My next social modeling goal is to work with colleagues in my department, college, university, various professional organizations, and the readers of this chapter to further develop the belief in our students that cheating is inappropriate behavior. I look forward with anticipation to the journey.

CONCLUDING REMARKS

Surprisingly, to date, the assessment of business student strengths of character has received minimal attention (Wright & Huang, 2008). To the best of my knowledge, the program initiated by me at Kansas State University constitutes the only attempt to systematically assess business student strengths of character. This current lack of awareness and attention is unfortunate as the ethical and strength of character development of our students should be made an integral part of our stated mission in higher education. In fact, the assessment of student strengths of character has never been more important, as evidenced by the shocking increase in student cheating behavior. In this chapter I have proposed that business ethics professors consider the merits of Peterson and Seligman's (2004) VIA-IS strengths of character framework. In particular, the assessment and subsequent further development of such student signature strengths as integrity, fairness and self-regulation will undoubtedly make a significant contribution to the moral betterment of our students, business operations, and society at large (including ourselves).

REFERENCES

Baldwin, D. C., Jr., Daugherty, S. R., Rowley, B. D., & Schwartz, M. R. (1996). Cheating in medical school: A survey of second-year students at 31 schools. *Academic Medicine, 71*(3), 267-273.

Bandura, A. (1977). *Social learning theory.* Englewood Cliffs, NJ: Prentice Hall.

Bandura, A. (1989). Human agency in social theory. *American Psychologist, 44*(9), 1175-1184.

Bandura, A. (1991). Social cognitive theory of self-regulation. *Organizational Behavior and Human Decision Processes, 50*(2), 248-287.

Bandura, A. (1997). *Self-efficacy: The exercise of control.* New York, NY: W.H. Freeman.

Bandura, A., Ross, D., & Ross, S.A. (1963). A comparative test of the status envy, social power, and secondary reinforcement theories of identificatory learning. *Journal of Abnormal and Social Psychology, 67*, 527-534.

Bandura, A., Walters, R.H. (1963). *Social learning and personality development.* New York, NY: Holt.

Bartlett, T., & Smallwood, S. (2004, June 25). Psst. Wanna buy a Ph.D.? The *Chronicle of Higher Education*, pp. A9, A17-19.

Beatty, J. E. (2004). Grades as money and the role of the market metaphor in management education. *Academy of Management Learning and Education, 3*(2), 187-196.

Brown, B. S. (1995). The academic ethics of graduate business students: A survey. *Journal of Education for Business, 70*(3), 151-156.

Callahan, D. (2004). *The cheating culture.* Orlando, FL: Harcourt.

Cropanzano, R., Rupp, D. E., Mohler, C. J., & Schminke, M. (2001). Three roads to organizational justice. In G. R. Ferris (ed.), *Research in personnel and human resources management* (Vol. 20, pp. 1-113). Kidlington, Oxford, England: Elsevier Science.

Dahlsgaard, K., Peterson, C., & Seligman, M. E. P. (2005). Shared virtue: The convergence of valued human strengths across culture and history. *Review of General Psychology, 9*(3), 209-213.

Dalrymple, M. (2004, October 31). More taxpayers say it's ok to cheat. *San Francisco Chronicle*, p. B1.

Dean, J., Brandes, P., & Dharwadker, R. (1998). Organizational cynicism. *Academy of Management Review, 23*(2), 341-352.

Drake, C. A. (1941). Why students cheat. *Journal of Higher Education, 12*(7), 418-420.

Eisenberger, R., Armeli, S., Rexwinkel, B., Lynch, P., & Rhoades, L. (2001). Reciprocation of perceived organizational support. *Journal of Applied Psychology, 86*(1), 42-51.

Fainaru-Wada, M. (2004, July 8). Steroids the rule in track, some say. *San Francisco Chronicle*, pp. A1, A4.

Festinger, L. (1957). *A theory of cognitive dissonance*. Evanston, IL: Row, Peterson.

Filter, R. O. (1921). An experimental study of character traits. *Journal of Applied Psychology, 5*(4), 297-317.

Folger, R. (2001). Fairness as deonance. In S. W. Gilliland, D. D. Steiner, D. P. Skarlicki (Eds.), *Research in social issues in management* (Vol. 1, pp. 3-33). Greenwich, CT: Information Age.

Franklin, B. (1961). The autobiography. In L. J. Lemisch (Ed.), *The autobiography and other writings* (pp. 15-180). New York, NY: Signet Classic. (Original work published ca. 1790)

Friedman, M. (1970, September 13). A Friedman doctrine: The social responsibility of business is to increase its profits. *The New York Times Magazine*, p. 32.

Genereaux, R. L., & McLeod, B. A. (1995). Circumstances surrounding cheating: A questionnaire study of college students. *Research in Higher Education, 36*(6), 687-704.

Gouldner, A. W. (1960). The norms of reciprocity: A preliminary statement. *American Sociological Review, 25*(2), 161-178.

Gross, M. A., & Hogler, R. (2005). What the shadow knows: Exploring the hidden dimensions of the consumer metaphor in management education. *Journal of Management Education, 29*(1), 3-16.

Hunter, J. W. (2000). *The death of character: Moral education in an age without good or evil*. New York, NY: Basic Books.

Johnston, D. K. (1996). Cheating: Limits of individual integrity. *Journal of Moral Education, 25*(2), 159-171.

Kahneman, D., Knetsch, J. L., & Thaler, R. H. (1986). Fairness and the assumptions of economics. *Journal of Business, 59*(4), S285-S300.

Kant, I. (1964). *Groundwork of the metaphysics of morals* (H. J. Paton, Trans.). New York, NY: Harper & Row.

McCabe, D. L., & Trevino, L. K. (1995). Cheating among business students: A challenge for business leaders and educators. *Journal of Management Education, 19*(2), 205-218.

McCabe, D. L., Treviño, L. K., & Butterfield, K. D. (1996). The influence of collegiate and corporate codes of conduct on ethics-related behavior in the workplace. *Business Ethics Quarterly, 6*(4), 461-476.

Park, N. (2004). Character strengths and positive youth development. *The Annals of the American Academy of Political and Social Science, 591*, 40-54.

Peterson, C., & Park, N. (2006). Character strengths in organizations. *Journal of Organizational Behavior, 27*(8), 1149-1154.

Peterson, C., Park, N., Hall, N., & Seligman, M.E.P. (2009). Zest and work. *Journal of Organizational Behavior, 30*(2), 161-172.

Peterson, C., Park, N., Seligman, M. E. P. (2005). Assessment of character strengths. In G. P. Koocher, J. C. Norcross, & S. S. Hill, III (Eds.), *Psychologists' desk reference* (2nd ed., pp. 93-98). New York, NY: Oxford University Press.

Peterson, C., & Seligman, M. E. P. (2004). *Character strengths and virtues: A handbook and classification*. New York, NY: Oxford University Press

Rawls, J. (1971). *A theory of justice*. Cambridge, MA: Harvard University Press.

Rousseau, D. M. (1995). *Psychological contracts in organizations: Understanding written and unwritten agreements.* Thousand Oaks, CA: Sage.

Salancik, G. R (1977). Commitment and control of organizational behavior and belief. In G. R. Salancik & B. M. Staw (Eds.), *New directions in organizational research* (pp. 1-54). Chicago, IL: St. Clair Press.

Schwesinger, G. C. (1926). Slang as an indication of character. *Journal of Applied Psychology, 10*(2), 245-253.

Skitka, L. J. (2000, September). *The moral mandate hypothesis.* Paper presented in K. van den Bos (Chair) Recent advances in social psychological theories of justice, a symposium conducted at the International Society for Justice Research, Rishon LeZion, Israel.

Slawson, J. (1922). The reliability of judgment of personal traits. *Journal of Applied Psychology, 6*(2), 161-171.

Spencer, H. (1970). *Social statics.* New York, NY: Augustus M. Kelley. (Original work published in 1851)

Stern, E. B., & Havlicek, L. (1986). Academic misconduct: Results of faculty and undergraduate student surveys. *Journal of Allied Health, 15*(2), 129-142.

Velasquez, M. G. (2002). *Business ethics: Concepts and cases* (5th ed.). Upper Saddle River, NJ: Prentice Hall.

Weber, M. (1947). *The theory of social and economic organization* (A.M. Henderson & T. Parson, Trans. & Eds.). New York, NY: Oxford University Press.

Whitley, B. E., Jr., & Keith-Spiegel, P. (2001). *Academic dishonesty: An educator's guide.* Mahwah, NJ: Erlbaum.

Wright, T. A. (2004). When a student blows the whistle [on himself]: A personal experience essay on 'delayed' integrity in a classroom setting. *Journal of Management Inquiry, 13*(4), 291-306.

Wright, T. A. (2006). Toward the development of a truly relational approach to the study of organizational behaviors: Further consideration of the committed-to-participant research perspective. In O. Kyriakidou & M. Ozbilgin (Eds.), *Relational perspectives in organizational studies* (pp. 278-305). Cheltenham, United Kingdom: Edward Elgar.

Wright, T. A., & Goodstein, J. (2007). Character is not "dead" in management research: A review of individual character and organizational-level virtue. *Journal of Management, 33*(6), 928-958.

Wright, T. A., & Huang, C. -C. (2008). Character in organizational research: Past directions and future prospects. *Journal of Organizational Behavior, 29*(7), 981-987.

Wright, T. A., & Wright, V. P. (2000). How our 'values' influence the manner in which organizational research is framed and interpreted. *Journal of Organizational Behavior, 21*(5), 603-607.

Yearley, L. H. (1990). *Mencius and Aquinas: Theories of virtue and conceptions of courage.* Albany, NY: State University of New York Press.

Zell, D. (2001). The market-driven business school: Has the pendulum swung too far? *Journal of Management Inquiry, 10*(4), 324-348.

CHAPTER 20

THE CHARACTER JOURNAL

An Assessment Tool
for Advancing Character Learning

Martin Stuebs

The universe is made up of stories, not atoms.

—Muriel Rukeyser

INTRODUCTION

Stories and experiences provide valuable opportunities for character learning and development. But how can students assess their personal stories and experiences to access the lessons and learning they contain? How can administrators demonstrate that character learning has indeed occurred?

Recent accounting scandals (e.g., Enron, WorldCom, Global Crossing, Waste Management, etc.) contain stories that have focused attention on the need for business education reform (Ghoshal, 2005). Reforms call for "business school graduates who are capable of ethical business action"

Toward Assessing Business Ethics Education
pp. 381–401
Copyright © 2011 by Information Age Publishing
All rights of reproduction in any form reserved.

(Kracher, 1999, p. 291). This call for ethical business actors has led to a rethinking of the business ethics paradigm. Grounded in the work of Kohlberg (1969), traditional business ethics education tends to "address cognitive goals and focus on teaching students tools and skills they need to be able to make ethical decisions in business" (Kracher, 1999, p. 292). The narrow focus is on moral judgment.

Equipping students to make good judgments, however, is not enough. The business ethics paradigm has moved to a call for more comprehensive character education (Mintz, 1995, 1996a) and for character development (Berkowitz & Fekula, 1999; see also the chapter by Wright in this book). Character education extends moral education to include virtue and character development in addition to Kohlberg's (1969) cognitive and intellectual capabilities (Hill & Stewart, 1999). This shift in paradigm broadens the learning objectives of ethics education beyond moral judgment to include moral motivation and moral character. Implementing these expanded objectives in the classroom requires new pedagogical tools to assess and advance character education (Kracher, 1999).

Although the idea of a broader, character-based approach to ethics education is plausible, implementing and assessing it is the challenge. How can character education be advanced and assessed in the classroom? The purpose of this chapter is to introduce the character journal, a pedagogical tool that can advance students' moral motivation and moral character through reflection and assessment. The character journal integrates two pedagogical strategies commonly used in character education: (a) the narrative (Bennett, 1993) and (b) self reflection (Mintz, 2006). Each character journal entry combines a moral short story or stories with a reflective personal journal entry. The catalyst moral stories focus student attention on specific character virtues. The reflective personal entries respond to the catalyst story and allow for personal introspection and self assessment. The students' self assessments provide an avenue for instructor assessment of character learning and development. Because each journal entry is simple, short, and concise, the character journal can be nonintrusively integrated into a number of courses as a useful character education tool with intended assessment benefits for students, instructors, and administrators.

WHY USE THE CHARACTER JOURNAL?
BACKGROUND AND SUPPORT

Developing trustworthiness in our students is paramount because a key objective of business education is to develop trustworthy business people. Trust is a function of two necessary and equally important components:

(a) competence (the ability to do something), and (b) character (the integrity to do something) (Baier, 1986; Covey, Merrill & Merrill, 1994). While business education primarily focuses on developing professional competence, professional character development has received less attention.

Recent advances in ethics education advocate a shift in learning objectives to include character education and character development (Armstrong, Ketz & Owsen, 2003; Melé, 2005; Mintz, 1995; Mintz, 1996a; Mintz, 2006). Ethics education's traditional focus on moral reasoning competence (Melé, 2005; Mintz, 1995, 1996a) has its roots in Kohlberg's (1969) six-stage moral development theory, which deals with moral reasoning development (Kohlberg & Hersh, 2001). A major implication of Kohlberg's moral development theory is that an individual's moral reasoning changes over time (Rest, 1980). Moral reasoning seems to develop as people grow older and as people continue their education (Rest, 1980). However, even Kohlberg recognized that developing moral judgment competence is a necessary, but insufficient condition, for moral action (Kohlberg & Hersh, 2001).

Rest (1984) and Rest and Narvaez (1994) extend moral development beyond moral judgment by describing it as a multifaceted phenomenon (Guthrie, 1997). In his four-component model, Rest models moral behavior as a function of:

1. *Moral sensitivity:* the awareness of possible courses of action and how each could affect involved parties. Moral sensitivity includes interpreting the situation and identifying the moral problem (Guthrie, 1997).

2. *Moral judgment:* deciding the most moral action from the possible alternatives. The person weighs choices and determines what ought to be done in such a situation (Navarez & Rest, 1995). Kohlberg's (1969) work on the stages of moral development advanced this component.

3. *Moral motivation:* the priority given to moral values relative to competing values (Guthrie, 1997).

4. *Moral character:* the skills needed to carry out the chosen action (Navarez & Rest, 1995).

This more comprehensive view of morality (Guthrie, 1997) provides a foundation for a broad-based approach to moral education (Bebeau & Thoma, 1999).

How can these additional components of morality be advanced and assessed? Virtue ethics offers perspective. Virtue ethics categorizes virtues into two broad groups: intellectual virtues and character virtues. Intellectual virtues are virtues that enable someone to reason and make right decisions. They relate to an individual's intellectual competence. Character virtues are virtues that enable someone to carry out well what he thinks he should do (Cheffers & Pakaluk, 2007; Mintz, 1996b). Virtues, then, are character traits that enable individuals to make choices (i.e., intellectual virtues) that lead to action (i.e., character virtues) (MacIntyre, 1984).

Thorne (1998) integrated this classification of virtues with Rest's (1986) four-component model (Armstrong et al., 2003). According to Thorne, Rest's first two components—moral sensitivity and moral judgment—deal with intellectual virtues, or the way people think about ethical issues. This has been the focus of accounting and business ethics education. Rest's last two components—moral motivation and moral character—deal with character virtues, or the importance a person places on acting morally (Mintz, 1996b).

How then can intellectual and character virtues be advanced and assessed? Intellectual virtues generally are taught through instruction and study (Cheffers & Pakaluk, 2007). Intellectual virtues, therefore, are more amenable to classroom instruction exercises. Character virtues, on the other hand, are learned through practice and experience (Cheffers & Pakaluk, 2007). Effective character education requires experiential learning and assessment tools. Experiential learning forms and builds the habits of character. Creating genuine experiences and practice in the confines of a controlled, artificial classroom setting can be difficult. As a result, character virtues can be much more challenging to advance and assess in the classroom setting. The challenge is to uncover valid avenues for advancing the experiential learning process in the classroom.

The Cyclical Experiential Learning Process

The cyclical experiential learning process, depicted in Figure 20.1, involves two interrelated steps: (a) experience and practice that can lead to opportunities for learning, and (b) reflection and assessment that can lead to opportunities for development (Esmond-Kiger & Stein, 1998; Hatcher & Bringle, 1997; Kolb, Rubin, & Osland, 1991). The latter step, in turn, can inform future experiences and practice.

As shown in Figure 20.1, experiences are necessary, but insufficient, to foster effective experiential learning. Assessment activities are also needed. Since experience and practice create opportunities for learning (discussed in more detail below), I use narratives as a way to bring experiences involving specific character virtues into the classroom. I then use reflection and assessment activities to harvest the lessons and knowledge from the learning opportunities that experiences create. In this way, the

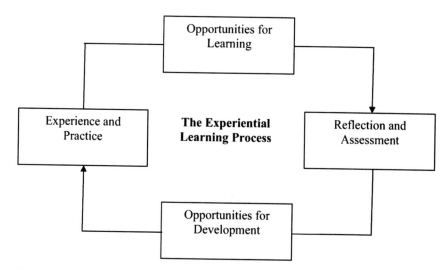

Note: Based on the definition and the components of experiential learning at http://en.wikipedia.org/wiki/Experiential_learning

Figure 20.1.   The experiential learning process.

journal is a tool that combines and connects narratives and experiences to reflective self-assessment activities focused on character learning. The harvested lessons and knowledge lead to opportunities for development that future practice and experience can utilize and internalize in the cyclical experiential learning process. As I discuss later in this chapter, the character journal also offers assessment opportunities for the instructor and administrators.

Using Narratives in the First Step of the Learning Process

Narratives are a common tool for bringing the first step, experiences, into the classroom. Traditional character education (Bennett, 1993, 1995; Wynne & Ryan, 1997) uses stories to instill character traits. The experiences conveyed in stories help students rehearse moral decisions, organize their own experiences, and understand the basis for future action (Lockwood, 1996). This is a basic and powerful instructional form since human memory is experience-based (Lockwood, 1996; Schank, 1990). Stories are used by some of the most successful communicators (DeBruyn, 2007). For example, Jesus often used parable stories to convey lessons to his disciples and others.

The experiences created by stories foster affective as well as cognitive development. Students not only hear, but also experience stories. A story's experiences can translate students' interconnections with others into emotionally felt moral dimensions (Wight, 2006). This hold on the imagination helps to create an emotional attachment and commitment to goodness (Lockwood, 1996). Because of this possible outcome, Plato advocated that the young should learn character traits via stories that develop a love for what is good before acquiring discipline-specific knowledge (Hill & Stewart, 1999; Meilaender, 1984).

Stories can also provide meaning and moral direction (Lockwood, 1996). Moral stories give students a chance to actualize basic moral issues and reflect on and understand why they should act morally (Knapp, Louwers, & Weber, 1998; Lockwood, 1996; Stewart, 1997). Stories frame life and reality and can provide structure and meaning (Lockwood, 1996). Storytelling is a way for people to know themselves (Lockwood, 1996). Through reflection "one can understand, on a conscious level, the reasons for moral behavior, what it means to be moral, and why one should be moral" (Lockwood, 1996, p. 60).

In sum, stories can affect the head, heart, and hands. Stories can convey intellectual concepts (a cognitive effect on the head). Stories can affect the imagination and generate an emotional attachment to goodness (an affective effect on the heart). And stories can clarify the meaning of activities (a behavioral effect on the hands). "Linking student knowledge and convictions to action makes heads, heart, and hands all work together" (Hill & Stewart, 1999, p. 184).

Using Reflective Exercises in the Second Step of the Learning Process

The second step in the experiential learning process, reflective learning exercises, provides an opportunity for students to reflect on and assess their own personal experiences. Reflective learning and self assessment are intentional, cognitive activities that occur after concrete experiences in an attempt to ascribe meaning to events (Esmond-Kiger & Stein, 1998; Hatcher & Bringle, 1997; Nelson, 1993). Mintz (2006) advocates reflective learning to aid deep learning and help students internalize virtues. Structured reflection exercises provide a means through which instructors can facilitate the recognition of lessons by students. Mintz (2006) provides a variety of pedagogical examples that incorporate reflective learning exercises into assignments and courses including reflective discussion, minute papers, role-playing exercises and reflection logs. Each of these techniques involves critical thought and introspective self-assessment.

The character journal can be added to the reflective learning techniques identified by Mintz (2006).

Reflection and self-assessment are important ingredients in character learning (Berkowitz & Fekula, 1999). They create cognitive perspective (Wight, 2006) that can form generalizations influencing future action (Glenn & Nelson, 1988; Hatcher & Bringle, 1997; Sheckley, Allen, & Keeton, 1993). These self-assessment activities help develop moral conscience (Wight, 2006) and enable an individual to know his/her moral self (Esmond-Kiger & Stein, 1998).

In the next section I discuss the use of narratives and reflective exercises in terms of the character journal.

WHAT IS THE CHARACTER JOURNAL? DESCRIPTION AND STRUCTURE

Teaching virtues vis-à-vis narratives and reflective exercises are appropriate and complementary "strategies ... to reorient business education" (Hill & Stewart, 1999, p. 184). At its microfoundational level, each individual character journal entry combines both: (a) the narrative catalyst story and (b) the reflective personal story. At its most general, the character journal process is about making connections (Mintz, 2006). It asks students to relate the virtue content in the narrative catalyst story to their own personal experiences (Bourner, O'Hara, & Barlow, 2000) and then connect them to personal virtue development conclusions and lessons. In this way the character journal can embody the experiential learning steps illustrated in Figure 20.1 of experience and practice on the one hand and reflection and assessment on the other.

Using Narratives in the Character Journal

The narrative catalyst story is a story from outside the personal experience of the student (Lockwood, 1996). The catalyst story can take a variety of forms (DeBruyn, 2007) including fictional stories (e.g., Aesop's fables), nonfictional stories (McCain & Salter, 2005), the use of moral exemplars (Dobson & Armstrong, 1995; Knapp et al., 1998) or moral exhortations (Armstrong et al., 2003). The moral literacy and character education movement (e.g., William Bennett, Kevin Ryan, Thomas Lickona, and William Kilpatrick) provide literature and resources for catalyst stories. Table 1 identifies and describes several possible resources for catalyst stories. By no means collectively exhaustive, this list provides sufficient resources for those who are interested in finding appropriate catalyst stories.

Table 20.1. Resources for Narrative Catalyst Stories

Resource	Description
The Book of Virtues, William Bennett (1993)	*The Book of Virtues* is a collection of hundreds of stories along with a useful anthology. Instructive introductions accompany each virtue and are followed by the collection of stories.
Moral Compass: Stories for Life's Journey, William Bennett (1995)	This is a companion volume to *The Book of Virtues*
The Book of Virtues for Young People: A Treasury of Great Moral Stories, William Bennett (1997)	*The Book of Virtues for Young People* is a treasury of timeless stories, poems, and fables.
Character is Destiny, John McCain and Mark Salter (2005)	*Character is Destiny* tells the stories of celebrated historical figures and lesser-known heroes whose values exemplify the best of the human spirit.
A Call to Character: Family Treasury of Stories, Poems, Plays, Proverbs and Fables to Guide the Development of Values for you and Your Children, Colin Greer and Herbert Kohl (1995)	*A Call to Character* is a 450-page collection of 217 stories, fables, and poems using the best of children's literature. The collection is rich and varied, divided into chapters of general characteristics, such as creativity, courage, generosity, compassion, adaptability, responsibility, and love, among others.
Bringing Out Their Best: Values Education and Character Development through Traditional Tales, Norma J. Livo (2003)	This is a collection of more than 60 tales organized into 12 thematic sections. Each cluster of stories is followed by a section that offers discussion and activity ideas.
Dale Carnegie's Scrapbook, Dorothy Carnegie (1959)	This is a collection of quotations that Dale Carnegie found inspirational, interspersed with excerpts from his own writings.
Core Virtues: A Literature-Based Program in Character Education, Mary Beth Klee (2003)	*Core Virtues* provides a comprehensive character education program. A section of the book also provides a critical resource guide to literature organized by virtue.

Using Reflective Exercises in the Character Journal: Connecting the Narrative to Personal Experience

The narrative catalyst story focuses on reflective self-assessment. Students respond to the narrative catalyst story with a reflective personal story. The purpose of the reflective personal story is to connect the catalyst story to personal life experiences. It is "told by the student about his own experience" (Lockwood, 1996, p. 35) and can be a way for students to sort out their thoughts.

Preparation of the reflective personal story requires the student to identify lessons from the catalyst story (i.e., review), relate past experiences to these lessons (i.e., reflect), and draw conclusions for current and future action (i.e., digest) (Bourner et al., 2000; Race, 1993). In the aggregate, the character journal entries combine narratives and reflection in a useful way to focus on professional awareness and character development (Bourner et al., 2000). The appendix to this chapter provides an example of the character journal's fundamental elements: (a) the catalyst story and (b) the reflective personal story.

Character Journal Entries: Building Blocks for Character Learning

Each catalyst story and related personal story forms one character journal entry. The character journal entry is the foundational building block, or "brick." The character journal continues to add these bricks to build character learning. Each entry can cover a different virtue or vice. Certain virtues have been recognized and certain vices condemned in all cultures (Hill & Stewart, 1999; Ryan, 1993; Schwehn, 1993).

The character journal entries can cover a number of virtues. Classical ethical theory's four cardinal virtues—courage, temperance, justice, and wisdom (Cheffers & Pakaluk, 2007)—are a good starting point. All other virtues, according to classical ethical theory, depend on the cardinal virtues. Using the cardinal virtues as a foundation, the character journal can then examine a number of other virtues. For example, Peterson and Seligman (2004) provide a handbook that identifies a number of virtues and classifies them around the four cardinal virtues and two additional foundational virtues. Klee (2003) provides another useful source that identifies a number of virtues. Based on Peterson and Seligman, I present a nonexhaustive list of possible virtues in Table 20.2 that can be used in the character journal.

In addition to the general virtues (Panel A), Cheffers and Pakaluk (2007) identify a set of cardinal virtues that specifically apply to business professionals and accountants. These are presented in Panel B of Table 20.2.

Virtues, however, can be organized in a number of ways. Table 20.3 presents two additional possibilities. Presented in Panel A, McCain and Salter (2005) organize virtues around several identified cardinal or fundamental virtues: (a) honor, (b) purpose, (c) strength, (d) understanding, (e) judgment, (f) creativity, and (g) love. Presented in Panel B, Greer and Kohl (1995) organize virtues around the individual: (a) virtues that relate to one's self, (b) virtues that relate to people, and (c) virtues that relate to

Table 20.2. Nonexhaustive List of Possible Virtues That can Be Used in the Character Journal

Panel A: General Virtues of a Good Person

1. Wisdom and Knowledge
   - Creativity: Originality, ingenuity
   - Curiosity: Interest, novelty-seeking, openness to experience
   - Open-mindedness: Judgment, critical thinking
   - Love of learning
   - Perspective: wisdom

2. Courage
   - Bravery: Valor
   - Persistence: Perseverance, Industriousness
   - Integrity: Authenticity, Honesty
   - Vitality: Zest, Enthusiasm, Vigor, Energy

3. Justice
   - Citizenship: Social responsibility, loyalty, teamwork
   - Fairness
   - Leadership

4. Temperance
   - Forgiveness and mercy
   - Humility and modesty
   - Prudence
   - Self-regulation: Self-control

5. Humanity
   - Love
   - Kindness: Generosity, nurturance, care, compassion, altruistic love, niceness
   - Social Intelligence: Emotional intelligence, personal intelligence

6. Transcendence
   - Appreciation of Beauty and Excellence: Awe, wonder, and elevation
   - Gratitude
   - Hope: Optimism, future-mindedness, future orientation
   - Humor: Playfulness
   - Spirituality: Religiousness, faith, purpose

Panel B: Instrumental Virtues of a Good Business Professional or Accountant

1. Wisdom and Knowledge
   - Competence
   - Objectivity

2. Courage
   - Due diligence

3. Justice
   - Sense of public interest

4. Temperance
   - Independence
   - Integrity

love. The second item, virtues that relate to people, is divided into two parts: virtues that relate to people one knows and virtues that relate to people one doesn't know. Nature is included in the latter category. The two structures presented in Table 20.3 can help students understand interdependent, connected relationships among virtues. For example, students can connect the secondary virtues in McCain and Salter's (2005) structure to their corresponding cardinal virtue. Greer and Kohl's (1995) structure, for instance, shows that love is an overarching, guiding virtue that affects personal virtues (i.e., love for one's self) and interpersonal virtues (i.e., love for others).

Table 20.3.   Examples of Structures to Organize Character Journal Content

Panel A: *Character is Destiny* Structure

Honor	1. Honesty, 2. Respect, 3. Authenticity, 4. Loyalty, 5. Dignity
Purpose	1. Idealism, 2. Righteousness, 3. Citizenship, 4. Diligence, 5. Responsibility, 6. Cooperation
Strength	1. Courage, 2. Self-control, 3. Confidence, 4. Resilience, 5. Industry, 6. Hopefulness
Understanding	1. Faith, 2. Compassion, 3. Mercy, 4. Tolerance, 5. Forgiveness, 6. Generosity
Judgment	1. Fairness, 2. Humility, 3. Gratitude, 4. Humor, 5. Courtesy
Creativity	1. Aspiration, 2. Discernment, 3. Curiosity, 4. Enthusiasm, 5. Excellence
Love	1. Selflessness and contentment

Panel B: *A Call to Character* Structure

Virtues that relate to one's self	1. Courage, 2. Self-Discipline, 3. Integrity, 4. Creativity, 5. Playfulness
Virtues that relate to people one knows	1. Loyalty, 2. Generosity, 3. Empathy, 4. Honesty, 5. Adaptability
Virtues that relate to people one doesn't know and nature	1. Idealism, 2. Compassion, 3. Responsibility, 4. Balance, 5. Fairness
Virtues that relate to love	1. Love

The character journal can include entries on vices in addition to virtues. For example, pride can be a vice that corresponds with the virtue of humility or gluttony can be a vice that pairs with the corresponding virtue of self control. From my experience, catalyst stories on virtues have been sufficient. Students naturally make connections to vices and virtue deficiencies when reflectively assessing past experiences in their personal stories.

IMPLEMENTATION SUGGESTIONS: TIPS AND TRICKS FOR EFFECTIVE USE OF THE CHARACTER JOURNAL

The character journal can be useful because it breaks character education into brief, regular, focused self-assessment sessions. Individually, each character journal entry functions like a nonintrusive brick giving the journal both flexibility and strength. When mortared together, these bricks can build consistent, repetitive, connected attention on character learning and assessment over time. Because it consists of brief, regular entries, the character journal can be integrated into any course or across the curriculum. In my classes, students compile their character journal over the course of the semester, organizing each entry in a three-ring binder. Each reflective personal story is filed behind the corresponding catalyst story or stories. I provide an index that lists the character journal stories, topics, and structure that represents a table of contents at the front of the character journal. At the end of the semester, students leave with a collection of stories accompanied by personal reflections on the importance of certain character attributes.[1]

The character journal can easily be used in many business and accounting courses. It is a relatively nonintrusive, repetitive way to infuse character education and assessment consistently across the curriculum. This method is consistent with Berkowitz and Fekula's (1999, p. 18) assertion that "institutions that want to engage in truly comprehensive character education must put in place a wide array of elements and implement them throughout the educational environment." Because of the brief, regular nature of each entry, the character journal only takes about five to ten minutes at the beginning of each class. Hence, it "can be used in any class" (Lockwood, 1996, p. 103) and introduced at any point in a student's course of studies (Knapp et al., 1998). I have successfully used the character journal in many courses across the accounting curriculum.

Certain steps can smooth implementation of the character journal. My suggestions are aimed at creating comfort for both students and instructors. There can be serious resistance among students (Haigh, 2001) to the character journal because of the discomfort caused by lack of familiarity. Lack of familiarity can be overcome by providing students with careful guidance. Students need to understand what a good reflective personal story entry contains. Many students express worries about what should be written in a journal entry (Haigh, 2001). It is important that students understand that a good reflective personal story identifies and references key concepts in the catalyst story, reflects on and assesses past personal experiences, and digests conclusions for current and future action (Bourner et al., 2000; Race, 1993). The instructor should communicate to students that an effective journal entry is personal, should be written in the first-person singular tense, be reflective, and contain past personal experiences that relate to the catalyst story. The instructor needs to communicate that an effective journal entry uses specific past experiences, not general statements about past tendencies. The entry should analyze the catalyst story and personal experiences in order to draw conclusions. Providing students with examples of good and bad journal entries can help students become comfortable with writing journal entries. Checking the first few student journal entries thoroughly and providing brief, helpful comments also helps students become familiar with journaling and can increase their comfort.

Communicating respect to students in the assessment process can help students feel comfortable in using the character journal. An effective journal entry requires honesty. Honesty results in vulnerability. It is important for students to feel respected and secure when expressing honest thoughts in their journals. Communicating empathy and understanding to students can help an instructor connect with students and communicate respect.

Certain steps can ease an instructor's transition to using the character journal. The first suggestion is to consider gradual implementation to smooth the transition. Practically speaking, this can take a variety of forms. For example, the character journal can initially begin with a manageable handful of stories and entries. Beginning with oral catalyst stories and student discussion of them at the beginning of class with no formal written requirement is another way to begin using character journal concepts. Breaking character journal implementation into smaller manageable steps can build students' familiarity and comfort with using the character journal and increase the likelihood of success.

ASSESSMENT CHARACTERISTICS OF THE CHARACTER JOURNAL

Assessment Benefits

At its foundational level, the journal entries translate character education into brief, regular, reflective self-assessment sessions that can be easily implemented on a repeated and consistent basis within a business ethics course or across the curriculum. This provides students with a chance for personal self-assessment of experiences and instructors and administrators with a qualitative assessment of character learning.

Collectively, the character journal entries meet guidelines for effective reflection and self-assessment activities (Hatcher & Bringle, 1997), especially since these entries: (a) are guided, (b) link experience to learning, (c) foster the exploration and clarification of values, (d) occur regularly, and (e) allow for feedback and assessment. Each individual entry satisfies these first three guidelines. First, the narrative catalyst story guides a student's attention to specific virtues of character. Second, the reflective personal story allows a student to link personal past experiences to the catalyst story and to learning. In this way, students can learn from past actions, emotions, and thoughts with the result of a richer learning experience. Third, both stories work together to foster the exploration and clarification of values. Overall, each journal entry can foster character learning through self-assessment in the experiential learning process.

The character journal can provide instructors and administrators with a qualitative measure of character development. While many tools develop and assess student intellect, the character journal can provide a measure of student character. Asking students to prepare a summary of their journal entries provides a concise, qualitative growth assessment. In the summary entry, students reflect on and assess their character journal experience, review their character strengths and weaknesses, reflect on how their character has changed during the journaling process, and digest future actions and character changes identified as a result of the character journal process. The summary entry represents a final reflection that provides qualitative documentation of character journal benefits. Pre and post measures of character development, such as the Moral Competency Inventory (Lennick & Kiel, 2005), can also be used in concert with the character journal summary entry to provide a more quantitative assessment for the program. The Moral Competency Inventory measures the resolve to have moral courage and can be used to assess the effects the journal process has on resolve and character (Christensen, Barnes & Rees, 2007a, 2007b).

Assessment Challenges

The character journal provides opportunities for assessment, but not without challenges. Two notable challenges are: (a) the subjectivity in grading and assessment and (b) the time required for analysis.

Subjectivity in the grading of the journal can create undue uncertainty for students, causing them to worry about how their journals will be assessed (Haigh, 2001). Indeed, there is some question as to whether or not journals should even be graded, due to their private nature (see Bourner et al., 2000). With these concerns in mind, it is important to develop and communicate to students a set of criteria that can be applied fairly to all (Mintz, 2006). For example, criteria can communicate that journal entries should be personal—written in the first person singular tense. Moreover, personal stories should contain three parts: (a) a review of the main point of the catalyst stories, (b) a reflection on related past personal experiences that is specific, and (c) a summary of lessons from the catalyst story and personal experiences for future growth. Mintz also recommends collecting the character journals on an unannounced basis to serve as a check on students' disciplined consistency with the journaling process.

Because of its personal and subjective nature, the character journal can be evaluated on a satisfactory/unsatisfactory basis (Bourner et al., 2000). Some characteristics of unsatisfactory journals can include: (a) review without reflection: a description of the catalyst story with no personal application, (b) impersonal entry: a general, not personal, character journal entry, (c) insufficient reflection: a journal entry that fails to reflect on personal past experiences, and (d) impersonal reflection: a reflective journal entry that is general and not specific. The character journal can also be graded as an extra credit activity. Either way, the point is to reduce student unease about assessment and grading and facilitate comfort with free expression within the boundaries of the assignment. Despite potential student concerns, my experience and that of others (Haigh, 2001; Hodges, 1995; Snadden, Thomas, Griffin, & Hudson, 1996) has been that they appreciate its value for promoting learning and encouraging introspection. The comments of my students reveal that the character journal helped them see how they can improve and change.

Journals require a significant amount of reading (Haigh, 2001). In order to reduce instructor workload, a sample of a student's character journal entries can be read and assessed with comments. Another alternative is to have students assess their own journals by providing a summary journal entry where students evaluate and discuss their complete character journal. How have they grown? What have they discovered when looking at their character journals? In addition to motivating students to consciously identify personal growth benefits, the summary entry can be used to direct instructor assessment to the most important entries written or lessons learned by the student, potentially eliminating the need to read all journal entries.

CONCLUSION

This chapter described the character journal as a pedagogical tool for advancing and assessing character learning. The character journal is important and useful because it addresses an often neglected area of education, character development, by facilitating experiential learning. Each journal entry is made up of two parts: (a) the narrative virtue-identifying catalyst stories and (b) the student's responsive virtue-assessing personal story. The character journal is easy to integrate in individual classes or across the curriculum, since each entry is small and nonintrusive. Taken as a whole, the character journal's entries facilitate consistent, repetitive character learning and assessment. Because the character journal is divided into flexible journal entry pieces, instructors can tailor journal implementation to instructor, student, and situational characteristics. It can be seen that the character journal offers attractive character learning and assessment benefits for students, instructors, and programs.

NOTE

1. Interested readers can contact the author for an example character journal that contains materials for implementing the character journal. The example character journal contains a story index along with an accompanying collection of catalyst stories for nineteen journal entries. It is ready for use in any class.

APPENDIX: AN EXAMPLE OF CHARACTER JOURNAL NARRATIVE CATALYST STORY AND A REFLECTIVE PERSONAL STORY

This appendix contains an example of a character journal entry. The narrative catalyst story (along with a catalyst quotation in this case) covers a character journal topic—the importance of character—and would be used in one class period. The narrative catalyst story is followed by an actual journal entry (i.e., reflective personal story) written by one of my students.

EXAMPLE: THE IMPORTANCE OF CHARACTER

Narrative Catalyst Story: The Frog and the Scorpion

There is an old African folk tale about a frog and a scorpion. A frog and a scorpion were standing by the edge of a river. Both wanted to get to the other side. The frog could swim. The scorpion could not. So the scorpion approached the frog and persuasively said, "Let me climb on your back when you swim across the river so that we both can get to the other side." The frog quickly replied, "No! It's not reasonable for me to let you climb on my back. You're a scorpion. Half-way across the river you're going to sting me. Then I will drown and die. It's not reasonable for me to let you climb on my back." The scorpion scoffed, "What are you talking about? If I sting you half-way across the river, you will drown and die. I cannot swim. Therefore, I will drown and die as well. It certainly is **not reasonable for me to sting you!**" Convinced by the scorpion's logic, the helpful frog let the scorpion climb on his back and they started out across the river. Half-way across the river the scorpion stung the frog. The frog was in complete shock! "Why did you sting me? Now I will surely drown and die. You cannot swim. You will drown and die as well. It's **not reason-**

able for you to sting me!" "Aaah," the scorpion replied, "**I do not act out of reason. I act out of character.**"

Catalyst Quotation: A. C. Ernst Quotation

If you believe that there is such a thing as a business future, and your vision of the possibilities of the accounting profession is broad enough, you will realize some of the opportunities offered by the firm of Ernst & Ernst, opportunities offered those who measure up, in **character, ability** and **industry**, to the standards Ernst & Ernst have set. As a member of the Ernst & Ernst organization, you are one of the **custodians of a trust.** The trust and the confidence the business and investing public reposes in Ernst & Ernst should be always in your mind. It has taken years, it has meant many sacrifices, material and otherwise, to create this trust. It must be preserved. Its value must be enhanced. In the performance of your work spare no time or effort. Be satisfied only with perfection, a perfection based on honesty, on efficiency, and on simplicity. We can afford to lose money, to lose time, but we cannot afford to lose the confidence of those we serve. **Integrity is your greatest asset in life**, it is your life, for without it you lack **self-respect. Be fair** to our clients, to their employees and to yourself and you will be fair to Ernst & Ernst. Avoid mental reservations, be frank, and you will be respected. And finally, and always do your work well, **do it honestly**, keep on the job.

—A.C. Ernst (1920 Ernst & Ernst Employee Manual)

Example of a Student's Reflective Personal Story

I really like the story about the frog and the scorpion. The story helps me to understand better why it is so important to take this ethics class and develop my character. I always assume that if put in a situation like the scorpion's, I will act with reason. This story proves the opposite. One acts out of character or habit. This story shows me that I do need to work on my character. I am very competitive and tend to see things as a competition, similar to the scorpion competing with the frog over survival. Friday, I went to a Ropes obstacle course and I saw the competitiveness in myself and many of my classmates. We were all told to put ourselves on four corners of a square and to all get to the opposite side by stepping on circular rubber pads. Once the pads were stepped on, they were picked up. My group thought it was a competition and, as a result, raced across the pads to take them away from the other teams. In fact, one member of my team intentionally sabotaged the other teams. It turned out that all four groups were supposed to aid each other in reaching the respective corners. It hit me when I was doing this exercise that teamwork is very important, especially in the workplace. It is definitely something that I need to work on. I get so competitive that sometimes I want to do things myself. When we all worked together it showed me the value of group collaboration. The exercise also taught me that when I am in a group with other competitive people, I become more competitive.

The Ernst & Ernst Employee Manual really makes me think. I have always known that integrity and honesty are important attributes for individuals; however, until this year I did not realize that once you lose your integrity, it can only very rarely be regained. Once in high school, I told my parents a lie because I wanted to do something at the time that they didn't want me to do. They ultimately found out. When they found out, it was the most strained that our relationship had ever been. Now I understand why. They had always thought of me as honest, and I had lost that trust that they had in me. Their disappointment in me was worse than any anger that they had ever expressed. It is funny how an experience from so long ago is so meaningful in today's business environment. Even though my situation was not very serious, it still caused me to lose a great deal of their confidence.

REFERENCES

Armstrong, M. B., Ketz, J. E., & Owsen, D. (2003). Ethics education in accounting: Moving toward ethical motivation and ethical behavior. *Journal of Accounting Education, 21*(1), 1-16.

Baier, A. (1986, January). Trust and antitrust. *Ethics, 96,* 231-260.

Bebeau, M. J., & Thoma, S. J. (1999). 'Intermediate' concepts and the connection to moral education. *Educational Psychology Review, 11*(4), 343-360.

Bennett, W. J. (1993). *The book of virtues* (1st ed.). New York, NY: Simon & Schuster.

Bennett, W. J. (1995). *The moral compass: Stories for a life's journey.* New York, NY: Simon & Schuster.

Bennett, W. J. (1997). *The book of virtues for young people: A treasury of great moral stories.* New York, NY: Simon & Schuster.

Berkowitz, M. W., & Fekula, M. J. (1999). Educating for character. *About Campus, 4*(5), 17-22.

Bourner, T., O'Hara, S., & Barlow, J. (2000). Only connect: Facilitating reflective learning with statements of relevance. *Innovations in Education & Training International, 37*(1), 68-75.

Carnegie, D. (1959). *Dale Carnegie's scrapbook.* Hauppauge, NY: Dale Carnegie and Associates.

Cheffers, M., & Pakaluk, M. (2007). *Understanding accounting ethics* (2nd ed.). Sutton, MA: Allen David Press.

Christensen, D. S., Barnes, J., & Rees, D. (2007a). Developing the resolve to have moral courage—An experiment with accounting students. *Journal of Accounting, Ethics & Public Policy 7*, 1-25.

Christensen, D. S., Barnes, J., & Rees, D. (2007b). Developing resolve to have moral courage: A field comparison of teaching methods. *Journal of Business Ethics Education 4*, 79-96.

Covey, S. R., Merrill, A. R., & Merrill, R. R. (1994). *First things first*. New York, NY: Simon & Schuster.

DeBruyn, R. L. (2007). Six types of stories to enhance instructional and counseling effectiveness. *The Professor in the Classroom, 13*(18), 2-4.

Dobson, J., & Armstrong, M. B. (1995). Application of virtue ethics theory: A lesson from architecture. *Research on Accounting Ethics, 1*, 187-202.

Esmond-Kiger, C., & Stein, D. M. (1998). A self-reflective approach to teaching ethics in the accounting curriculum. *Advances in Accounting Education, 1*, 217-234.

Ghoshal, S. (2005). Bad management theories are destroying good management practices. *Academy of Management Learning & Education, 4*(1), 75-91.

Glenn, S., & Nelson, J. (1988). *Raising self-reliant children in a self-indulgent world: Seven building blocks for developing capable young people*. Rocklin, CA: Prima Publishing and Communications.

Greer, C., & Kohl, H. (1995). *A call to character: Family treasury of stories, poems, plays, proverbs, and fables to guide the development of values for you and your children*. New York, NY: HarperCollins.

Guthrie, V. L. (1997). Cognitive foundations of ethical development. *New Directions for Student Services, 77*, 23.

Haigh, M. J. (2001). Constructing Gaia: Using journals to foster reflective learning. *Journal of Geography in Higher Education, 25*(2), 167-189.

Hatcher, J. A., & Bringle, R. G. (1997). Reflection: Bridging the gap between service and learning. *College Teaching, 45*(4), 153-158.

Hill, A., & Stewart, I. (1999). Character education in business schools: Pedagogical strategies. *Teaching Business Ethics, 3*(2), 179-193.

Hodges, H. F. (1995). Journal writing as a mode of thinking for RN-BSN students: A leveled approach to learning to listen to self and others. *Journal of Nursing Education, 35*(3), 137-141.

Klee, M. B. (2003). *Core virtues: A literature-based program in character education*. Libertyville, IL: The Link Institute.

Knapp, M., Louwers, T., & Weber, C. (1998). Celebrating accounting heroes: An alternative approach to teaching ethics. *Advances in Accounting Education, 1*, 267-277.

Kohlberg, L. (1969). Stage and sequence: The cognitive developmental approach to socialization. In D. A. Goslin (Ed.), *Handbook of socialization theory* (pp. 347-480). Chicago, IL: Rand McNally.

Kohlberg, L., & Hersh, R. H. (2001). Moral development: A review of the theory. *Theory into Practice, 16*(2), 53-59.

Kolb, D. A., Rubin, I. M., & Osland, J. (1991). *Organizational behavior: An experiential approach*. Englewood Cliffs, NJ: Prentice-Hall.

Kracher, B. (1999). What does it mean when Mitchell gets an 'A' in business ethics? Or the importance of service learning. *Teaching Business Ethics, 2*, 291-303.

Lennick, D., & Kiel, F. (2005). *Moral intelligence.* Upper Saddle River, NJ: Prentice-Hall.

Livo, N. J. (2003). *Bringing out their best: Values education and character development through traditional tales.* Santa Barbara, CA: Libraries Unlimited

Lockwood, J. H. (1996). *The moral of the story: Content, process, and reflection in moral education through narratives.* Unpublished manuscript, University of Florida.

MacIntyre, A. (1984). *After virtue.* Notre Dame, IN: University of Notre Dame Press.

McCain, J., & Salter, M. (2005). *Character is destiny: Inspiring stories every young person should know and every adult should remember.* New York, NY: Random House.

Meilaender, G. C. (1984). *Theory and practice of virtue.* Notre Dame, IN: University of Notre Dame Press.

Melé, D. (2005). Ethical education in accounting: Integrating rules, values and virtues. *Journal of Business Ethics, 57*(1), 97-109.

Mintz, S. M. (1995). Virtue ethics and accounting education. *Issues in Accounting Education, 10*(2), 247-267.

Mintz, S. M. (1996a). Aristotelian virtue and business ethics education. *Journal of Business Ethics, 15*(8), 827-838.

Mintz, S. M. (1996b). The role of virtue in accounting education. *Accounting Education, 1*(1), 67-91.

Mintz, S. M. (2006). Accounting ethics education: Integrating reflective learning and virtue ethics. *Journal of Accounting Education, 24*, 97-117.

Navarez, D., & Rest, J. (1995). The four components of acting morally. In W. Kurtines & J. Gewirtz (Eds.), *Moral behavior and moral development: An introduction* (pp. 385-400). New York, NY: McGraw-Hill.

Nelson, K. (1993). The psychological and social origins of autobiographical memory. *Psychological Science, 4*, 7-14.

Peterson, C., & Seligman, M. E. P. (2004). *Character strengths and virtues: A handbook and classification.* New York, NY: Oxford University Press.

Race, P. (1993). *The open learning handbook.* London, England: Kogan Page.

Rest, J. (1980). Moral judgment research and the cognitive-developmental approach to moral education. *Personnel and Guidance Journal, 58*, 602-605.

Rest, J. (1984). The major components of morality. In W. Kurtines, & J. Gewirtz (Eds.), *Morality, moral behavior, and moral development* (pp. 24-40). New York, NY: Wiley.

Rest, J. (1986). *Moral development: Advances in research and theory.* New York, NY: Praeger.

Rest, J., & Narvaez, D. (Eds.). (1994). *Moral development in the professions of psychology and applied ethics.* Hillsdale, NJ: Erlbaum.

Ryan, K. (1993). Mining the values in the curriculum. *Educational Leadership, 51*(3), 16-18.

Schank, R. C. (1990). *Tell me a story: A new look at real and artificial memory.* New York, NY: Charles Scribner's Sons.

Schwehn, M. R. (1993). *Exiles from Eden.* New York, NY: Oxford University Press.

Sheckley, B. G., Allen, G. J., & Keeton, M. T. (1993). Adult learning as recursive process. *Journal of Cooperative Education, 28*, 56-67.

Snadden, D., Thomas, M. L., Griffin, E., & Hudson, H. (1996). Portfolio-based learning and general practice vocational training. *Medical Education, 10*(3), 148-152.

Stewart, I. (1997). Teaching accounting ethics: The power of narrative. *Accounting Education, 2*(2), 173-184.

Thorne, L. (1998). The role of virtue in auditors' ethical decision making: An integration of cognitive-developmental and virtue-ethics perspectives. *Research on Accounting Ethics, 4*, 291-308.

Wight, J. (2006). Adam Smith's ethics and the "Noble arts" 1. *Review of Social Economy, 64*(2), 155-180.

Wynne, E., & Ryan, K. (1997). *Reclaiming our schools: A handbook on teaching character, academics and discipline.* New York, NY: Merrill.

ABOUT THE AUTHORS

Ann K. Buchholtz is a professor of leadership and ethics and research director of the Institute for Ethical Leadership at Rutgers University. She received her PhD from the Stern School of Business at New York University. She is past division chair of the Social Issues in Management Division of the Academy of Management and was a member of the ethics task force that designed a code of ethics for the academy. She then served as the inaugural chairperson of the academy's ethics adjudication committee. Her work has been published in *Business and Society, Business Ethics Quarterly, Academy of Management Journal, Academy of Management Review,* and *Organization Science,* among others. She is coauthor, with Archie Carroll, of *Business and Society: Ethics and Stakeholder Management* (8th ed., South-Western CENGAGE Learning, 2012) and serves on the editorial boards of *Business & Society* and *Business Ethics Quarterly.*

Robert L. Braun is the Charles Wesley Merritt Professor of Accounting at Southeastern Louisiana University. His research and teaching focus is on auditing and ethical decision making in business and accounting. His work has been published in *Accounting Organizations and Society, Issues in Accounting Education, Advances in Accounting, Journal of Accountancy, Advances in Accounting Education, Accounting Educator's Journal, Managerial Auditing, CPA Journal,* and other outlets. His teaching and research awards include the Business Partnership Excellence in Teaching Award and the Outstanding Dissertation Award by the Auditing Section of the American Accounting Association. He currently serves as an ad hoc reviewer for several journals and as a member of the editorial board for *Issues in Accounting Education.*

Rogene A. Buchholz is the Legendre-Soule Chair in Business Ethics Emeritus in the College of Business Administration at Loyola University of New Orleans. He has published more than 75 articles and is the author or coauthor of 12 books in the areas of business and public policy, business ethics, and the business environment. Before moving to Loyola, he taught in business schools at the University of Minnesota, Washington University in St. Louis, and the University of Texas at Dallas, where he was also an associate dean and undergraduate program director. Professor Buchholz is on the editorial board of several journals and served as chair of the Social Issues in Management Division of the Academy of Management. He received the Sumner Marcus Award from this division in 1996 for distinguished service to the division and the field of social issues in management. Dr. Buchholz is currently retired and lives with his wife in Denver, Colorado.

Archie B. Carroll is director of the Nonprofit Management and Community Service Program and professor emeritus in the Terry College of Business, University of Georgia. Dr. Carroll received his three academic degrees from The Florida State University, and he has been on the faculty of UGA since 1972. His teaching and research interests have been in business ethics, business and society, and stakeholder management. His most recent books include *Business and Society: Ethics, Sustainability, and Stakeholder Management* (8th ed., South-Western CENGAGE Learning, 2012) with Ann K. Buchholtz and *Business Ethics: Brief Readings on Vital Topics* (Routledge/Taylor & Francis Group, 2009). His research has been published in *Business and Society, Business Ethics Quarterly, Academy of Management Journal, Academy of Management Review,* and other outlets. He is a fellow of the Academy of Management and Southern Management Association and past president of the Society for Business Ethics.

Ángel Castiñeira holds a BA and PhD from the University of Barcelona and a diploma of executive leadership from ESADE where he directs the Department of Social Sciences and holds the chair in leadership and democratic governance. He is also the director of the Values Observatory for the Lluis Carulla Foundation. Previously he directed the Center for Contemporary Studies of the autonomous government of Catalonia. His current areas of expertise are applied ethics and values, leadership, and geopolitical thought.

Diane C. Chase is director of academic resources at Babson College and was formerly director of institutional assessment. She has presented at regional and national conferences on collaborative practices in assessment as well as on her research interests in composition and rhetoric. She received a BA in English from Boston University, an MA in higher education administration from Boston College, and is pursuing a PhD in composition and rhetoric at University of Massachusetts Amherst.

Denis Collins is a professor of business at Edgewood College in Madison, Wisconsin, where he teaches classes in management and business ethics and is a Sam M. Walton Free Enterprise Fellow. He holds a PhD in business administration from the University of Pittsburgh. He has published a number books and articles. His latest book, *Essentials in Business Ethics: Creating an Organization of High Integrity and Superior Performance* (2009, John Wiley & Sons), provides practical how-to examples and best practices on every area of managing ethics inside organizations. Professor Collins serves on the editorial boards of several academic journals and has served on the board of governance for several professional organizations. He is the recipient of the Estervig-Beaubien Outstanding Professor Award at the School of Business at Edgewood College for excellence in teaching and mentoring. Three times he was voted the outstanding MBA faculty member at the University of Wisconsin-Madison in *Business Week*'s survey of alumni.

Dann Fisher, CPA, PhD, is an associate professor and the Deloitte & Touche Faculty Fellow at Kansas State University where he teaches undergraduate and graduate courses in taxation. He is coeditor of *Advancing Business Ethics Education*. His work on accounting ethics has been published in numerous journals, including *Behavioral Research in Accounting*, *Advances in Accounting Behavioral Research*, *Research on Accounting Ethics*, *Issues in Accounting Education*, *Accounting Education: An International Journal*, and *Journal of Business Ethics*. He ranked 13th in a 2005 article, appearing in *Research on Professional Responsibilities and Ethics in Accounting*, that examines the productivity of accounting ethics authors for the period 1968 to 2002.

R. Edward Freeman is the Olsson Professor of Business Administration at The Darden School and academic director of the Business Roundtable Institute for Corporate Ethics. Previously he was director of Darden's Olsson Center for Applied Ethics. Freeman is an adjunct professor of stakeholder management at the Copenhagen Business School in Denmark. His most recent books are *Managing for Stakeholders: Survival, Reputation and Success* and *Stakeholder Theory: The State of the Art*.

Linda Kidwell is associate professor and director of graduate programs in the accounting department at the University of Wyoming. Her teaching focuses on accounting ethics and auditing, and her research focuses on ethics, governmental accounting, and interdisciplinary topics. Her work has appeared in the *Journal of Business Ethics, Journal of Accounting and Public Policy, Accounting Education: An International Journal, Journal of Markets & Morality, Teaching Business Ethics,* and several other journals. She has also developed the Standardized Client method of educating auditors.

Barrie E. Litzky is an associate professor of management and organization in the Great Valley School of Graduate Professional Studies at The Pennsylvania State University. She received her PhD in organizational science and psychology at Drexel University. Her primary research interests include social issues in management with a focus on gender and career-related issues, ethical decision-making, and workplace deviance. Her work has appeared in a variety of peer reviewed journals including *Academy of Management Executive, Academy of Management Perspectives, Career Development International, Group and Organization Management, Entrepreneurship Theory and Practice,* and *Journal of Management Education.*

Tammy L. MacLean is an associate professor of management in the Sawyer Business School at Suffolk University, Boston, Massachusetts. She earned her PhD in organization studies at Boston College. Her primary research interests focus on how decoupling organizational programs and initiatives from core business functions affect organizational behavior at multiple levels of analyses. She also does research in the areas of managing diversity and organizational identity. Her work has been published in a variety of journals, including *Academy of Management Review, Academy of Management Journal, Academy of Management Learning & Education,* and *Journal of Business Ethics.*

Richard P. Mandel is an associate professor of law at Babson College where he teaches a variety of courses in business law, taxation, and meteorology and has served as both acting and associate dean of the undergraduate school as well as chair of its finance division. Mr. Mandel is also of counsel to the law firm of Bowditch and Dewey, of Worcester, Boston and Framingham, Massachusetts, where he specializes in the corporate, tax, and securities law issues affecting small businesses. Mr. Mandel has written a number of articles regarding the legal issues of small businesses and is a frequent contributor to the *Portable MBA* series. He holds an AB in political science and meteorology from Cornell University and a JD from Harvard Law School.

Janette Martell is currently a PhD candidate in management sciences at ESADE Business School. Her research interests focus on organizational change in terms of social responsibility in universities and business schools. Her work has been published in the *Journal of the World Universities Forum,* and she is coauthor of a chapter in a book by the rectors and deans of the Community of European Management Schools (CEMS). Martell holds two masters degrees, one in organizational development and the other in business administration. She also holds a BS in industrial engineering from the Tecnológico de Monterrey, Mexico where she has worked for 16 years in different administrative posts, including one as general director of a campus. She has been a lecturer at the Tec de Monterrey and has been at ESADE since 2010.

Nancy McGaw is deputy director of the Business and Society Program at the Aspen Institute and director of the Center for Business Education. She leads research initiatives to identify trends in corporate leadership and management education. She oversees the center's programs, including Beyond Grey Pinstripes, a global database and alternative ranking of MBA programs; CasePlace.org, an online resource to help faculty integrate social, ethical, and environmental issues into their teaching and research; and an MBA student attitude research project. She also created and directs the Aspen Institute's First Movers Fellowship program, an innovation lab for exceptional business professionals who have demonstrated an ability and passion for imagining new products, services, and business models that achieve profitable business growth and lasting, positive social impacts.

Jeremy Moon is a professor and the founding director of the International Centre for Corporate Social Responsibility (ICCSR), Nottingham University Business School. He won a Beyond Grey Pinstripes European Faculty award for preparing MBAs for social and environmental stewardship in 2005. He is a fellow of the Royal Society for the Arts and has held visiting positions at the European University Institute, Florence; McGill University; University of Toronto; Churchill College, Cambridge University; Institute for Advanced Studies, Princeton; and the University of Manchester. Professor Moon is coeditor of *The Oxford Handbook of CSR* (Oxford University Press, 2008) and coauthor of *Corporations and Citizenship* (Cambridge University Press, 2009). His journal publications include *Academy of Management Review, British Journal of Management, Journal of Management Studies, Journal of Business Ethics, Business Ethics Quarterly, Corporate Governance: An International Review,* and *Business and Society.* His current research includes the relationship between CSR and government, comparative CSR, and theories of corporate citizenship.

Brian P. Niehoff is the associate provost at Kansas State University and a professor of management in the College of Business Administration. He earned his BS degree in 1977 in mathematics from St. Joseph's College (Indiana), and his MBA and PhD from Indiana University, the latter earned in organizational behavior in 1988. His research has focused on leadership, workplace justice, organizational citizenship behaviors, mentoring, and international aspects of teaching and workplace behavior. His work is published in *Academy of Management Journal, Organizational Behavior & Human Decision Processes, Journal of Organizational Behavior, Group and Organizational Management, Journal of Psychology, Employee Responsibilities & Rights Journal, International Journal of Public Administration, Human Resource Management Journal, Asian Journal of Social Psychology, Career Development International, Information and Management,* and *Irish Journal of Management.* He was the department head of management in the KSU College of Business Administration from 2000 to 2009.

Marc Orlitzky (PhD, University of Iowa) is an associate professor of management at the Pennsylvania State University, Altoona. Previously, he served on the faculty of the University of New South Wales and University of Auckland (senior lecturer above the bar) and, in 2007-2008, was a visiting research fellow at the ICCSR at the University of Nottingham. His main research program of the past decade is synthesized in the book *Integrative Corporate Citizenship: Research Advances in Corporate Social Performance,* coauthored with Diane Swanson. His work has been published in *Organization Studies, International Journal of Human Resource Management, Business & Society, Journal of Business Ethics, Small Group Research, Personnel Psychology, Journal of Management Education, Academy of Management Review, Academy of Management Learning & Education,* two *Oxford University Handbooks,* and several other publication outlets. He has won several research awards and, in 2007, was the recipient of an Outstanding Reviewer Award from the *Academy of Management Journal.*

Steve Payne's academic career, following his doctorate at Arizona State University, included positions at the University of Louisiana-Lafayette (1981-1989), Eastern Illinois University (1989-1995), and Georgia College & State University (1995-2008). He was formerly the Bertrand P. Holley Professor of Social Responsibility in Business at Eastern Illinois University. Professor Payne has focused on issues of ethics education in his most recent publications.

Joseph A. Petrick is the Brage Golding Distinguished Professor of Research in the Department of Management and International Business at Wright State University. His research and teaching focuses on ethics in economics and business, management and leadership ethics, and integrity capacity as a strategic asset. He has coauthored four books including *Management Ethics: Integrity at Work* and published articles in the *Journal of Business Ethics, Business and Society Review, Business and Professional Ethics Journal, Academy of Management Executive, Journal of Managerial Psychology, Global Business and Economics Review, International Journal of Human Resource Management,* and *Global Business and Finance Review.* He is the founding director of the Institute for Business Integrity in the Raj Soin College of Business and faculty coach for regional/national award-winning ethics bowl teams. He was the former president of the Midwest Society for Human Resources and now serves as the president of the International Business Honor Society.

Andreas Rasche is assistant professor of Business in Society at the Governance and Public Management Group at Warwick Business School, University of Warwick. He is a consultant to the United Nations Global Compact Office in New York and is visiting professor at European Business School, Germany. Professor Rasche holds a PhD (political science) from European Business School, Germany and a Habilitation (Dr. habil.) from Helmut-Schmidt-University, Hamburg. He has published widely in the field of corporate responsibility and transnational governance, including contributions to *Organization Studies, Journal of Management Inquiry, Business & Society, Business Ethics Quarterly, Business Ethics: A European Review, Journal of Business Ethics, Corporate Governance, Research in the Sociology of Organizations,* and *Corporate Social Responsibility and Environmental Management.* His latest edited book is *The United Nations Global Compact: Achievements, Trends and Challenges* with Georg Kell.

Lisa A. Stewart is the program manager for the Business Roundtable Institute for Corporate Ethics. She is the lead author on the report *Shaping Tomorrow's Business Leaders: Principles and Practices for a Model Business Ethics Program* as well as the producer of the *Masters Seminars in Business Ethics* online video series.

Martin T. Stuebs, Jr., PhD, CPA, CMA, CIA, and CFM, is an assistant professor of accounting at Baylor University in Waco, Texas. He received his doctoral degree from the University of Arkansas. His research addresses important relationships between ethics, human resources, and company performance. Professor Stuebs has published articles in several journals, including *Strategic Finance, Journal of Accounting and Public Policy, Accounting & the Public Interest, CPA Journal,* and *Issues in Accounting Education.*

Diane L. Swanson, PhD (University of Pittsburgh), is the von Waaden Professor of Business at Kansas State University where she chairs the Business Ethics Education Initiative. The recipient of international awards for research and teaching, she has published widely on business ethics and corporate social performance in such journals as *Academy of Management Review, Behavioral Science, Human Relations, Business & Society, Journal of Business Ethics*, and *Systems Research and Behavioral Science*. Her two books published prior to this one are *Toward Integrative Corporate Citizenship* (coauthored with Marc Orlitzky) and *Advancing Business Ethics Education* (coedited with Dann Fisher). Swanson served as an associate editor for the award-winning *Encyclopedia of Business Ethics and Society* and currently serves on the editorial boards of the *Academy of Management Review, Business Ethics Quarterly*, and *Business & Society*. For the past 6 years, she has taught business ethics in a program for executive managers held at Dartmouth College

Gregory C. Unruh is the director of the Lincoln Center for Ethics at Thunderbird School of Global Management. Previously he was the Alumni Professor of Corporate Social Responsibility at the IE Business School in Madrid, Spain. He cofounded the Center for Eco-Intelligent Management with green architect William McDonough and has held positions at Columbia University in New York City, The Fletcher School in Boston, The Rotterdam School of Management, and INCAE in Costa Rica. His research has appeared in academic and business journals, including *Harvard Business Review* and *Energy Policy*, as well as news outlets such as *Financial Times, Business Week*, and *Boston Globe*.

Sandra Waddock is the Galligan Chair of Strategy and Professor of Management at Boston College's Carroll School of Management. Her forthcoming book with Malcolm McIntosh is on *SEE Change: The Great Transformation to the Sustainable Enterprise Economy* (Greenleaf, 2010). Other recent books include *The Difference Makers: How Social and Institutional Entrepreneurs Build the Corporate Responsibility Movement, Leading Corporate Citizens*, and *Total Responsibility Management: The Manual* (with Charles Bodwell). Holding MBA and DBA degrees from Boston University, Professor Waddock has published over 100 articles and book chapters on corporate responsibility, corporate citizenship, and intersector collaboration in a wide array of outlets. Waddock is a founding faculty member of the Boston College Leadership for Change Program and cofounder of the Institute for Responsible Investing. She initiated *Business Ethics'* 100 Best Corporate Citizens ranking with coauthor Samuel Graves and then editor Marjorie Kelly and edited the *Journal of Corporate Citizenship* from 2003-2004. She received the 2004 Sumner Marcus Award for Distinguished Service from the Social Issues in Management Division of the Academy of Management and the 2005 Faculty Pioneer Award for External Impact from the Aspen Institute Business in Society Program and World Resources Institute. Waddock has also been a visiting scholar at the Harvard Kennedy School of Government (2006-2007) and University of Virginia Darden Graduate School of Business (2000).

James Weber (PhD University of Pittsburgh) is a professor business ethics and management, chair of the Management Department, and founding director of the Beard Center for Leadership in Ethics at Duquesne University. His research interests include the assessment of values, moral reasoning, and ethical behavior on both the individual and organizational levels. He has been published in numerous academic and practitioner journals and is the coauthor, along with Anne T. Lawrence, of the 13th edition of *Business and Society: Stakeholders, Ethics, Public Policy*, published by McGraw-Hill/Irwin, Inc.

Patricia H. Werhane is the Wicklander Chair of Business Ethics and executive director of the Institute for Business and Professional Ethics at DePaul University. She was formerly the Peter and Adeline Ruffin Professor of Business Ethics and senior fellow at the Olsson Center for Applied Ethics in the Darden School at the University of Virginia where she is now professor emeritus. Professor Werhane has published numerous articles and is the author or editor of more 20 books including *Adam Smith and His Legacy for Modern Capitalism, Moral Imagination and Managerial Decision-Making, Organization Ethics for Health Care* (Oxford University Press), and *Employment and Employee Rights* with Tara J. Radin and Norman Bowie (Blackwell Publishing). She is the founder and former editor-in-chief of *Business Ethics Quarterly*, the journal of the Society for Business Ethics. Professor Werhane is a member of the academic advisory team for the Business Roundtable Institute for Corporate Ethics housed at the University of Virginia. Her latest book is *Alleviating Poverty through Profitable Partnerships* with Laura P. Hartman, Dennis Moberg, and Scott Kelley.

Thomas A. Wright is currently the Jon Wefald Leadership Chair and a professor of organizational behavior at Kansas State University. He received his PhD in organizational behavior and industrial relations from the University of California, Berkeley. He has published his work in many outlets, including the *Academy of Management Review, Journal of Applied Psychology, Psychometrika, Journal of Organizational Behavior, Journal of Management, Organizational Dynamics*, and *Journal of Management Inquiry*. He is a past associate editor for the *Journal of Management* and currently serves as an associate editor for the *Journal of Organizational Behavior*. In recognition

LaVergne, TN USA
25 February 2011

217987LV00001B/2/P